COMPUTER PROGRAMMING   Made Simple

The Made Simple series
has been created
especially for self-education
but can equally well
be used as
an aid to group study.
However complex the subject,
the reader is taken
step by step,
clearly and methodically,
through the course. Each volume
has been prepared by experts,
taking account of modern
educational requirements, to
ensure the most effective way
of acquiring knowledge.

In the same series

Accounting
Acting and Stagecraft
Additional Mathematics
Administration in Business
Advertising
Anthropology
Applied Economics
Applied Mathematics
Applied Mechanics
Art Appreciation
Art of Speaking
Art of Writing
Biology
Book-keeping
British Constitution
Business and Administrative
    Organisation
Business Economics
Business Statistics and Accounting
Calculus
Chemistry
Childcare
Commerce
Company Law
Computer Programming
Computers and Microprocessors
Cookery
Cost and Management Accounting
Data Processing
Dressmaking
Economic History
Economic and Social Geography
Economics
Effective Communication
Electricity
Electronic Computers
Electronics
English
English Literature
Export
Financial Management
French
Geology

German
Housing, Tenancy and Planning Law
Human Anatomy
Human Biology
Italian
Journalism
Latin
Law
Management
Marketing
Mathematics
Metalwork
Modern Biology
Modern Electronics
Modern European History
Modern Mathematics
Money and Banking
Music
New Mathematics
Office Administration
Office Practice
Organic Chemistry
Personnel Management
Philosophy
Photography
Physical Geography
Physics
Practical Typewriting
Psychiatry
Psychology
Public Relations
Rapid Reading
Russian
Salesmanship
Secretarial Practice
Social Services
Sociology
Spanish
Statistics
Teeline Shorthand
Twentieth-Century British History
Typing
Woodwork

COMPUTER PROGRAMMING   Made Simple

J. Maynard, MBCS

Made Simple Books
HEINEMANN : London

Made and printed in Great Britain
by Richard Clay (The Chaucer Press), Ltd., Bungay, Suffolk
for the publishers William Heinemann Ltd.,
10 Upper Grosvenor Street, London W1X 9PA

First Edition, September 1972
Reprinted, June 1975
Reprinted, December 1976
Reprinted, April 1978
Reprinted, March 1979
Second (enlarged) Edition, May 1980
Reprinted, April 1981
Reprinted, March 1982
Reprinted, January 1983

British Library Cataloguing in Publication Data

Maynard, Jeff
    Computer programming made simple.—2nd ed.—
    (Made simple books)
    1. Electronic digital computers—Programming
    I. Title   II. Series
    001.64'2   QA76.6

ISBN 0-434-98482-5

Preface

A glance at some of the paperwork in a computer department might easily prompt the question: *Can* computer programming be made simple? The answer is a very definite "yes".

The major barrier between computer people and the layman is one of initiation. The rows of flashing lights, the reams of numbers and the jargon are all part of a continuing but unnecessary mystique, and a small amount of carefully planned and well-presented instruction can open up new horizons for anyone interested enough to pay attention.

Modern techniques in programming enable anyone to participate in the writing of small programs after a brief training, and only by encouraging such participation will the benefit of computers be appreciated by everyone. The computer is becoming more and more a part of our daily lives and we must learn to live with it. Man must be the master not the slave.

Thus, from the outset, *Computer Programming Made Simple*, which requires no previous knowledge of mathematics or electronics, was planned to be of value and interest to a very wide circle of readers: to the man in the street who wishes to satisfy his curiosity about computers without becoming enmeshed in technical detail; to the aspiring programmer who wants a grounding in the subject before seeking a job; to the line manager who has an involvement with computers and wishes to know something of the problems encountered in preparing work for them; to the engineer who would like to use a computer as a problem-solving tool; and, finally, to school-leavers and undergraduates who wish to expand their background knowledge before entering the world of commerce or industry.

In conclusion, I am indebted to Roger Marshallsay and Honeywell Information Systems for their assistance in the computerized preparation of the index for the book.

J. MAYNARD

Preface to Second Edition

The decade of the seventies will be remembered for the tremendous growth that took place in computing—not just in the commercial applications of large computers (described in Parts One, Two and Three) but in the use of computers in the home.

The home computer was made possible by the enormous reductions in price and increases in power of integrated circuits or chips "spun off" from the American space programme. Initially seen in pocket calculators and television games, chips soon offered the hobbyist the chance to do his own thing. Playing chess, teaching children elementary mathematics, playing tunes, decoding morse, keeping personal accounts, running small businesses; those and many, many more are the uses of the home computer. (In addition, of course, to just playing. . . .)

The aspiring computer programmer can still gain a good grounding for a future career by reading *Computer Programming Made Simple*. So too can the hobbyist or small system user learn from this book the fundamentals of the home computer (in Part Five) and the ins and outs of a typical BASIC language (in Part Four). The additions to the Second Edition are written with an approach that requires no technical or other foreknowledge. Computer programming, especially in the home, really can be made simple.

I am indebted to MOSTEK for their help.

J. MAYNARD

Acknowledgment

To
Margaret and Sara Jane

By the same author
MODULAR PROGRAMMING
COMPUTER PROGRAMMING MANAGEMENT
BASIC PL/1
DICTIONARY OF DATA PROCESSING

In the same series

Computers and Microprocessors Made Simple, by G. Olsen and I. Burdess, provides a readable introductory survey of the field of computers. Although not a formal examination text the book should prove useful to those taking A level GCE, City and Guilds and TEC courses. Some mathematical background is assumed, but in general no prior knowledge of computers is needed. With the emphasis nowadays on digital electronics, the major part of the book deals with microprocessors and digital computers, but other forms of computing have also been discussed.

Data Processing Made Simple, by Susan Wooldridge, provides an introductory text for students of computer science at schools, universities and higher education establishments. The book will also be helpful to those who are preparing for a more detailed study of the subject through professional bodies or by working as an operator, programmer or systems analyst, and it will be of interest to anyone seeking a wider understanding of commercial data processing.

Contents

PREFACE AND PREFACE TO SECOND EDITION   v

ACKNOWLEDGMENT   vii

PART ONE: INTRODUCTION TO COMPUTER SYSTEMS

1	INTRODUCTION	3
2	COMPUTER STRUCTURE	5
	Input Unit	7
	Backing Store	7
	Memory Unit	7
	Output Unit	7
	Program	7
	Exercises	9
3	INPUT DEVICES	9
	Punched Cards	10
	Punched Paper Tape	12
	Keyboard	15
	Magnetic Ink Character Recognition	15
	Optical Character Recognition	15
	Optical Mark Reading	15
	Encoders	16
	Exercises	16
4	OUTPUT DEVICES	16
	Printing	16
	Line Printers	16
	Exercises	18
5	BACKING STORE DEVICES	19
	Backing Store Devices	19
	Magnetic Tape Devices	19
	Magnetic Disc Devices	22
	File Organization	25
	File Sequencing	27
	File Security	28
	Exercises	29
6	LOGIC AND FLOWCHARTING	29
	Flowcharting	30
	Flowcharting Symbols	30
	Exercises	39

7	PROGRAM SPECIFICATION ANALYSIS	39
	Program Specifications	39
	Introduction	40
	Input	40
	Output	40
	Throughput	-41
	Exercises	45
8	OPERATING SYSTEMS	45
	The Supervisor	47
	Program Scheduling	47
	Operator Communication	48
	JCL Interpretation	48
	Compilers	49
	Compiler Functions	49
	Operating Systems	50
	Library Maintenance	50
	Sorting	50
	Utilities	51
	Error Recovery	51
	Software	51
	Exercises	51
9	DATA AND NUMBERS	52
	Data Sets and Numbers	52
	Structures	52
	Arrays	53
	Number Systems	54
	The Decimal System	54
	The Binary System	55
	The Octal System	58
	The Hexadecimal System	59
	Number Notations	61
	Exercises	61

PART TWO: COBOL PROGRAMMING LANGUAGE

10	INTRODUCTION TO COBOL	65
	Language Structure	65
	The COBOL Character Set	65
	Punctuation	66
	Program Divisions	67
	Exercises	67
11	WORD TYPES AND CONSTANTS	68
	Reserved Words	68
	Keywords	68
	Optional Words	68
	Connectives	68

Names 69
   Data Names 69
   Condition Names 69
   Procedure Names 70
Constants 70
   Literal Constants 70
   Figurative Constants 71
General Format Notation 71
Exercises 72

12 THE COBOL CODING FORM 73
Sequence Numbers 73
Continuation of Lines 73
Area A and B 73
Blank Lines 76
Exercises 76

13 ARITHMETIC STATEMENTS 76
ROUNDED Option 77
GIVING Option 77
SIZE ERROR Option 78
The ADD Statement 78
The SUBTRACT Statement 80
Exercises 81

14 MULTIPLY AND DIVIDE 81
The MULTIPLY Statement 81
The DIVIDE Statement 82
The COMPUTE Statement 84
Arithmetic Expressions 84
Exercises 86

15 PROGRAM FLOW 86
Procedure Name 86
The GO TO Statement 86
The ALTER Statement 88
Exercises 90

16 PROGRAM CONTROL 91
The PERFORM Statement 91
Embedded PERFORM Statement 94
The EXIT Statement 95
The STOP Statement 96
Exercises 96

17 THE DATA DIVISION 97
Data Division—Organization 97
Organization of External Data 97
Description of External Data 98
The DATA DIVISION 98
Data Division Entries 99
Level Numbers 99
Special Level Numbers 101
Exercises 101

18   FILE DESCRIPTIONS—1   102
     BLOCK CONTAINS Clause   102
     RECORD CONTAINS Clause   103
     Recording Mode   104
       Fixed-Length Recording Mode   104
       Variable-Length Recording Mode   104
       Undefined-Length Recording Mode   104
       Spanned-Length Recording Mode   105
     RECORDING MODE Clause   105
       F Mode   105
       V Mode   105
       Other Modes   106
     Exercises   106

19   FILE DESCRIPTIONS—2   107
     File Labelling   107
     Generation Numbers   107
     LABEL RECORDS Clause   108
     VALUE OF Clause   109
     DATA RECORDS Clause   109
     Data Record Descriptions   109
     The FD in Use   110
     Exercises   111

20   DATA CLASSES IN COBOL   111
     Alphabetic Class   112
     Numeric Class   112
     Alphanumeric Class   112
     Data Description   113
     General Rules   113
     Data-name Clause   113
     Exercises   114

21   DATA DESCRIPTION—1   115
     PICTURE Clause   115
     Symbols Used in the PICTURE Clause   115
     Other Combinations of PICTURE Characters   116
     Symbol Repetition   117
     The PICTURE Clause in Use   117
     The USAGE Clause   118
     Exercises   119

22   DATA DESCRIPTION—2   119
     Further Data Description Entry Clauses   119
     The OCCURS Clause   120
     Subscripting   122
     Redefinition   123
     The REDEFINES Clause   123
     Exercises   124

23 DATA VALUES 125
    Data Item Content 125
    The VALUE IS Clause 125
    BLANK WHEN ZERO Clause 126
    Exercises 127

24 EDITING 127
    Types of Editing 128
    Editing in Use 130
    Exercises 131

25 THE DATA DIVISION IN USE 132
    File Section Entries 133
    Working Storage Section Entries 134
    Notes on Data Division Entries 135
    Exercises 136

26 THE PROCEDURE DIVISION 136
    Organization 136
    Statement Types 137
    Conditional Statements 138
    Imperative Statements 138
    Compiler Directing Statements 139
    Exercises 139

27 CONDITIONS 139
    Class Condition 140
    Sign Condition 140
    Relation Condition 141
    Condition Names 142
    Compound Conditions 143
    Exercises 144

28 THE IF STATEMENT 145
    Nested IF Statements 146
    Exercises 148

29 DATA MANIPULATION—1 148
    The MOVE Statement 148
    Alphanumeric to Alphanumeric 149
    Numeric to Numeric 149
    Numeric to Alphanumeric 150
    Alphanumeric to Numeric 150
    Exercises 151

30 DATA MANIPULATION—2 152
    The EXAMINE Statement 152
    UNTIL FIRST Option 152
    ALL Option 153
    LEADING Option 153
    TALLY 153
    REPLACING Option 154
    The TRANSFORM Statement 154
    Exercises 155

31 PREPARING DATA FILES   156
    The OPEN Statement   156
    The CLOSE Statement   157
    Exercises   158

32 DATA TRANSFER   159
    The READ Statement   159
    The WRITE Statement   162
    Print Files   163
    Printing by Channel   164
    Exercises   164

33 COMMUNICATION WITH THE COMPUTER OPERATOR   165
    The DISPLAY Statement   165
    The ACCEPT Statement   166
    Exercises   168

34 FILE PROCESSING   168
    File Matching   168
    Exercises   173

35 PROCESSING PRINT FILES   173
    Printing on Plain Stationery   174
    Printing on Pre-printed Stationery   175
        Stationery Line-up   177
    Exercises   178

36 QUALIFICATION   178
    CORRESPONDING Option   179
    Exercises   180

37 TABLE HANDLING   181
    PERFORM VARYING Option   182
    Exercises   186

38 TABLE SEARCHING   186
    Keys in Serial Order   188
    Table Optimization   188
    Exercises   189

39 SUBROUTINES   190
    Parameters   190
    The ENTRY Statement   191
    The CALL Statement   192
    Exercises   192

40 PROGRAM TERMINATION   193
    Program Controls   193
    Exercises   194

41 DOCUMENTATION AIDS   194
    The COPY Statement   195
    Mixed Programming Languages   197
    Exercises   197

42 THE SORT FEATURE 198
    Sorting 198
    Using the SORT Statement 200
    Exercises 201

43 PROGRAM TESTING FACILITIES 201
    The TRACE Statement 201
    The EXHIBIT Statement 202
    The DEBUG Statement 202
    Exercises 203

44 EJECT AND SKIP 203
    The EJECT Statement 204
    The SKIP Statement 204
    Exercises 204

45 THE IDENTIFICATION DIVISION 204
    Required Entries 205
    Optional Entries 205
    Exercise 206

46 THE ENVIRONMENT DIVISION—1 206
    The Environment Division 207
    The Configuration Section 207
    Special Names 207
    Exercise 208

47 THE ENVIRONMENT DIVISION—2 208
    Input–Output Section 208
    The FILE-CONTROL Paragraph 208
    The I-O-CONTROL Paragraph 209
    Exercises 210
    REVISION QUESTIONS SETS 1–4 210

PART THREE: FORTRAN PROGRAMMING LANGUAGE

    HISTORY 215

48 INTRODUCTION 217
    Time-Sharing Computer Systems 217
    FORTRAN Coding 219

49 CONSTANTS AND VARIABLES 220
    Constants 220
    Variables 222
    Initial Value (Time-Sharing) 224
    Initial Value (Non-Time Sharing) 224
    Exercises 224

50 THE ASSIGNMENT STATEMENT   225
      Arithmetic Expressions   225
      The Assignment Statement in Use   227
      Exercises   230

51 PROGRAM CONTROL STATEMENTS   231
      The GO TO Statement   231
      The Computed GO TO Statement   231
      The Assigned GO TO Statement   233
      Exercises   234

52 PROGRAM DECISIONS AND LOOPS   234
      Additional Program Control Statements   234
      Relational Expressions   235
      The DO Statement   238
      Exercises   240

53 ARRAYS   241
      Variable Subscripting   242
      The DATA Statement   244
      Exercises   245

54 INPUT AND OUTPUT STATEMENTS   246
      The INPUT Statement   246
      The PRINT Statement   247
      Formatting   250
      Exercises   250

55 BACKING STORE HANDLING   251
      File Layout   251
      Outputting Data   251
      Inputting Data   252
      Arrays and Files   253
      Exercises   254

56 SUBROUTINES   255
      Passing Parameters   255
      Arrays in Subroutines   257
      Exercises   258

57 FUNCTIONS   259
      Built-in Functions   260
      Functions in Use   263
      User Defined Functions   264
      Exercises   265

      REVISION QUESTIONS. SET 5   266

PART FOUR: BASIC PROGRAMMING LANGUAGE

58 INTRODUCTION   269
    Instruction Format   269
    BASIC Statements   271

59 CONSTANTS AND VARIABLES   271
    Data   271
    Numbers   272
    Texts   272
    Variables   273
      Numeric Variables   273
      String Variables   274
    Exercises   274

60 THE LET STATEMENT   274
    Expressions   275
    Order of Evaluation   276
    Strings   277
    Functions   278
    Exercises   280

61 FURTHER FUNCTIONS   280
    More Intrinsic Functions   281
    Exercises   281

62 INPUTTING DATA   282
    DATA and READ Statements   282
    The INPUT Statement   283
    Exercises   283

63 THE PRINT STATEMENT   284
    The TAB Feature   285
    PRINT USING   286
    Blank Lines   288
    Exercises   288

64 PROGRAM CONTROL   288
    The GO TO Statement   288
    The IF THEN Statement   289
    Extensions to the IF THEN Statement   289
    The ON . . . GO TO Statement   291
    Exercises   291

65 LOOPS AND SUBROUTINES   292
    The FOR and NEXT Statements   292
    The GOSUB Statement   293
    Exercises   295

66 ARRAYS AND SUBSCRIPTS   296
   Arrays   296
   Subscripts   297
   Exercises   299
   REVISION QUESTIONS. SET 6   299

   PART FIVE: THE MICROPROCESSOR EXPLAINED

67 THE HOME COMPUTER   303
   Random Access Memory—RAM   303
   Read Only Memory—ROM   304
   Programmable Read Only Memory—PROM   304
   Erasable PROM—EPROM   304

68 THE HOME COMPUTER I/O SYSTEM   305
   Input   305
   Output   306
   Backing Storage   307
   Other Input/Output   307

69 THE BUS SYSTEM   308
   REVISION QUESTIONS. SET 7   311

   APPENDIX ONE: GLOSSARY OF TERMS USED   313

   APPENDIX TWO: COBOL—LIST OF RESERVED WORDS   322

   APPENDIX THREE: ANSWERS TO EXERCISES   324
   Exercises: Part One   324
   Exercises: Part Two   325
   Revision Questions: Sets 1–4   332
   Exercises: Part Three   338
   Revision Questions: Set 5   341
   Exercises: Part Four   343
   Revision Questions: Set 6   344
   Revision Questions: Set 7   345

   INDEX   346

PART ONE

INTRODUCTION TO COMPUTER SYSTEMS

CHAPTER ONE

INTRODUCTION

The popular conception of a computer sees it as a most complicated electronic machine performing incredibly complex calculations at incomprehensible speeds to the accompaniment of hundreds of flashing light bulbs. Any attempt to elicit information as to the workings of a computer from a computer programmer will produce a stream of technical jargon interspaced with amazing statistics chosen to fill the questioner with awe and admiration.

The popular press and radio and television have done little to curb the mystique surrounding the operation of computers, with their emphasis on the spectacular or exciting applications to which computers are being applied. Presumably news editors consider their readership figures are more likely to be improved with stories of computers playing chess, composing music, or sending gas bills for thousands of pounds rather than if they filled their pages with explanations of the real benefit society is getting from these machines. Indeed some popular media would have us believe that computers are giant electronic brains monitoring our every move in preparation for the day they take over all our decision-making and many of our thought processes.

The people who work with computers, the programmers, analysts, and operators who seem to live by rules of their own and seldom leave their own environment, tend to be very cynical towards the stories of electronic brains. This attitude will appear hardly surprising when one eventually learns that the computer is basically a very simple device and is as far removed from an electronic brain as a bicycle from a spaceship. Programmers in particular are the people most aware that computers are no substitute for the human brain; in fact the preparation of work to be run on a computer is one of the most mind-bending exercises likely to be encountered in everyday life. No doubt in time, as the computer becomes more a daily fact of life, the individualistic computer experts will emerge from their shells to embroil us all in the workings of their interesting machines. Perhaps when the world at large discovers the truth about computers they will recoil at the disillusionment although I hope this will not be the case. Indeed the man credited with the invention of the computer—Charles Babbage—received as part of a letter about his "Analytical Engine" (the name he gave to his computer) the following advice:

It is desirable to guard against the possibility of exaggerated ideas that might arise as to the powers of the Analytical Engine. In considering any new subject, there is frequently a tendency, first, to overrate what we find to be already interesting or remarkable; and secondly, by a sort of natural reaction, to undervalue the true state of the case when we do discover that our notions have surpassed those that were really tenable. The analytical engine has no pretensions whatever to originate anything. It can do whatever we know how to order it to perform.

Considering that it was written more than 100 years ago the last sentence in that letter is remarkably profound and provides the key to the whole problem of computers. If a computer programmer does not himself know the method required to perform a certain calculation or process then he cannot instruct the computer to solve that calculation. It is most important to appreciate, at this stage, that a computer cannot tell its user how to solve a problem but can only perform those calculations which it has been instructed to do. The computer is just a tool (albeit a very powerful tool) and, as with any tool, the benefits to be gained from its use depend upon the skill and experience of the people who direct and control the uses to which it is put.

The reader with little or no previous knowledge of computing may perhaps feel a little cheated at this point—the prospect of controlling a vast electronic brain has gone forever and with it perhaps the desire to learn more about computer programming. The effectiveness of computers and the potential benefit to society lies, not in their complexity or ability to think, but in their versatility and speed. It is the ability to relate everyday problems to the language of computers and the ability to harness the computer's speed that is the challenge of computer programming. The computer is a simple machine, or rather a collection of simple machines, some electronic and some mechanical, whose activities are co-ordinated by a central control unit. These machines, when working together, are able to perform arithmetic and simple logical processes such as comparing two numbers. They can also read in information, store this information for later use, and issue results in a form understandable by human operators.

The versatility of the computer lies in the fact that the way in which the central control unit controls the activities of the other machines can be changed as often as required. The specific activities to be carried out for any one job are given to the computer in the form of a program. This consists of a series of instructions which tell the computer every step it is required to take in order to perform the calculations required of it. The purpose of this book is to give the reader the knowledge required to write computer programs. In order to do this he will need to understand more than just the language of programming. Part One provides an introduction to the structure of computer systems, an outline of the available machines that can be attached to the central control unit (these are called peripheral units), and a detailed explanation of the methods used to analyse a problem prior to writing a program to solve that problem.

Once the programmer has analysed the problem to be programmed he must decide which programming language is the best to use for the particular problem. A program to solve a business problem (such as calculating payroll, or maintaining a sales ledger) would be written in COBOL (an acronym of COmmon Business Oriented Language) which is described in detail in Part Two. The solution to a more mathematical problem (such as working out the lengths of suspended cables) would be written in FORTRAN (from FORmula TRANslation) which is explained in Part Three. The reader who has not studied mathematics very deeply, will find no difficulty in reading Parts One and Two but may omit Part Three, if desired, since a knowledge of FORTRAN is not normally required by commercial computer programmers.

CHAPTER TWO

COMPUTER STRUCTURE

The computer as we have already seen, consists of a **central control unit** and a number of **peripheral units** collectively known as the **computer system**. The work carried out by a computer system is often known as EDP (**Electronic Data Processing**) which means the use of electronic machines to derive results from data input to them by means of arithmetic and logic. The term EDP is most commonly applied to the use of computers in business for routine office work but is equally suitable for their application as scientific calculators. However, the examples used in Part One to describe the workings of computer systems will concentrate on business systems although the principles discussed apply to scientific work.

The computer has already been described as a very simple machine whose main advantage is speed. How then can such a machine produce, with unfailing accuracy, the wage-slips of a large factory payroll each week? The computer system will not use any new methods for producing payrolls but will beat the human wage clerk every time by virtue of its speed and accuracy. Indeed a computer has been called a very fast, highly competent (but unoriginal) clerk. In order, therefore, to discover the constituent parts of a computer system and the way in which they are used to solve an everyday problem let us first look at the methods used by its human counterpart.

Consider, for example, the wages clerk in a factory whose job it is each week to produce pay-slips for each of the factory employees. To complete this task the clerk will use, at his desk, the following items:

1. *In-tray*. This will be used by the clerk for the receipt of new or changed information likely to cause a change in the pay-slip of an employee. For example, the overtime worked by each hourly-paid worker must be notified to the clerk every week, as must changes in tax code, time off due to illness and so on.
2. *File*. Each employee for whom the clerk will make up a pay-slip, will have a record in the file (entered on a filing-card or kept in a folder) containing such permanent or seldom varying information as the man's name, grade, pay code, and salary. The file will also contain various items of accumulated data to be up-dated each week, such as the employee's tax to date, gross pay to date, and any other deductions to which the man's pay may be subjected. As each pay-slip is made up, the clerk will refer to this file for the standing information and will also up-date the financial information.
3. *Memory*. As each new pay-slip is to be produced, the clerk will read the various items of information about the employee and his wages. The information is then held in the man's memory where it can be referred to instantly or worked on as required. If any employee has a very large record in the file which cannot be remembered all at once, the clerk will probably deal with each section of the file in turn.
4. *Calculator*. The clerk will use some form of desk-calculator (or adding-machine) as well as, perhaps, a scrap pad and a ready-reckoner to perform

the various calculations involved in producing a pay-slip. This will normally involve calculations using information both from the in-tray and from the employee's file (e.g. overtime hours multiplied by rate to give overtime pay).

5. *Out-tray.* Once the clerk has calculated the net pay, having entered the various details on to the pay-slip and pay-sheet and up-dated the file he will wish to pass the information on to either the employee or another department. To do this he will put the various items into his out-tray from where it will be distributed as required.

6. *Procedure Manual.* Each step to be taken by the clerk in producing a pay-slip will be laid down in a procedure manual to which he can refer at will. This manual must also provide information about the procedure in unusual cases—for example the clerk must be able to read what to do if a man's tax code is missing or if, due to a clerical error, he is shown as having worked overtime while he has been away on holiday.

It is easy to visualize the wages clerk sitting at his desk receiving, say, clock-cards, referring to the employee's file and, after some calculations, producing a pay-slip. But is it as easy to visualize an EDP system performing similar functions? Surprisingly, the answer to this question is *yes*, as can be seen from the following:

The computer system performing an identical payroll job would require, basically, the same six functional units as the wages clerk and would operate in the same manner. Figure 1 shows the corresponding units of the computer system:

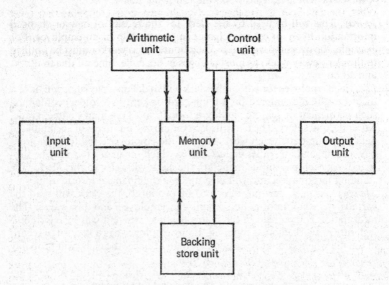

Fig. 1. Organization of a computer system

Input Unit

In order for the computer system to process details of each employee's weekly pay variations these will be converted into a machine-readable format and passed through an **input device** or **unit**. This unit will transmit the data as a series of electrical pulses into the computer's memory unit where it is available for processing. A full description of input devices will be found in Chapter Three.

Backing Store

The file for each employee containing his standing and accumulated information will be held on some form of **backing store** (the various types of which are described in detail in Chapter Five). When the computer reads in each employee's details from the input device it will request the backing store to provide the **file record** (sometimes called a history record). After the calculations have been performed (see below) the file will be **updated** by returning the record to its place on the backing store.

Memory Unit

The data read from an input device or backing store are transmitted to the computer's **memory unit** where they are available for processing. This processing can consist of **arithmetic computations** (for example subtracting the employee's deductions from his gross pay to produce his net weekly wage) or **logical operations** such as examining the employee's staff-grade to determine his bonus or overtime rate. The data held in the memory unit are also available for transmission to output devices.

Output Unit

When the details of an employee's pay-slip have been computed they must be made available in a human readable form. This is the function of an **output unit** or **device** which transmits data held in memory to an external medium (this will normally consist of paper on which the computer's output is printed). Output devices are described in Chapter Four.

Program

The set of instructions (called a **program**), corresponding to the clerk's procedure manual, tells the computer how each step in the production of the pay-slip is to be carried out. The program is held in a reserved part of the computer's memory and is actioned by the **Control Unit**. Each instruction is selected (one at a time) and **decoded** by the control unit which will instruct which of the other units is required to perform a particular function. For example, if the control unit selects as the next instruction a READ command it will instruct the input device to transmit data into the computer's memory.

The flow of data within the computer system is shown by the lines in Fig. 1. Data flow from the **input unit** to the **memory unit** where they are held until, with data read from the **backing store**, they are transmitted to the **arithmetic unit** for computations before being transmitted to the **output unit**. *These operations are regulated by the control unit obeying instructions in the program stored in the memory unit.* The arithmetic, memory, and control units are collectively known as the **Central Processor Unit** (usually shortened to **CPU**).

The reader may treat the CPU as a single unit since the computer programmer is not able to distinguish between the three constituent units when coding his program. (Note the term **coding** which is preferred to **writing** when referring to a computer program.)

Before proceeding to a description of the individual items consider the set-up of a specific computer system to perform an everyday task. Most consumers now receive their gas bills via a computer so let us consider the manner in which they are produced.

Figure 2 illustrates the computer system set up to produce consumers' quarterly gas bills. The history file recorded on magnetic tape (see Chapter Five) contains for each consumer such details as his name, address, account number, charging tariff, outstanding balance, and hire-purchase commitments. This information is recorded in sequence (of, say, account number) to make it easier for the computer to **retrieve** any particular record.

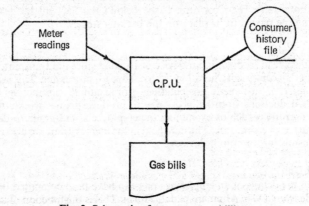

Fig. 2. Schematic of gas-consumer billing

The object of this job is to produce, for each consumer, a bill showing the amount charged for gas used this quarter plus outstanding debts and hire-purchase charges, if any. (Note—the reason for the different-shaped boxes in Fig. 2 is explained fully in Chapter Six.)

The amount of gas used by the consumer as recorded by the meter reader is transcribed on to an input medium (in this case punched cards—see Chapter Three) which are **sorted** into the same sequence as the consumer history file. The first stage in running this job is to load the program into the CPU (see Chapter Eight), the computer operator will then press the start button and the CPU will begin executing the program.

The program will begin by reading the first record from the consumer history file into the memory unit. It will then instruct the input device to transmit the first card into memory. The account number on the card will be compared with that of the consumer history record. If they are the same the program will proceed to produce a gas bill. To do this the computer will calculate the total number of gas units consumed and multiply it by the tariff code rate indicated on the consumer's history file in order to arrive at the cost of this quarter's gas used. This amount will be transmitted to the output device to be printed. The program will then check to see if the consumer's history record contains any outstanding debts or hire-purchase charges; if so these will also be sent to the output device to be printed. The last task will be the printing of the total amount payable. The program will now repeat these functions for the next consumer. If the account number on a card does not **match** that of the consumer history record the program will read further records from the backing store until a match is achieved. When the final card has been processed the program will re-wind the magnetic tape and will transmit a message to the computer operator stating that the program has finished.

This example makes the business of programming a computer look very simple indeed. How then, one might ask, do mistakes occur which result in consumers receiving gas bills for thousands of pounds? To answer this, first remember how the wage clerks' procedure manual had to cater for every possible combination of situations. So it must be with the computer program. The computer cannot think and if, for example, the programmer does not code his program to cater for erroneous input data then an incorrect bill could easily be produced. This is often referred to as a GIGO system—garbage in, garbage out!

Incorrect input data and program errors or omissions are two of the main reasons why computers produce faulty information. The programmer must cater for every possibility in his program. Indeed this, rather than the act of coding, is where the art of computer programming lies.

Exercises

1. What does CPU stand for?
2. What three units form the CPU?
3. What are the two main causes of computer program failure?
4. Where is the computer program held during its execution?
5. Besides the CPU what are the other constituent parts of a computer system?

CHAPTER THREE

INPUT DEVICES

Input devices on computer systems are required to transmit data prepared by or readable by humans into the computer memory unit from where they can be processed under control of a computer program. It is not the intention of this book to describe in detail the electronic workings of computers (the interested reader is referred to *Electronic Computers Made Simple*). However, a little must be said to enable the reader to appreciate the need for the various input devices described below. Data in a computer memory, whether they represent the instructions of a program or the name of a customer, are stored as a series of **electrical pulses** each of which can be a **negative** or a **positive** pulse (conventionally represented diagrammatically by the digits 0 and 1). Any character, number, or instruction is therefore represented, in the computer memory, as a unique **set of pulses** (e.g. the letter A might be represented as 11110001). A stream of data being input to a computer could be likened therefore to a string of morse-code characters, the major difference being that in a computer system each digit or character is represented by the same number of pulses.

As already mentioned, a detailed account of the internal workings of a computer is beyond the scope of this book; however, the reader should now appreciate that data understandable to himself such as:

JOHN SMITH 12 HIGH STREET ANYTOWN

cannot be understood by a computer. Indeed, as will be seen below, this data cannot even be understood by an input device.

An input device is therefore a means of transmitting data into the computer memory as a series of electrical pulses. The input device will read (see below) an **input media** coded with the information the human operator wishes to give to the computer and will transcribe it somehow into a string of pulses.

Scientists and engineers are still endeavouring to design input devices which read human handwriting and translate it into the required string of pulses. Unfortunately, however, the vast variation found in different samples of such writing presents a major obstacle and these type of input devices are still very much in the experimental stage.

In order to input data to a computer it is necessary therefore to have an intermediate stage during which the handwritten data is mechanically transcribed by a clerk into a format readable by an electro-mechanical machine. This intermediate stage, known as **data preparation**, is used to produce one of two types of computer input media depending upon the particular computer system in use. These two media are **punched cards** and **punched paper tape**.

Punched Cards

A punched card (or more simply a card) consists of a thin piece of card measuring $7\frac{3}{8}'' \times 3\frac{1}{4}''$ and divided into **80 columns**, each of which can contain one character (letter or number). A **character** is represented by a combination of one or more holes punched in a particular column.

For punching holes in each column the card is divided into **12 rows**. An unpunched card showing the rows and columns is illustrated in Fig. 5. A particular character is represented by a combination of holes according to a certain conventional code. For the purpose of this code the rows of the card are divided into two areas; the rows labelled 0 to 9 are the **numeric rows** and the rows labelled 12, 11, and 0 are the **zone rows**. Notice that 0 row can be both a numeric and a zone row.

Representation of the numbers 0 to 9 is by the occurrence of a punched hole in the appropriate row (e.g. a hole punched in row labelled 3 represents the number 3). Each column on a card can represent a single number. A larger number like 347 would be represented by punched holes in three columns. The letters of the alphabet and special symbols such as ? / , * & @ are represented by combinations of zone and numeric row punching. For example the letter "A" is represented by punched holes in the 12 row and the 1 row, the letter "B" by punched holes in the 12 row and the 2 row.

A unique code exists therefore for each character that can be input to the computer although the reader need not concern himself with attempting to memorize any such code. (A card punched with input data is illustrated in

Fig. 6.) Some punch machines, e.g. those machines used in the data-preparation stage to prepare punched cards, print the character punched in each column along the top of the card. This of course, obviates the need for anyone to memorize the punching code. Since a card contains 80 columns it may contain 80 characters of data. It is quite usual to split a card up into fields when deciding how a particular set of data should be punched. A **field** will consist of one or more columns which collectively represent a particular data function. For example, in a payroll application, we could decide that columns 1 to 20 would contain the employee's name and columns 21 to 25 his clock-number. We would then refer to the name field (meaning columns 1 to 20) or the clock-number field (meaning columns 21 to 25). When a card is divided up into fields a particular item of information will occupy only that field and even if the item is shorter than the field, no other item will appear in the field. In the example above if an employee's name consisted only of 12 characters then these could be punched in columns 1 to 12. However, the man's clock-number would still be punched in columns 21 to 25 with columns 13 to 20 left blank, i.e. unpunched.

We now have our data punched into a series or **pack** of cards ready to be input to the computer. In order to transmit these data we will use a **card-reader**. A card-reader is a device for reading packs of cards electro-mechanically and transcribing the pattern of punched holes into a series of electric pulses which are then sent to the computer memory. A card-reader is shown schematically in Fig. 3 which should be referred to in relation to the following text.

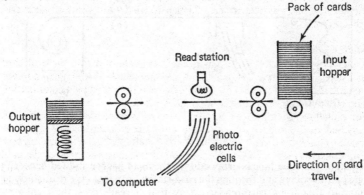

Fig. 3. Schematic of card-reader

The pack of cards is loaded into the **input hopper** which consists of a U-shaped metal channel into which the cards are slid face down. On command from the computer the cards are drawn one by one from the input hopper and are passed by a series of rubber wheels through the **read-station**. The read-station consists of a powerful light shining through the punched holes on to a set of twelve photo-electric cells. The light falling on a particular photo-electric cell generates an electric pulse. The pattern of holes on each card is therefore reproduced, column by column, as a series of electric pulses which are transmitted to the computer memory. Once the card has passed through the read-station it is sent to an **output hopper** for later removal and storage. The output hopper usually has a spring-loaded base-plate which will move down to accommodate an increasing pack of cards. Typical modern card-reading equipment can operate at speeds of over 1000 cards per minute resulting in a minimum transfer of 80,000 characters per minute into the computer. With speeds of this order in a largely mechanical piece of equipment it is obviously important to ensure that each card in a pack is in prime condition. A card which has been creased or stapled or has become damp will often be either rejected by the card-reader or, even worse, will cause the read-station to jam. It is important therefore to treat cards with respect!

The end of a pack of cards will be detected by the card-reader which will send a special end of pack **signal** to the computer.

Punched Paper Tape

Paper tape, for use on computer systems, is 1″ wide and is supplied in rolls up to 50 feet in length. Tape which has not been prepared with data contains only a row of sprocket holes (see Fig. 7) which are offset from the centre to ensure that the tape is always loaded the correct way in the paper tape reader. Data are punched into paper tape as a series of holes across the tape, each character having a unique set of holes (see Fig. 8). A **paper tape reader** is illustrated schematically in Fig. 4.

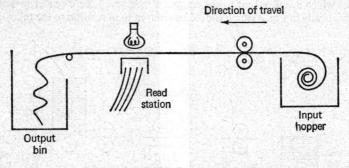

Fig. 4. Schematic of paper tape reader

The roll of punched tape is dropped into the **input hopper** and fed between a single pair of rollers and through the **read-station**. A paper tape read-station is similar to that for a card-reader except that it reads only the eight rows punched on to the tape. After passing through the read-station the paper tape is allowed to fly into an **output bin** which literally consists of a large box or bin. (Note—mechanical problems prevent the tape being wound on to a spool after it has been read.)

The tape is read under computer control again although a special character must be punched on to the tape to indicate the end of a group of fields (i.e. corresponding to the end of a card). Each group of fields (known as a **record**) is therefore delimited by the special character and another special character signifies the end of the reel of tape. (Note—spare tape must always be run out at the end of a punched tape to enable the tape-feeding mechanism to function correctly.)

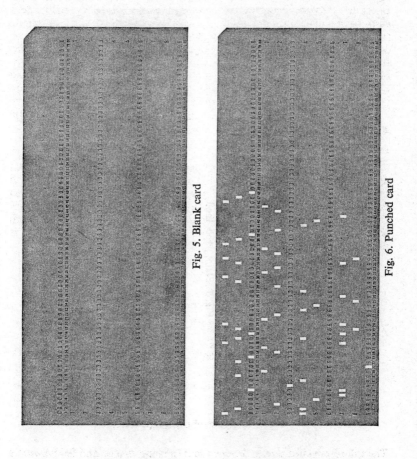

Fig. 5. Blank card

Fig. 6. Punched card

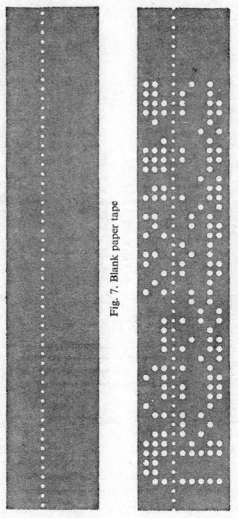

Fig. 7. Blank paper tape

Fig. 8. Punched paper tape

Typical reading speed for a modern paper tape reader would be up to 1,000 characters per second.

Punched cards and punched paper tape represent between them something over 95% of the input media currently in use in commercial computer installations. There are other methods of inputting data to a computer system although their use tends to be rather specialized. However, for completeness these methods are described briefly below.

Keyboard

Most computer systems have attached to them a device resembling an electric typewriter (in fact the device usually is a slightly modified electric typewriter). These can be used for inputting data although only at the comparatively very slow rate of human typing. Their main function is to enable the computer to communicate with the **computer operator** who would only be required to type very brief responses to questions (typically YES or NO or a date). Keyboards cannot be considered for inputting a large quantity of data.

Magnetic Ink Character Recognition

MICR tends to be used mostly by the clearing banks for inputting data relating to cheques. Each cheque, when it is issued, will have encoded on it the account number of the customer together with the sorting code of his bank branch. When the cheque is received at the bank's computer centre it will have encoded on it the value of the cheque. As the name implies the data on MICR documents are encoded magnetically, each character being identified by a unique arrangement of the **magnetic ink**. The MICR documents are read by a machine similar to a card-reader except that the read-station contains a device sensitive to magnetic fields.

Optical Character Recognition

OCR extends at present only to the reading of machine-printed type. Despite many years of research the infinite variety of handwriting styles make their reading by machine still an engineer's dream.

Each character on an OCR document is scanned by a photo-electric device to determine its outline or shape. This shape is then compared with a sample set to identify the particular character whose electronic code can then be sent to the computer. Early OCR machines were able only to recognize a single font (or type style) although the more sophisticated machines can now "read" typewritten or computer-printed documents.

OCR techniques are unlikely to be widely used until they can accept handwritten documents.

Optical Mark Reading

OMR denotes the use of reading devices which can detect the presence or absence of a **mark** (e.g. a pencilled cross). The full perms on some football coupons are read by OMR devices where each selection by the punter generates a pulse which can be fed to the computer. The heavy black marks sometimes seen on the side of such coupons are called **timing lines** and are used by the reading device to synchronize the read station with the match entries. Another popular use for OMR devices is in the reading of gas and electricity meters. The meter reader has a form supplied to him for each consumer whose meter he is to read and by making a series of marks with a pencil, he can record the units of gas or electricity used. Using OMR techniques avoids the necessity for a separate data-preparation stage between meter reading and computer input.

Encoders

Many computer installations are now using magnetic tape encoders to transcribe data directly from a keyboard unit to a magnetic tape. The tape is then read at high speed by a magnetic tape unit of the type described in Chapter Five.

Exercises

1. How many characters can a punched card contain?
2. How many rows are available for coding each character in a punched card?
3. Where is the combination of punched holes translated into a series of electrical pulses?
4. If a punched card contained a name (10 columns), an address (40 columns), and an account number (6 columns), how many fields would it be said to contain?
5. How many holes are available to represent each character on punched paper tape?

CHAPTER FOUR

OUTPUT DEVICES

A number of different **output devices** are available for use on computer systems and various combinations of them will be found in common use. The two input media, examined in detail in the previous chapter—punched cards and punched paper tape—may themselves be produced by an output device under control of the computer. However, because of the complicated mechanical component (involved in actually cutting the holes) these devices are very slow compared with the speed of the computer itself. The main form of computer output for human use is the **printed report** and this chapter will concentrate therefore on the output device used to produce it.

Printing

The typewriter discussed in Chapter Three as a means of inputting data can be used also to print out result from computer programs. However, since the speed of such devices is rarely greater than 30 characters per second they are clearly unsuitable for high-volume printing. Instead the main printed output from a computer system will be on a **Line Printer**, so called because, as we shall see below, a complete line is printed at one time.

Line Printers

A number of methods of producing high-speed printing on computer systems have been evolved during the past few years. However, the most popular method only is described here. This consists of the barrel printer. The main constituent of the **barrel printer** is the **print barrel** consisting of a metal block, circular in cross-section, with a length equal to the required width of printing. The characters to be printed are embossed on the surface of this barrel in such a way that each character appears as a complete row across the barrel. For example, if the printer is designed to print lines of 120 characters in width then there will be a row of 120 A's, a row of 120 B's, and so on. This is illustrated in Fig. 9.

Fig. 9. Print barrel layout

The print barrel revolves at high speed in front of a carbon ribbon and the paper to be printed. Behind the paper is a row of tiny **hammers**, each one corresponding to a print position on each line. In the example above there will therefore be 120 hammers. This general arrangement is illustrated in Fig. 10.

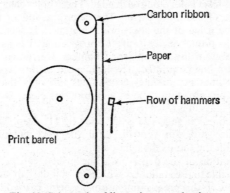

Fig. 10. Schematic of line-printer mechanism

In order for a character to be printed it is necessary for the hammer to be **fired** (or struck) causing the paper to strike the character image through the carbon ribbon. During the printing of a line the paper is stationary but the print barrel continues to revolve at high speed. As each row of characters moves behind the hammers then all the occurrences of that character in the line are printed.

Figure 11 shows this operation. As the row of A's, on the print barrel, comes level with the hammers then the hammers are fired for those positions, in the line to be printed, in which an A occurs; all the A's on the sample line are therefore printed at the same time. Similarly the B's in the line are printed, then the C's and so on until the entire line has been printed. If a particular character does not appear in a line then no hammers will be fired as that character passes them. Since each print character occurs once around the barrel a line can be printed during one revolution of the barrel. The speed with which the hammers are fired is such that the characters are printed

Computer Programming Made Simple

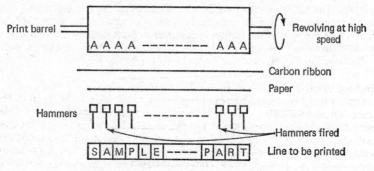

Fig. 11. Sequence of character printing

clearly and without smudging. After a line has been printed the paper is advanced to the next line position.

In order that the paper advancement can be controlled accurately the paper has a row of **sprocket holes** along each edge. These holes engage with sprocket pins either side of the print barrel. The determination of the print barrel position and the firing of the appropriate hammers is accomplished by the electronics of the printer device itself; the programmer has merely to issue the appropriate program instruction (see Chapters Thirty-two and Fifty-four) requesting that a line be printed. The high speed of this type of line printer (typically 1300 lines per minute) necessitates not only that the paper has sprocket holes but also that it be in a continuous piece. However, to make paper handling easier it is usual to divide it, with perforations across the paper, into pages. A common page size is 15″ wide by 11″ deep. The paper can be advanced, under program control, until the next line-printing position corresponds with the top of the next page.

Since the position of the paper on a line printer can be accurately controlled it is possible to use stationery which has standard or static information pre-printed on to it (this pre-printing normally being carried out by the paper manufacturers). Typical applications of **pre-printed stationery** include invoices, statements, gas bills and so on where the pre-printing would include a mixture of text (e.g. gas tariffs) and lines (e.g. the box in which name is printed on an invoice). The additional program instructions required when controlling the positioning of pre-printed stationery are discussed in detail in Part Two.

Exercises

1. What is the most popular form of the line printer?
2. How many hammers would there be on a line printer designed to print lines up to 132 characters in width?
3. How many revolutions of the print barrel are required to print each line?
4. How is the feeding and alignment of the paper controlled in a line printer?
5. What is the common page size for use on line printers?

CHAPTER FIVE

BACKING STORE DEVICES

Backing Store Devices

During the processing of any application data will have to be input to the computer and following the calculations done by the program, data will be output. In addition to this input and output data the computer will require, in a number of cases, to refer to historical data of some kind. For example in a works payroll application the computer would require access to each employee's year-to-date data to produce cumulative totals on pay-slips and so on. Clearly, while it would be possible to maintain this data on punched cards, it would be not only impractical but extremely slow in relation to the speed of the computer. These historical data are stored on a **backing store device** in the form of a **file,** in this context a file being a collection of related data records. Information can only be written to or read from a backing store device by the computer, although it is done under program control. The computer control of backing store devices enables their speed of operation to be increased (see below) and improves the security of the data stored thereon. Note that when we talk of the computer reading historical data from a backing store device we do not necessarily mean data that was prepared a long time ago. However, it is important to remember that only a computer can put data on to a backing store device and before data can be read from such a device a computer program must have put the data in place.

A backing store device can hold data that were created some time ago, as in the case above where the details of an employee's past wages are held. However, data which are newly created can also be held providing an intermediate stage is utilized. For example, suppose a deck of cards is to be read by a number of different programs. Rather than have each program read the actual physical deck of cards a special program can precede the others which transfers the contents of the pack of cards on to a backing store device. Each program then requiring access to the cards can read their images from the backing store device thereby reducing the time taken to input the data and increasing the security of the data (since the "pack of cards" is effectively under control of the computer there is no danger of their being dropped, etc.).

Two main types of backing store devices are in common use—**magnetic tapes** and **magnetic discs.** Although based on the same basic principle the methods utilized to store the data differ between these two types of device. However, the use of either type of device requires much the same type of programming to handle the data. Accordingly the physical operation of these devices is described separately followed by a discussion on the general programming requirements of backing store devices.

Magnetic Tape Devices

Magnetic tape can vary in width according to the particular computer system in use, although $\frac{1}{2}''$ wide tape is becoming increasingly popular. The tape consists of a plastic or mylar tape coated, on one side, with a substance capable of being magnetized such as iron oxide. The actual tape is not unlike that used on domestic tape-recorders except that it is of a much higher quality. A reel of tape may consist of 1200, 2400, or 3600 feet held on a plastic spool.

The reel of tape on which data are to be recorded is placed on the tape-deck and the tape threaded through the **read/write head assembly** on to a **take-up spool**. The general layout of a tape-deck, complete with reel of tape, is shown in Fig. 12—the purpose of the tape reservoirs is explained later in the text. Note that separate heads are provided for writing and reading data. Allowing for a length of spare tape to be fed through the right-hand reservoir and on to the take-up spool a special marker is placed on the back of the tape to identify the starting-point of the data on the tape. This marker usually consists of a piece of self-adhesive metallic strip which is detected by a photo-electric cell assembly following the read/write head assembly. This metallic strip acts as a reference point for the start of the data on the tape. A second metallic strip, which can be detected by a photo-electric cell before the read/write head assembly, will be attached to the tape a few feet from the end of the tape. This second strip will inform the computer when the reel of tape is almost full. (The action taken at that point is described later.)

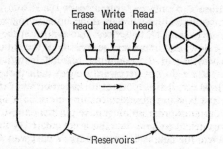

Fig. 12. Schematic of magnetic tape unit

Once a reel of tape has been positioned at its **load point** (i.e. the point identified by the first metallic strip) it can have data recorded on it by the sequence of events described below. The computer will first **interrogate** the tape-deck to verify that the tape is at load point and that the deck is ready to commence writing. Once this has been done, data can be recorded on (or written to) the tape.

The data to be written to the tape are in an area of the computer's core storage and will be transferred to the tape-deck when the computer issues the write instruction (Chapters Thirty-two and Fifty-four). When the write instruction is issued the **erase head** is switched on (to ensure that any previously recorded data are removed from the tape) and the tape is set in motion. The speed of the tape at which data are recorded varies from deck to deck but can be in the range 30–200 inches per second. During the time taken for the tape to accelerate from rest to the recording speed no data are being recorded (although the erase head is switched on).

When the correct tape speed has been reached the data to be written are transferred character by character from core storage to the tape-deck **write head**. Each character is recorded as a magnetic pattern across the tape as the tape passes the write head. Recording continues until all the data required have been copied from core storage to the tape (the data in core storage are not destroyed or altered in any way during this writing). The density of recording varies from system to system but will be in the range 200 to 1600 characters per inch (i.e. each inch of tape could contain the magnetic patterns for 1600 separate characters). When the last character from the area of core storage has been transferred to the tape the write head is switched off and the tape is allowed to come to rest. During this deceleration the erase head remains switched on. Since the erase head is switched on from the moment the tape starts to accelerate until the moment it comes to rest each block of data on the tape will be preceded and followed by a portion of unmagnetized tape. Thus when a number of blocks of data are recorded each will be separated from its neighbours by a length of unmagnetized tape. These are referred to as **inter-block gaps** and will be used to delimit the data when it is to be read (see below). When all the data blocks that are required have been written to the tape a special **end-of-file** pattern is written to the tape. (Note—a complete set of data blocks on a tape is referred to as a file.) This end-of-file marker will be detected during the reading process and will inform the computer program that the file is finished. If the end-of-tape metallic strip is detected (automatically) before the file has been completely written to the tape then another special pattern (**end-of-reel**) will be written to the tape and the file continued on another reel. Conversely, if an end-of-reel marker is detected during the reading process the next reel of tape will be called for so that reading of the file can continue. Data will be read from the tape, under program control, by the issuance of a **read** instruction (Chapters Thirty-two and Fifty-four).

Initially, when the tape is aligned on the first metallic strip, the read head will be positioned over an inter-block gap. When a read instruction is issued the read head is switched on and the tape accelerated. By the time the data reaches the read head the tape will be travelling at full speed. The data on the tape will be transferred into a designated area of core storage until the next inter-block gap is reached. Reading of data blocks can continue until the end-of-file marker is identified. (Note that the transference of reels when an end-of-reel marker is identified will be accomplished automatically and the programmer will not be aware of its occurrence.) Once a file has been completely read the computer program can issue an instruction requesting that the tape be rewound to its load point.

Because of the high speed with which the tape moves on a modern tape-deck it is not possible to match the acceleration of the (comparatively heavy) tape reels with that of the tape itself. To overcome this difficulty the tape passes through a **reservoir** either side of the read/write head assembly. This reservoir consists of a loop of tape maintained by a vacuum underneath the loop. When the tape is accelerated past the read/write heads the reservoir is depleted slightly and the supply reel is allowed to turn to fill it up again. The take-up reel works conversely.

Typical speeds for tape-deck reading and writing are between 30,000 and 300,000 characters per second transferred between the deck and core storage. A reel of magnetic tape can hold up to 20 million characters of information. However, this transfer rate and storage capacity can be effectively reduced if the size of the blocks of data recorded is not chosen carefully. Each inter-block gap on a tape will be about $\frac{1}{2}''$ long: on a deck recording at 800 characters per inch a 400 character block would require $\frac{1}{2}''$ of tape. Since each data block is preceded by an inter-block gap the effective block size for this example is 1″ rather than ¼″. The capacity of the tape would therefore be halved. If instead the block size was 1600 characters the amount of tape required for the block would therefore be 2″ and the inter-block gap would represent only one-quarter of this. The effective increase in block size would therefore be reduced from double to one-quarter. The total amount of data that could be recorded on the tape would therefore be increased. Similarly if the data blocks are larger, and therefore fewer in number, the number of inter-block gaps to be read are fewer and the total time required to read the file is reduced. One might be expected to say at this point "why don't we record a single data block the size of the tape and have no inter-block gaps?". This might seem an easy solution, unfortunately things do not work out so easily usually because there is insufficient core storage to write such a large data block. Additionally it must be appreciated that the data on a file cannot be processed until it has been read and we do not want the computer waiting for the tape-deck to complete its data transfer.

Despite the speeds of magnetic tape-decks they are relatively slow compared to the central processor unit. It is possible to overlap processing (in the CPU) with magnetic file transfer. Once a read instruction has been initiated the CPU can continue its own computing while the data from a magnetic file is being transferred into core storage. (Note that the following comments apply equally well to both types of magnetic storage devices as well as other peripheral units.)

Obviously, though, we cannot continue processing if we wish to work on the data block that is being read in. However, if while processing, say, the 3rd block of data on a file we could at the same time be reading the 4th block a considerable amount of time could be saved (when processing on the 4th block commences we would be reading the 5th block and so on).

This overlap of processing and input or output (the same technique being applied to the writing of data) can be achieved by **double-buffering**. This technique involves the allocation of two areas in core storage into which data from a file are to be read (or from which it is to be written). When a data block is being processed in area 1 the next block is being read into area 2. When the block in area 2 is being processed the next block is being read into area 1 and so on. The two areas allocated are called **buffers** (hence double-buffering) since they act as a buffer between the (relatively) slow peripheral and the computer program processing the data. The reader should note, however, that in the programming languages described later in this book double-buffering is provided automatically and does not require any special coding techniques.

Magnetic Disc Devices

Data are recorded on magnetic discs as a series of magnetic patterns as with magnetic tape above although the mechanics of the system are quite different. A disc store consists typically of six circular **plates**, fixed to a central **spindle**, each surface of which is coated with a magnetic medium such as iron oxide. Both surfaces of each plate are used to contain data except for the top and bottom plates when only the inner surfaces are used. A set of disc plates (called a **disc pack** or **cartridge**) can thus have 10 surfaces on which data can be recorded. Disc packs can be removed from the disc transport mechanism for storage enabling different data to be made available to the computer. For each recording surface there is a read/write head assembly, the five assemblies being joined in a comb-like structure (see Fig. 13) and therefore moving in unison.

To use a disc-recording device the disc packs are placed on the **transport mechanism** (while the head assembly is retracted in a protective housing—to the left in Fig. 13) and the drive engaged. The disc pack is rotated at high speed (about 2500 revs per min.) and when the full speed is reached the head assembly is automatically moved to the first recording position of the outer periphery of the disc surfaces. Each arm of the head assembly contains two read/write heads—one for each of the surfaces between which the heads are positioned. Note that the heads do not actually touch the disc surfaces but **float** on a minute cushion of air (to avoid the disc surface being scratched).

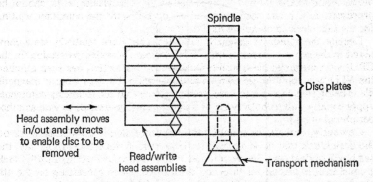

Fig. 13. Schematic of magnetic disc unit

Each head on the disc drive can be positioned at each of typically 100 concentric recording bands on each surface. Since all the heads move together the same recording band is selected on each recording surface at the same time. For any single head movement the computer can therefore access 10 bands of information (one per surface). These 10 bands, or **tracks** as they are also called, together form a **cylinder**. There are therefore 100 cylinders per disc pack. The dotted line in Fig. 14 shows one particular cylinder on a disc pack.

Data held on a single cylinder can be accessed without any head movement. A large number of data blocks recorded would therefore follow the line of a cylinder rather than go from track to track on a single surface. Only when the cylinder is full will the head assembly be moved to another cylinder. In this way the amount of, relatively slow, head movement required is reduced to a minimum.

Each cylinder has a specially recorded **home address marker** on it to identify the beginning (in a circular direction) of that cylinder. Data blocks are recorded on the disc surfaces with inter-block gaps in the same manner as tape units. However, since the disc pack is continually revolving the heads do not remain over an inter-block gap once a data block has been read (or written). Instead the disc unit "remembers" how far round the track it has just read (or written) and when next asked to read (or write) will "know" how far the disc can revolve from the home address marker before the transfer operation has to be initiated.

The comments made earlier about the relationship of inter-block gap size to record size apply again to disc packs. In addition, the person designing the layout of the files to be recorded on the disc pack must also remember that each track may only hold a certain number of characters. If the block size is badly chosen it may be found that a large proportion of the recording surface is wasted because the unused portion remaining at the end of a track may be just less than the amount required for a data block (causing the block to be written on to the next track of the cylinder). Fortunately, the computer manufacturers provide tables from which optimum data-block sizes can be established.

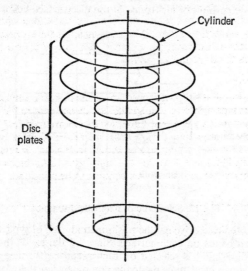

Fig. 14. Concept of disc cylinder

When processing a file serially (i.e. reading each block on the file one after the other) the disc unit will automatically provide the computer program with the next block and will also move the head assembly from cylinder to cylinder as required. It is quite usual to record more than one file on a disc pack and each will be identified by start-of-file and end-of-file markers recorded on the pack. Note that there is no equivalent, on disc packs, to the metallic strips used on magnetic tapes since a disc pack is always of a specified size (e.g. 100 cylinders each of 10 tracks).

Since the head assembly of a disc drive can be positioned at any of the cylinders and then any of the 10 tracks can be read from (or written to) it is not necessary to read an entire file serially. Because of this feature disc drives are often referred to collectively as **Direct Access Storage Devices**. However, if a file is to be accessed in a direct manner (i.e. data blocks are to be selected in any order as they are required rather than serially) the file must be set up in a special manner. This is because the program, accessing the data directly, must be able to supply the disc unit with cylinder number, track number, and block number of the desired piece of data. In order that this can be done the programmer must establish a relationship between the key of the data block he requires (the key being the data-block identifier—e.g. a customer account number) and the three location identifiers already mentioned. The complexity of this type of programming renders it beyond the scope of this book and subsequent discussions on file organization and handling will relate only to serial files. However, the reader should remember the direct access capability of disc drives which provides the key to many of the newer and more exciting computer developments. (Note that the complexities mentioned above will diminish in stature as the reader gains experience in programming.)

A typical disc pack can hold about 30 million characters of information which can be transferred to the CPU at a rate of up to 300,000 characters per second. It is quite common to find commercial installations with up to eight disc-drive units connected to the CPU providing immediate access to up to 240 million characters of information. Further data can of course be stored on other disc packs to be loaded as required.

File Organization

In the discussion that follows the recording medium for a file can be taken to be a magnetic tape device or a magnetic disc device used in the serial mode. From the programming viewpoint these two media are identical.

We have already seen that data blocks are recorded on a backing store device separated by inter-block gaps as shown in Fig. 15. We have also seen that the optimum block size is chosen to minimize the inter-block gap wastage while occupying only those storage areas that can be allocated.

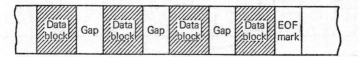

Fig. 15. Inter-block gaps

However, what would be the answer if the information we wished to hold on the file was in units smaller than the block size. For example, suppose the manufacturers tables indicate that for a particular application we should use a data-block size of 600 characters. However, the units of information (called **records**) which we wish to hold on the file—customer name and address details—are only 200 characters in length. Rather than reduce the data-block size we will so construct the file that each data block contains three records. This technique is called **blocking** and a file can be said to be **blocked** in threes (or however many records are contained in a block). When the record size is equal to the required block size the file is said to be **single-blocked**. The layout of part of a file blocked in fours is shown in Fig. 16. Thus we can now choose the block size which is a multiple of the record size and is closest to the optimum block size (e.g. in the example above the optimum block size may have been 420 characters).

Within each record on the file will be the fields of data making up the file

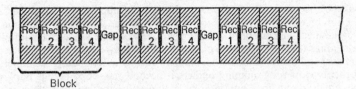

Block

Fig. 16. Blocked file schematic

(fields being similar to those described in Chapter Three). Each field will be composed of one or more individual characters although, when referring to files, it is not usual to specify smaller units than fields. Thus for the customer name and address records mentioned above the layout of the fields within the file might be as shown in Fig. 17.

When a file is to be used by a program it must be completely described within that program so that it can be handled correctly. Four levels of file definition are required as seen above and these are summarized in Fig. 18.

Once this information has been supplied (Chapters Eighteen, Nineteen, and Fifty-four) the programmer need no longer concern himself with the physical organization of the file. He will instruct his program to read (or write) a single record at a time. The blocking or de-blocking (for writing or reading respectively) will be done automatically—see Chapter Eight.

Account no.	Name 20 chars	Address line 1 30 chars	AL 2 30	AL 3 30	AL 4 30	AL 5 30	Delivery instructions

10 chars

20 chars

AL = Address line

Fig. 17. Sample record layout

So far we have only considered the case when all the records on a file were of equal size. It is possible to record records of varying lengths if the application requires it. For example in the case quoted above (Fig. 17) each line of the address is allocated 30 characters within the record, giving 150 characters in all for this part of the data. However, on average an address will require much less than this amount of space (although we must allow for a large maximum size address). We could decide therefore to abandon the separate lines of the address and store only the complete address in as many characters as it required. Clearly, then, the records (and therefore the blocks) on the file will be of varying lengths.

A **variable-length block** can be read satisfactorily since the end of it will be signified by the inter-block gap. How though will the program know the length of each record? Each record in a variable-length file is preceded by a

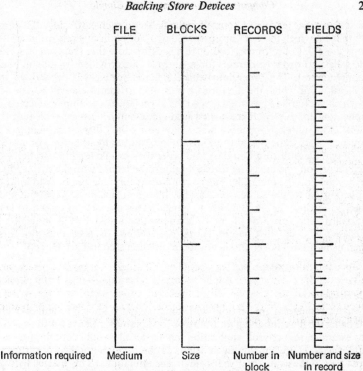

FILE	BLOCKS	RECORDS	FIELDS

| Information required | Medium | Size | Number in block | Number and size in record |

Fig. 18. The levels of file definition

field containing a count of the total number of characters contained in that record (including the count itself). Each variable-length block also contains a field at its beginning containing a count of the total number of characters in the block. A variable-length block is illustrated in Fig. 19. A variable-length file will have specified for it a **maximum block size** in order that the buffers can be allocated the (maximum) amount of core storage they require.

As with fixed-length files the de-blocking of variable-length files is done automatically. A detailed discussion on the programming required for records with a variable number of fields will be found in Part Two.

Block count	Rec cnt	Record 1	Rec cnt	Record 2	Rec cnt	Record 3

Fig. 19. Variable-length block layout

File Sequencing

Files held on a backing store device will be processed in a particular sequence or order. When information is punched on to cards it will be in no particular order (except of course for the fields on each card) since the documents from which the data are prepared will not be in any particular order, Once these data are transcribed on to a backing store file, they will be sorted into a desired order (programs for sorting files are provided by the computer manufacturers). The order into which a file is sorted will depend on the application for which the file forms a part. A particular field will be selected on which the file is to be sorted (called the **key field**). For example, in a payroll application the file could be sorted into clock-number order, such that the lowest clock-number appeared first, followed by the other clock-numbers in sequence. Such a file is said to be **serially** or **sequentially** organized or sorted. When two files are sorted in the same order they can be read in parallel with each record on one file being **matched** against the record with the corresponding key field on the other file. Thus amendments for a file can be read in from cards, sorted to the same order as the file on to magnetic tape and then matched against the file they are to amend. This obviates any need to skip backwards and forwards along a file attempting a match. File matching is discussed in detail in Chapter Thirty-four. (Note—its need does not arise when using FORTRAN and is not therefore discussed in Part Three.)

File Security

Most commercial applications will contain what is known as a **master file**, this being the file containing the (more or less) permanent data for the system. For example, in a payroll application the master file would contain, for each employee, a record showing such details as name, clock-number, department, gross pay, bonus rate, and year-to-date accumulations. This master file will need to be amended or **updated** on a regular basis to reflect changes in the basic information it contains. For example, in the payroll application the master file will need to have new starters added, leavers deleted, and the year-to-date figures brought up to date weekly.

To update this master file another file, containing the amendments, will be created in the same sequence as the master file. The two files will be **matched** and the master file records amended according to the details on the **amendments file**. It is rarely possible to overwrite a block on magnetic tape with another block (even of the same length) without disturbing the data block which follows. When updating a magnetic tape file it is necessary therefore to create a new file that is a copy of the original, except for those records which have been amended (plus any new records that have been created). Note that when processing sequential files every record on the file must be processed anyway.

This creation of a separate updated master file improves the security of that file. The new master file is carried forward to the next run of the program when it becomes the input master file. The tape containing what is now the old master file is not overwritten until a new master file has been produced on a succeeding processing run. Thus at any one time there will be in existence **three generations** of master file. If the current master file becomes accidentally damaged or destroyed the previous version of the master file can be re-run against its amendments and the current master file recreated (see Chapter Thirty-four).

Exercises

1. Name the two main types of backing store devices.
2. How is the beginning of a reel of tape identified?
3. How are data blocks separated?
4. What limits the size of a data block?
5. Name the technique requiring two storage areas for reading or writing data.
6. How many tracks form a cylinder in the example given?
7. How many cylinders are available on a disc pack in the example given?
8. How much data-recording area is accessible without moving the disc heads?
9. Name the four levels of file definition required by a program.
10. How many generations of master file are kept for security?

CHAPTER SIX

LOGIC AND FLOWCHARTING

A computer program is a series of **statements** or **instructions** which instruct the computer how to solve a given problem. The computer cannot "think", it will do only that which it has been instructed to do and no more. A computer program will, in almost every case, be a generalized procedure and will not contain specific sets of instructions relating to each data item to be processed. For example, in a payroll application we cannot instruct the computer to look for every specific employee's name and calculate a wages amount accordingly. The program to calculate employees' pay will contain only one routine for actually calculating pay; where the pay of an employee is arrived at differently from another the information on the master file must reflect this.

As a simple example of this consider a payroll program to calculate the gross pay of each employee. Suppose this gross pay is made up of a number of items which may or may not be present for each employee. The gross pay will be computed by adding together the contents of each of these fields on the master file. The master file record of an employee will contain a zero amount in the fields for which he receives no additional pay. In this way the coding required for each employee's gross pay calculation is the same, i.e. all the fields on the master file are added together. (Those with a zero amount being effectively ignored since they make no difference to the final amount.) Remember the clerical example quoted earlier (Chapter Two)—the computer program relates to the payroll Procedure Manual. This manual refers to all cases but will produce the correct result according to the data supplied.

As an analogy consider a bagatelle board—only one way exists in and one way out although there are a considerable number of paths available within the board—choice being dependent on the variations of the input (i.e. speed of ball, weight of ball, etc.). *Similarly a program will have only one start and one end point but a number of possible paths between these points.* The exact path taken each time will depend on the values of the data input. In our payroll application each employee's details will be read from the master file; a program path will be followed depending on the data read, then, when this record has been processed, the next record will be read from the master file and the procedure will be entered again. This will continue until all the records have been processed on the file. Despite the possibility of different paths being followed, as just introduced, we still have a single procedure or program for all records on the master file although every record may not utilize all the steps in the program. For example at one point in the program it may be necessary to calculate a weekly bonus. The value of this bonus could depend on the sex of the employee, thus if male one path would be followed and if female another path (although both paths would return to the same point further down the program). If this were the case then the master file could contain a field identifying the sex of the employee—i.e. it could contain an "M" for male and an "F" for female. The program would then examine this field and decide which path was to be taken depending upon the value of the field.

Before a program can be written it is necessary to identify every step and path making the solution to the problem at hand. *It is most important to clearly isolate every single step and every single condition that can possibly occur during the solving of the problem.* This is the area in which most mistakes originate during the development of a computer program; it is all to easy to be slipshod and not ensure that every possibility is catered for. Unfortunately the definition of a computer programs **logic paths** (as they are often called) is not an area which can be readily taught to the newcomer—expertise will normally only come with experience. However, the job is made easier, and in some cases foolproof, by the use of a technique to represent the program logic diagrammatically.

Flowcharting

A **flowchart** is a diagrammatic representation of the logic paths contained within a computer program and **flowcharting** is the technique of drawing the flowchart. The acts of identifying the logic paths and actually drawing the flowchart are difficult to split into separate areas and are normally undertaken as a single exercise. Flowcharting is illustrated below but first the symbols used to make up a flowchart are described.

Flowcharting Symbols

1. PROCESS

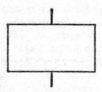

This symbol indicates any complete **process** or **step** which is always executed when the path it is in is followed. A process, in this context, could include almost any simple operation (excluding those shown later as having their own symbol), some examples of which are shown below (as a series of processes to be executed one after another):

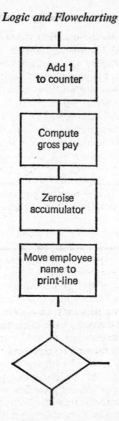

2. DECISION

A **decision** box, which is normally entered from the top, represents a point at which different process paths may be selected. In other words, it represents the occurrence of a question—the answer to which will determine the path to be taken. The decision box must, as shown above, have at least two exits although a third may be added if desired. A decision box may contain a simple question (with a YES or NO answer) with the two exits being labelled Y or N (for YES or NO respectively) as shown below:

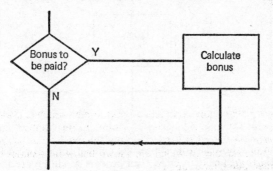

In this case if the answer to the question is yes (i.e. there is a bonus to be paid) then the exit marked Y is taken, the process to calculate the bonus is executed and the logic paths join up again. (Note—unless otherwise indicated with arrowheads the program along connecting lines on a flowchart is left to right or top to bottom.) A decision of this type may have two different processes before the paths rejoin:

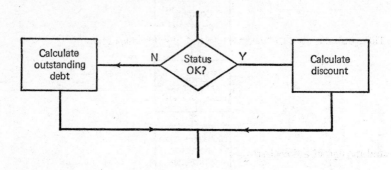

The two different process paths may of course go in completely different directions only to meet at the end of the program. This will be illustrated in the more fuller examples later.

A decision box may also be used to represent the **comparison** of two fields with the exit points being labelled with the possible outcomes of the comparison (i.e. equal and not equal, or less than, equal to, and greater than). A decision containing a comparison is shown below:

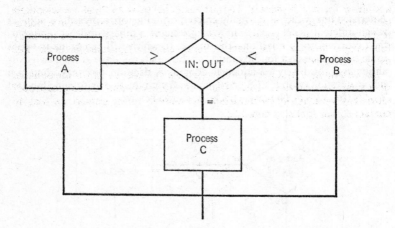

This section of a flowchart illustrates the comparison of two fields (IN and OUT); if IN is greater than OUT then process A will be executed, if IN is less than OUT then process B will be executed, and if IN is equal to OUT process C will be executed.

3. TERMINATORS

This symbol is used to illustrate the start of a flowchart thus:

and the end of a flowchart thus:

There are several more symbols available for use in flowcharting. However before discussing them, let us examine a problem (not related to a computer) and draw for it a flowchart. The problem chosen is to "make a telephone call"—something which comes naturally to all of us and may seem a ridiculously simple task. However, as we shall see if this call is to be made by following a flowchart the chart becomes quite complicated in order that every contingency can be catered for.

Let us assume that a telephone is available and that we know the name of the person we wish to contact. What will be the first step in this procedure? Obviously we must know the telephone number of the person we wish to contact so our first step could be:

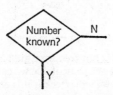

If the number is not known then we must look up the number—to do this requires a telephone directory:

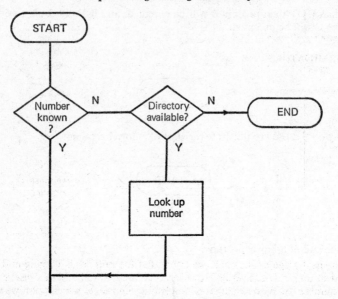

The next stage would seem to be to dial the required number; however, this can only be done if the telephone is not in use by another person. The next stage of our flowchart could therefore be:

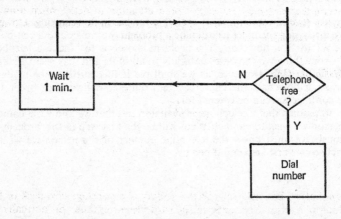

Note that if the telephone is not free we wait 1 minute before attempting a further call. Once the telephone is available we can dial the required number. Having dialled the number we will check if it is engaged, and if so will return to the "wait 1 min." process: if the number is not engaged we will need to know if it is ringing. If it is not ringing (and is not engaged) something is amiss and the call must be retried. The next stage of the flowchart will there-fore be:

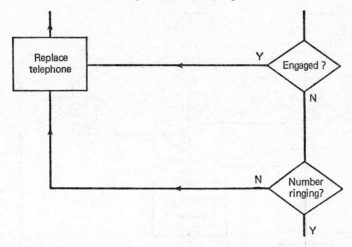

For the next stage of the chart we know that the number is ringing and we must wait until it is answered. However, it is essential to build in a test to see if the number has been ringing too long (say 2 minutes) at which point we will hang-up. If the telephone is answered we must then inquire if the person we wish to speak to is available and if so we can finally conduct the conversation. The final complete flowchart is illustrated in Fig. 20.

Quite a lengthy process for such a simple task! No doubt you will now appreciate the earlier points made about attention to detail when drawing flowcharts from which computer programs are to be written. We will now look at the remainder of the flowcharting symbols:

4. PUNCHED CARD

This symbol can be used to signify the reading of a punched-card deck or the punching of a deck. The name of the card file being used will normally be entered in the box:

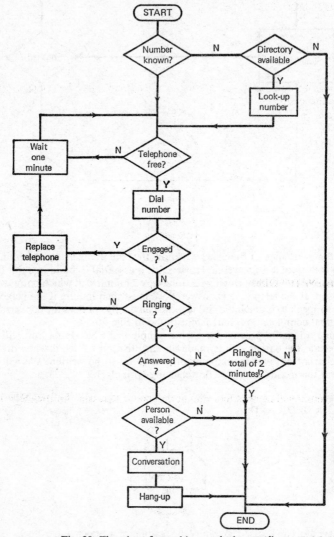

Fig. 20. Flowchart for making a telephone call

5. PAPER TAPE

This will signify input (or output) of paper tape and will again contain the name of the file in use.

6. MAGNETIC TAPE

Indicates an input or an output magnetic tape the exact use being specified inside the symbol:

7. MAGNETIC DISC

This symbol will be used in a similar manner to that used for magnetic tape:

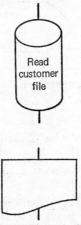

8. PRINTER DEVICE

The printed output of a program is indicated with this symbol, the name of the report being contained within the box:

A program may produce more than one report in which case two overlapped symbols can be used:

9. PREDEFINED PROCESS

This symbol identifies a **subroutine** or **predefined process** which is described in detail in Chapters Thirty-nine and Fifty-six.

10. OPERATOR CONSOLE

A communication with the computer operator will be signified by the use of the symbol shown:

The flowcharting symbols shown above represent those most commonly used and will be sufficient for the reader to draw any flowcharts he requires. The use of flowcharts when designing a computer program layout is discussed in Chapter Seven.

Exercises

1. How many start and end points can a computer program have?
2. Will a payroll program contain the name of each employee and, if not, where will the name be held?
3. How can the logic of a program be represented diagrammatically?
4. Identify the use of the following flowcharting symbols:

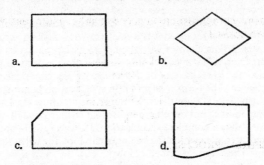

5. Identify the following flowcharting symbols:

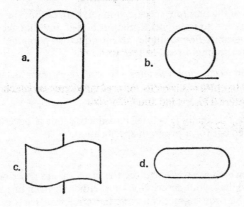

CHAPTER SEVEN

PROGRAM SPECIFICATION ANALYSIS

Program Specifications

The programmer may on occasion prepare the specification for a program himself. However, it is more common for the program specification to be prepared by a Systems Analyst and passed to the programming department for coding (see *Computer Programming Management* (London: Butterworths, 1972 by the present author)). Many trainee programmers, despite being fully conversant with a programming language (see Parts Two and Three) stare at a blank sheet of paper for a long time when given their first program to code: when asked why they reply "I don't know where to start." A strange response perhaps—but where *does* one begin?

This aspect of programming is in fact very difficult to teach to a newcomer; indeed little research appears to have been done in this area by the computer industry. The major stumbling-block to producing a computer program (at least for the beginner) is the conversion of a program specification or narrative into a flowchart. Once the flowchart has been produced and verified as representing the logic required it is a relatively easy task to actually code the processing steps. This chapter will attempt to assist the reader in producing his flowchart from a first specification. As with most aspects of programming this one becomes less and less of a problem as the experience of the practitioner increases. The form of a program specification is not something that can be described in standard terms. Some installations do have their own individual guide-lines but even here individual writers have their own idea as to what constitutes a complete specification. However, there are a number of minimum requirements which the beginner can look for when reading his first specification. These are described below.

Introduction

This section of the program specification serves to outline the basic function of the program and to specify the relationships if any that the program has with other programs. For example, an introductory paragraph for a simple card validation run might read as follows:

This program reads and validates the weekly payroll amendment cards, writing accepted data to magnetic tape. This program is the first in the payroll run and is followed by the master file up-date.

As you can see this really is a brief introduction but is nevertheless an important requirement for a program specification.

Input

All the files which are to be read by the program are described here. Note that a complete file layout description must either be given or referred to here in order that the programmer can code those relevant parts of the program without reference elsewhere. The input section of the program specification quoted above could be as follows:

Card File. Payroll weekly amendments are read from a punched-card file prior to validation (see below). The layout of the cards is as shown in App. 1 to this specification.

Output

The files which are to be written by the program are listed here in the same manner as for input files above. The sample program specification could contain the following output files list:

Tape File. Accepted amendments, read from cards above, are written to a magnetic tape file blocked in fours. Record layout is the same as the input card file.

Print File. All input cards rejected by the validation routine are listed on standard stationery in card image format. Headings, including a page number, should be selected to reflect the nature of the printout.

Throughput (also called Processing)

This section is the most important in the program specification since it describes the procedures which the program is to contain and represents the problem to be solved by the program. The manner in which this section is specified varies from being minutely detailed to being extremely vague depending on the individual who has written the specification. The ideal format of a specification is a subject of some controversy but would seem to be somewhere about the middle of the two extremes mentioned above (for a further discussion on the content of program specifications see *Computer Programming Management* by the same author). However, this section of the specification must give all the processing steps required and must be unambiguous. In other words, it must be sufficiently clear to enable the program to be coded without reference to the specification writer. Continuing with our sample specification we might have a throughput section written thus:

Throughput. The program will read payroll amendment cards and validate according to the following rules. Each card read must be either a type 148 or type 150 although these types may appear in any order. Type 148 contains the employee's new address and/or clock number; if an address is present it must consist only of alphabetic characters; the clock-number if present must consist only of numeric characters. Card type 150 specifies new deductions to be made from an employee's pay—up to 6 new deductions may be on a card—each consisting of a 2 digit identifier and an amount in pence. Spaces in the amount field would indicate the withdrawal of a deduction from the employee's pay.
Cards which are accepted as valid are written to the amendments tape. Invalid cards are listed with an appropriate comment.

The program specification would be completed by appendices giving detailed layouts of all the records on each of the files used; however these are of no concern to us for the present exercise. The problem now is to translate the above program description into a flowchart. How is this to be done? Where in fact do we start?

The first and most important task is to make certain that the specification is understood, it must be clear and unambiguous. Before commencing to draw a flowchart the programmer must be quite sure, in his own mind, that he understands what the program is expected to do. As an example of a potential error the above specification implies that on a card type 148 it is possible to have neither an address or a clock-number although the specification does not give the required action if this does happen. It is fairly clear however that if a card type 148 is read with no amendment data then it can be considered to be invalid and rejected accordingly.

Most programs can be divided roughly into three parts—input, processing, and output. The sample shown above is no exception—we will read in cards, process them (i.e. validate them) and depending on the result of the validation, will either write a record to tape or will print a line on the printer device. We have therefore a basis on which to begin our flowcharting and can draw an initial chart:

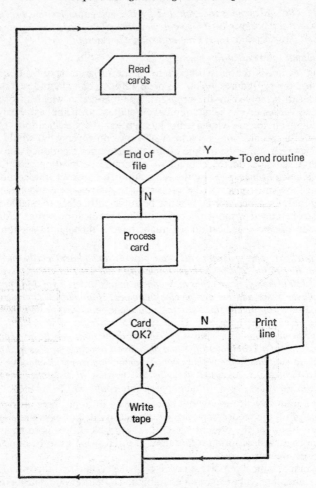

It can be seen that once started this program will continue until the end-of-file condition is reached on the card input file (see Chapter Thirty-two). Before the files used by the program can be processed it is necessary to prepare them by using some special statements (discussed in detail in Chapter Thirty-one) and similarly, they must be terminated in a special manner. The flowchart can therefore be expanded as shown on page 43.

The next step is to expand the box labelled "process card" to reflect the full specification as shown above. The first stage of this is to select different paths depending on whether the card type is 148 or 150 although note particularly that we must specifically test for each type—if the card type is not 148 we cannot assume it will be 150. Each of the valid card type paths will then contain coding to perform the required validation; as each (if any) error is found a marker will be set to indicate this and it is this marker which is examined in

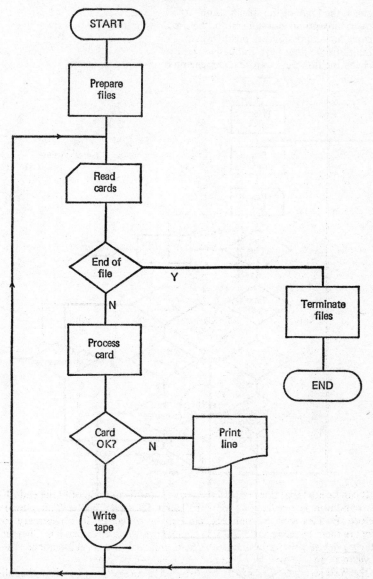

the "card OK?" decision box. Note that the marker must be reset to the OK state before each card is examined (otherwise all cards after the first rejected one would be also rejected). The complete flowchart will now be as Fig. 21.

There, briefly, is a demonstration of the way in which a flowchart can be produced from a specification. When actually doing this yourself remember the most important points made above:

check the logic of the specification
query any points not understood before flowcharting
cater for all possibilities positively
build up the flowchart gradually
check the flowchart before commencing to code the program.

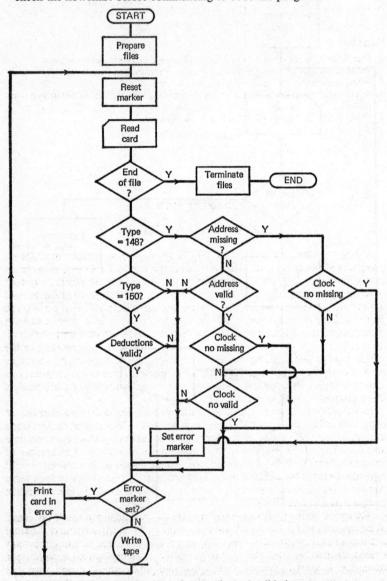

Fig. 21. Complete flowchart for sample card validation program

Any errors or omissions in your flowchart will become apparent during the testing of the program. It is very rare to write a computer program that works first time. Remember however that only by having a correct flowchart can you hope to have a correct program. Flowcharting is often derided by some experts—but it is a valuable tool the perfection of which (from experience) will be the sign of a truly competent programmer.

Exercises

1. Name the four areas which must be present in a program specification.
2. What details are required in the program specification of files to be used?
3. What three parts can most programs be divided into?
4. What must be done with the program specification before flowcharting commences?
5. What is the final step before coding your program?

CHAPTER EIGHT

OPERATING SYSTEMS

A large modern computer has the ability to run a number of different programs at the same time. The way this is done is to start the first program and allow it to perform its processing until it requests an input or output operation to a peripheral device (i.e. until it, say, issues the instruction to read a punched card into core storage). While this input/output operation is being performed the program that issued the instruction will be idle (note: even with techniques designed to speed up the effective data transfer rate—such as double-buffering—the speed of any peripheral device is slow relative to the CPU). During this idle time the CPU can permit a second program (in another area of core storage) to begin execution. Ultimately this second program will also request an input/output operation and while this is being performed, a third program can be executing.

In theory this system could be continued for an unlimited number of programs although in practice this is not the case. A number of factors place limitations on the number of programs that can be in core storage at one time and the effect of these will vary from computer to computer. The number of programs involved in this technique (called **multi-programming**) would typically be three for a medium-sized computer and up to about 16 for a large computer (small computers are not usually capable of handling more than one program at any one time).

The major limiting factor on the number of programs in a multi-programming environment is the speed and size of the CPU itself. Obviously the total number of storage locations required by all the programs in storage cannot exceed the number available within the CPU. Even though an input/output operation is relatively slow it will eventually be complete and then the program that requested it must be allowed to continue from the point the input/output request was issued with the data now available. The sequence of events for a CPU with three programs being run is illustrated in Fig. 22.

We can see the points mentioned above in this figure. When execution of program 1 is suspended for the first input/output operation program 2 is allowed to execute. Similarly when program 2 is suspended program 3 is allowed to execute. Two further points are illustrated in the diagram. Firstly when the input/output request is made by program 3 all the programs are waiting for an input/output operation to be completed; the CPU is therefore idle for a short time until one of these operations (in the example that for program 1) is complete. As soon as one is complete the relevant program is allowed to continue executing. The second point introduced in the diagram is

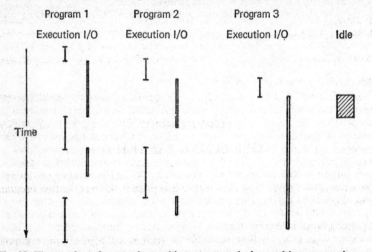

Fig. 22. The overlap of processing and input/output during multi-programming

at the end of the second input/output operation for program 2. Since at this point program 3 is still waiting for input/output completion the next program to be allowed to execute is program 1.

To summarize, therefore, we can say that multi-programming is a system to enable a number of programs to interleave with each other such that the execution of one program is overlapped with the input/output operation(s) of other programs. Clearly there are a number of potential problems associated with multi-programming—for example if several input/output operations finished simultaneously which program would be given control? It could be arranged that this was always the first program to issue an input/output request, but if things were organized in this manner, it would be possible for a program started last in a large series to be almost completely ignored. It is necessary for some system to be initiated to control or schedule the flow of work through the CPU. This scheduling will need to control not only multi-programming but also such things as peripheral device allocation (to make sure two programs do not attempt to use the same printer at the same time for example), computer operator communication and so forth. These tasks are all undertaken by a routine known as the **Supervisor** or **Executive**.

The Supervisor

The Supervisor is a program supplied by the computer manufacturer which is designed to control the flow of work through the computer. The Supervisor is termed a **permanently resident program** since it will be held in part of core storage all the time the computer is in use. Note however that it is not part of the computer, it is basically only another program (although it will of necessity be more complicated than the average commercial program). It is normal practice to load the Supervisor into core storage at the start of each working day; it should only be necessary to reload it if a serious error develops causing the Supervisor itself to be corrupted (i.e. altered) in core storage (although this is very rare). As will be seen below the Supervisor is used to load the normal production programs into core storage; the Supervisor itself is loaded by a special facility built into the computer.

Communication with a Supervisor is by one of two methods—using the console typewriter (mainly for use by the computer operators—see below) or by means of a **Job Control** or **Job Description Language** (often referred to simply as JCL or JDL).The programmer will request the various functions he wants by use of the JCL; for example in a system using punched cards as the main input media he would precede his program punched-card deck with the appropriate JCL cards. The Supervisor would read the JCL cards and either carry out the requested function itself or instruct another (manufacturer supplied) program to undertake the request. The format of JCL cards varies from system to system and is beyond the scope of this book; however, given an understanding of the basic facilities offered by a Supervisor it is a simple task to select the required JCL statements from the computer manufacturer's manual. The facilities provided by an average Supervisor are described below.

Program Scheduling

This is perhaps the most important function of a Supervisor since it is designed to maximize the utilization of the CPU by the introduction and control of multi-programming. For the purpose of running several programs at one time the core storage in the CPU is divided into a number of **partitions**, each of which can contain one program. (Note—the boundaries between partitions are conceptual only, there is no physical barrier within the CPU, the size of partitions can be changed as required by giving the appropriate JCL command to the Supervisor.) For a system running three programs the CPU will be divided into four partitions as shown in Fig. 23.

At the start of operations the Supervisor will load the three programs and

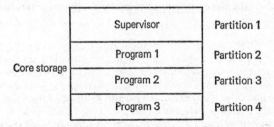

Fig. 23. Division of core storage into partitions

then pass control to program 1 which will commence executing. When program 1 issues an input or output command (see Chapters Thirty-two and Fifty-four) control is transferred to the Supervisor which will process the command. The Supervisor will verify that the device at which the command is directed is not **busy** (if the device is already actioning an earlier command—i.e. is busy—the current command will be placed in a **queue** for later processing when the device is free). Once an I/O command is actioned or queued, control is returned to the program that issued that command (remember double-buffering). However, the program will shortly need the data from the second buffer but cannot yet use it because the input/output operation is not complete. It will therefore inform the Supervisor that it is **waiting** and the Supervisor can pass control to program 2. Similarly, control will eventually pass to program 3. As soon as a particular input/output operation is complete the CPU is automatically **interrupted**; this means that the program currently executing is temporarily stopped and control is passed to the Supervisor. The Supervisor will verify that the input/output operation completed successfully (if not it will attempt the same operation again) and will return control to the next program to be executed (which one will depend on the system of priorities built in to the Supervisor).

The Supervisor therefore schedules the execution of all the programs within the CPU and within each program schedules the operation of input/output commands. The scope of this work is indicated by an experiment conducted by the author which demonstrated that a program designed to read a magnetic tape file and print pay-slips on a line printer generated over 3000 CPU interruptions every minute.

Operator Communication

The Supervisor will keep the computer operators informed as to the current **status** of the system and the programs running at any one time. For example if an input/output operation is unsuccessful—perhaps a record on magnetic tape cannot be read—the Supervisor will print out a message to that effect on the computer operator's console typewriter. Often in a case like this the operator will be asked what action he wants taking—for example the record which cannot be read could be by-passed or the program could be terminated.

The computer operator can request information from the system by pressing his "call" or "interrupt" button. This causes control to be passed to the Supervisor which can then read the operator's request from the console typewriter and print out the information he requires.

The operator will be informed as each program ends and in some systems he can instruct the Supervisor to start a new program by typing the appropriate commands.

JCL Interpretation

The Supervisor is responsible for reading, interpreting, and actioning the JCL commands supplied to the system. These can be of two types—direct and indirect. A **direct command** is one that the Supervisor itself can action without reference to any other procedure. An **indirect command** is one that requires a procedure not normally held within the Supervisor itself (if all such routines were permanently resident in core storage no room would be available for ordinary programs!). Within the Supervisor is a mini-partition area into which special routines can be loaded, by the Supervisor, to supplement the standard facilities. As far as the user is concerned these two types of commands are the same—it is only the manner in which they are actioned within the Supervisor that is different.

The major function of the Supervisor under the heading of JCL interpretation is the loading of programs. All programs which have been supplied by the computer manufacturer and all those user-written programs which have been compiled (see below) are stored on a backing store device. When available this will be a disc storage device with the programs being accessed directly by the Supervisor. To load a program the Supervisor will refer to the backing store device containing the program and will instruct the device to transfer the program into core storage (note the stored program is considered by the backing store to be just another set of data). Once the program has been read into core storage the Supervisor will transfer control to the program which can then begin its processing.

Compilers

The programming languages, COBOL and FORTRAN, which you will read about in Parts Two and Three of this work are known as **high-level languages**. This name derives from the pseudo-English syntax used in these particular languages. In the early days programming consisted of writing down long strings of numbers which represented the processing to be carried out. These numbers, when read into the CPU, were directly understandable and therefore executable by the computer. However, their very nature made them difficult to understand, prone to error, and slow to produce. Computers still function internally in much the same way—i.e. they examine and execute instructions represented by strings of numbers—however, it is no longer necessary to code programs in this basic form. As we shall see later in the book we can now write straightforward English language statements such as

ADD TRANSACTION-VALUE TO BALANCE.

The computer can read this type of coding (via, say, a punched-card input device—the statements having been transcribed on to cards in the datapreparation department) but it cannot execute the statements in this form because it recognizes only strings of numbers as a program. The computer manufacturers supply with each machine a program written to translate the English-type statements of our program into the strings of numbers that the computer can execute. This type of program is known as a **compiler** and a separate one will be supplied for each programming language in use (e.g. COBOL and FORTRAN).

Compiler Functions

The major function of a **compiler** is, as already mentioned, to translate the statements written by the programmer into machine executable number strings. The actual mechanics of this translation (or **compilation** as it is known) is beyond the scope of this book, although the reader will appreciate that it is quite a complicated task.

The compiler will perform additional functions depending on the nature of the program being compiled (known as the **source program**). If a program manipulates a blocked backing store file it is necessary for coding to be present in the program to block or de-block the file records as required. It is not, however, necessary for the programmer to write the coding to do this work. Such coding is automatically inserted into a program by the compiler when the description of a blocked file (Chapters Sixteen and Seventeen) is encountered in the source program.

The compiler will verify as much as is feasible, that the program being compiled does not contain any logic errors. For example any attempt to add into a field which has been defined as containing only alphabetic (i.e. the letters A–Z) characters will be identified as an error. Similarly a reference to a field which has not been defined in the program will not be accepted. (Note—definition of data fields is described fully in Parts Two and Three.)

The output from a compiler will be in two parts: (a) all the statements forming the program (i.e. the details making the source program) will be printed out (on a line-printer device) together with comments generated by the compiler (showing errors which have been discovered—these errors are said to be **flagged**). This **source listing**, as it is called, will be used by the programmer as a record of precisely what was compiled when he wishes to make corrections to the original following any tests of the program. (b) A program may be required to be run several times but it obviously is un-desirable to compile it each time. The compiler will therefore produce the executable program (called an **object program**) as its second output. This can be directed to any output device other than the line printer although it is usual to store object programs on a disc backing store. From this backing store the program can be retrieved by the Supervisor, loaded into core storage and executed as often as the user desires.

Operating Systems

The Supervisor and the Compiler described above are the most important of a whole series of programs supplied by the computer manufacturer known collectively as an **Operating System**.

The main aims of an operating system are those already given for a Super-visor—*to maximize the amount of work undertaken by the computer and to minimize the amount of human operator intervention*. Additional capabilities commonly present in operating systems are described below:

Library Maintenance

The programs held on a backing store device (called a **Library of Programs**) have to be kept in a tidy condition. For example those programs no longer required have to be deleted from the backing store and the space allocated to other programs. The programmer must be able to find out what programs are stored in the Library and how much space is available for new programs. An Operating System will contain programs to perform all these Library functions.

Sorting

It is often convenient to have backing store files organized in a particular sequence, for example a payroll master file could be organized in ascending clock-number order. The Operating System will contain a **sort program** to accomplish any required ordering of backing store files. The program will be generalized and the programmer will supply for each particular sort run details about the file to be sorted and the way in which it is to be organized (these details are called **parameters**).

Utilities

A number of simple tasks occur frequently in a computing environment and rather than have a special little program written for each one the Operating System contains a number of **generalized utility programs**. By supplying the necessary parameters to the appropriate program a number of simple jobs can be performed. These jobs will include:

copying a file from one device to another (and optionally altering the blocking factor)
listing the contents of a file on the line printer
counting the number of records or blocks on a file
combining two files into one (i.e. merging two files).

Error Recovery

Various types of error can occur while a computer system is running—a program can fail (due to an incorrect or illogical instruction)—a backing store device can malfunction—the CPU could develop a faulty circuit and so on. The Operating System will contain routines and programs to deal with all these types of error (some of the routines will effectively form part of the Supervisor by being read into the mini-partition). In the case of a peripheral device error the Operating System will attempt to correct the fault (by re-trying the data transfer causing the error a set number of times). If the fault cannot be corrected the computer operator will be informed and the appropriate action can be taken (i.e. the faulty unit can be replaced).

When a program fails (frequently during the testing stage!) the Operating System will first of all **dump** the contents of core storage—i.e. it will print out (on the line printer) the current contents of the computer memory to enable the programmer to investigate the error and make the necessary corrections to his source program prior to re-compilation. Secondly it will delete the failed program from its current schedule so allowing the next program to be read in and executed.

Software

This term is often used as an alternative to Operating System but strictly speaking it refers to all the programs in use at an installation (i.e. Operating System programs and the user written programs). **Software** is complementary to **Hardware** which refers to the electronic and mechanical components of a computer system.

Exercises

1. What name is given to the technique of running more than one program at the same time?
2. What schedules the programs and input/output operations of a computer?
3. How are programs loaded into core storage?
4. How does the computer operator request status information about the running of the computer?
5. What is JCL?

6. How is a COBOL program translated into a form executable by the computer?
7. What is the input to and output from the program given as the answer to question 6?
8. Name four components of an Operating System.
9. Why is COBOL called a high-level language?
10. What makes multi-programming possible?

CHAPTER NINE

DATA AND NUMBERS

Data Sets and Numbers

When designing files and subsequently handling them in a program, it is common to organize the data into sets to identify the relationship(s) which exist between the different items of data within the set. These organizational methods are of two types—**arrays** and **structures** although they can be combined when necessary.

Structures

A structure is merely a **hierarchical** description of a set of data items, showing individual items, individual items arranged in groups, and groups themselves arranged in larger groups.

Every set of data will contain individual items (fields) which will hold particular pieces of information and will have unique names to identify them (described in detail in Parts Two and Three). For example, a set of data relating to the name and address of an individual may have the following fields:

Christian Name
Surname
Address Line 1
Address Line 2
Address Line 3

When referring to this data it may be convenient to refer, for example, to the Christian Name and Surname fields with one collective name such as "Identity". The word "Identity" is a group name referring to the two subordinate fields Christian Name and Surname. Similarly we could allocate the term "Location" to be the group name for the three address lines. The two group names so far defined (Identity and Location) could themselves be combined into a group (with the name "Customer" for example). Since now the name Customer refers to the group items Identity and Location it also refers to the five data fields (called **elementary items**) making up the data set. The complete data structure can be represented as a hierarchical **tree structure** as shown in Fig. 24.

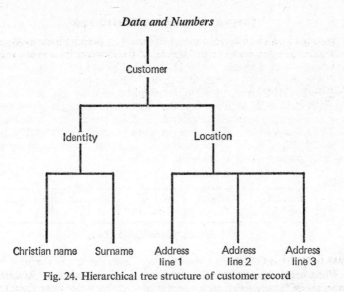

Fig. 24. Hierarchical tree structure of customer record

It is more common to represent such structures as a block diagram as shown in Fig. 25.

Customer				
Identity		Location		
Christian name	Surname	Address line 1	Address line 2	Address line 3

Fig. 25. Block structure of customer record

It is important to appreciate that only those names on the bottom of such a diagram (i.e. the elementary items) refer to reserved areas of core storage (the method of reserving such areas is described in Parts Two and Three). The **group names** merely allow the programmer to refer to more than one elementary item within a single expression. The most common use for structure is in the specification of data layouts for input/output files. Each record on such a file will have a structural organization and as will be seen in Part Two, this layout can be transcribed into COBOL thus enabling the programmer to relate the physical properties of the file to the requirements of his program.

Arrays

An **array** could be called a structure with only one group item in which all the elementary items are of the same size. An array could therefore be the computer representation of a set of pigeon holes. Each of these holes would correspond to an **element** of the array. Those readers with a mathematical background will appreciate that an array is an alternative description for a matrix.

Arrays are used to hold **tables** of information where a certain type of value is to be repeated a number of times. For example, suppose in a stock-control application details were to be maintained of the movements of stock over the twelve months of the year. We could define twelve like fields (called January, February, and so on) and refer to them individually; however, as will be seen later, this could be tedious (imagine, for example, an array with 200 elements!). The ideal method of defining these data items is to specify a twelve-element array, which could be called Monthly-Sales. Each element can, as will be seen later, be referenced by use of the array name (in this case "Monthly-Sales") followed by the number of the element in the array. An array can be represented diagrammatically as shown in Fig. 26.

Array

Element 1	Element 2	Element 3	Element 4	Element 5

Fig. 26. Layout of an array

An array can occur within a structure with each element of the array forming an elementary item within the structure. This is illustrated in Fig. 27 which shows the structure used earlier amended such that the three lines of the address are held in a three-element array. Note that each element in the array has the same name.

Customer				
Identity		Location		
Christian name	Surname	Address (1)	Address (2)	Address (3)

Fig. 27. Structure containing an array

The methods used to define and manipulate structures and arrays are dealt with in Parts Two and Three.

Number Systems

The high-level languages taught later in this book require only that the programmer be able to count in the decimal system as in normal everyday use. Earlier programming languages, as mentioned in Chapter Eight, required the programmer to specify long strings of numeric digits. The method of writing these down used different number systems depending on the particular computer in use. Although these alternative number systems are no longer a prerequisite to programming they do occur from time to time particularly when working on complicated tasks. A review of these systems is presented below therefore for the sake of completeness.

The Decimal System

Before looking at the more unusual number systems in use we will review the **decimal system** to learn something of the make-up and terminology of these systems. In the decimal system we count in "tens" using the **marks** 0–9 to represent our values. When a particular position overflows its maximum value (9) then it recycles to zero after **carrying** one to the next (left-hand) position. Let us consider a decimal number and analyse its significance; the number 32 for example means $3 \times (10) + 2 \times (1)$. Each digit in the number has **positional significance** and represents the number of occurrences of the **weight** in that position. In the example quoted the weights are 10 and 1 or 10^1 and 10^0. (Note—any number raised to the power zero is equal to 1.) Each positional weight is equal to the previous (right-hand) weight multiplied by the **base** or **radix** of the system. The base of the decimal system is 10. The number 4281 for example is really a shorthand method of writing

$$4 \times 10^3 + 2 \times 10^2 + 8 \times 10^1 + 1 \times 10^0$$

Remember, that for any number system there are *n* marks used to represent the values in the system where *n* is the base or radix of the system. *Each digit in a number has a positional value and represents the number of occurrences of the weight of that position.* The weight of the right-hand position is always one, succeeding weights are derived by multiplying the previous weight by the base of the system. In other words the weights, working to the left, are successive powers of the base starting from the power zero. The weights for the first six positions in a decimal system are therefore:

$$10^5 \quad 10^4 \quad 10^3 \quad 10^2 \quad 10^1 \quad 10^0$$

The Binary System

The base of the **binary number system** is 2 and it therefore uses only two marks (0 and 1) to represent its numeric values. The rules for binary arithmetic are much simpler than for any other system and it is this simplicity that makes the system ideal for the internal workings of electronic computers. Whereas the decimal system uses powers of 10 the positional weights for the binary system are expressed as powers of 2. To visualize the positional values of the binary system we will write down the weights for the first six positions (to the left of the decimal point). Below each binary weight will be shown the equivalent decimal value of that binary position. These values are shown in Fig. 28.

Binary positional weight	2^5	2^4	2^3	2^2	2^1	2^0
Equivalent decimal value	32	16	8	4	2	1

Fig. 28. The decimal equivalents of the binary weights

Remembering that the binary system allows only the marks 0 and 1 we can see that each position in a binary number represents either the equivalent decimal value (mark 1) or zero (mark 0)—since the positional value is equal to the weight multiplied by the mark. If, therefore, all the six positions above had a 1 mark (giving the binary number 111111) the value of the number would be equivalent to 63 (i.e. the sum of the equivalent decimal values in

Fig. 28). Our earlier example of decimal 32 can be represented in binary as 100000 which is a shorthand method of writing the complete values of

$$1 \times (2^5) + 0 \times (2^4) + 0 \times (2^3) + 0 \times (2^2) + 0 \times (2^1) + 0 \times (2^0)$$

This positional representation demonstrates an easy method of converting decimal numbers to their binary equivalent. Suppose we wish to convert the decimal number 41 into its binary equivalent. We will first of all decide which is the largest power of two that can be contained within the number to be converted. This of course is 32 or 2^5. We place therefore a 1 mark in the sixth binary position (reading from right to left) remember that 2^0 also occupies a position. We then must decide which next lower power of two can be contained within the remainder $(41 - 32 = 9)$. This is 8 or 2^3 which gives a 1 mark in the fourth position. The remainder this time is $1 (9 - 8)$ which gives a 1 mark in the first (2^0) position. The binary equivalent of decimal 41 is therefore

101001

An alternative method of converting from decimal to binary is by successive division by the binary base 2. The remainders from these divisions (always either 0 or 1) are read, in reverse order, to obtain the binary number. Figure 29 illustrates the conversion of decimal 41 by this method.

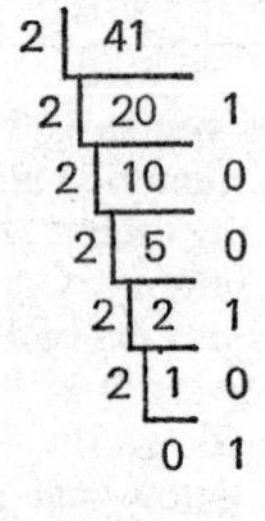

$$
\begin{array}{r r l}
2 & \underline{41} & \\
2 & \underline{20} & 1 \\
2 & \underline{10} & 0 \\
2 & \underline{5} & 0 \\
2 & \underline{2} & 1 \\
2 & \underline{1} & 0 \\
  & 0 & 1 \\
\end{array}
$$

Fig. 29. Decimal to binary conversion by division

The binary number is obtained by reading the remainders from bottom to top and as can be seen gives the same result as earlier—101001.

Binary Arithmetic

The rules of **binary arithmetic** are very simple indeed and are as shown:

Addition	*Multiplication*
$0 + 0 = 0$	$0 \times 0 = 0$
$0 + 1 = 1$	$0 \times 1 = 0$
$1 + 0 = 1$	$1 \times 0 = 0$
$1 + 1 = 10$	$1 \times 1 = 1$

Note that in the case of the addition $1 + 1$ there is a carry of one into the second position; the result (10) is pronounced "*one-oh*" not ten. $(1 + 1 = 10$ in binary is equivalent to the decimal $1 + 1 = 2$ since binary 10 is equivalent to decimal 2.) Binary addition, with its decimal equivalent, is illustrated in Fig. 30.

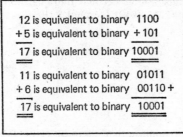

```
12 is equivalent to binary   1100
+ 5 is equivalent to binary  + 101
17 is equivalent to binary  10001

11 is equivalent to binary   01011
+ 6 is equivalent to binary  00110 +
17 is equivalent to binary   10001
```

Fig. 30. Binary addition

Subtraction can be carried out as the reverse of addition:

$$101101$$
$$-1011$$
$$\overline{}$$
$$100010$$

It can also be carried out by **complement addition**. To do this the **subtrahend** (the number to be subtracted) is **complemented** and then added to the other number; if any carry is made at the left-hand end of the addition it is added to the result. To complement a binary number the marks are reversed, i.e. one's are changed to zeroes and zeroes to ones. The complement of 01100110 is therefore 10011001.

Let us subtract two numbers by complement addition. Suppose we wish to subtract 1011 (decimal 11) from 1101 (decimal 13), we could use direct subtraction as shown:

$$1101$$
$$-1011$$
$$\overline{}$$
$$0010 \quad \text{(answer} = \text{decimal 2)}$$

By the alternative method we will first complement the subtrahend:

$$\text{complement } 1011 = 0100$$

the complement addition is now:

$$1101$$
$$+0100$$
$$\overline{}$$
①0001
↳ 1 (carry from left-hand end of previous line)
$$\overline{}$$
$$0010$$

This can be seen to give the same result as direct subtraction and the reader may care to verify for himself that it will always do so. Complement addition is used internally by computers as the means of performing subtraction although it is presented here for the sake of completeness only.

Multiplication is simply carried out using the rules already specified, in the same manner as ordinary long decimal multiplication. For example, to multiply 1011 (decimal 11) by 0101 (decimal 5):

$$
\begin{array}{r}
1011 \\
0101 \\
\hline
1011 \\
1011.. \\
\hline
110111
\end{array}
$$

The reader may care to confirm that the result (110111) is the equivalent of decimal 55.

Division is carried out either by a series of subtractions or by the long-division method.

The Octal System

The **octal number system** has the base 8 and uses the marks 0–7. The weights for digit positions are successive powers of 8 therefore as shown in Fig. 31

Octal positional weight	8^5	8^4	8^3	8^2	8^1	8^0
Equivalent decimal value	32768	4096	512	64	8	1

Fig. 31. The decimal equivalent of the octal weights

Thus the Octal number 231 can be converted to its decimal equivalent thus

$$2 \times (64) + 3 \times (8) + 1 \times (1) = 153$$

Each of the marks used in the Octal number system can be given its equivalent in only three binary marks as the table below shows:

Octal	Binary Equivalent
0	000
1	001
2	010
3	011
4	100
5	101
6	110
7	111

We have, therefore, a very convenient method of representing large binary numbers. The binary marks are split into groups of three from the right-hand end (with zeroes added at the left to make up a multiple of three if required) and each group is represented by its octal mark equivalent. Thus to represent the binary number 1101011100011111 we could proceed as shown:

Binary number	001	101	011	100	011	111
Octal equivalent	1	5	3	4	3	7

Converting octal to binary is very straightforward, each octal digit being replaced by the equivalent three binary marks. (Note—three must always be used.) For example to convert octal 14732:

$$
\begin{array}{ccccc}
1 & 4 & 7 & 3 & 2 \\
001 & 100 & 111 & 011 & 010
\end{array}
$$

gives the binary number 001100111011010.

To convert a decimal number to its octal equivalent the original number is divided successively by 8 in a similar manner to the decimal to binary conversion above. The remainders are read in reverse order to give the octal number required:

To convert decimal 1967 into its octal equivalent:

$$
\begin{array}{r|rl}
8 & 1967 & \\
8 & 245 & \mathbf{7} \\
8 & 30 & \mathbf{5} \\
8 & 3 & \mathbf{6} \\
 & 0 & \mathbf{3}
\end{array}
$$

Octal equivalent therefore is 3657.

To convert an octal number to decimal directly (i.e. rather than converting it to binary and then converting the binary to decimal) the following procedure can be used:

1. Multiply the left-hand digit by 8 (i.e. 3 in the number 3657).
2. Add the next digit to the product of step 1 (i.e. add 6 to 8×3).
3. Using the sum derived in step 2 (30) as the new multiplicand repeat steps 1 and 2 until the last right-hand digit (7 in the example) is added. The sum at this point is the decimal value.

The workings of this method are shown diagrammatically below:

$$
\begin{array}{rl}
3657 & \text{octal number} \\
\times 8 & \\
= 24 & \\
+6 & \\
\hline
30 & \\
\times 8 & \\
= 240 & \\
+5 & \\
\hline
245 & \\
\times 8 & \\
= 1960 & \\
+7 & \\
\hline
1967 & \text{decimal equivalent}
\end{array}
$$

The Hexadecimal System

This number system uses the base 16 and requires, therefore, 16 marks for its representation. These must be single characters and the following set is conventionally used:

0 1 2 3 4 5 6 7 8 9 A B C D E F

The weights used in a **hexadecimal system** are successive powers of 16, the first four being

4096   256   16   1

The hexadecimal system is used because like the octal system it is easily derived from the binary system. Each hexadecimal mark is derived from four binary marks split from the right-hand end of the binary number. The hexadecimal marks with their binary and decimal equivalents are shown in Fig. 32.

Hexadecimal	Binary	Decimal
0	0000	0
1	0001	1
2	0010	2
3	0011	3
4	0100	4
5	0101	5
6	0110	6
7	0111	7
8	1000	8
9	1001	9
A	1010	10
B	1011	11
C	1100	12
D	1101	13
E	1110	14
F	1111	15

Fig. 32. The decimal and binary equivalents of the hexadecimal marks

Conversion between binary and hexadecimal is simply accomplished by grouping the binary data into four marks and replacing each group with hexadecimal equivalent. Conversely hexadecimal can be converted into binary by replacing each mark by the appropriate four binary marks.

For example, binary   1101   1001   1111   0101   is equivalent to

D   9   F   5

Conversely, the hexadecimal value   3   D   A   7   is equivalent to

0011   1101   1010   0111   in binary

Decimal to hexadecimal conversion can be carried out using the remainder technique (as shown above for binary and octal) with the division being by 16. Hexadecimal can be converted to decimal by multiplying each mark by the positional weight and adding the results together.

As has already been stated computers work internally with strings of numbers which are in fact binary numbers. A core dump printout (see

Chapter Eight) in binary would be a rather daunting prospect for the programmer wishing to read it.

To make these dumps quicker to print and easier to read they are formatted in the octal system or the hexadecimal system depending on the computer in use.

Number Notations

When a number with a decimal portion (such as 27·34) is held in core storage the actual decimal point does not exist (since it would require an additional storage location to itself). Instead the computer "remembers" where the decimal point is meant to be and can align the various numbers in a calculation correctly. (Note—coding to achieve this is automatically generated by the compiler.) Note that a number without a decimal point is assumed to be an **integer** with the decimal point to the right of the least significant digit. When studying Parts Two and Three of this book you will come across numbers specified with a single V thus—27V34. The V specifies the location of an **assumed decimal point**.

Because of the way computers are organized internally they cannot hold very large or very small numbers (such as 124,000,000,000,000 and 0·000,000,000,000,41 respectively) as strings of digits. Numbers such as these are held in **Floating-point format**. This consists of two parts—a **mantissa** and an **exponent**. The mantissa of a floating-point number indicates the numeric quality of the number. In the first example above the mantissa would be 1·24. The exponent gives the order or magnitude of the number and is expressed as a power of ten. In the example the exponent could therefore be 10^{14}. The number $1·24 \times 10^{14}$ is obviously equivalent to 124,000,000,000,000 but requires far less space. A shorthand method is used to write down floating-point numbers when used in programming—1·24E14. The letter separates the mantissa (before the E) and the exponent power. Very small numbers are represented with a negative exponent (equivalent to dividing the mantissa by a positive exponent value). For example 0·000456 could be represented by 4·56E–4.

Exercises

1. How many elementary items are in the structure below?

Record						
Details						
Credit		Account		Details		
Count	Status	Ident	Name	Trans (1)	Trans (2)	Trans (3)

2. In the structure above what, if any, are the properties of the array(s) within the structure?
3. Convert the following binary numbers into their decimal equivalent:
   (a) 1011   (b) 101   (c) 011   (d) 111001
4. Convert the following decimal numbers into binary, octal, and hexadecimal:
   (a) 16   (b) 25   (c) 8   (d) 46
5. Write down the following numbers in floating-point format:
   (a) 123,000   (b) 60   (c) 2,000,000   (d) 0·00812

PART TWO

COBOL PROGRAMMING LANGUAGE

CHAPTER TEN

INTRODUCTION TO COBOL

Language Structure

COBOL was designed to be as much like ordinary English language as possible while containing those elements required by the computer system in use. Like English, then, COBOL has **grammar**, **punctuation**, a **character set**, and **words** and **names**. The grammar of the language will not be required until later on and is explained, in detail, in Chapter Twenty-six; the methods used for formulating words and names are described in Chapter Eleven.

The COBOL Character Set

When writing programs in COBOL the programmer must use only the allowable **characters** and **symbols**. Any other entry on his **coding form** will not be recognized by the COBOL compiler and will cause an error to be flagged. The character which must be used is described below:

Character	Meaning
Character	*Meaning*
0 to 9	The numeric digits
A to Z	The letters of the alphabet
	Blank or space (where it is important to specify a space its occurrence will be indicated in this book, for identification purposes only by ƀ)
+	Plus sign—denoting addition (see Chapter Fourteen) or a positive number
−	Negative sign—denoting subtraction (see Chapter Fourteen) or a negative number. Also used as a hyphen (to join two words together)
*	Asterisk
/	Slash (also called stroke and oblique)
=	Equal sign
£	Currency sign
,	Comma
;	Semi-colon
.	Full-stop (also called period) used to terminate sentences (see Chapter Twenty-six) and to indicate a decimal point in a number (e.g. 321.3)
"	Quotation mark
(	Left parenthesis
)	Right parenthesis
>	Greater than symbol (e.g. 3 > 2 means 3 "greater than" 2)
<	Less than symbol (reverse of greater than)

The human reader will differentiate between the *letter* O and the *number* 0 by the context of the entry; the computer however must be given distinct electronic patterns for the two characters (since they are logically different). In order that the data-preparation department can code the two characters differently (there being two distinct keys on their keyboards) it is important to indicate the precise code required on each coding form.

A number of different methods have been used over the years to indicate the difference between the letter O and number 0; the most popular system is as described below.

The letter "oh" is written   O

The number zero is written   Ø

Throughout this part of the book any text representing computer input, output, or contents will use the slash mark to indicate a numeric zero (Ø).

For clarity of reading the text of this part, too, has been set in standard printers' characters. In practice the characters available to the computer user are limited to those found on a typewriter. The reader will find, when studying computer print-out, that the quotation symbols and those for minus and hyphenation differ slightly from those shown herein.

Punctuation

The use of punctuation in COBOL has two main functions—to improve the readability of the program listing and to indicate to the compiler different elements of the coding (e.g. a period is used to terminate a sentence—see Chapter Twenty-six). However, even when used purely as a documentation aid punctuation must follow certain rules in order that the compiler will be able to interpret the symbols used. The following general rules must therefore be observed when using punctuation symbols.

1. Any **punctuation mark** shown in the **general format** examples of COBOL expressions later in this book must be used where shown. For example the general format of the EXIT expression (Chapter Sixteen) is shown as:

paragraph-name. <u>EXIT</u> <u>PROGRAM</u>.

Therefore the two periods shown must be used when coding a statement of this type.
2. Any **period, comma,** or **semi-colon** used in the coding of a program must not be preceded by a space but must be followed by at least one space.

e.g. ADD NET, TAX, DEDUCTIONS TO GROSS.

(for a full description of ADD see Chapter Thirteen).
3. A **left parenthesis** must not be immediately followed by a space and a **right parenthesis** must not be immediately preceded by a space.
4. At least one space must appear between successive words and expressions. Two or more successive spaces will be treated as a single space (except within certain types of constants—see Chapter Eleven).
5. Any **arithmetic operator** (e.g. $+$) or an **equal sign** must be preceded by and followed by at least one space.
6. A **comma** may be used between **successive operands** (Chapter Eleven) in a statement to improve readability, e.g.

DATA-RECORDS ARE TYPE-1, TYPE-2, TYPE-3, TYPE-4.

7. A **semi-colon** or a **comma** may be used to separate **clauses** in a long statement (see Chapter Twenty-six).

e.g. MOVE NET TO PAYOUT, MOVE TAX TO DEDUCTION1;
GO TO PRINT.

Program Divisions

A COBOL program is written in four separate **divisions**, each of which can be coded separately during program development. When all the divisions are complete they must be submitted for compilation in the following order

> IDENTIFICATION DIVISION
> ENVIRONMENT DIVISION
> DATA DIVISION
> PROCEDURE DIVISION

The **Identification Division** identifies the name and author of the program and the date it was written and compiled. A complete description of this division is given in Chapter Forty-five.

The **Environment Division** describes the configuration of the computers on which the program is to be compiled and executed. This feature is incorporated since any COBOL program may be run on different computers. This division also allows the programmer to assign names (called special-names—see Chapter Forty-six) to particular peripheral units attached to the computer to be used for program execution. A full description of the Environment Division is given in Chapters Forty-six and Forty-seven.

The **Data Division** contains descriptions of all the data areas, constants, and input and output files to be used by the program. The Data Division is described in Chapters Seventeen to Twenty-five.

The **Procedure Division** describes the operations to be performed by the program. This division is not related to any specific computer and will refer to those items defined in the Data Division. A discussion of the Procedure Division is contained in Chapters Thirteen to Sixteen and Twenty-six to Forty-five.

Exercises

1. What are the two functions of punctuation in a COBOL program?
2. What is wrong with this expression?

ADD FIELDA ,FIELDB ,TO ANSWER.

3. Name the four COBOL divisions.
4. Where is the programmer's name specified in a COBOL program?
5. How can clauses in a long statement be separated?

CHAPTER ELEVEN

WORD TYPES AND CONSTANTS

The basic unit of a COBOL program is the **word**. A word is a combination of up to 30 characters chosen from the **word set**:

A to Z
Ø to 9
- (hyphen)

A word cannot contain a space and it cannot start or terminate with a hyphen. A word is terminated with a space, period, right parenthesis, comma, or semi-colon depending upon how it is used. Examples of COBOL words are:

READ
MASTER-FILE
READ-IN-ITEM-TYPE-10
(SUBSCRIPT)

Note that in the last example the left and right parentheses do not form part of the word but are shown to illustrate a word terminated by a right parenthesis.

Reserved Words

A certain number of words are known as **reserved words** and cannot be used as names by the programmer. Reserved words identify certain functions to the compiler and can be split into three types:

1. *Keywords.* A **keyword** is one which must appear in the relevant COBOL statement when used in a program. Keywords are identified in the general format entries later in this book by appearing underlined and in upper case. Keywords themselves fall into three broad categories; these are **verbs** (such as ADD, MOVE, WRITE), **required words** which appear in various statements (such as TO in a MOVE statement), and words with a **special functional meaning** such as ZERO, DIVISION, and so on.
2. *Optional Words.* These are words available in certain statement formats to improve the legibility of a statement. For example in the statement

READ MASTER-FILE RECORD INTO WORK-AREA

the reserved word RECORD can be omitted by the programmer if he so desires. However only the word RECORD can appear in this position and it cannot be used elsewhere. An **optional word** is shown in the general formats in upper case but is not underlined.
3. *Connectives.* These are reserved words used to connect two data names or literals (see below) together with some special relationship. For example, the words OF and IN are used as qualifier **connectives** (see Chapter Thirty-seven) as shown:

MOVE NAME OF INPUT-FILE TO NAME IN OUTPUT-FILE.

The logical operators (ADD, OR, NOT discussed in Chapter Twenty-seven) are also reserved words used as connectives:

IF PAY-CODE IS NOT EQUAL TO BONUS-CHECK ...

A complete list of COBOL reserved words will be found in Appendix Two and the use of each will be explained as it is encountered in the text.

Names

The reserved words we have just examined are already built-in to the COBOL compiler and cannot be changed or augmented in any way by the programmer. However, all names used in a program are unique to that program and are selected for use by the programmer as coding proceeds. **Names** will be used to identify items of **data, ranges of value,** and **procedures.**

Data Names

A **data name** is a word (formed according to the rules described above) containing at least one alphabetic (A to Z) character and identifies an item of data in the Data Division. By using this name the programmer can refer to the item of data in his Procedure Division coding. Some programmers invent names for data items on a random basis and use such expressions as FRED, JIM, JOE, etc. This is very bad practice and should not be used under any circumstances; *all data names should be derived from the contents or use of the data item to produce meaningful names which will themselves help to identify the use of the data item.* For example some of the data names used in a payroll file record could be:

> PAYGROUP
> CLOCK-NUMBER
> STAFF-GRADE
> BONUS-CODE
> TAX-CODE

Any statement then manipulating these data items immediately becomes clearer because the data names themselves mean something. This is demonstrated by the following statement (do not worry at this stage about the verbs used):

IF STAFF-GRADE IS EQUAL TO "W" MOVE
> > CLOCK-NUMBER TO CLOCK-PRINT.

Condition Names

This is the name given to a specific value or range of values that a particular data item may contain. For example, in the example above the data item STAFF-GRADE might have three possible values: W for weekly staff, M for monthly staff, and T for temporary staff. It is possible to allocate **condition names** to these values (Chapter Twenty-seven) such that for example the value M in STAFF-GRADE would have the name MONTHLY. This enables more meaningful statements to be coded:

> IF STAFF-GRADE IS WEEKLY MOVE CLOCK-NUMBER
> TO CLOCK-PRINT.

Condition names must be formed according to the same rules as data names.

Procedure Names

A **paragraph** in the Procedure Division may be given a name in order that the paragraph may be referred to in another part of the program. A **paragraph name** may consist of numeric characters only. Examples of paragraph names:

> COMPUTE-GROSS-PAY.
> PRINT-PAYSLIP.
> READ-INPUT-FILE.
> CALCULATE.
> 212.

Note that these names refer only to the paragraph following, they do not themselves perform the functions they describe.

Constants

A **constant** is a predetermined unit of data, the value of which is not expected to change. Constants can be **literal** or **figurative**.

Literal Constants

A **literal constant** (usually known simply as a **literal**) is a string of characters whose value is made up of the characters composing that literal. A literal is either **numeric** or **non-numeric**. A **numeric literal** is a string of characters made up of the digits 0–9 plus, optionally, a plus or minus sign and a decimal point. A numeric literal can consist of 1 to 18 characters only one of which may be a sign. If the literal does not have a **sign character** it is assumed to be **positive**. A numeric literal may contain only one **decimal point** which may appear anywhere except at the right-hand end. A literal without a decimal point is assumed to be a **whole number**. Note that the decimal point in a numeric literal is only assumed and does not actually occupy any storage space. Numeric literals are usually used in arithmetic calculations. Some examples are shown below:

> 327
> +21934
> −7
> −70.34279
> 1.34

A **non-numeric literal** can consist of 1 to 120 characters chosen from the entire COBOL character set (described in Chapter Ten) and is enclosed in **quotation marks**. Any space within the quotation marks is treated as part of the constant and therefore occupies core storage within the constant. Examples of non-numeric literals:

> "BONUS THIS WEEK"
> "GRAND TOTAL"
> "ERROR 32—PROGRAM TERMINATED"
> "END OF JOB"
> "PLEASE REFEED LAST CARD"
> "NO MORE PAPER"

Figurative Constants

Certain values are used frequently in programming and these have been allocated specific data names. These data names, which are not enclosed in quotation marks, are reserved words.

A **figurative constant** may be used wherever "literal" is shown in a general format. The plural values of the figurative constants are identical with the singular and may be used interchangeably.

Figurative Constant	*Value*
ZERO ZEROES ZEROS	The value Ø or one or more occurrences of the character Ø depending upon the context.
SPACE SPACES	Represents one or more blanks or spaces.
HIGH-VALUE HIGH-VALUES	Represents one or more occurrences of the character with the highest collating sequence for the computer in use.
LOW-VALUE LOW-VALUES	Represents one or more occurrences of the character with the lowest collating sequence for the computer in use.
QUOTE QUOTES	Represents one or more occurrences of the quotation-mark character. Note that the word QUOTE cannot be used in place of the quotation mark to enclose a non-numeric literal.
ALL literal	Represents one or more occurrences of the characters composing the (non-numeric or figurative) literal following the word ALL. When a figurative constant is used the word ALL is used for improved readability only. Example: MOVE ALL "*" TO LONG-FIELD. the receiving field in this MOVE statement (LONG-FIELD) will be filled with asterisks.

General Format Notation

As each element of the COBOL language is introduced it is preceded by the **General Format** showing the basic method of use of the element together with any available options. For example the format of the MOVE statement is shown thus:

```
┌─────────────────────── Format ───────────────────────┐
│                                                       │
│                                                       │
│          ⎧ identifier-1 ⎫                             │
│   MOVE   ⎨             ⎬  TO   identifier-2  [identifier-3] ... │
│          ⎩ literal      ⎭                             │
│                                                       │
└───────────────────────────────────────────────────────┘
```

This format does not itself form part of the COBOL language specification but it is used extensively to describe the language. Each format therefore follows the same rules which will aid the programmer when writing his own statements. The following rules apply *only* therefore to the general formats in Part Two of this book.

1. All words printed in upper case are **reserved words** and have specific meanings to the COBOL compiler. In all general formats words in upper case represent an actual occurrence of those words.

2. All underlined words are required when coding a statement unless the portion containing the word is itself optional (see 6 below). Words underlined are **keywords** and must be spelt exactly as shown in the format. Reserved words not underlined are **optional words** and may be omitted or included at the programmer's option.

3. The characters $+$, $-$, $<$, $>$, $=$ will not be underlined but, when appearing in formats, are required when such formats are used.

4. All punctuation shown in general formats represents an actual occurrence and must be used where shown. Note—additional punctuation can be inserted according to the rules already given.

5. Words printed in lower case represent information to be supplied by the programmer as explained in the accompanying text.

6. Square brackets ([ ]) indicate that the enclosed item is optional as required by the program. When square brackets contain more than one item one or more may be used as required.

7. Braces ({ }) enclosing a number of items indicate that one of the items must be used.

8. Ellipsis (. . .) indicate that the preceding unit may be repeated as many times as required. Note that if the unit is enclosed in brackets or braces the entire unit must be repeated (when repetition is required).

9. Any comments and full explanations about each general format are in the accompanying text.

Exercises

1. Under what circumstances may the programmer use a reserved word as a name?
2. Which of the following are valid numeric literals?

(a) 327.4.6
(b) 329.6
(c) 428+
(d) +29.1

(e) 37−2
(f) .764
(g) 412.
(h) +0.7

3. What is the maximum number of characters that can be contained within:

(a) a numeric literal
(b) a non-numeric literal

4. Write down one version of each of the figurative constants.
5. Which of the following are NOT valid words:

(a) ZQY37X
(b) −SIGN
(c) 374
(d) NEXT−
(e) READ(4)IN

(f) TYPE/4
(g) T−Y−P−E−4
(h) £P
(i) WORD

CHAPTER TWELVE

THE COBOL CODING FORM

All COBOL source programs are coded on a COBOL coding form, the format of which is shown in Fig. 33. When coding is complete the coding form is transcribed, line by line, on to an input medium. The usual input medium for COBOL compilers is punched cards which must be punched in the same format as that shown in Fig. 33.

Columns 1–6   contain the sequence number of the coded line
    ,,   7   may contain the continuation character
    ,,   8–11 represents Area A
    ,,   12–72 represents Area B
    ,,   73–80 may be used to identify the program.

Coding examples used in this book are, for improved readability, not shown on coding forms. However, the rules for spacing described below take precedence over any implied rule in the textual examples.

Sequence Numbers

A six-digit **sequence number** is used to numerically identify each line to be processed by the compiler. The use of sequence numbers for any program is optional; however, if present sequence numbers must be in ascending sequence. Any out-of-sequence lines read will be flagged as an input error. (Note that this will not affect the compilation of the lines as read.)

Continuation of Lines

When any entry or sentence cannot all be coded on a single line (up to column 72) it may be continued by starting following line(s) in Area B. These subsequent, or continuation, lines are identified by the appearance of a hyphen in column 7.

When a non-numeric literal is to be continued, a hyphen is placed in column 7; and a quotation mark indicating the continuation of the literal, may be placed anywhere in Area B. Note that any spaces at the end of the initial line and any following the quotation mark on the continuation line are considered to be part of the literal. The continuation of a word or numeric literal is indicated by a hyphen in column 7, and the first non-blank character in Area B of the continuation line follows the last non-blank character in the preceding line.

Any number of continuation lines may be used although readability may be impaired by so doing.

Area A and B

Area A (columns 8–11) is reserved for the beginning of **division headers, section names, paragraph names,** and certain **level numbers** as described below. Area B is used for coding COBOL source statements.

Division Header. The name of the division (e.g. ENVIRONMENT DIVISION), which must be the first entry in a division, starts in Area A.

73

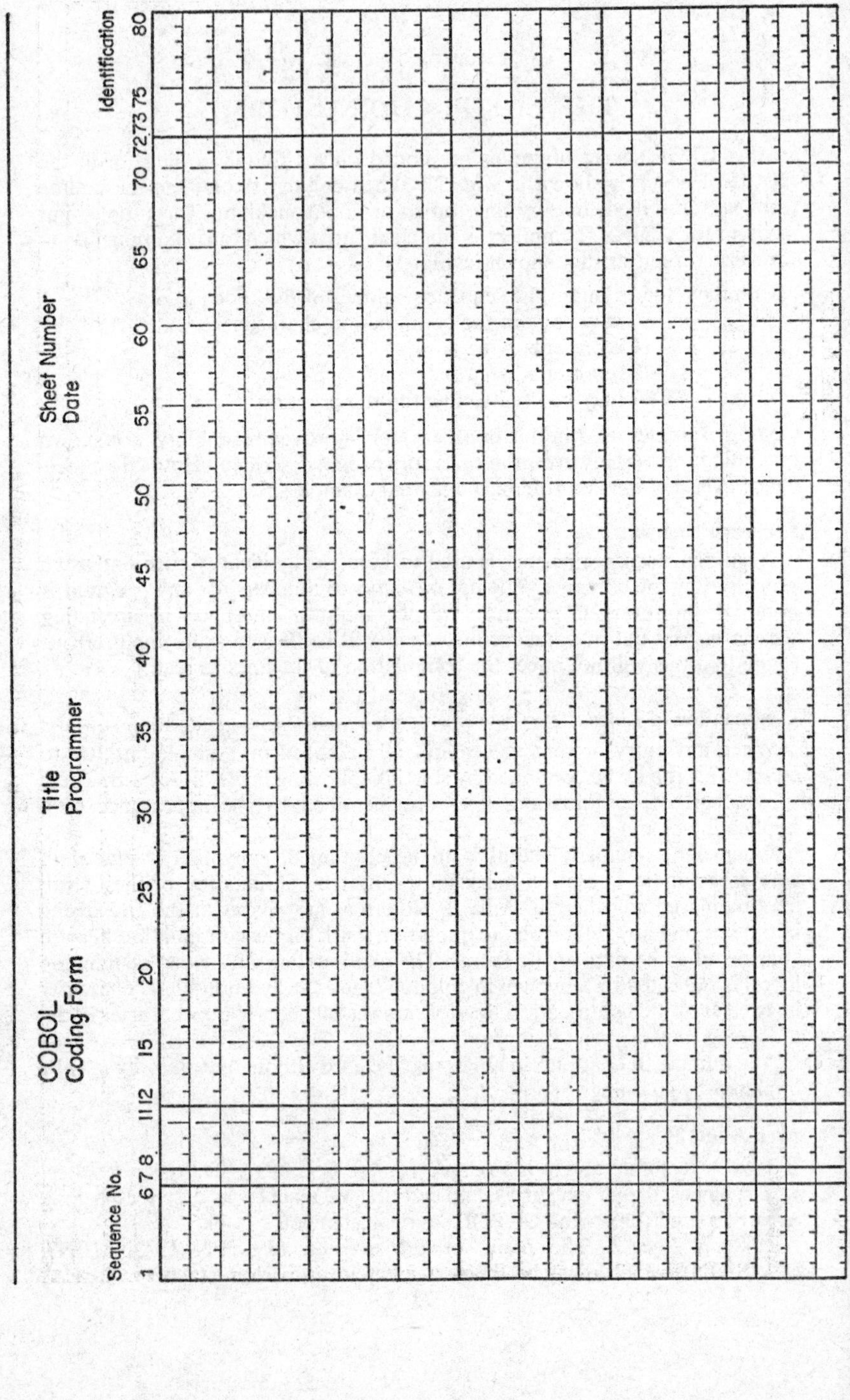

COBOL
Coding Form

Title
Programmer

Sheet Number
Date

Sequence No.				Identification
1	6 7 8	11 12	15 20 25 30 35 40 45 50 55 60 65 70 72 73 75	80

COBOL
Coding Form

Title
Programmer

Sheet Number
Date

Identification

Sequence No.																
1	678	1112	15	20	25	30	35	40	45	50	55	60	65	70 7273 75	80
Ø1Ø1Ø1Ø	Ø1	FILLER-AREA													
Ø1Ø1Ø2Ø		Ø2	CLOCK-NUMBER	PICTURE X(5).											
Ø1Ø1Ø3Ø		Ø2	WAGE-CODE	PICTURE 9.											
Ø1Ø1Ø4Ø		Ø2	TAX-TO-DATE	PICTURE 99(4)V99.											
Ø1Ø1Ø5Ø		Ø2	GROSS-TO-DATE	PICTURE 99(6)V99.											
Ø1Ø1Ø6Ø		Ø2	DEDUCTIONS	PICTURE 99V9.											
Ø1Ø1Ø7Ø		PROCEDURE DIVISION.													
Ø1Ø1Ø8Ø		CALCULATE SECTION.													
Ø1Ø1Ø9Ø		BEGIN.	PERFORM OPEN-ROUTINE.												
Ø1Ø1ØØ		READ-IN.													
Ø1Ø11Ø			PERFORM READ-ROUTINE.	PERFORM WAGE-ROUTINE.											
Ø1Ø12Ø		CALCULATIONS.													
Ø1Ø13Ø			IF WAGE-CODE IS EQUAL TO "M" MOVE "WEEKLY WAGE EARNE												
Ø1Ø14Ø	1		"R CODE M" TO PRINT-LINE-1.												
Ø1Ø15Ø															
Ø1Ø16Ø			MOVE CLOCK-NUMBER TO CLOCK-PRINT. MOVE TAX-TO-DATE TO TA												
Ø1Ø17Ø	1		X-PRINT.												
Ø1Ø18Ø			MOVE STATUS-CODE-3 TO LATEST-STATUS.												
Ø1Ø19Ø				ADD CALCULATED-TAX TO TAX-TO-DATE.											
Ø1Ø2ØØ				ADD CALCULATED-GROSS TO GROSS-TO-DATE.											
Ø1Ø21Ø				PERFORM PAYSLIP-PRINT.											
Ø1Ø22Ø				GO TO READ-IN.											
Ø1Ø23Ø															

Fig. 34. COBOL coding sheet in use

A space must separate the two words and a period must immediately follow the word DIVISION. No other text may appear on a division header line.

Section Header. The section name (e.g. ROOT SECTION see Chapter Twenty-six) follows the same rules as a division header.

Paragraph Names. The name of a **paragraph** (consisting of one or more **sentences**) starts in Area A of any line following the division header and is followed by a period followed by at least one space. Each successive line of a paragraph starts anywhere in Area B.

Level Number. The **level number** of a data item (see Chapter Seventeen) may appear anywhere in Area A followed by its descriptive information in Area B. Level numbers 02–49, 66, and 88 may also appear in Area B followed immediately by their descriptive information.

Blank Lines

A **blank line,** as defined for the COBOL compiler, is one containing spaces in columns 7 to 72 inclusive. A blank line may be used to improve the readability of a program and can appear anywhere except immediately preceding a continuation line.

The use of the COBOL coding form is illustrated in Fig. 34. Do not at this stage attempt to understand the actual coding used in this example—all the expressions used will be explained as the book proceeds.

Exercises

1. Write down the columns reserved for Area A and Area B.
2. In which column does the continuation character appear?
3. In which areas do the following occur?

    (*a*) Division header
    (*b*) Paragraph name
    (*c*) Level 01 entries
    (*d*) Level 02 entries

4. In which columns does the sequence number appear?
5. Can a blank line be followed immediately by a continuation line?

CHAPTER THIRTEEN

ARITHMETIC STATEMENTS

Some courses in COBOL programming would, at this point, launch straight into the details of the Data Division. This division is normally coded before the Procedure Division and so learning about it first might seem quite logical. However, without knowing what can be done with the data, it can be difficult to understand the details of data definition. A further complication is that a full explanation of most Procedure Division statements requires a knowledge of the Data Division! Something of a chicken and egg problem . . . The solution adopted in this book is firstly to explain some simple Procedure

Division statements, then to examine the Data Division, and finally to cover the remaining Procedure Division statements.

This and the next three chapters will therefore describe some of the basic and simplest to understand procedure statements beginning with those used for arithmetic computation. The **arithmetic statements** in COBOL share certain optional additions which, having similar effects for each statement, are described first.

ROUNDED Option

After an arithmetic calculation it is possible for the result of that calculation to contain more decimal places than the programmer has provided for in his result field. For example, in the following calculation the result field may only have provision for two decimal places:

$$\frac{202.13 \times 3}{15} = 40.426$$

However, as can be seen, the correct answer requires three decimal places. **Alignment** of arithmetic data items is on the **decimal point** so therefore the **least significant digit** in the result of the example shown will be lost (or truncated).

If, however, ROUNDED is specified the least significant digit of the **result field** (in this example the figure 2) will be rounded depending on the value of the digits truncated. If the leading truncated digit (in the example the figure 6) is greater than or equal to 5 the least significant digit of the result field will be incremented by 1. If the leading truncated digit is not greater than 5 no increase is made to the result field.

The following examples will demonstrate the use of ROUNDED with a result field having three decimal places:

Result of Arithmetic Calculation	Result field without ROUNDED	Result field with ROUNDED
127.3267	127.326	127.327
934.3005	934.300	934.301
842.3014	842.301	842.301
876.9995	876.999	877.000

(Note, in particular, the last example which shows that any rounding may affect the entire result field when the least significant digit in the result is a 9.)

GIVING Option

A calculation such as A + B = C, which adds A and B into C, would include the original value of C in the result. If this is not required the value zero can be moved into C before the addition is carried out. The COBOL language provides this facility in one statement by use of the GIVING option. When the GIVING option is specified the result of the arithmetic calculation is placed in the identifier specified immediately following the word GIVING. This identifier is not itself involved in the calculation. Examples showing the use of the GIVING option will be shown following the description of each arithmetic statement.

SIZE ERROR Option

If, after decimal-point alignment, the value to be placed in the result field exceeds the largest value that that field can hold a **size error condition** is said to exist. This applies only to the integer part of the answer and not to the decimal position since excess decimal places will be truncated. For example, if a result of 1269 is to be placed in a field with only three digits capacity then a size error condition exists for the calculation. Checking for a size error condition is only carried out on the final result of the calculation and is therefore done after rounding if the ROUNDED option has been specified.

If a size error condition exists for a computation that did not specify the SIZE ERROR option the value of the result field is unpredictable.

If a size error condition exists and the SIZE ERROR option has been specified the statement following the SIZE ERROR option will be executed (following the completion of the arithmetic calculation). Note, however, that in this case the value of the result field is again unpredictable.

An attempt to divide by zero will always raise a size error condition. Examples of size error conditions appear in the following text.

The ADD Statement

The ADD statement allows the programmer to sum two or more numeric fields and store the result. The result can be stored in one of the fields being summed or in another field.

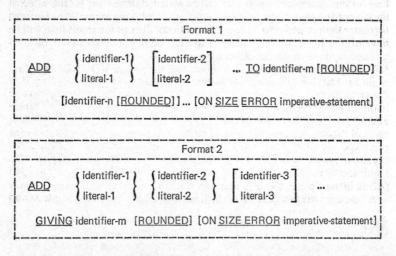

Format 1. The values of each of the items (**operands**) preceding the word TO are added together and the result is added to the value of each of the fields following the word TO. The result of the calculation is therefore stored in the field(s) following the word TO. The number of fields preceding and the number of fields following the word TO is dependent on the program but must be at least one in each case.

Any literal used (preceding the word TO only) must be of the numeric type —see Chapter Eleven.

Examples: In its simplest form the ADD statement will be used to sum two fields:

ADD SOCIAL-FUND TO DEDUCTIONS.

In this case the value of SOCIAL-FUND will be added to the value already in DEDUCTIONS. If it were desired to add more than one value to the receiving field the following could be used:

ADD SOCIAL-FUND, PENSION, BUPA TO DEDUCTIONS.

Suppose that before this statement was executed the values in these fields were 00014, 00270, 00300, and 01296 respectively the value of DEDUCTIONS after execution would be 01880. Note that the values in the other fields would not be changed by the execution of this statement. If the fields preceding the word TO had two decimal places each while the receiving field had only one the ROUNDED option could be used:

ADD SOCIAL-FUND, PENSION, BUPA TO DEDUCTIONS ROUNDED.

A final result of, say, 01234.67 would be stored in DEDUCTIONS as 01234.7. The ADD statement may, as shown in the general format, be used to add one or more fields to more than one receiving field:

ADD DEDUCTIONS TO DED-THIS-YEAR, TOTAL-DEDUCTIONS.

If the values in these fields prior to execution of this statement were 00125, 02239, and 00469 they would be 00125, 02364, and 00594 following execution.

If the programmer considered that a size-error condition could arise he could include the SIZE ERROR option. An imperative-statement is one directing the computer to do a specific task—for a full list of such statements see Chapter Twenty-six.

ADD THIS-MONTHS-COST TO YEARS-COSTS ON SIZE ERROR
GO TO ERROR.

If when the two values were added together the resultant value exceeded the capacity of YEARS-COSTS the size error condition would be raised and GO TO ERROR would be executed (GO TO is explained fully in Chapter Fifteen).

Format 2. The values of the operands preceding the word GIVING are added together and the result **replaces** the value of the operand identifier-m (note that the -m is used only to enable reference to be made to separate identifiers within a general format and does not signify a special type). At least two operands must precede the word GIVING.

Examples: Consider the case of an invoice program which has to produce the gross cost of an item from the unit cost, the tax on the unit, and the delivery charge for that unit. Any value in the receiving field (invoice cost) refers to a previous item and must not therefore be added to the result:

ADD UNIT-COST, UNIT-TAX, DELIV-CHARGE GIVING INVOICE-COST.

If the values of the fields before execution of this statement had been 100, 200, 100, and 337 respectively the values after execution would be 100, 200, 100, and 400.

As with format 1 ADD statements this format may be used to add numeric literals to data items:

ADD 327, 489, FIELDA GIVING FIELDB ON SIZE ERROR GO TO CHECK.

The SUBTRACT Statement

The SUBTRACT statement is used to subtract one or more values from another value.

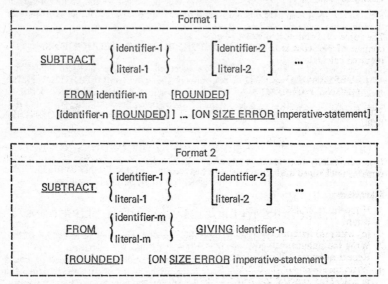

Format 1. The values in the data items preceding the word FROM (identifier-1, identifier-2, etc.) are added together and their sum is subtracted from the items following the word FROM (identifier-m, etc.). The number of identifiers preceding and following the word FROM is dependent upon the program but must be at least one in each case.

Examples: The simplest form of the SUBTRACT statement will be used to subtract the value of one item from the value of another:

SUBTRACT TAX FROM GROSS.

The statement may also be used to subtract a value from more than one field:

SUBTRACT 47 FROM FIELDA, FIELDB ROUNDED.

Note that in this case only FIELDB will be rounded, to round both fields the following format would be used:

SUBTRACT 47 FROM FIELDA ROUNDED, FIELDB ROUNDED.

A number of fields may be subtracted from one or more fields as shown:

SUBTRACT TAX, BUPA, SOCIAL-FUND FROM GROSS, GROSS-TO-DATE.

In this case the values of the first three fields will be added together and this sum will be subtracted from each of the remaining fields in turn.

Format 2. The values of the data items listed in front of the word FROM are added together and this value is subtacted from identifier-m, the result replacing the previous value of identifier-n. Note that the value of identifier-m is *not* changed. Only one identifier may appear after the word FROM and only one after the word GIVING.

Examples: Suppose it is desired to perform the following calculation:

$$\text{Net cost} = \text{Total cost} - (\text{Discount} + \text{Rebate} + \text{Credit})$$

The value of Total cost is not to be changed by the calculation and the previous content of Net cost is to be ignored. The following statement could perform the required calculation:

> SUBSTRACT DISCOUNT, REBATE, CREDIT FROM TOTAL-COST
> GIVING NET-COST.

This format can also be used to place the difference between two fields in another field:

> SUBTRACT A FROM B GIVING C.

It is particularly important to remember that in this example the value of field B remains unchanged after the statement has been executed.

Exercises

1. If the value 27.496 is moved to a field with two decimal places what will be the result:
   (*a*) with; (*b*) without the ROUNDED Option?
2. Write the statement to add the value of FIELD-1 to the value of FIELD-2.
3. Repeat question 2 but place the answer in FIELD-X.
4. Write the statement to subtract the values in fields SA, SB, and SC from the value in field TOT placing the result in field RESULT.
5. Write the statement to add 327.6 to the values in fields AA, AB, AC, and AD with field AC rounded.

CHAPTER FOURTEEN

MULTIPLY AND DIVIDE

The MULTIPLY Statement

The MULTIPLY statement is used to obtain the product of two data-item values.

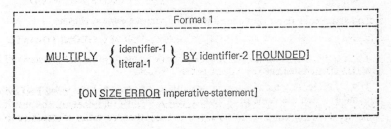

```
┌--------------------------------------------------------------------┐
|                              Format 2                              |
|--------------------------------------------------------------------|
|                                                                    |
|    MULTIPLY   { identifier-1 }  BY  { identifier-2 }  GIVING identifier-3 |
|               { literal-1    }      { literal-2    }               |
|                                                                    |
|                                                                    |
|       [ROUNDED]      [ON SIZE ERROR imperative-statement]          |
|                                                                    |
└--------------------------------------------------------------------┘
```

Format 1. The value in identifier-1 (or the value of literal-1) is multiplied by the value of identifier-2 and the result replaces the original value of identifier-2. Note that a field may be multiplied by itself.

Example: The area of a circle is calculated from the formula $A = \pi r^2$ where π is the constant 3.142 and r is the radius of the circle. Suppose the radius of a circle is held in a field called RADIUS which, it is required, is to be made to contain the area of the circle. The following two statements could be used to achieve this result.

MULTIPLY RADIUS BY RADIUS.
MULTIPLY 3.142 BY RADIUS.

After execution of the second statement RADIUS contains a value equal to the area of the circle.

Care should always be taken with the result fields used for multiplication since the number of digits required can often far exceed the number in either of the original operands. The SIZE ERROR option can of course be used with the MULTIPLY statement:

MULTIPLY SMALL BY LARGE SIZE ERROR GO TO OVERFLOW.

Note the omission of the optional reserved word ON in this example.

Format 2. The value of identifier-1 or literal-1 is **multiplied** by the value of identifier-2 or literal-2 and the result (**product**) replaces the value of identifier-3. The values of the first two fields are not changed by the execution of this statement.

Example: If in the example quoted above the value of RADIUS was not to be destroyed during the calculation of the circles area a format 2 multiplication statement could have been used.

MULTIPLY RADIUS BY RADIUS GIVING AREA.
MULTIPLY 3.142 BY AREA.

The item AREA is used in the first statement as an **intermediate work area.** The second statement's result is of course stored in AREA when the calculation is complete.

The DIVIDE Statement

The DIVIDE statement is used to calculate the **quotient** (and optionally the **remainder**) when the value of one data item is **divided** by the value of another data item.

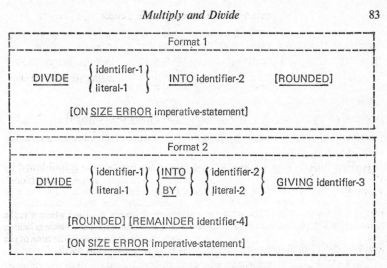

Format 1. The value in identifier-1 (or the value of literal-1) is divided into identifier-2 and the quotient replaces the value of identifier-2; any remainder is discarded. This calculation can be summarized thus:

$$\text{identifier-2} = \frac{\text{identifier-2}}{\text{identifier-1}}$$

Examples: To convert a number of minutes (held in data item TIME) to hours the field must be divided by 6Ø:

DIVIDE 6Ø INTO TIME.

If the number of hours is to be rounded to the nearest hour the statement would be coded:

DIVIDE 6Ø INTO TIME ROUNDED.

A program involving an average speed calculation could contain the following statement:

DIVIDE HOURS INTO DISTANCE.

Format 2. The value in identifier-1 is divided into or by identifier-2 (depending on whether INTO or BY respectively is specified) and the quotient replaces the value of identifier-3. If a remainder is required it can be obtained by specifying an identifier-4.

Example: The conversion of minutes into hours can be carried out using this format without losing the value of HOURS as in the example above. Suppose the initial values of the fields HOURS and MINUTES are 32 and 64 respectively. The following statement is then executed:

DIVIDE 6Ø INTO MINUTES GIVING HOURS ROUNDED.

The values are HOURS–Ø1, MINUTES–64. (Note that the value of MINUTES remains unaltered while the quotient from the division has replaced the original value of HOURS.) If the original number of minutes is to be converted into hours and minutes the DIVIDE statement with the REMAINDER option can be used:

DIVIDE MINUTES BY 6Ø GIVING HOURS REMAINDER MINS-LEFT.

If the original values of these fields had been in the above example the values now will be Ø1-HOURS 04-MINS-LEFT and the original 64 in MINUTES. The last statement is identical with this alternative format:

DIVIDE 6Ø INTO MINUTES GIVING HOURS REMAINDER MINS-LEFT.

The average speed calculation could also be improved by using a format 2 DIVIDE statement:

DIVIDE HOURS INTO DISTANCE GIVING AVERAGE ROUNDED.

Notes. If the ROUNDED and REMAINDER options are both specified in one statement the quotient is rounded after the remainder has been calculated (by subtracting the product of the quotient and divisor from the dividend). An attempt to divide by a data item with a value of **zero** will always raise the **size error condition.**

The COMPUTE Statement

The COMPUTE statement can be used to give to a data item the value of (i) the value of another data item, (ii) the value of a literal, or (iii) the value of an arithmetic expression (see below).

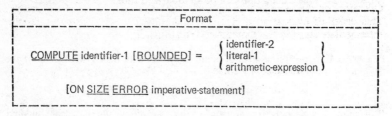

```
                              Format
────────────────────────────────────────────────────────────

                                         ⎧ identifier-2          ⎫
    COMPUTE identifier-1 [ROUNDED] =     ⎨ literal-1             ⎬
                                         ⎩ arithmetic-expression ⎭

         [ON SIZE ERROR imperative-statement]
```

The **expression** to the right of the equals sign is evaluated and its value replaces the value of identifier-1.

Example: The first two options for the **expression** to the right of the equal sign provide two simple methods of assigning values to data items:

COMPUTE FIELDA = 47.
COMPUTE FIELDB = FIELDC.

The second example has the effect of making the value of FIELDB equal to the value of FIELDC.

Arithmetic Expressions

An **arithmetic expression** is a combination of **identifiers, numeric literals,** and **arithmetic operators.** As might be expected the arithmetic operators specify arithmetic operations and are as follows:

      +   **addition**
      −   **subtraction**
      *   **multiplication**
      /   **division**
    **   **exponentiation** (or raised to the power of)

It is possible therefore to specify, in a single statement, a complicated arithmetic calculation:

$$\text{COMPUTE RESULT} = A + B + C * D$$
$$\text{COMPUTE RESULT} = A**B$$
$$\text{COMPUTE RESULT} = A/B*3-24*C$$

Obviously in certain cases the final answer to the calculation could depend on the sequence in which the arithmetic operators were evaluated. For example, the statement 3*2**3 will produce two different results depending on whether the * operator (multiply) or the ** operator (exponentiate) is acted upon first (the results would be 216 and 24 respectively). To avoid this uncertainty an **arithmetic operator hierarchy** is specified which lays down the order in which the operators are to be evaluated. The order is as follows:

1. $-$ (minus sign)
2. **
3. * and /
4. + and $-$ (addition and subtraction)

So in the example already looked at (3*2**3) the exponentiation will be carried out first followed by the multiplication. (Giving a result of 24.) Operators on the **same level** are evaluated **left to right** in the expression used. This order of evaluation is demonstrated in the table below showing the intermediate steps in the evaluation of a complex statement:

		24*3/8 + 6*3 $-$ 12/3
intermediate stage	1	72/8 + 6*3 $-$ 12/3
,,	,, 2	9 + 6*3 $-$ 12/3
,,	,, 3	9 + 18 $-$ 12/3
,,	,, 4	9 + 18 $-$ 4
,,	,, 5	27 $-$ 4
final stage		23

If the calculation to be performed requires operator evaluation different from that given above then the order of evaluation is altered using parentheses. *Operators within parentheses are evaluated first and multiple parentheses are evaluated from the innermost pair to the outermost.* This is shown in the following stage-by-stage evaluation:

		24* (6 $-$ 2) + (18 $-$ (3*4/6) + 1)
intermediate stage	1	24* (6 $-$ 2) + (18 $-$ 2 + 1)
,,	,, 2	24* 4 + (18 $-$ 2 + 1)
,,	,, 3	24* 4 + (16 + 1)
,,	,, 4	24* 4 + 17
,,	,, 5	96 + 17
final stage		113

Examples: The calculation for the area of a circle used at the beginning of the chapter can now be coded in one statement:

$$\text{COMPUTE AREA} = 3.142 * \text{RADIUS} **2.$$

A payroll program to calculate a bonus based on the average weekly overtime and the staff grade could use the COMPUTE statement as shown:

COMPUTE BONUS = (MONTH-OTIME/4 + STANDARD-BONUS) *
                      (RATE*GRADE +1).

Exercises

1. Where is the result stored in the statement MULTIPLY AREA BY DEPTH?
2. How could the statement in question 1 be altered to put the same answer in the data item called VOLUME?
3. How could the answer to question 2 be rewritten using the COMPUTE statement?
4. List the hierarchy of arithmetic operators.
5. What will be the result of statement 2 shown below?:

> 1. SUBTRACT FIELDA FROM FIELDA.
> 2. DIVIDE FIELDB BY FIELDA GIVING FIELDC.

CHAPTER FIFTEEN

PROGRAM FLOW

The execution of statements, sentences, and paragraphs normally follows a sequential pattern. After each one is executed the one immediately following it is executed. This is analogous to reading a book; after each sentence is read the reader continues with the sentence immediately following, similarly after each page the immediately following page is read. It is frequently necessary to divert the flow of a program from its sequential operation, for example, a group of instructions may have to be by-passed or a group may have to be re-executed. The **procedure branching** statements—GO TO, ALTER, PER-FORM, STOP, and EXIT—allow the programmer to alter the sequential flow of a program.

Procedure Name

A **procedure name** is the name given by the programmer to a statement or group of statements and as seen in Chapter Eleven is a paragraph name. A procedure name will therefore begin in Area A and is terminated by a period.

The selection of procedure names for a given program is largely a matter of choice—some programmers like to allocate these names sequentially (using such names as A10, A20, A30, etc.). While others prefer to use meaningful names designed to identify the function of the procedure (such as READ-INPUT-FILE, CALCULATE-BONUS, TERMINATE). The latter method will be followed throughout this part of the book.

The GO TO Statement

The GO TO statement permits the execution flow to be transferred from one part of the program to another.

```
┌─────────────────────────────────────────────────────────────┐
│                          Format 1                           │
├─────────────────────────────────────────────────────────────┤
│    GO TO procedure-name-1                                   │
└─────────────────────────────────────────────────────────────┘
```

```
┌─────────────────────────────────────────────────────────────┐
│                          Format 2                           │
├─────────────────────────────────────────────────────────────┤
│    GO TO procedure-name-1 [procedure-name-2] ...            │
│         DEPENDING ON identifier                             │
└─────────────────────────────────────────────────────────────┘
```

```
┌─────────────────────────────────────────────────────────────┐
│                          Format 3                           │
├─────────────────────────────────────────────────────────────┤
│    GO TO.                                                   │
└─────────────────────────────────────────────────────────────┘
```

Format 1. This statement causes program flow to be transferred to the statement or group of statements identified by procedure-name-1. If a GO TO appears where an imperative-statement is permitted (for example following the SIZE ERROR option) it must be the last or only statement in that imperative-statement.

Examples: To transfer control to the statement called NEXT:

GO TO NEXT.

To use the GO TO in an imperative-statement position the coding would be like this:

ADD TAX TO DEDUCTIONS ON SIZE ERROR GO TO OVERFLOW.

If the size error condition was raised the GO TO would be executed and control would be immediately transferred to the statement called OVERFLOW. When this condition is raised other imperative processing may be executed prior to the control transfer:

SUBTRACT JUMP FROM LINE-COUNT ON SIZE ERROR ADD
1 TO ERROR-COUNT GO TO CHECK-ROUTINE.

The most usual occurrence of a format 1 GO TO will, however, be the straight-forward transference of control to another statement or group of statements:

GO TO READ-NEW-RECORD.
GO TO END-OF-JOB.
GO TO OVERFLOW.

Format 2. By using this statement the programmer is able to transfer control to one of a number of procedures depending on the value of identifier. If the valuer of identifier, at the time this statement is executed, is 1 control will be transferred to procedure-name-1; if the value is 2 control will be transferred to procedure-name-2, and so on up to procedure-name-n (for a value n in identifier). If the value in identifier is not a positive whole number or is not in the range 1 to n (where n is the number of procedure names after the words GO TO) the entire statement will be ignored.

Examples: Consider the statement shown:

GO TO ONE, TWO, THREE DEPENDING ON CONTROL.

If, at the time this statement is executed, the value of CONTROL is 3 then control will be transferred to the procedure named THREE. If the value is 2 control will be transferred to the procedure named TWO. Any value of CONTROL outside the range 1–3 will cause this statement to be ignored and control will pass to the next sequential statement. A payroll program may have as part of its processing a number of routines to calculate the annual staff bonus which is different for each of four grades of staff. Each time that part of the program dealing with bonus calculation is executed the necessary transfer of control could be accomplished by use of a format 2 GO TO as shown below:

GO TO BONUS-1, BONUS-2, BONUS-3, BONUS-4 DEPENDING
ON STAFF-GRADE.

So, with this statement, control will be automatically transferred to the appropriate bonus calculation routine each time it is executed. If an erroneous staff code is in the field STAFF-GRADE the programmer may want control to be transferred to an error routine. He cannot obviously cater for every possible value of STAFF-GRADE but could use coding such as:

GO TO BONUS-1, BONUS-2, BONUS-3, BONUS-4, DEPENDING
ON STAFF-GRADE. GO TO ERROR-ROUTINE.

Format 3. This is a special case of the GO TO statement and can be considered in its coded form as a **dummy statement.** Coded as shown in the general format this statement will have no effect on the program when executed. However, a procedure containing a format 3 GO TO can be the subject of an ALTER statement (see below) and its use will be seen once ALTER has been studied.

The ALTER Statement

The ALTER statement is used to change the transfer point specified in a GO TO statement.

```
                               Format
  ALTER procedure-name-1 TO [PROCEED TO] procedure-name-2

       [procedure-name-3 TO [PROCEED TO] procedure-name-4] ...
```

Procedure-name-1 (and procedure-name-3, etc., if used) must refer to a paragraph containing only a GO TO statement:

PARAGRAPH-1.
                        GO TO END-ROUTINE.
PARAGRAPH-2.
                              .
                              .
                              .
                              .
                              .

PARAGRAPH-1 as shown could be the subject of an ALTER statement. The names specified for paragraph-name-2 (and paragraph-name-4, etc., if used) must be the name(s) of paragraph(s) within the Procedure Division. The effect of the ALTER statement is to replace the procedure-name operand of the GO TO statement (called procedure-name-1) with procedure-name-2.

Example: Consider the out-line Procedure Division shown below. The first time execution of these statements occurs paragraph SEQ-CHECK is to be by-passed, on subsequent executions the paragraph is to be executed following the paragraph READ-IN.

```
        READ-IN.
             .
             .
             .
             .
             .
        SWITCH. GO TO CALCULATE.
        SEQ-CHECK.
             .
             .
             .
        CALCULATE.
             ALTER SWITCH TO PROCEED TO SEQ-CHECK.
             .
             .
             .
```

When paragraph SWITCH is first executed control will be transferred to CALCULATE whereupon the ALTER statement will be executed. Any subsequent execution of SWITCH will cause control to be transferred to SEQ-CHECK.

The original function of SWITCH can be restored with another ALTER statement as shown:

```
        ALTER SWITCH TO PROCEED TO CALCULATE.
```

The ALTER statement may be used conveniently to swop processing paths on alternate executions. Suppose a program consists of three parts (MAIN-LOOP, CALCULATE-1, CALCULATE-2) for each data item processed MAIN-LOOP is to be executed followed by CALCULATE-1 for odd-numbered items and CALCULATE-2 for even-numbered ones. The following coding could accomplish this:

```
MAIN-LOOP.       .
             .
             .
             .
TRANSFER-SWITCH. GO TO CALCULATE-1.
CALCULATE-1.
             ALTER TRANSFER-SWITCH TO PROCEED TO CALCULATE-2.
             .
             .
             .
        GO TO MAIN-LOOP.
```

CALCULATE-2.
      ALTER TRANSFER-SWITCH TO PROCEED TO CALCULATE-1.
      .
      .
      .
      .

      GO TO MAIN-LOOP

A format 3 GO TO statement can be the subject of an ALTER statement and after such is no longer a dummy statement.

      INPUT-READS.
      .
      .
      .

      ALTER SWITCH TO PROCEED TO ERROR.
      .
      .
      .
      .

      SWITCH. GO TO.
      NEXT-CARD. .
      .
      .
      .

Exercises

1. Write the statement to transfer control to the procedure-named END-OF-RUN.
2. Write the statement to cause control to be transferred to CARD-1 if TYPE is 1 or 4, CARD-2 if TYPE is 3, or ERROR if TYPE is 2.
3. What is wrong with this statement?:

      SWITCH. GO TO ERROR1. GO TO ERROR2.

4. Write the statement to change the transfer point at MAIN-LOOP from CALCULATE to SUBSID-LOOP.

5. What is wrong with the following coding?:

      FIRST-TIME. ALTER CHECK TO PROCEED TO SWITCH.
      .
      .
      .

      CHECK. GO TO ERROR.
            ADD 1 TO LOOP-COUNT

CHAPTER SIXTEEN

PROGRAM CONTROL

The PERFORM Statement

The PERFORM statement is used to depart from the normal sequence of statements in order to execute a statement or series of statements, a given number of times; or until a specified condition exists. After the statements are executed control is returned to the statement following the PERFORM.

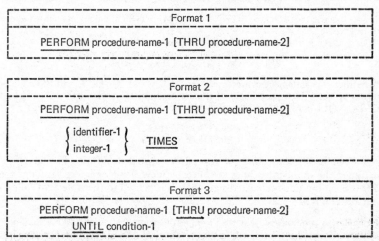

```
Format 1

PERFORM procedure-name-1 [THRU procedure-name-2]
```

```
Format 2

PERFORM procedure-name-1 [THRU procedure-name-2]
    { identifier-1 }   TIMES
    { integer-1    }
```

```
Format 3

PERFORM procedure-name-1 [THRU procedure-name-2]
    UNTIL condition-1
```

General. Each time a PERFORM statement is executed control is transferred to the first statement of the procedure with the name procedure-name-1. Control is always returned to the statement following the PERFORM; the point from which this control is passed is determined according to the following rules:

1. *If procedure-name-2 is not specified*—return is made after the execution of the last statement of procedure-name-1.
2. *If procedure-name-2 is specified*—return is made after the execution of the last statement of procedure-name-2.

Format 1. This statement causes the procedure(s) named to be executed once only.

Examples: Consider the coding shown below:

```
CALC-1.
    ADD OVERTIME TO TIME GIVING TOTAL-TIME.
    SUBTRACT FREE-TIME FROM TOTAL-TIME.
CALC-2.
    MULTIPLY TOTAL-TIME BY RATE GIVING BONUS.
CALC-3.
    DIVIDE LOSS-FACTOR INTO BONUS.
```

In the program using these procedures it may be desired to execute one or more of the calculations in different parts of the program. Rather than repeat the statements each time they are required, the PERFORM statement can be utilized.

To execute CALC-1 (i.e. the ADD and the SUBTRACT statements) the following could be used:

PERFORM CALC-1.

When CALC-1 has been executed control will return to the statement following the PERFORM (which can be on the same or next line). If the programmer wished to execute CALC-1 and CALC-2 he could use:

PERFORM CALC-1 THRU CALC-2.

This will cause the ADD, SUBTRACT, and MULTIPLY statements shown above to be executed.

To execute all three procedures the following would be necessary:

PERFORM CALC-1 THRU CALC-3.

Note that this statement causes execution of CALC-1, CALC-3, and those statements between these procedures. If it were required to execute only CALC-1 and CALC-3 (and *not* CALC-2) the following two statements would be required:

PERFORM CALC-1.
PERFORM CALC-3.

Format 2. The procedure or procedures specified (as with format 1) are executed the number of times specified by identifier-1 or integer-1. Once the TIMES option has been exhausted control is passed to the statement following PERFORM.

Examples: A programmer may wish to repeat a group of statements a given number of times. For example, to repeat the procedure called ADD-UP 4 times the statement below could be used:

PERFORM ADD-UP 4 TIMES.

The number of times a paragraph is to be executed can be determined by the value of a data item. If the content of the field LOOP was 10 the following statement would cause execution of the paragraph named ROUND-UP to be performed 10 times:

PERFORM ROUND-UP LOOP TIMES.

As with format 1 PERFORM statements this format can specify the execution of more than one paragraph. The first statement in the coding below will cause the three paragraphs CALC-1, CALC-2, and CALC-3 to be executed 4 times:

```
        PERFORM CALC-1 THRU CALC-3 4 TIMES.
CALC-1. ADD 1 TO STAFF-COUNT.
        MULTIPLY STAFF-COUNT BY HOURS GIVING TOT-
        HOURS.
CALC-2. ADD TOT-HOURS TO GRAND-TOT-HOURS.
CALC-3. ADD COUNT TO INDICATOR.
        SUBTRACT 1 FROM LOOP-TIMES.
```

Note that the three paragraphs are performed as a group for each of the PERFORM TIMES. The sequence of execution of the paragraphs following this PERFORM statement will therefore be:

CALC-1
CALC-2
CALC-3
CALC-1
CALC-2
CALC-3
CALC-1
CALC-2
CALC-3
CALC-1
CALC-2
CALC-3

When the PERFORM format 2 statement is used with an identifier specifying the number of times execution is required this number will not be affected if the value of identifier-1 is amended by the paragraphs being performed. For example, consider these statements:

PERFORM TOTALING COUNT TIMES.
TOTALING.   ADD BASIC-AMOUNT TO TOTAL-1.
ADD BONUS-AMOUNT TO TOTAL-2.
SUBTRACT 1 FROM COUNT.

If the value of COUNT was 6 when the PERFORM statement was encountered then the paragraph TOTALING would be executed 6 times regardless of the fact that the third statement in TOTALING amends the value of COUNT.

Format 3. When this format is used the paragraph(s) specified are performed until the UNTIL condition is satisfied. If this condition exists when the PERFORM is encountered then the paragraph(s) are not executed.

Examples: A stock-control program may require the procedures allocating items held in stock to be performed until the stock-level is zero.

PERFORM ALLOCATE UNTIL STOCK-LEVEL EQUALS ZERO.

Care must be exercised when coding this type of statement to ensure that the specified condition will occur every time the PERFORM is executed. Suppose the paragraph ALLOCATE in the above example contained the following statement:

SUBTRACT ORDER-QUANTITY FROM STOCK-LEVEL.

If these two values were not equal it is possible for STOCK-LEVEL to become negative without ever having been equal to zero. If this happens the PERFORM statement would be executed endlessly. An alternative would be to code the PERFORM statement thus:

PERFORM ALLOCATE UNTIL STOCK-LEVEL LESS THAN 1.

Now the execution will be terminated as soon as STOCK-LEVEL becomes zero or negative. In the program mentioned above it would be more likely that the paragraph ALLOCATE would be executed only as long as the value of STOCK-LEVEL exceeded the value of ORDER-QUANTITY (in other words as long as the available stock was sufficient to satisfy the next order). The PERFORM statement would now be rewritten:

PERFORM ALLOCATE UNTIL STOCK-LEVEL LESS THAN
ORDER-QUANTITY.

This format of the PERFORM can again be used to execute a group of paragraphs:

PERFORM REORDER THRU STOCK-UPDATE UNTIL CODE EQUALS 7.

Embedded PERFORM Statement

A PERFORM statement contained within the range of another PER-
FORM statement is said to be **embedded** or **nested**. For example, the second
PERFORM shown below is an embedded PERFORM:

> PERFORM MAIN-CALC.
> .
> .
> .
> .

MAIN-CALC.   ADD 1 TO LOOP-COUNT.
                PERFORM SMALL-CALC.
  NEXT.

*The range of an embedded PERFORM statement must be either totally included
or totally excluded from the range of the original PERFORM statement.* In
other words the exit point for the first PERFORM cannot be within the
range of the second PERFORM. This is best illustrated by the two examples
shown below:

Totally excluded nested PERFORM:

MAIN-PROC.   PERFORM CALC-ROUTINE.
                  .
                  .
                  .

CALC-ROUTINE.   ADD 1 TO INDICATOR.
                  SUBTRACT HOURS FROM TOTAL GIVING
                  SUB-TOTAL.
                  PERFORM SUBSID-CALC.
                  ADD RATE TO RATE-TOTAL.
NEXT.   .
                  .

SUBSID-CALC.   MULTIPLY SUB-TOTAL BY R-FACTOR
                  GIVING WORK.
                  ADD WORK TO BONUS GIVING RATE.
NEXT-2.   .
                  .
                  .
                  .

Totally included nested PERFORM:

START.   PERFORM RATES THRU BONUS.
                  .
                  .
                  .

```
RATES.          ADD RATE TO RATE-TOTAL.
                PERFORM RATE-CALC.
                MULTIPLY CALC-RATE BY EFFICIENCY
                GIVING WORK.
                    .
                    .
                    .
                    .
                GO TO BONUS.
RATE-CALC.      ADD RATE-1, RATE-2, RATE-3, GIVING WORK.
                DIVIDE WORK BY 3 GIVING CALC-RATE.
BONUS.          MULTIPLY BONUS-HOURS BY RATE
                GIVING BONUS-AMOUNT.
                ADD 1 TO LOOP-COUNT.
```

Note in the second example the use of a GO TO within the range of a PER-FORM statement. Any such embedded GO TO must refer to a point within the range of the original PERFORM.

The EXIT Statement

The EXIT statement provides a common exit point or end point for a series of procedures.

```
┌─────────────────────────────────────────────────────────────┐
│                          Format                              │
├─────────────────────────────────────────────────────────────┤
│    paragraph-name.   EXIT.                                   │
└─────────────────────────────────────────────────────────────┘
```

When a series of procedures is being executed by a PERFORM statement it is sometimes necessary to transfer control to the end point from within the group of procedures. In other words it is necessary to terminate the PER-FORM from several points within the group being performed.

Example

```
MAIN-CALC.      PERFORM RATE THRU RATE-EXIT.
                    .
                    .
                    .
                    .
                    .
RATE.               .
                    .
                    .
                    .
SPECIAL-EXIT. GO TO RATE-EXIT.
                    .
                    .
                    .
                    .
```

PARA-1.   .
.
.
.
.
.
PARA-2.   .
.
.
.
.GO TO RATE-EXIT.
.
.
.
.
RATE-EXIT.   EXIT.

If the procedure named SPECIAL-EXIT is executed then control is transferred to RATE-EXIT. Since this is procedure-name-2 in the associated PERFORM it represents the end of the PERFORMed group of procedures. If an EXIT statement is encountered that is not the subject of a PERFORM statement then it is ignored.

The STOP Statement

The STOP statement is used to halt execution of the program.

```
-------------------------------------------------------
|                        Format                       |
-------------------------------------------------------
|         STOP   { RUN     }                          |
|                { literal }                          |
-------------------------------------------------------
```

When the RUN option is used program execution is terminated and control is returned to the operating system.

Example

STOP RUN.

When the literal option is used program execution is suspended. The value of the literal is communicated to the computer operator and program execution is only resumed when the operator gives the necessary instruction.

Example

STOP "PLEASE CHANGE PAPER".

Exercises

1. Write a single statement to execute the statements contained in paragraphs BONUS and RATE.
2. How many times will the paragraph LOOP be executed here (COUNT has initial value of 6)

PERFORM LOOP COUNT TIMES.
LOOP.   ADD BONUS TO TOTAL.
SUBTRACT 1 FROM COUNT.

3. Write the statement to execute the paragraph PAY until RATE-CODE is smaller than 7.
4. Write the statements to (*a*) terminate the execution of your program; (*b*) suspend the operation of your program after telling the computer operator that an error has occurred.
5. Where must the range of an embedded PERFORM lay?

You should now attempt Revision Questions, Set 1, on page 210.

CHAPTER SEVENTEEN

THE DATA DIVISION

Data Division—Organization

We have now learned some of the basic COBOL statements and can perform simple arithmetic statements without too much trouble. However, in the examples used in the foregoing chapters it has been assumed that the data to be operated upon have already existed in core storage and that the data items manipulated did not require some form of definition to the compiler. Clearly this will not normally be the case in practice—the programmer will find it necessary to input some data to his program (via an input unit) and he will need to tell the compiler the way in which his various fields and data items are structured. Some of the programmer's data will be read in from input units and some will be defined within the program (constants). In addition to data read in or defined the programmer will often require core storage space to be reserved for intermediate work areas. In the context of the Data Division, work areas and constant definition areas can be regarded as the same.

A COBOL program may therefore basically process two types of data: information recorded externally on data files and information created internally during the execution of the program. The purpose of the Data Division is to give the descriptions of these two types of data to be processed by the program.

Organization of External Data

External data are held, as we have seen in Part One, on data files which can be input units or backing store units. A **file** is a collection of **records** which can be of two types—**physical records** and **logical records.** A physical record is a group of characters which is treated as a single unit when transferred to or from core storage. For example the complete content of a punched card is a physical record.

A logical record is a number of related data items (or a structure—see Chapter Nine). A logical record may also be a physical record in that each physical unit of data transferred to core storage represents a logical record. A logical record may also be one of several logical records contained within a physical record. Occasionally a logical record may be made up of more than one physical record.

To avoid confusion in the following text physical records will be referred to as **blocks** and logical records simply as **records**. When more than one record occurs in a block the file is said to be **blocked** and the number of occurrences is called the **blocking factor**.

File Blocking is illustrated below:

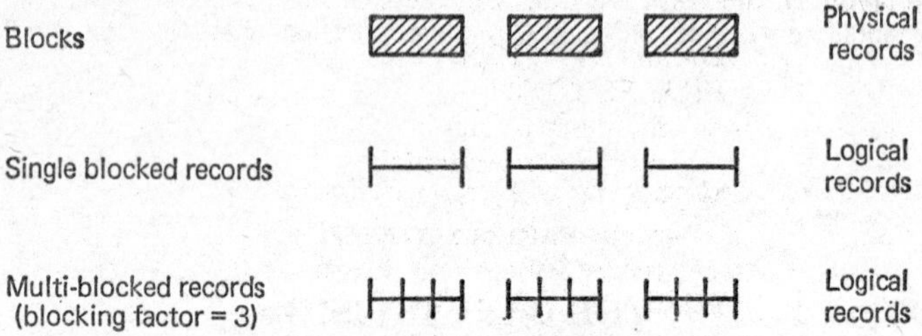

Fig. 35. Schematic of file blocking

Statements are provided in COBOL for describing the relationship between blocks and records on a file. However, once this relationship is established the programmer need not concern himself with the physical structures of the file. A COBOL programmer only has access to the records on a file, the so-called **unblocking** (separating the logical records from the block) is done by the operating system and makes the job of file handling much simpler for the beginner.

Description of External Data

Before a file can be described in a COBOL program it is necessary to distinguish between the external description of the file and the internal contents of the file.

The external description of a file refers to the way in which it is physically organized on the input or backing store unit. For example the number of records in each block indicates how the data is grouped on the file. These physical aspects are described in file-description entries (see below). Each record on a file will normally be in the form of a structure and the description of this structure (describing the type of data to be held in each field) represents the internal contents of the file. The details of each field in a particular type of record are given in a Record Description.

The DATA DIVISION

The Data Division is divided into three sections which, when used, must appear in the correct order and be identified by their correct headers:

> FILE SECTION.
> WORKING-STORAGE SECTION.
> LINKAGE SECTION.

The **File Section** is used to describe all data that is stored externally, to be processed by the program. Such data cannot be processed by a COBOL program unless it is described in a File Section entry. The File Section header is followed by one or more **file descriptions**. All data to be generated internally by the program is described in the **Working-Storage Section**. Single or **non-**

contiguous items are described first, followed by **record (or structure)** descriptions.

Data to be passed between programs (see Chapter Thirty-nine) is defined in the **Linkage Section**. Once again non-contiguous items are defined first followed by structure definitions.

The layout of the Data Division will therefore be:

> DATA DIVISION.
> FILE SECTION.
> > file description
> > record description(s) . . .
> WORKING-STORAGE SECTION.
> > non-contiguous item definitions
> > record (or structure) definitions
> LINKAGE SECTION.
> > non-contiguous item definitions
> > record (or structure) definitions

Whenever a particular section is not required it may be omitted completely.

Data Division Entries

Each entry in the Data Division is preceded by a **level number** (see below) except the file-description clause which is preceded by a **level indicator**. The description of a file is identified by the level indicator FD (File Description) which appears in Area A; the name of the file follows in Area B. Full details of file definitions are given in Chapters Eighteen and Nineteen.

Level Numbers

Level numbers are used to identify the subdivisions within a record or structure for the purpose of data reference. Each level may be likened to a level of division in a structure hierarchy as described in Chapter Nine. How-

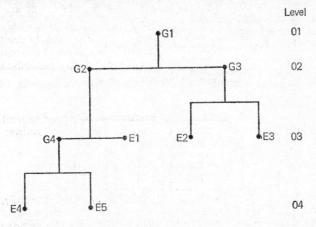

(G = Group, E = Elementary item)

Fig. 36. Relationship between group and elementary levels

ever, note that once a subdivision has been established there is no restriction on the programmer further subdividing the item to establish a more detailed reference.

The lowest units within a structure, that is those units which are not them-selves subdivided, are called **elementary items**. Normally a record will consist of a sequence of elementary items, although if the record is not subdivided then the record itself is an elementary item. A set of elementary items may be combined together to form a **group item**. A group item, which must be named to exist, consists of a sequence of elementary items; a number of groups may themselves be combined into a larger group. *An elementary item may therefore belong to one or more groups.* Level numbers and grouping are shown dia-grammatically in Fig. 36.

This structure could be defined within the program as shown below. (Note the descriptive details of the elementary items have been omitted for clarity.)

```
Ø1   GROUP1.
     Ø2   GROUP2.
          Ø3   GROUP4.
               Ø4   ELEMENTARY4 . . .
               Ø4   ELEMENTARY5 . . .
          Ø3   ELEMENTARY1 . . .
     Ø2   GROUP3.
          Ø3   ELEMENTARY2 . . .
          Ø3   ELEMENTARY3 . . .
```

Note how elementary item ELEMENTARY4 is a member of groups 4, 2, and 1. This system of level numbers indicates the relationship between different items and groups of items within a record. The **level number 1** (always written as Ø1) is assigned to the highest level or largest group which will always be the complete record. Less inclusive items are assigned level numbers numerically higher (but not necessarily consecutive) than the group to which they belong up to a maximum of level number 49. A group is ter-minated when a level number equal to or higher than the group level number is encountered.

As a further example of level numbers used to define record structures, consider the data to be read in via punched cards with the following fields:

Account no	Credit limit	Name	Street	Town

Basically there are five fields on this card, however, the program to process this file may wish to access individual fields and groups of fields in the format shown:

Card				
Financial		Address		
Account	Credit	Name	Delivery	
no	limit		Street	Town
*	*	*	*	*

*indicates elementary item.

In order to be able to access these groups (with the names shown) the programmer could code the record layout as shown below (once again omitting the elementary item definition details for clarity):

        Ø1   CARD.
        Ø2   FINANCIAL.
                 Ø5   ACCOUNT-NO . . .
                 Ø5   CREDIT-LIMIT . . .
        Ø2   ADDRESS.
             Ø3   NAME . . .
             Ø3   DELIVERY.
                 Ø5   STREET . . .
                 Ø5   TOWN . . .

Special Level Numbers

In addition to the level numbers in the range Ø1–49 discussed above for record structure definition two **special level numbers** are provided.

Level 77. **Non-contiguous items** of data, that is elementary items which are not part of a group, are defined with level number 77.

                77   NON-CONTIG-AREA . . .

A fuller description of level 77 items will be found in Chapter Twenty-one.

Level 88. It is permissible to associate a particular **condition** with a data item by defining that data item under level 88:

            88   CONDITION   condition-definition.

Conditions are discussed fully in Chapter Twenty-seven.

Level numbers Ø1 and 77 must appear in Area A, followed in Area B by their associated data names and descriptive information. All other level numbers may appear in either Area A or Area B followed, in Area B, by their data name and descriptive information. All level numbers will be written with two digits (i.e. Ø1, Ø7, Ø9, etc.).

Exercises

1. What three sections comprise the Data Division?
2. What is the maximum level number for record structuring?
3. What are the special level numbers and what are they used for?
4. What level number is used for the complete record description?
5. When a block contains, say, 3 records how is the file described?

CHAPTER EIGHTEEN

FILE DESCRIPTIONS—1

For each file to be used during the execution of a program the programmer must code a **file description** which outlines the characteristics of each file. The file description is identified by the level indicator FD which is followed by a number of independent clauses. The entry for each file is terminated by a period (full-stop).

```
┌─────────────────────────────────────────────────────────┐
│                      General Format                     │
├─────────────────────────────────────────────────────────┤
│ FD file-name                                            │
│                                                         │
│     [BLOCK CONTAINS Clause]                             │
│                                                         │
│     [RECORD CONTAINS Clause]                            │
│                                                         │
│     [RECORDING MODE Clause]                             │
│                                                         │
│     LABEL RECORDS Clause                                │
│                                                         │
│     [VALUE OF Clause]                                   │
│                                                         │
│     [DATA RECORDS Clause] .                             │
│                                                         │
└─────────────────────────────────────────────────────────┘
```

The level indicator FD must precede the file description and the FD must be followed by the name the programmer wishes to assign to the file. This **file name** is formed according to the rules already given for data names. The clauses which follow the file name are in some cases optional and can in any event appear in any order between file name and the period.

The clauses shown in the general format above will mean little to the reader at this stage, however, they are all described below (and in Chapter Nineteen), individually and where necessary further explanation is given of the properties of files of interest to the COBOL programmer.

BLOCK CONTAINS Clause

This clause is used to specify the size of each block (physical record) on the file.

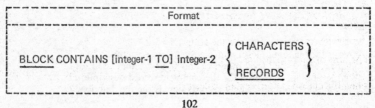

```
┌─────────────────────────────────────────────────────────┐
│                         Format                          │
├─────────────────────────────────────────────────────────┤
│                                        ⎧ CHARACTERS ⎫    │
│ BLOCK CONTAINS [integer-1 TO] integer-2 ⎨           ⎬    │
│                                        ⎩ RECORDS    ⎭    │
└─────────────────────────────────────────────────────────┘
```

This clause need not be specified if each block contains only one record, however, it will be used in all other cases.

The RECORDS option may only be used when each block contains a whole number of records and the length of each record is **fixed** (see below). Since in this case the block size is fixed integer-1 is omitted from the clause.

Consider the case of a file containing blocks each of which holds 3 records:

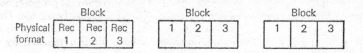

the clause describing the block size for this file could be thus:

BLOCK CONTAINS 3 RECORDS

This clause can be rewritten using the CHARACTERS option as shown below (assume each record contains 100 characters):

BLOCK CONTAINS 300 CHARACTERS

The CHARACTERS option is mainly used when the block length is **variable** (see below) because the records themselves are of variable length. As will be seen below, when records are of variable length the block size will vary, however, the program must be given a maximum block size and a minimum block size. For example, consider a variable-length file which may have blocks varying from 120 characters in length to 316 characters in length; the clause required would be as follows:

BLOCK CONTAINS 120 TO 316 CHARACTERS

The CHARACTERS option is also used for **spanned** files (see below) when the maximum block size is specified for each file. Note that the RECORDS option cannot be used for this type of file.

BLOCK CONTAINS 200

This clause specifies a block size of 200 (CHARACTERS being the assumed option). A BLOCK CONTAINS clause is required for all files except those of a single-blocked nature (i.e. those with one record per block).

RECORD CONTAINS Clause

This clause is used to specify the size of the records on a file.

```
┌─────────────────────────────────────────────────────┐
│                      Format                          │
├─────────────────────────────────────────────────────┤
│                                                      │
│  RECORD CONTAINS [integer-1 TO] integer-2 CHARACTERS │
│                                                      │
└─────────────────────────────────────────────────────┘
```

The size of each record is completely specified when the record description is coded (Chapter Nineteen) and this clause is therefore optional. However, when the clause is used certain rules apply.

When only integer-2 is used the file must contain records which are all the same, fixed, length.

RECORD CONTAINS 80 CHARACTERS

This clause indicates a file containing fixed-length records each of 80 characters. When a file contains variable-length records the maximum record size and the minimum record size are specified using this clause in full:

RECORD CONTAINS 70 TO 412 CHARACTERS

Normally the programmer will omit this clause and the compiler will calculate the size of each record from the descriptions given following the FD entry.

Recording Mode

We have already seen mention of the existence of fixed-length and variable-length records. The COBOL language also recognizes Undefined-length records and Spanned-length records. These four **recording modes** are described below:

Fixed-length Recording Mode

Each record on the file will be the same fixed length and each record will be wholly contained within a block. A block may contain more than one record; the number of records in each block will be constant for each file.

Since the size of each record is known and fixed it is not necessary to indicate, within the record itself, the length of the record.

Variable-length Recording Mode

Each record on the file is of variable length although each must be wholly contained within a block. A block may contain more than one record; however, the length of the block will vary (up to a specified maximum—see BLOCK CONTAINS clause) according to the lengths of the records it contains.

In order that the program may determine the length of each variable-length record read, each record is preceded by a field containing the length of the record. Similarly, each block is preceded by a field containing the length of the block. This is illustrated below:

Block	Length of block	Length of record 1	Record 1	Length of record 2	Record 2	Length of record 3	Record 3

These length fields do not have to be described, in the Data Division, by the programmer and their contents are not available to him. (Note—the compiler will automatically reserve the space for the length fields when a file requiring them is defined.)

Undefined-length Recording Mode

Each record may be of fixed or variable length and must be wholly contained within one block. No length-indicator fields are included and the programmer must therefore determine, within the program, the length of each record read. This mode is not normally used in general COBOL programming.

Spanned-length Recording Mode

Each record may be of fixed or variable length and may extend over more than one block. If a record is larger than the available space in a block then a segment of the record is written to fill the block. The remaining portion of the record is written in the next block or blocks. Each segment (or portion) of a block is preceded by a segment-length field (which is not available to the programmer) although only complete records are presented to the program. A spanned record (occupying 2 blocks) is illustrated below:

Block length	Segment 1 length	Segment 1		Block length	Segment 2 length	Segment 2

If the program read this file only a single record could be provided:

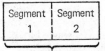

complete record

This method again is rarely used; however, if required the splitting into segments (and subsequent joining up) will be handled by the operating system.

RECORDING MODE Clause

This clause is used to specify the recording mode used by the file.

```
┌────────────────────────────────────────────────────────┐
│                          Format                         │
├────────────────────────────────────────────────────────┤
│                                                         │
│   RECORDING MODE IS mode                                │
│                                                         │
└────────────────────────────────────────────────────────┘
```

Mode may be given F, V, U, or S.

F Mode

This may be specified when each record on the file is of **fixed length** and wholly contained within one block. More than one record may be contained within a block (see BLOCK CONTAINS clause above).

If more than one record description is specified (see Chapter Nineteen) then the lengths of each description must all be the same.

Any file assigned to a card-reader must be mode F.

RECORDING MODE IS F

V Mode

This may be specified when each record is of **variable length** but wholly contained within one block. As already mentioned each variable-length record is preceded by a field containing the length of that record; however, since this length field requires no involvement from the programmer it can be ignored. The range of block sizes for variable-length files is specified with a

BLOCK CONTAINS clause. For example a file whose blocks can be between 100 and 300 characters could have the clause:

BLOCK CONTAINS 100 TO 300 CHARACTERS

The programmer may specify as many data-record descriptions (Chapter Nineteen) as he wishes, and each of them may be of a different length. When a record is to be written (WRITE is fully described in Chapter Thirty-two) the programmer will quote the name of the data record to be written. From the description of this record the compiler will have determined its length and can determine therefore if it can be accommodated within the current block. For example, consider the case mentioned above where the block can contain between 100 and 300 characters. Suppose that the data records can be 50, 100, or 250 characters in length. A number of block lengths are now possible, for example, if a 100 character record is followed by a 250 character record the first record will be written in a single block. If now the second record is followed by one of 50 characters then records 2 and 3 will be written as one block. If the third record had been 100 characters then the second record would also have been written as a single block. Some of the combinations of records making up this file are shown below:

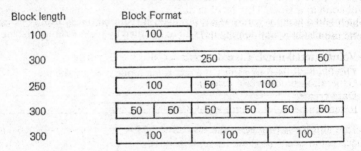

Block length	Block Format
100	100
300	250 / 50
250	100 / 50 / 100
300	50 / 50 / 50 / 50 / 50 / 50
300	100 / 100 / 100

The variable-length recording mode is indicated with the following clause:

RECORDING MODE IS V

Other Modes

The other recording modes available, **undefined** and **spanned**, are specified in a similar manner (as shown below); however, since these modes are not used very much a detailed description is omitted from this book.

RECORDING MODE IS U
RECORDING MODE IS V

(Note—the use of the above-mentioned clauses is shown in detailed examples at the end of Chapter Nineteen.)

Exercises

1. Write the clause to specify a block size of
   (a) 4 records
   (b) minimum 100 characters, maximum 370 characters

2. Write the clause to specify a record size of 80 characters.
3. Write down the four recording modes with their single letter abbreviations.
4. Can the programmer access the field-length indicators in a variable-length file?
5. Write the first entry for a file description of a file named MASTER.

CHAPTER NINETEEN

FILE DESCRIPTIONS—2

File Labelling

When a backing store file is made available to the computer it is important that checks can be made to ensure the acceptability of the file. When a file is to be read by a program checks must be made to ensure that the correct file has been supplied by the operators. When a file is to be written the program must check that the data already on the file, which will be overwritten, is no longer required. In order that these checks can be made all backing store files will contain a **label**. This label is simply a specially formatted data record which is the first record on the file. The type of information held on a magnetic tape label could include the following fields:

Volume serial number (i.e. the number of the reel of tape)
File name of data on tape
Generation number (see below)
Data created
Retention period (i.e. number of days this file is to be retained).

Before any file is processed the operating system will read the file label and check some or all of these fields, depending on whether it is to be read or written.

File to be read—the operating system will verify that the file name and generation number are correct.

File to be written—the operating system will check that the retention period has expired [i.e. the current date is greater than (date created + retention period)].

If any of these checks fail a message will be sent to the computer operator requesting that he supply the correct file. The details against which the file is to be checked are supplied to the operating system by the computer operators. **Label checking is performed automatically by the operating system** and requires no action by the programmer except that he must specify in each file description whether or not labels are present (see LABEL RECORDS clause).

Generation Numbers

The **generation number** of a file is simply a count of the number of times this particular file has been created. For example, a Payroll Master File (held on magnetic tape) might be updated weekly; this means that each week the file would be read in, together with amendments to the file read from, say, cards, and a new Payroll Master File written out to a new reel of tape.

If the old Payroll Master File had a generation number of 307 then the new one written out by the update program would be generation 308.

When file generation number 308 was itself to be updated, the following week, it would be possible to overwrite generation number 307 and create 309. However, for security reasons it is normal to operate the "grandfather–father–son" cycle of generation numbers. This means that generation number 309 would be created by overwriting 306. Supposing, then, that a disaster occurred in the computer room and generation number 306 and 308 (and the half-created 309) were destroyed, generation number 307 would still exist and the master file would not have been lost.

LABEL RECORDS Clause

This clause specifies whether or not labels are present on a file.

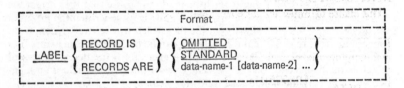

This clause is required in every FD coded in your program.

The OMITTED option specifies that no labels exist on the file being described. The OMITTED option must be specified for punched-card files and printer files and may, if desired, be specified for magnetic tape files. It is not recommended, however, that magnetic tape files be created without standard labels.

LABEL RECORDS ARE OMITTED

The STANDARD option specifies that labels exist for the file and they conform to the standard for the operating system. The specification of this option will ensure that the labels on the file are checked as described above.

LABEL RECORDS ARE STANDARD

In addition to the standard system labels the user is permitted to have his own labels on the file. These, when present, will physically follow the standard labels. **User labels** are the same length as system labels (usually 80 characters) but may contain any information the user wishes.

To specify one or more user labels the third option of this clause is used:

LABEL RECORD IS OWN-LABEL

This clause will ensure that the standard system labels are processed and that the user label is made available to the program for any processing desired. More than one user label may be present on a file:

LABEL RECORDS ARE OWN-LABEL1,OWN-LABEL2

VALUE OF Clause

This clause identifies the content of particular field(s) in the user label.

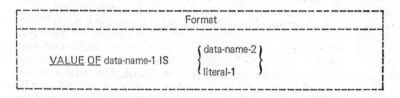

If this clause is present it is treated as a comment and is therefore only used as a documentation aid by the programmer.

VALUE OF LABEL-CODE IS "FILE 7"

DATA RECORDS Clause

This clause identifies the different types of records in the file by name.

```
┌──────────────────────────────────────────────────────────┐
│                          Format                          │
├──────────────────────────────────────────────────────────┤
│          ⎧ RECORD IS   ⎫                                 │
│   DATA   ⎨ RECORDS ARE ⎬   data-name-1 [data-name-2] ... │
│          ⎩             ⎭                                 │
└──────────────────────────────────────────────────────────┘
```

Any given file may contain records with different layouts (even when they are the same length). For example, the Payroll Master File referred to above might contain departmental-summary records and employee records. This would be shown thus:

DATA RECORDS ARE DEPT-SUMMARY, EMPLOYEE

It is most important to realize that only *one area is reserved in core storage for these two records*. In the above clause we are merely saying that two different formats can exist for this one area. This is particularly important when creating a variable-length record file, since the compiler will only know the size of the different record types by examining the data-record descriptions which follow the FD (see below) and which are named in the DATA RECORDS clause.

When a file is defined as being of fixed length the data descriptions given in the DATA RECORDS clause must all be of the same length. Data-name-1, data-name-2, etc., must be the names of level 01 entries following the FD.

Data-Record Descriptions

Following each FD the programmer will code the layout of each data-record type to occur on the file. This is done in the same way as we have already seen for structures. In the examples which follow the individual field descriptions are omitted for clarity.

The FD in Use

Let us, first of all, consider an FD for the Payroll Master File already discussed. Suppose it is to be of variable length, DEPT-SUMMARY being 40 characters in length and EMPLOYEE 60 characters. The maximum block size is to be 200 characters. The FD for this could appear as follows:

```
FD   PAY-MASTER
        BLOCK CONTAINS 200 CHARACTERS
        RECORD CONTAINS 40 TO 60 CHARACTERS
        RECORDING MODE IS V
        LABEL RECORDS ARE STANDARD
        DATA RECORDS ARE DEPT-SUMMARY, EMPLOYEE.
01   DEPT-SUMMARY.
        02  DEPT-DETAILS.
            03  DEPT-CODE ...
            03  DEPT-NAME ...
            03  DIVISION-CODE ...
        02  DEPT-TOTALS.
            03  NO-EMPLOYEES ...
            03  GROSS-TOTAL ...
01   EMPLOYEE.
        02  PERSONAL.
            03  EMP-NAME ...
            03  EMP-DEPT ...
            03  EMP-CLOCK ...
        02  PAY.
            03  GROSS-TO-DATE ...
            03  TAX-TO-DATE ...
            03  GROSS-TW ...
            03  TAX-TW ...
        02  CODES.
            03  TAX-CODE ...
            03  NHI-CODE ...
        02  OTHERS.
            03  PENSION ...
            03  SOCIAL-CLUB ...
            03  DEDUCTIONS ...
        02  SPARE ...
```

The above coding completely describes this file and should be readily understood by the reader. If you do not completely understand this FD please re-read Chapters Eighteen and Nineteen before proceeding.

As one more example of an FD, consider the punched-card file used to update the Payroll Master File. The FD itself should be self-explanatory:

```
FD   AMENDS
        RECORD CONTAINS 80 CHARACTERS
        RECORDING MODE IS F
        LABEL RECORDS ARE OMITTED
        DATA RECORD IS CARDIN.
```

```
Ø1    CARDIN.
      Ø2   CARD-CODE ...
      Ø2   COMPARE.
           Ø3   DEPT-CODE-A ...
           Ø3   CLOCK-NO-A ...
      Ø2   AMENDMENTS.
           Ø3   FIELD-NO ...
           Ø3   CHANGE ...
```

Note that in the FD the BLOCK CONTAINS clause has been omitted since each block contains one record.

Exercises

1. Write the clause to specify that a file contains standard labels.
2. Write the clause to indicate two data-record types called ONE and TWO.
3. How many labels does a punched-card file contain?
4. Write the clause to indicate the answer to question 3.
5. Write an FD for a magnetic tape file containing two types of fixed-length records (DATA-B, DATA-C) each of 70 characters. The file has standard labels and a blocking factor of 4. The file is to be called MAIN-IN.

CHAPTER TWENTY

DATA CLASSES IN COBOL

We have now reached the stage where we wish to describe to the compiler all the data items or data fields which the program will process. In order to do this we obviously need to know the type of data each field will hold and the size of each field (i.e. the number of characters it will contain). The major problem here would seem to be knowing the types of data that can occupy a given field. Let us look therefore at the **classes of data** available to the COBOL programmer. The COBOL compiler recognizes three classes of data—**alphabetic, numeric,** and **alphanumeric.** Within the alphanumeric class a number of categories is available when editing is to be undertaken; however, since editing is fully described in Chapter Twenty-four it will be disregarded during the present discussion.

Every elementary item used within a program will belong to one of the three classes of data. The particular class in each case will be identified by the use to which the item is to be put or by the content of the item when the program is run. Since each of these items has to be defined when the program is first coded it is the responsibility of the programmer to identify the class to which each item belongs. This may seem to be another problem for the programmer to cope with; however, once the data classes have been studied (see below) the reader will appreciate that little thought will be required to determine the class for each item.

Alphabetic Class

A data item defined as being of the **alphabetic class** is one that will contain only a combination of the letters A to Z (the alphabet) plus the space character. Valid alphabetic data-item values could be as follows:

ABCDEFG
ZXYQ   R
P
YOUR NAME

This class in fact will not be used a great deal since the omission of numeric characters is something of a drawback (for example, a name and address would no doubt require a number in the address).

Numeric Class

A **numeric** item is one consisting of the digits 0–9 and optionally a sign (+ or −) character. Note, however, that the sign character does not occupy a separate location in core storage (the manner in which the sign is stored varies from computer to computer and will not be described here).

A numeric item can be stored either in **decimal** or **binary** form. A decimal number will require one storage position for each digit in the number. A binary number will require less than one storage position per digit although the exact number of digits which can be stored in each location will depend upon the computer in use. The reader need only remember that binary numbers are written in the same manner as decimal ones and that the correct storage allocation will be made by the compiler.

In view of the differences between different computers when binary numeric items are handled all examples in this part will refer to decimal items. Valid numeric data values could be:

+1
−2
2367
+Ø123

Note. The method of specifying the location of a decimal point for a numeric item is described in Chapter Twenty-one. You will remember from Chapter Nine that a numeric constant can take the form 27.3 where the period or full-stop represents a decimal point. The decimal point is not stored in storage when a numeric constant is moved to a data field of numeric class. Instead the compiler "remembers" where the decimal point is to be kept and so ensures that the correct calculations are performed.

Alphanumeric Class

A data field in this class can contain a combination of any of the allowable characters for the COBOL compiler (see Chapter Ten). An **alphanumeric class** data item could contain a combination of just the numeric digits:

7894

However, this field could not be used for arithmetic calculations; these may only be done with data fields defined as being of numeric class. In order that alphanumeric (and alphabetic) fields can be distinguished from numeric ones they are usually enclosed in quotation marks when written in a program (the quotation marks themselves are not stored in core storage).

Note. A group item is always treated as an alphanumeric class regardless of the class of the elementary items making up the group.

Data Description

A **Data-Description Entry** is the clause or clauses that specify the characteristics of a particular non-contiguous data item, or of a data item within a record. The data description consists of a **level number**, a **data name** plus the required **data-description clauses**. A **record-description entry** is a collection of **data-description entries** arranged in a hierarchical manner to specify the structure of the record.

A data-description entry defining a non-contiguous item (i.e. using special level number 77) can occur in the Working-Storage and Linkage Sections. A record-description entry can occur in the File, Working-Storage, and Linkage Sections.

```
                         General Format

  level number { data-name }
               { FILLER    }

       [REDEFINES Clause]
       [BLANK WHEN ZERO Clause]

       [OCCURS Clause]
       [PICTURE Clause]

       [USAGE Clause]
       [VALUE Clause]
```

General Rules

This general format may be used for record-description entries in the File, Working-Storage, and Linkage Sections and for non-contiguous data-item descriptions in the Working-Storage Section and the Linkage Section. As we have already seen the level number may be in the range 01–49 for record-description entries or 77 for non-contiguous data-item descriptions (see Chapter Twenty-seven for special level 88). The optional clauses can be specified in any order except that the REDEFINES clause (Chapter Twenty-two), if used, must appear first. The PICTURE clause (Chapter Twenty-one) must be specified for all elementary items. Each data description will be terminated with a period although commas or semi-colons may be used to separate the clauses.

Data-name Clause

This clause specifies the name of the data item which is to be described. The **data name** is the name which the programmer wishes to give to this particular data item. *This name refers to the area in storage and not to a particular value*; the item to which the name refers may assume different values during execution of the program.

```
┌─────────────────────────────────────────────────────────────┐
│                           Format                              │
├─────────────────────────────────────────────────────────────┤
│                                                               │
│                       ⎧ data-name ⎫                           │
│       level number    ⎨ FILLER    ⎬                           │
│                       ⎩           ⎭                           │
│                                                               │
└─────────────────────────────────────────────────────────────┘
```

The keyword FILLER is used to describe data items which will not be referenced in the program. For example, a program may read in a file with large records but only need to access, say, the first and last fields. The intermediate fields must be defined to the compiler in order that the following fields are accessed correctly although no reference will be made to the intermediate fields.

Examples

77 SWITCH
Ø2 PENSION-FUND
Ø3 INDICATOR
2Ø FILLER

Notes. All level 77 data item descriptions must appear in the Working Storage or Linkage Sections before any record-description entries. Each data name allocated by the programmer must be unique within the program (i.e. no two data names may be the same).

The other clauses in the data-description entries are described in the following chapters.

Exercises

1. Name the classes to which the following data item values belong:

   (a) 1234
   (b) "1234"
   (c) "FRED SMITH"

2. How many storage positions would be required for the data item with a value of +23.7?
3. What class can a group item belong to?
4. What keyword is used to name a data item which will not be referenced in the program?
5. What are the two methods of storing numeric data?

CHAPTER TWENTY-ONE

DATA DESCRIPTION—1

PICTURE Clause

The class of a data item and its size (i.e. the number of characters it can contain) is described by means of the PICTURE clause in its data-description entry.

```
┌─────────────────────────────────────────────────────────────────┐
│                            Format                                 │
├───────────────────────────────────────────────────────────────────┤
│                                                                   │
│   ⎰ PICTURE ⎱   IS character string                              │
│   ⎱ PIC     ⎰                                                     │
│                                                                   │
└───────────────────────────────────────────────────────────────────┘
```

The character string following the keyword PICTURE (or its abbreviated form PIC) is a combination of one or more of the symbols available for PICTURE descriptions. These symbols are described individually below and are followed by detailed examples of the use of this clause.

Symbols Used in the PICTURE Clause

A   When used this symbol will be the only one used in a PICTURE and it indicates a data item of the alphabetic class. As with all PICTUREs the size of a data item is indicated by the number of symbols. For example, a data item of the alphabetic class which was to contain 5 characters would be described thus:

PICTURE IS AAAAA.

An alphabetic data item of length 3 characters could be described thus:

PIC IS AAA.

9   Each occurrence of a 9 in the character string represents a storage location that will contain a numeric digit. The length of the field will be determined by the number of 9's in the PICTURE character string:

PICTURE IS 9999.

represents the description of a numeric data item, 4 characters in length.

X   The character X specifies a data-item position of the alphanumeric class (which may therefore hold any character). An alphanumeric data item of length 6 characters would be defined thus:

PICTURE IS XXXXXX.

S   The letter S is used to indicate that a numeric data item contains a sign. The letter S may only occur once in a PICTURE character string and, if used, must be the first such character. As already mentioned this sign does not occupy a storage location and is not therefore included in the length of the data item. The definition of a 4 character signed numeric data item would therefore appear thus:

PICTURE IS S9999.

V   As mentioned in Chapter Nineteen a numeric data item may contain an assumed decimal point. In other words a numeric data item, of, say, 4 characters in length could hold the values 207.3, 20.73, 2.073, or .2073, depending upon the location of the decimal point. Although this decimal point is not actually stored the compiler "remembers" where it is located by the occurrence of a V in the PICTURE character string. For example, if the 4 character numeric item mentioned above were to be used as a field with two places of decimal it could be defined thus:

PICTURE IS 99V99.

and could hold the value, say, 37.29. Now to demonstrate the use of assumed decimal points let us add this value to a field defined:

PICTURE IS 999V9.

and containing the value 412.7. Even though both these fields are 4 characters in length, one character will be lost (for the addition) from the first field. This is because the numbers are aligned on their decimal points and the final answer can only hold four digits (999V9). The addition, as performed, would look like this:

$$412.7$$
$$37.2(9)$$
$$\overline{}$$
$$449.9$$

If the V character is omitted from the PICTURE of a numeric item it is assumed to follow the right-hand 9 (i.e. the item being defined is assumed to be an integer). The V character can be used in conjunction with the S character to define a signed number with a decimal part:

PICTURE IS S99V9.

This field could hold a value of, say, −37.2.

Other Combinations of PICTURE Characters

In addition to the combination of S, V, and 9 already studied, the other characters allowable in the PICTURE description X and A, can be combined with 9 or with each other. However, if this is done the overall result will be equivalent to a definition using all X's. For example, consider the data item:

03 NUM PICTURE IS 99XX9,

which could hold a value of, say, 12AB7. It is not possible to perform arithmetic of this field, because of the alphabetic content, so the definition is effectively the same as:

03 NUM PICTURE IS XXXXX.

Symbol Repetition

To save the programmer the trouble of writing very long character strings (for, say, an alphanumeric field 30 characters in length), the COBOL compiler recognizes a **repetition factor**. The PICTURE characters A, X, and 9 may have following them an integer enclosed in parentheses. This integer indicates the number of occurrences of the PICTURE character. For example, in the case mentioned above, rather than write a PICTURE clause with thirty X's the programmer could write:

PICTURE IS X(3∅).

Similarly, long numeric fields may be defined easily:

PICTURE IS 9(8).

When a V character is in use both the parts of the number may be defined with the repetition factor:

PICTURE IS 9(4)V9(5).

Similarly, the S character may be prefixed to a definition with a repetition factor:

PICTURE IS S9(6).

The PICTURE Clause in Use

To see the use of the PICTURE clause let us consider once again the Payroll Master File seen in an earlier chapter. One of the types of record on this file has the following layout:

Dept. Code	Dept. Name	Division Code	Number of Employees	Gross Pay

The entire record is to be called DEPT-SUMMARY, the first two fields are to have the group name DEPT-DETAILS and the remaining fields the group name DEPT-TOTALS. Note particularly that **group names do not have PICTURE clauses** (since their size is determined by the total of the sizes of the elementary items making up the group; the class of a group is always alphanumeric).

The record in question can be defined thus:

```
∅1   DEPT-SUMMARY.
     ∅2   DEPT-DETAILS.
          ∅3   DEPT-CODE PICTURE IS 9999.
          ∅3   DEPT-NAME PICTURE IS A(2∅).
          ∅3   DIVISION-CODE PICTURE IS 99.
     ∅2   DEPT-TOTALS.
          ∅3   NO-EMPLOYEES PICTURE IS 9(7).
          ∅3   GROSS-TOTAL PICTURE IS 9(7).
```

The group item DEPT-TOTALS has a size of 14 characters (9(7) plus 9(7)) and could be moved, if required, to a field defined thus:

77 DEPT-SAVE PICTURE X(14).

When defining numeric items with decimal points (character V in PICTURE string) it is helpful if all the fields to be manipulated together have the same number of decimal places. If this is not done the compiler will generate extra coding to align the decimal points correctly.

For example, consider these two fields:

> 77 NUM-1 PICTURE IS S999V99.
> 77 NUM-2 PICTURE IS S99V9.

If, in the Procedure Division, the following statement occurred:

> ADD NUM-2 TO NUM-1.

the correct result would be given; however, because the (assumed) decimal points do not align directly, additional coding would be generated (by the compiler) to arrive at the correct result. The efficiency of your program can be improved if these misalignments can be removed. In the example quoted above this could be achieved by redefining NUM-2 thus:

> 77 NUM-2 PICTURE IS S99V99.

Note also the use of the S (sign) character in the PICTURE clause of numeric items, this too will improve the efficiency of computations done on these fields in the Procedure Division.

The USAGE Clause

This clause specifies the manner in which the data are stored in core storage.

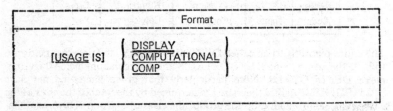

```
                            Format

                      ┌ DISPLAY        ┐
      [USAGE IS]      │ COMPUTATIONAL  │
                      └ COMP           ┘
```

This clause tells the compiler the manner in which the data are to be stored in memory and can be specified for elementary items or group items. If a USAGE clause is specified for a group name then that USAGE applies to all the elementary items making up the group.

The DISPLAY option specifies that the data is to be stored in character fashion. In other words each location in core storage will hold one character of data. If USAGE clause is omitted then USAGE IS DISPLAY is assumed by default. All the data definitions seen so far have therefore been of DISPLAY items.

> 77 SAMPLE PICTURE 999 USAGE IS DISPLAY.

Since this option is obtained by default the above definition is equivalent to

> 77 SAMPLE PICTURE 999.

The COMPUTATIONAL (or shortened form COMP) option specifies that the data is to be held in binary form. As already mentioned the number of character positions required to hold a given binary number depends upon the computer in use. However, each machine's compiler will take care of the allocation for the programmer.

A binary field can be defined thus:

77 BINARY-COUNT PICTURE S9999 USAGE IS COMPUTATIONAL.

If the programmer has a group item containing a number of binary fields the USAGE clause can be specified at the group level:

```
Ø2   BINARY-GROUP USAGE IS COMPUTATIONAL.
     Ø3   BIN-1 PICTURE IS S9(6).
     Ø3   BIN-2 PICTURE IS S9(6).
     Ø3   BIN-3 PICTURE IS S9(6).
     Ø3   BIN-4 PICTURE IS S9(6).
```

All four elementary items have the USAGE IS COMPUTATIONAL clause applied to them.

Exercises

1. Name the three data classes and give the PICTURE character that identifies each.
2. Define a non-contiguous data area as being signed numeric, total length six digits, two of which follow the decimal point.
3. Define an alphanumeric field of length 90 characters called NAME.
4. Define the record with the following layout:

RECORD-1				
ACCOUNT		PAYMENTS		
ACC-NO	ACC-STATUS	PAY-1	PAY-2	PAY-3
5 digits	1 character	all 3 digits each in binary		

5. What characters may the field defined below hold?

77 NAME PICTURE IS A(2Ø).

CHAPTER TWENTY-TWO

DATA DESCRIPTION—2

Further Data-Description Entry Clauses

In the exercise for the previous chapter the reader was asked to define a group containing three identical fields:

Ø2   PAYMENTS USAGE IS COMPUTATIONAL.
  Ø3   PAY-1 PICTURE IS S999.
  Ø3   PAY-2 PICTURE IS S999.
  Ø3   PAY-3 PICTURE IS S999.

Defining three fields in this way does not present too much of a problem; neither would the Procedure Division coding to handle these fields. However, what would the situation be with 200 identical fields? Obviously the programmer would not wish to write out 200 field definitions. Neither would he wish to write 200 sets of statements to do the computations with these fields. Instead he would use the OCCURS clause in the data-entry descriptions and subscripting in the Procedure Division.

The OCCURS Clause

This clause specifies the number of occurrences of identical fields within a record.

```
┌─────────────────────────────────────────────────────┐
│                      Format                          │
├─────────────────────────────────────────────────────┤
│  OCCURS integer   TIMES                              │
└─────────────────────────────────────────────────────┘
```

Perhaps the easiest method of understanding this clause is by example. Consider the definition of the group called PAYMENTS above. Rather than define it as shown we can use the OCCURS clause to specify the three occurrences.

Ø2   PAYMENTS USAGE COMP PIC S999 OCCURS 3 TIMES.

Notice in particular how the three names PAY-1, PAY-2, PAY-3 are no longer used. Instead we have said that there are three identical fields called PAYMENTS (how to refer to an individual field is shown below) each with the attributes USAGE COMP PIC S999. The amount of core storage used is the same as in the first example but obviously the amount of writing is considerably reduced. If the programmer wished to retain the name PAYMENTS as a group name he could code the definitions thus:

Ø2   PAYMENTS USAGE COMPUTATIONAL.
  Ø3   PAY PIC S999 OCCURS 3 TIMES.

Now the three (identical) fields are called PAY.

In the Payroll Master File updating program mentioned already in some examples the amendments to the files are supplied on punched cards. Each of these cards can contain up to ten amendments; the cards have the following format:

Card code	Dept code	Clock number	Amend 1	Amend 2	. . . .	Amend 10

Each amendment consists of two fields:

> FIELD-NO 2 numeric characters
> CHANGE 4 characters of amended data

Although some of the fields on the Payroll Master File are longer than 4 characters they can be updated using the 4 character amendment field; each field on the master file is allocated a number and this is used on the card file to identify the field requiring amendment. Any field longer than 4 characters is split into 4 character sections each of which is given a separate field number.

This technique is useful because it enables the amendment cards to have a simpler, more uniform format. In our particular case only five fields on the Payroll Master File exceed 4 characters in length—DEPT-NAME, EMP-NAME, NO-EMPLOYEES, GROSS-TOTAL, CLOCK-NO—these fields are unlikely to be amended very frequently and so the multiple amendment field technique is quite practical in this case. The reader should note, however, that in an application involving a number of large fields requiring frequent amendment a more complicated amendment card layout would be required (with a consequent increase in the complexity of the update program).

The record-description entry for the card file could be defined thus:

```
Ø1  CARDIN.
    Ø2  CARD-CODE            PICTURE XXX.
    Ø2  COMPARE.
        Ø3  DEPT-CODE-A      PICTURE 9999.
        Ø3  CLOCK-NO-A       PICTURE 9(6).
    Ø2  AMENDMENTS OCCURS 10.
        Ø3  FIELD-NO         PICTURE 99.
        Ø3  CHANGE           PICTURE XXXX.
```

Note that the OCCURS clause is written at the group level—this in effect defines ten groups each containing two elementary items (FIELD-NO and CHANGE). It is not possible to refer to all the amendments in one statement as this definition stands, if this facility were required the record-description entry would need to be rewritten thus:

```
Ø1  CARDIN.
    Ø2  CARD-CODE            PICTURE XXX.
    Ø2  COMPARE.
        Ø3  DEPT-CODE-A      PICTURE 9999.
        Ø3  CLOCK-NO-A       PICTURE 9(6).
    Ø2  AMENDS-A.
        Ø3  AMENDMENTS       OCCURS 1Ø.
            Ø4  FIELD-NO     PICTURE 99.
            Ø4  CHANGE       PICTURE XXXX.
```

With this definition there are still ten group items called AMENDMENTS (each containing two elementary items FIELD-NO and CHANGE), but there is also a group item AMENDS-A containing the ten groups called AMENDMENTS. This description can be represented diagrammatically thus (showing only the amendment fields):

Amends-A						
Amendments (1)		Amendments (2)		....	Amendments (10)	
Field-no (1)	Change (1)	Field-no (2)	Change (2)	....	Field-no (10)	Change (10)

This diagram gives a clue to the method used for referring to individual fields defined with the OCCURS clause. Any individual field can be referenced by use of a **subscript**.

Subscripting

A subscript is used to refer to an individual field within a list that has not been assigned individual names (i.e. that has been defined with an OCCURS clause).

```
Format

    data-name (subscript)
```

The subscript to identify a list entry is enclosed in parentheses, following the entries data name and separated from it by a space.

The **first element** in a **list** (also called a **table**) has the **subscript number** 1, the second subscript number 2, and so on. The maximum value of a subscript is equal to the number of TIMES the data name OCCURS.

To refer to the third amendment in the card layout above we could therefore use the name:

AMENDMENTS (3)

or to refer to the two elementary items within this group:

FIELD-NO (3)
CHANGE (3)

Suppose in a sales program a table has been set up to contain a count of the number of sales in each area:

```
Ø1   SALES-TOTALS.
     Ø2   AREA-TOT OCCURS 2Ø PICTURE 9999.
```

(assuming there are twenty sales areas).

To add 1 to the count of the number of sales in area 7:

ADD 1 TO AREA-TOT (7).

To add the number of sales in area 8 to the number in area 12:

ADD AREA-TOT (8) TO AREA-TOT (12).

A subscript may, in addition to being specified as an integer value, be specified as a data name—the value of the data item each time the statement is executed being used as the subscript. The use of such so-called variable subscripts is a subject in itself and is discussed in detail in Chapter Thirty-seven.

Redefinition

It is sometimes necessary for a field of data to be given different formats at different times during the execution of a program. For example, a 4 character field might contain the characters 2179 which at one point in the program are to be treated as a number of pence. The definition for the field would then be:

77 PENCE PICTURE 9999.

However, later in the program the same value might require to be treated as £21.79 which of course would require the definition:

77 POUNDS PICTURE 99V99.

It is not possible simply to move the value in PENCE to the value in POUNDS since automatic alignment of the decimal points (assumed in PENCE) would result in POUNDS having a value of 79.00. The problem is overcome by using the REDEFINES clause.

The REDEFINES Clause

This clause is used to permit the same storage area to contain different data items or to provide different descriptions for the same item.

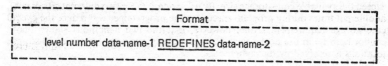

Format

level number data-name-1 <u>REDEFINES</u> data-name-2

The level numbers of data names and the data-name-2 must be the same (and cannot be level 88). Data-name-2 refers to the previous data-item description entry and data-name-1 is an alternate name for this area.

Example: Take the case above:

77 PENCE   PICTURE 9999.
77 POUNDS REDEFINES PENCE PICTURE 99V99.

The data names PENCE and POUNDS both refer to the same 4 character location in core storage; the difference being that POUNDS has an assumed decimal point in the middle. Note that the use of a REDEFINES clause does not alter the content of an area in storage but only the manner in which it is used.

The REDEFINES clause can also be used to give different layouts to structures or group items. Consider an area, within a record description, that is to contain a date in the format dd/mm/yy (for example 19/02/73). The definition for this could be:

03 DATE PICTURE X(8).

If at some stage in the program it was necessary to perform arithmetic calculations on all or part of the date (for example to add 1 to the month to arrive at a new reminder date) the definition given would be unsatisfactory. This can be overcome by redefining this elementary item as a group:

```
Ø3 DATE PICTURE X(8).
Ø3 NEW-DATE REDEFINES DATE.
   Ø4 DAY PICTURE 99.
   Ø4 FILLER PICTURE X.
   Ø4 MONTH PICTURE 99.
   Ø4 FILLER PICTURE X.
   Ø4 YEAR PICTURE 99.
```

Note the use of FILLER to by-pass the locations containing the two oblique (/) characters. The desired calculation can now be performed thus:

ADD 1 TO MONTH.

An area can be given two group item definitions also by use of the REDEFINES clause. A group may be used to hold both alphabetic and numeric class data at different times during execution of the program.

```
Ø2 ALPHA-HOLD-AREA.
   Ø3 ALPHA-1            PICTURE X(1Ø).
   Ø3 ALPHA-2            PICTURE X(1Ø).
   Ø3 ALPHA-3            PICTURE X(1Ø).
Ø2 TEMP-TOTAL-AREA       REDEFINES ALPHA-HOLD-AREA.
   Ø3 TOTAL-1            PICTURE 9(6).
   Ø3 TOTAL-2            PICTURE 9(6).
   Ø3 TOTAL-3            PICTURE 9(6).
   Ø3 TOTAL-4            PICTURE 9(6).
   Ø3 TOTAL-5            PICTURE 9(6).
```

This technique can be particularly useful when the program is large and likely to exceed the available core-storage size. By using one area for two different sets of data, at different times during program execution, the programmer will reduce the overall core-storage requirement. Note, however, that the two definitions shown above cannot both be in use at the same time (since only one actual block of 30 storage locations is reserved by the compiler).

The REDEFINES clause may be used at any level except Ø1 in the file section. When specifying multiple record descriptions with the DATA RECORDS clause redefinition is automatically implied.

Exercises

1. Define a group called TOTAL containing 6 identical fields called TOT each 6 characters (numeric) in length.
2. Write the statement to add 1 to the second field mentioned in question 1.
3. Write the statement to redefine the area mentioned in question 1 as a 36 character alphabetic field.
4. Where is redefinition implied?
5. Define 6 groups (called MAIN) each containing two fields ONE and TWO (3 characters each) *or* one field of 6 characters.

CHAPTER TWENTY-THREE

DATA VALUES

Data-Item Content

Most of the data items we will define in the Working-Storage Section will have values assigned to them during execution of the program. However, it may be required to give an item an initial or starting value (which we may use as a **constant** throughout the program or which we may overwrite later).

Any data item could of course be given a value in the opening section of the Procedure Division by coding the necessary statements. However, this would be wasting time and storage since although the statements would be executed once only during each run of the program, they would occupy storage space throughout execution. It would be far more convenient if a value could be given to a data item at the time it was defined and so be allocated by the compiler and therefore not require any additional time or storage at the time the program was executed. This can be done by means of the VALUE IS clause.

The VALUE IS Clause

This clause is used to give to an elementary item, in the Working-Storage Section, an initial or starting value.

```
┌─────────────────────────────────────────────────────────┐
│                          Format                          │
├─────────────────────────────────────────────────────────┤
│                                                          │
│     VALUE IS literal                                     │
└─────────────────────────────────────────────────────────┘
```

The value specified by literal is given to the data item, the item assuming the specified value when program execution is started. Note that if this value is altered or amended in any way during program execution it is not restored (unless of course the program is reloaded, at which point everything returns to the original state).

The value specified with this clause must of course fit in with the PICTURE of the item. In other words, the programmer cannot specify a numeric value for an alphabetic field and so on. Any value specified must be within the range that the data item can hold, although, if specified with less characters than the PICTURE, automatic padding with spaces or zeroes (as appropriate) will take place.

```
77 PI PICTURE S99V999 VALUE IS 3.142.
```

In this example the value 3.142 will be the initial value of PI when program execution commences. Note that the actual value stored will be 03.142 (i.e. the compiler will automatically fill out the data item with zeroes as necessary).

```
77 HEADING1 PICTURE X(21),
   VALUE IS "SALES ANALYSIS REPORT".
```

Here we see an alphanumeric data item given an initial value which could be used to begin a printed report. (Note how the definition of the data item has been carried over to another line—each clause can be separated by a comma— the definition being terminated by a period.)

The programmer may use the figurative constants to specify initial values; although the value so specified must still match the data-items definition (i.e. the figurative constant SPACES cannot be used with a numeric elementary item).

```
77 COUNT-A PICTURE S9(7) VALUE ZEROES.
77 HEADING PICTURE X(2Ø) VALUE SPACES.
```

The individual items forming a group can all be given initial values as shown:

```
Ø2   TOTALS.
     Ø3   TOTA PICTURE S999 VALUE ZERO.
     Ø3   TOTB PICTURE S9(6) VALUE ZERO.
     Ø3   TOTC PICTURE S9(4) VALUE ZERO.
```

In a case like this where all the elementary items have a similar value description then the value can be specified at group level, providing a figurative constant or non-numeric literal is used (i.e. a group level VALUE clause may only be specified with a figurative constant or a non-numeric literal). The above example could therefore be rewritten:

```
Ø2   TOTALS VALUE IS ZERO.
     Ø3   TOTA PICTURE S999.
     Ø3   TOTB PICTURE S9(6).
     Ø3   TOTC PICTURE S9(4).
```

Each elementary item would therefore have the value zero. Care should be exercised when specifying values at group level since it is possible to inadvertently give an alphabetic value to a numeric item. If this happened a program error would occur when any arithmetic was attempted on the elementary item.

BLANK WHEN ZERO Clause

This clause specifies that an elementary item will be set to spaces (blanks) whenever its value is zero.

```
┌─────────────────────────────────────────────┐
│                  Format                      │
├─────────────────────────────────────────────┤
│   BLANK WHEN ZERO                            │
└─────────────────────────────────────────────┘
```

This clause may only be specified for elementary numeric items. Any computation during program execution resulting in the value of the data item being zero will result in this value being replaced with spaces.

```
77 EXAMPLE PICTURE S9(4) BLANK WHEN ZERO.
```

Suppose this field contains the value 1200 which is also contained in the field SUB. The following statement will result in the field EXAMPLE being set to spaces:

SUBTRACT SUB FROM EXAMPLE.

This clause is useful when the field in question is to appear in a printed report and the programmer does not wish to print zero fields.

Exercises

1. Define a 7 character numeric field (called NUM) to have an initial value of 6.
2. What will be the actual 7 characters stored as a result of the definition in question 1?
3. Define a group item called TOTALS containing six 5 character fields (called TOT) each of which has an initial value of zero.
4. Define a non-numeric item to have an initial value of "HEADING ONE".
5. Define a numeric field called EDIT (6 characters in length) which is to be set to spaces when given a value of zero.

CHAPTER TWENTY-FOUR

EDITING

Most programs used for commercial data processing will involve some form of printed output—e.g. invoices, sales analyses, pay-slips, etc. A file for an output unit (which may, as in this case, refer to a printer) is defined, as with any other file, by specifying the appropriate FD. We will be looking in Chapter Thirty-two at the program instructions used to direct information to an output device. However, while still considering the Data Division, it will be useful to examine some other aspects of printed reports.

Suppose the programmer wishes to produce a pay-slip for each employee. He may therefore write the necessary statements to output, say, two lines of print; one giving the headings and the second the data. However, if he did this the data would be printed exactly as it appears in core storage and could therefore look something like this:

```
NAME      GROSS  TAX  NET
JONES B.  003712 0210 003502
```

Clearly, this is unsatisfactory, the gross pay should be printed to indicate that it is an amount in sterling—for example like this—£37.12 or 37.12p; similarly the tax and net should be printed in "legible" formats (e.g. £2.10 and £35.02). In these cases we wish therefore to replace any leading zeroes with a £ sign and we wish to insert a period to delineate pounds from pence. This is called *editing* and is specified by means of the PICTURE clause in the Data Division. We will look firstly at the additional picture string characters that are allowable for the specification of editing requirements and then, at the end of the chapter, we will examine some uses of editing.

Note. The term **leading zeroes** has been mentioned once already and will occur frequently when looking at editing; so what is meant exactly by the term? A **leading zero** (also called a **non-significant zero**) is one that precedes the actual data value and is itself preceded only by zeroes. For example, in the field Ø0Ø42Ø6 the first three zeroes are leading or non-significant zeroes and can be removed without altering the value of the item—42Ø6. (Note that the length is of course altered but for printing purposes this does not matter.) The zero between the 2 and 6 is most significant, however, since if it were removed the value of the item would be altered to 426.

Types of Editing

Two basic types of editing exist within the COBOL language—**insertion** editing and **suppression** and **replacement** editing. We will first of all look at insertion editing which is the easier of the two types to understand.

Simple insertion editing consists of specifying the relevant insertion character(s) in the PICTURE character string; then when a value is moved to the edited item the insertion characters are inserted in the value in the position specified in the PICTURE. The simple insertion characters allowable in a COBOL PICTURE character string are , (comma) B (Blank) and Ø (zero). Suppose we have a value 1234567 which we wish to print as 1,234,567 we could move the value to an edited data item defined thus:

77 EDIT PICTURE 9,999,999.

Similarly, we could insert zero characters or blank character into a data item:

77 EDIT PICTURE 99B99B99Ø9.

A data value of 1234567 moved to this item would produce a result of:

12 34 56Ø7

Note that each 9 in the PICTURE character string corresponds to one digit in the data value, any insertion character being in addition to this. The total length of an edited item therefore includes the insertion characters. The period (full-stop) may also be used as an insertion character but may only occur once in the PICTURE character string and must correspond with the assumed decimal point in the value to be moved to the edited item. For example, suppose we wish to edit a data item containing the value 346V2 to contain a printed decimal point. We could move the value to an item defined thus:

77 EDITOR PICTURE 999.9

The resulting value of EDITOR would then be 346.2. Note that although a V in a PICTURE character string is an assumed decimal point and does not therefore occupy any storage, the period however in an edited PICTURE character string does occupy a storage location.

Fixed-insertion editing involves inserting a **sign** (+ or −) character at either end of the data item or inserting a **currency symbol** (£ or $) at the beginning of the data item.

The characters used to specify these fixed insertions are +, −, and £ respectively. (N.B. $ may be substituted for £ as required.)

If the + character is used it will be inserted as a plus if the value assigned to the edited data item is positive, or inserted as − if the value is negative.

The − editing character will be replaced by a blank if the assigned data value is positive or − if it is negative. Either of these characters may appear at either end of a PICTURE character string (and will be inserted where written in the string) but only one may appear in any PICTURE. As examples of fixed-insertion editing (as described above) consider the following table showing, in three columns, the PICTURE of an edited item, the value moved to the edited item, and the value of the item after editing.

Picture	Value	Result
£9999	27	£0027
+999	27	+027
+999	−27	−027
9999+	−31	0031−
£999,999	3146	£003,146
£999,999.99	37V12	£000,037.12

Fig. 37 Examples of fixed insertion editions

Notice how in the last example above we have now managed to insert the £ symbol and full-stop into our currency amount; however, the result is still not really satisfactory. We would prefer to print the result as £37.12, this could be done by defining a PICTURE of £99.99 but now the result field will only hold a maximum of two figures for pounds. In order to print the amount with the £ symbol immediately to the left of the highest figure we will use a **floating** editing symbol. This is done by specifying £ for each position where the symbol may occur, then when a value is moved to the edited item the £ symbol will appear as required. For example, an edited item defined as PICTURE ££££9 could have the value 377 moved to it and the result would be £327. Note how the additional left-hand £ symbols are replaced by spaces; the £ symbol is said to float to its required position. The simple insertion characters (, B Ø) when used within a floating edited item are themselves replaced with a space when occurring to the left of the floated £ symbol. This is illustrated in the table of examples below:

Picture	Value	Result
££££9	6	£6
££££9.99	37V12	£37.12
££££,££9.99	3133V08	£3,133.08
££££,££9.99	2V81	£2.81

Note that one more £ symbol than digits of pounds must be supplied in order that a space always exists for the £ at the left-hand end of the edited item. (In the last example above the maximum value that could be accommodated would be 999999V99.) At least one 9 character is always placed to the left of the period to ensure that (when the value moved to the edited item has zero pounds) the £ symbol does not appear next to the period. For example, suppose the value zero was moved to the edited item shown last in the above table, the result would be

$$£0.00$$

Suppression and replacement editing is used to remove leading zeroes from the value to be edited. The characters allowable in the PICTURE character string are Z, which will cause leading zeroes to be replaced by spaces, and * which will cause leading zeroes to be replaced by *. Only Z or * may be used in any single PICTURE character string and cannot be combined with £, +, or −. They may, however, be combined with the simple insertion characters (, B Ø) which, if occurring among the leading zeroes, will themselves be replaced with the insertion character (i.e. space or *).

When used the PICTURE character string characters Z and * must appear either (a) in every position in the string (excluding those positions occupied by the simple insertion characters or the decimal point) or (b) in any or all the leading numeric positions to the left of the decimal point (i.e. the Z or * character must start in the left-hand PICTURE position and cannot be interposed with 9's).

Note that if a value of zero is moved to an edited item containing all Z's the result will be a field of all spaces. The table below illustrates the use of these editing characters:

Picture	Value	Result
***.99	8V72	**8.72
ZZZZ.99	12V81	12.81
ZZZZ.99	ØØVØØ	.ØØ
ZZZZ.ZZ	ØØVØØ	
****.**	ØØVØØ	****.**
ZZ99.99	4V6	Ø4.6
ZZZZZZ	27	27

Editing in Use

Let us first of all reconsider the pay-slip example quoted at the beginning of this chapter in the light of the new information presented since then. Clearly we are now in a position to produce a much neater printed result. The working-storage definitions for the two print-lines involved in this example could look like this:

```
Ø1  PAY-HEAD.
    Ø2   HEAD-1 PICTURE X(34),
         VALUE "NAME          GROSS TAX NET".
Ø1  PAY-DETAIL.
    Ø2   P-NAME PICTURE X(2Ø).
    Ø2   FILLER PICTURE X.
    Ø2   P-GROSS PICTURE ££££9.99.
    Ø2   FILLER PICTURE X.
    Ø2   P-TAX PICTURE ££9.99.
    Ø2   FILLER PICTURE X.
    Ø2   P-NET PICTURE ££££9.99.
```

The coding required, within the Procedure Division, to produce these two lines might look like this (note the MOVE verb is fully described in Chapter Twenty-nine and need not be worried about here):

```
MULTIPLY RATE BY HOURS GIVING P-GROSS, GROSS.
MOVE TAX TO P-TAX.
SUBTRACT TAX FROM GROSS GIVING P-NET.
MOVE PAY-HEAD TO PRINT-LINE,
         PERFORM PRINT-ROUTINE.
MOVE PAY-DETAIL TO PRINT-LINE,
         PERFORM PRINT-ROUTINE.
```

Note that an edited numeric field cannot be used as identifier-1 or identifier-2 in an arithmetic statement; however, it can be the subject of a GIVING option.

The * replacement symbol is often called the **cheque-protect** symbol since it is mainly used to print amounts on cheques, or similar documents, in such a way that the amount cannot be altered. For example, a program to print dividend warrants (i.e. cheques) might contain this definition for the field to hold the printed amount of the cheque:

Ø5 PAY-AMOUNT PICTURE *(5)9.99.

(Note the use of a repetition factor with the * edit symbol.)

This field could have moved to it the value 71V31 giving the following result:

****71.31

If a £ symbol had also been required, preceding the cheque protect symbols, the PICTURE would have been rewritten thus:

Ø5 PAY-AMOUNT PICTURE £*(5)9.99.

(Note that the floating £ symbol cannot be used in conjunction with Z or *.)

Editing will be used considerably in any program producing printed reports in order to improve the readability of such reports. The most commonly used editing symbols will be Z to remove leading zeroes from numeric count fields and floating £ to indicate numeric sterling (and remove leading zeroes). The programmer will also make frequent use of the , (comma) and period to improve the legibility of his output printing. The editing symbols, as described in this chapter, are very simple to use if the programmer remembers their basic function—to improve the readability of printed reports. It is often a help for the programmer to try and visualize the printed result when specifying edited items.

The other thing to remember when coding edited items is that each character will occupy a storage location (including the period for decimal point) and so must be counted when working out the spacing of a printed report. This applies particularly when the program outputs to pre-printed stationery—i.e. stationery that has already printed on it, say, the "boxes" for an invoice or the general terms for a gas bill. When this is the case the program specification given to the programmer should contain a detailed description and layout of the pre-printed stationery.

Exercises

1. Write the results of moving the following values to a field with the PICTURE ZZZ9.99:

   (a) ØØVØØ
   (b) 2
   (c) Ø3Ø7V3
   (d) 2196V32

2. Write the results of moving the following values to a field with the PICTURE £**,***,**9.99:

   (a) 37V2Ø
   (b) 21364789V31

3. Write the results of moving the following values to a field with the PICTURE Z,ZZZ,Z99:

   (*a*) 1
   (*b*) 3174
   (*c*) Ø
   (*d*) 1234567

4. Define an item EDIT to receive a data item of maximum length 6 digits, with zero suppression of the leading 4 characters and a — sign to appear if the item is negative.

5. Define an item called POUNDS which would produce the result £3,127.ØØ from a value 3127 and £2.99 from a value 2V99.

CHAPTER TWENTY-FIVE

THE DATA DIVISION IN USE

We have now looked at the major constituent parts of the Data Division and are in a position to code the necessary elements of this division for an average program. However, the reader may feel that, although he understands the individual parts, he would not be too happy if asked to write a Data Division from a program specification. The purpose of this chapter then is to present an idea of the way in which a specification presented to the programmer would be interpreted in relation to the Data Division.

The coding of a Data Division for a given program will consist of two parts —firstly the programmer will pick out from the program specification all the "obvious" division entries (such as File Descriptions, accumulator areas, etc.) and secondly he will add to the Data Division during the coding of the Procedure Division as he discovers new areas or fields required by the program. At the moment we are concerned only with this first stage; picking out those Data Division entries which are implied by the program specification.

Let us consider therefore the specification of a simple, but realistic, program for which we wish to code the Data Division. The program specification is reproduced below:

Program Specification
Card Validate Program

Input	Card types 307 and 308 containing respectively details of payments received and credits given to customers. (Card layouts are as shown below.)
Output 1	Magnetic tape containing all input records accepted as valid by processing. Records are in card-image format blocked in fours.
Output 2	Printout listing all invalid cards read, identifying the field in error. At end of job a print will be given of the total accepted payments and total accepted credits.

Processing   Files will be opened and report headings printed. Each card
will be read and checked for validity against the following rules:

1. Card type can be 307 or 308.
2. Customer number must be numeric and check digit must be correct.
3. For each payment or credit:
      date must be valid ddmmyy (N.B. check for numeric only)
      payment must be numeric amount (leading spaces are acceptable)
   any unused payment/credit amount fields are to be set equal to zeroes.

Invalid cards are printed on the report (in card-image format) with the following line containing asterisks under the invalid field(s).

Valid cards are written to tape after the payment or credit amount has been added to the appropriate total. When all the cards have been processed the totals are printed out, the files closed, and the program terminated.

Card Layout   cc 1–3   Card type
                    4–9   Customer number
                    10   Check digit
                    11–34   1 to 4 occurrences of payment (card type 307) or credit (card type 308) each containing a date (in form ddmmyy) and an amount (max £9999.99)
                    35–80   Blank

File Section Entries

The first part of the Data Division to be coded is the File Section and we will examine the program specification to pick out the files used by the program. As can be seen this program requires three files—card-input file, tape-output file, and printer-output file—which can be defined in any order and can be given names chosen by the programmer.

The card-input file may contain two types of records (identified by 307 or 308 in the first three columns of the card) although since their layout is identical only one DATA RECORD description is given. The record descriptions for the other two files do not need to be broken down to elementary fields since no data manipulation will be carried out in these record areas. Instead, only complete groups will be moved into these areas prior to their being sent to the output device. This will become clearer later in this part when the complete program coding is shown.

The File Section for this program will therefore be coded as shown:

```
DATA DIVISION.
FILE SECTION.
FD CARD-IN,
    BLOCK CONTAINS 1 RECORD,
    RECORDING MODE IS F,
    LABEL RECORDS ARE OMITTED,
    DATA RECORD IS CARD.
```

```
Ø1 CARD.
    Ø2 CARD-TYPE          PICTURE XXX.
    Ø2 CUST-NUMBER.
        Ø3 CUST-ACCNO     PICTURE 9(6).
        Ø3 CHK-DIGIT      PICTURE 9.
    Ø2 ENTRY OCCURS 4.
        Ø3 ENTRY-DATE     PICTURE X(6).
        Ø3 ENTRY-AMOUNT   PICTURE S9(4)V99.
    Ø2 FILLER PICTURE X(46).
FD TAPOUT,
    BLOCK CONTAINS 4 RECORDS,
    RECORD CONTAINS 8Ø CHARACTERS,
    RECORDING MODE IS F,
    LABEL RECORDS ARE STANDARD,
    DATA RECORD IS VALID.
Ø1 VALID.
    Ø2 VALID-CARD-DATA    PICTURE X(8Ø).
FD PRINT,
    BLOCK CONTAINS 1 RECORD,
    RECORD CONTAINS 132 CHARACTERS,
    RECORDING MODE IS F,
    LABEL RECORDS ARE OMITTED,
    DATA RECORD IS PRINT-OUT.
Ø1 PRINT-OUT.
    Ø2 PRINT-DETAIL       PICTURE X(132).
```

Working-Storage Section Entries

This completes the File Section for this program and we can now go on to the Working-Storage Section. To do this we will examine the program specification again and pick out obviously required constants and work areas.

The first areas seen to be required are for the various print-lines which the program will write to the output-print file. We will need a line with heading information, a line to accept the contents of an invalid card, a line to accept the asterisks to indicate invalid card fields, and a line to contain the totals at the end of the program. As each of these lines is required to be output it will be moved to the area PRINT-DETAIL from where it can be sent to the printer-output file. Note that if only different print-line definitions are required the REDEFINES option could be used on one area; however, in this application more than one print area may be in preparation at one time.

In addition to the print-line image areas an examination of the program specification reveals that areas are required in which the total amount of cash written to tape can be accumulated. As each card is validated the amount(s) contained in the payment or credit field(s) is added to the appropriate accumulator if the card is accepted as passing the validation tests. The programmer may also decide that he would like to keep a count of the total number of cards read and the total number accepted as valid—again fields will be defined in the Working-Storage Section to act as accumulators. These would seem to be all the areas so far required and the Working-Storage Sections can now be coded thus far:

WORKING-STORAGE SECTION.
77 TOTAL-PAYMENTS PICTURE S9(6)V99.
77 TOTAL-CREDITS PICTURE S9(6)V99.
77 TOTAL-CARDS PICTURE S9(6).
77 TOTAL-REJECTED PICTURE S9(6).
01 PRINT-HEAD.
    02 FILLER PICTURE X(6), VALUE SPACES.
    02 FILLER PICTURE X(44), VALUE
       "CARD VALIDATION RUN—LISTING OF ERROR CARDS".
    02 FILLER PICTURE X(82) VALUE SPACES.
01 PRINT-CARD-DETAIL.
    02 FILLER PICTURE X(6) VALUE SPACES.
    02 CARD-IMAGE PICTURE X(80).
    02 FILLER PICTURE X(12),
       VALUE "bbbbbREJECTED"
    02 FILLER PICTURE X(34) VALUE SPACES.
01 PRINT-ERROR-FIELDS.
    02 FILLER PICTURE X(6) VALUE SPACES.
    02 PRINT-ASTERISKS VALUE SPACES.
       03 A-TYPE PICTURE XXX.
       03 A-NUMBER PICTURE X(7).
       03 A-ENTRY OCCURS 4.
          04 A-DATE PICTURE X(6).
          04 A-AMOUNT PICTURE X(6).
01 PRINT-TOTALS.
    02 FILLER PICTURE X(22),
       VALUE "TOTAL CASH-PAYMENTS".
    02 P-TOTAL-PAYS PICTURE ££££,££9.99.
    02 FILLER PICTURE X(10),
       VALUE "CREDITS".
    02 P-TOTAL-CRS PICTURE ££££,££9.99.
    02 FILLER PICTURE X(78) VALUE SPACES.

Notes on Data Division Entries

1. In the definition of some of the print-lines you will notice that the actual words we want to print (such as "TOTAL CASH-PAYMENTS") have been inserted with VALUE clauses; since we will not refer to these fields individually in the Procedure Division they have been defined with the keyword FILLER.

2. The print-line called PRINT-ERROR-FIELDS contains the sub-group item PRINT-ASTERISKS which you will note has the same layout as CARD in the File Section, except that all the fields are defined as being alphanumeric. When a card is found to be invalid it will be printed, as it was read, on one line, and on the line following will be printed the line PRINT-ERROR-FIELDS containing asterisks in the areas corresponding to the invalid card field(s). For example:

      30712345671204710123009904710001A40 REJECTED
                       ****

This will enable the Data-Control Clerks to quickly identify the erroneous fields.

3. Notice in the print-line PRINT-TOTALS the use of constants and edited items to enable an easily read output to be produced. For example, the following line could be output at the end of this program:

TOTAL CASH-PAYMENTS £3,174.02 CREDITS £3,784.00

4. Note that all the level 77 items occur before any group definitions—if this is not done the compiler will produce error diagnostics.

The initial Data Division coding for this program is now complete; however, it is quite possible that when coding the Procedure Division the programmer will realize a need for additional entries in the Data Division. In order to facilitate their easy insertion it is normal practice to code the level 77 and group-item definition on separate sheets of coding forms.

Exercises

There are no exercise questions for this chapter, however, you should now attempt Revision Questions, Set 2, on page 211.

CHAPTER TWENTY-SIX

THE PROCEDURE DIVISION

Organization

The Procedure Division is used to specify the set of instructions which the programmer wishes to use to solve a given data-processing problem. These instructions are specified by the use of COBOL statements, which may, at the discretion of the programmer, be combined to form **sentences**. The programmer may combine sentences to form **paragraphs** and paragraphs to form **sections**.

The Procedure Division is identified by the header:

PROCEDURE DIVISION.

which must appear in Area A and must immediately follow the last entry in the Data Division. Following this header the programmer will code his instructions consisting of statements, sentences, paragraphs, and sections at his discretion. These instructions must each be a valid combination of words and symbols and each must begin with a COBOL verb; additionally the programmer will attempt to ensure that his set of instructions is logically correct (i.e. will solve the problem to hand) although the compiler cannot check this aspect of the program.

The statement is the basic unit of the Procedure Division and will contain one instruction specified by a combination of COBOL words and programmer-defined words. The following are examples of statements:

ADD 1 TO ERROR-COUNT
MULTIPLY RATE BY BONUS GIVING GROSS
PERFORM PRINT-ROUTINE

The three types of statements are discussed below:

A **sentence** is a combination of one or more statements optionally separated by semi-colons. *Each sentence must be terminated by a period which must itself be followed by at least one space.* Examples of sentences are:

ADD 1 TO CARD-COUNT.
ADD 1 TO LOOP; MULTIPLY RATE BY 2; PERFORM BONUS.
PERFORM PRINT-ROUTINE; PERFORM HEAD-ROUTINE.

Although there is no limit to the number of statements making up a sentence it is good practice to limit this; preferably to one statement per sentence per line. If this is done then less effort is involved in replacing or correcting individual statements at the testing stage.

A **paragraph** is a combination of one or more sentences usually related by the procedure they are to compute (for example paragraphs could be formed to calculate gross pay, print pay-slips, read input files, and so on). Each paragraph must begin with a paragraph name (which is followed by a period) which appears in Area A. A paragraph is terminated by the occurrence of another paragraph name or a section name.

Examples of paragraphs and paragraph names appear below:

COMPUTE-PAY.
    ADD BONUS TO BASIC GIVING GROSS.
    PERFORM TAX-CALCULATION; ADD 1 TO COUNT-3.
    SUBTRACT TAX FROM GROSS GIVING NET.
SALES-ANALYSIS. MULTIPLY NO-SALESMEN BY TARGET.
    DIVIDE TARGET BY 52 GIVING AVERAGE.
    PERFORM PRINT-ROUTINE.
END-OF-RUN. STOP.

Notice that statements may appear on the same line as a paragraph name if desired. The last paragraph (END-OF-RUN) in the example above is terminated by the physical end of the program.

A **section** is composed of one or more paragraphs preceded by the section name. The section name is formed from a word identifying the use of the section followed by the word SECTION:

FIRST SECTION.
PARAGRAPH-1.
PARAGRAPH-N.
SECOND SECTION.
PARAGRAPH-2.
PARAGRAPH-2N.

Statement Types

The COBOL statements are classified into three types—**conditional** statements, **imperative** statements, and **compiler-directing** statements.

Conditional statements are those which can alter the flow of the program depending upon the state of a **condition**. At execution time the specified condition (see Chapter Twenty-seven) is tested and depending upon its state, alternate program paths will be selected.

Certain conditional statements (ADD ... ON SIZE ERROR ...) have already been described and the remainder follow later in Part Two. However, a complete list is presented here for reference:

IF

$$
\left.\begin{array}{l}
\text{ADD} \\
\text{COMPUTE} \\
\text{SUBTRACT} \\
\text{MULTIPLY} \\
\text{DIVIDE}
\end{array}\right\} \text{(ON SIZE ERROR)}
$$

$$
\left.\begin{array}{l}
\text{READ} \\
\text{SEARCH}
\end{array}\right\} \text{(AT END)}
$$

Note. If the options in parentheses above are not used then the particular statement is no longer a conditional statement. *The IF verb always produces a conditional statement.*

Imperative statements are those which, at execution time, specify that an unconditional action is to be taken. In other words imperative statements are always executed as they appear and do not have differing actions dependent upon any condition. The imperative statements used in COBOL are as in the following list:

Arithmetic	ADD
	COMPUTE
	DIVIDE
	MULTIPLY
	SUBTRACT
Procedure Branching	GO TO
	ALTER
	PERFORM
	STOP
	EXIT
Data-Manipulation	MOVE
	EXAMINE
	TRANSFORM
Input/Output	OPEN
	CLOSE
	READ
	WRITE
	ACCEPT
	DISPLAY
Others	SORT
	RETURN
	RELEASE
	SEARCH
	SET

Compiler-directing statements are those which direct the compiler to perform a certain action at compile time. Note that these types of statements are never executed when the program is running. The compiler directing statements are:

COPY
ENTER
NOTE

The above lists are presented for information only—it is not necessary to memorize the statement type to which each COBOL verb belongs.

Exercises

For the sample program below specify the number of:
1. Statements
2. Sentences
3. Paragraphs
4. Sections

    that are contained within the coding:

PROCEDURE DIVISION.
MAIN-SECTION.
PARA-2.   ADD 1 TO LOOP; ADD 2 TO LINE-FEED.
           PERFORM HEADING.
PARA-3.   PERFORM PRINT; PERFORM PAGE.
           MULTIPLY RATE BY 3.
           GO TO PARA-4.
SUB-SECTION.
PARA-4.   COMPUTE A = B + C + (D*E).
           ADD 1 TO LOOP; PERFORM PAGE; PERFORM PRINT.
PARA-5.   STOP.

5. What is the ideal number of statements to write on each line of your coding sheet?

CHAPTER TWENTY-SEVEN

CONDITIONS

As already mentioned in Chapter Twenty-six the conditional statements examine the state of a condition at the time the conditional statement is executed, and depending upon the state of the condition then, will alter the flow of the program. In fact the flow of the program will only be altered to proceed to one of two paths. The first path will be taken if the condition is **true** and the second path if the condition is **false**.

When a conditional statement is encountered during execution the necessary steps are taken to determine if the condition is true. A condition is said to be true if that condition exists. For example the condition A = B would be true if the values, at execution time, of variables A and B were identical; if the values were not identical the condition would be false.

Conditions are examined, and program flow therefore altered, by use of the IF statement. This statement is discussed in detail in the following chapter. However, in order to fully understand the IF statement it is necessary to be aware of the four types of conditions available within the COBOL program. Note that the state of a condition can be inverted (i.e. true made false and vice versa) by use of the NOT prefix; i.e. if CONDITION is true then NOT CONDITION is false. In the above example (condition A = B) if we had wished instead to determine if A was not equal to B we could have used the condition NOT (A = B).

Class Condition

This condition is used to determine whether an elementary item is numeric or alphabetic.

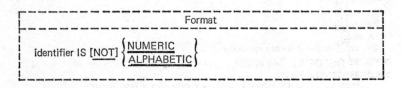

The identifier IS NUMERIC condition is satisfied if the content of the field identifier is made up only of the digits 0 to 9 (plus optionally a sign). The condition identifier IS ALPHABETIC is satisfied if identifier is made up only of the characters A through Z and the space character.

The NUMERIC test cannot be made on an identifier defined with the PICTURE attributes A or X; similarly the ALPHABETIC test cannot be made on an identifier defined with the PICTURE attribute 9.

Note that the condition NOT NUMERIC is not the same as ALPHABETIC since the value * ? + will be true for the first condition but false for the second. Some results of this conditional test are shown in the tables below:

Identifier description—PICTURE 9999.

Content	Condition	Result of Condition
1234	NUMERIC	true
1234	NOT NUMERIC	false
A23B	NUMERIC	false
A23B	NOT NUMERIC	true

Identifier description—PICTURE XXXX.

Content	Condition	Result of Condition
1234	ALPHABETIC	false
4321	NOT ALPHABETIC	true
AB D	ALPHABETIC	true
B CD	NOT ALPHABETIC	false
A?*C	ALPHABETIC	false

Sign Condition

This condition is used to determine whether the value of a numeric item is less than, equal to, or greater than zero.

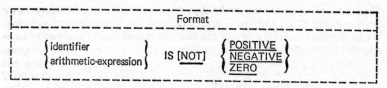

Note—a value is **POSITIVE** if it is greater than zero, and **NEGATIVE** if it is less than zero. However, an item with a value of zero is neither positive or negative. The following table will illustrate the result of this conditional test for a number of values of the data item defined as **PICTURE S999**.

Value	Condition	Result of Condition
123	POSITIVE	true
123	NEGATIVE	false
123	NOT NEGATIVE	true
123	ZERO	false
000	ZERO	true
000	POSITIVE	false

Note, in particular, the last example above which demonstrates the prior-mentioned rule.

Relation Condition

A relation condition involves the comparison of two identifiers according to the relational-operator used.

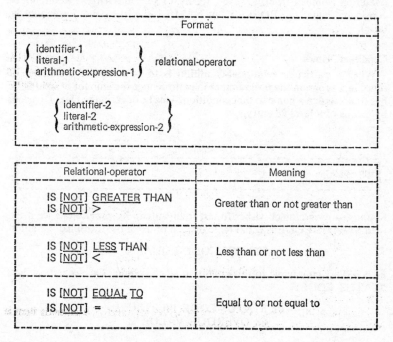

The relational-operator shows the type of comparison made between identifier-1 and identifier-2 and can be one of those shown in the table on p. 141. We have already seen the use of the last mentioned (=) of these relational-operators; the others are used in similar ways:

> TOTAL LESS THAN 10
> NAME = "SMITH"
> AREA IS NOT GREATER THAN MAXIMUM
> COUNT < 30

When two numeric items are compared in this way the comparison is done on their algebraic value; e.g. the value 0037 is numerically equal to 37. However when alphanumeric or alphabetic items of unequal length are compared the shorter item is considered to be extended, to the right, with spaces. For example, consider these definitions:

> 77 NAME-1 PICTURE X(6).
> 77 NAME-2 PICTURE X(9).

If these two items appeared with a relational-condition:

> NAME-1 EQUAL TO NAME-2.

then the whole of NAME-2 would be compared with the whole of NAME-1 plus three space characters on the right. So a value of "ROBERT   " in NAME-2 would be considered equal to "ROBERT" in NAME-1 (i.e. the condition would be true), however "ROBERTS   " in NAME-2 would not be considered equal to "ROBERT" in NAME-1 (i.e. the condition would be false).

Condition Names

When a particular relational-condition is to be examined a number of times in a program the programmer may, to reduce the amount of writing he has to do, assign a name to that condition. This he does, in the Data Division, by means of a level 88 entry.

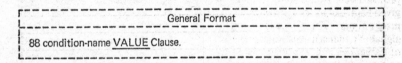

```
                          General Format

  88 condition-name VALUE Clause.
```

Suppose a programmer wishes to test frequently in his program to see if the field STATUS-CODE is equal to 1. Instead of using the relational-condition

> STATUS-CODE EQUAL 1

he could assign a name to this condition when defining the elementary item STATUS CODE:

> 02 STATUS-CODE PICTURE 9.
> 88 OVERDUE VALUE 1.

The expression OVERDUE now becomes the name of the relational-condition

STATUS-CODE EQUAL 1

and the programmer can replace this expression with

OVERDUE

(This condition will be true if STATUS-CODE has a value of 1 otherwise it will be false.)

Several condition names can be assigned to different values of a single elementary item:

```
Ø2 STATUS-CODE PICTURE 9.
   88 OVERDUE VALUE 1.
   88 CLOSED VALUE 2.
   88 OK VALUE 3.
   88 REFER VALUE 4.
```

This method of specifying relational-conditions can be quite useful, as shown, by giving meaningful names to tests made on a particular value.

Compound Conditions

Several conditions, as described above, can be combined to form a compound condition. (Note, however, that it is not recommended that more than two such conditions be combined in one statement.)

Single conditions are combined with each other by using the so-called logical operators AND and OR.

When combined with OR a compound condition is true if either of the single conditions is true.

When combined with AND a compound condition is true only if both of the single conditions are true. For example, the compound condition

A = Z OR C = 3

will be true if A has a value of 2 or C has a value of 3. However, this compound condition

A = Z AND C = 3

will only be true if the value of A is 2 and the value of C is 3.

In addition to AND and OR the operator NOT may be specified in compound conditions to negate one or all of the single conditions. For example, the expression:

NOT A = Z AND C = 3

will only be true if A has a value other than 2 and C has a value of 3. If NOT were to apply to both single conditions then parentheses would be used:

NOT (A = Z OR C = 3)

this compound condition would only be true if A did not have the value 2 and C did not have the value 3 (i.e. the compound condition here would only be true if the condition within the parentheses was false). The various combinations of the logical operators, and the compound condition result for the various single condition results, are shown in Table 1 below:

Single Condition		Compound Condition						
A	B	A AND B	A OR B	NOT A	NOT (A AND B)	NOT A AND B	NOT (A OR B)	A OR B
True	True	True	True	False	False	False	False	True
False	True	False	True	True	True	True	False	True
True	False	False	True	False	True	False	False	False
False	False	False	False	True	True	False	True	True

Table 1. Conditions resulting from compound logical operations

Note that in this table A and B each represent single conditions (such as COUNT = 3∅, LOOP = 7, etc.) and not elementary items. Thus the expression:

$$\text{NOT COUNT} = 1 \text{ AND STATUS} = 3$$

will only be true if COUNT = 1 (condition A) is false and STATUS = 3 (condition B) is true—see column 7 in the table.

Exercises

1. State whether each of the conditions listed below is true or false:

Definition	Value	Condition
(a) PICTURE 999	32	NUMERIC
(b) PICTURE XXX	A B	ALPHABETIC
(c) PICTURE XXX	***	ALPHABETIC
(d) PICTURE 999	3∅∅	POSITIVE
(e) PICTURE 999	−32	NOT NEGATIVE

2. For values of FLDA=27 and FLDB=30 state the result of the following conditions:

(a) FLDA > FLDB
(b) NOT FLDA = 27 AND FLDB = 3∅
(c) NOT FLDA > 27 AND FLDB = 3∅
(d) FLDA = 3∅ OR FLDB = 3.

CHAPTER TWENTY-EIGHT

THE IF STATEMENT

The IF statement is used to evaluate the result of a condition and causes alternate program action depending upon whether the condition is true or false.

```
┌─────────────────────────────────────────────────────────────────┐
│                            Format                                 │
│                                                                   │
│ IF condition THEN  ⎰ statement-1   ⎱ ⎰ ELSE      ⎱ ⎰ statement-2   ⎱│
│                    ⎱ NEXT SENTENCE ⎰ ⎱ OTHERWISE ⎰ ⎱ NEXT SENTENCE ⎰│
└─────────────────────────────────────────────────────────────────┘
```

When an IF statement is executed the condition is evaluated.

If the condition is true—the statement immediately following the condition, or the word THEN (statement-1) is executed. After execution of statement-1 control is transferred to the next sentence unless statement-1 was specified as a GO TO statement. If the condition is true and NEXT SENTENCE is specified then control is passed to the next sentence.

If the condition is false—statement-2 will be executed if present—if not present or if the NEXT SENTENCE option is used then control is passed to the next sentence.

Examples: Let us first of all consider some simple examples of the IF statement.
1. Suppose that the programmer wishes to transfer control to the paragraph END if the elementary item STATUS-CODE had the value of 1—he could write:

IF STATUS-CODE = 1 GO TO END.

If STATUS-CODE did not have the value 1 then control would be passed to the next sentence. You will remember from the previous chapter that STATUS-CODE has been given a condition-name:

Ø2 STATUS-CODE PICTURE 9.
88 OVERDUE VALUE 1.

The above IF statement could therefore be written:

IF OVERDUE GO TO END.

Note that both these IF statements will produce identical results.
2. Suppose a program, when dealing with a particular record, is to keep a count of the number of records whose field TRANSACTIONS is equal to spaces. The following statement could be used:

IF TRANSACTIONS = SPACES ADD 1 TO COUNT-A.

To count those records whose field TRANSACTIONS was not equal to spaces the following statement could be used:

IF NOT TRANSACTIONS = SPACES ADD 1 TO COUNT-B.
(or IF TRANSACTIONS NOT = SPACES ADD 1 TO COUNT-B.)

Now for some more complicated examples.

3. The two statements shown in (2) above could be combined thus:

IF TRANSACTIONS = SPACES ADD 1 TO COUNT-A ELSE ADD 1 TO COUNT-B.

Note that since TRANSACTIONS will either be equal to spaces or it will not be equal to spaces only one of the ADD statements above can be executed.

4. Suppose a program is to transfer control to END-OUT if the value of SWITCH is 1 and to END-IN if the value of SWITCH is not 1; the following statement could be used:

IF SWITCH = 1 GO TO END-OUT ELSE GO TO END-IN.

Note that in this case the statements following the IF will only be executed if given a name which appears in a GO TO statement.

5. Consider a program validating an input record—if the field ACCNO is not numeric then 1 is to be added to an error count field otherwise control is to be transferred to ACCNO-OK. If ACCNO is in error than the print-routine is to be performed and then control is to be transferred to READ-IN:

IF ACCNO NOT NUMERIC ADD 1 TO ERR ELSE GO TO ACCNO-OK.
PERFORM ERR-ROUTINE; GO TO READ-IN.

Note that if ACCNO is not numeric then ADD 1 TO ERR is executed then control is transferred to the next sentence where the PERFORM is executed.

6. The statements in (5) above could be rewritten:

IF ACCNO NOT NUMERIC NEXT SENTENCE ELSE GO TO ACCNO-OK.
ADD 1 TO ERR; PERFORM ERR-ROUTINE; GO TO READ-IN.

7. As a final example consider the case of a payroll program which determines the bonus rate for men as (bonus × 2) and for women as (bonus × $1\frac{1}{2}$):

IF SEX = "M" THEN BONUS = BONUS*2 ELSE BONUS = BONUS*1.5.

Nested IF Statements

Statement-1 or statement-2 in an IF statement may themselves be an IF statement, the second IF being called a **nested** IF statement. Although there is no limit to the number of levels of nesting it is not recommended that more than one IF statement be nested within another in order to avoid ambiguity. (Note—nested IF statements can always be recoded without the use of nesting.)

Consider the last IF statement example shown above. Suppose that, in addition to the test shown, it was desired to differentiate the male bonus rates between those under 21 and those over 21. The following nested IF statement could be used:

IF SEX = "M" THEN IF AGE < 21 THEN BONUS = BONUS*2
                              ELSE BONUS = BONUS*3
            ELSE BONUS = BONUS* 1.5.

The operation of this nested IF statement is best explained by means of the flowchart below:

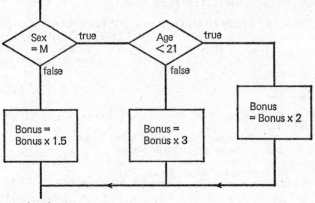

Fig. 38. Example of nested IF statement

Note how in all cases control eventually returns to next sentence.

The coding of nested IF statements is much simplified if the programmer remembers that an equal number of THEN and ELSE expressions will ensure the correct functioning of the statement (use the NEXT SENTENCE option where necessary). For example, consider the following paragraph from a program specification:

"If the customer is a supermarket the discount will be 30% for group members otherwise 25%. For non-supermarkets discount will be 10% unless credit status is 2 or 3 in which case no discount is given."

This could be represented with the following flowchart:

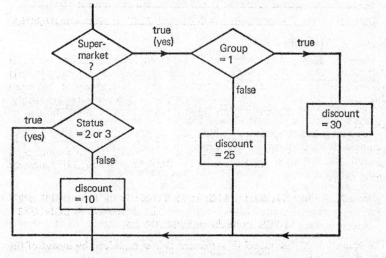

Fig. 39. Flowchart for discount rating procedure

and could be coded with the following nested IF:

IF TYPE = "S" THEN IF GROUP = 1 THEN DISCOUNT = 3∅
         ELSE DISCOUNT = 25
    ELSE IF STATUS = 2 OR 3 THEN NEXT SENTENCE
         ELSE DISCOUNT = 1∅.

Exercises

1. Write the statement to transfer control to END if ACC is numeric otherwise add 1 to ERR-COUNT.
2. Write the statement to multiply A by B if C has a value of ∅.
3. Is the value zero considered positive or negative?
4. Write the single statement to compare A and B and if they are equal add the larger of the two values of D and E to C.
5. Rewrite the answer to question 4 without using a nested IF.

CHAPTER TWENTY-NINE

DATA MANIPULATION—1

The MOVE Statement

The MOVE statement is used to transfer data from one field in the program to one or more other fields.

```
┌─────────────────────────────────────────────────────────┐
│                          Format                          │
├─────────────────────────────────────────────────────────┤
│                                                          │
│         ⎰ identifier-1 ⎱                                 │
│  MOVE   ⎱ literal      ⎰   TO identifier-2  [identifier-3] ... │
│                                                          │
└─────────────────────────────────────────────────────────┘
```

The data value of identifier-1, or the value of literal, is transferred to the items specified by identifier-2 (and then to the item specified by identifier-3 and so on if this option is used). Note that the contents of identifier-1 remain completely unchanged by the execution of this statement. Certain rules govern the permitted use of the MOVE verb and these must be borne in mind when coding a program—an attempt to execute an unpermitted MOVE may, as with any illegal instruction, cause the program to terminate abnormally. Even if this does not happen the contents of the receiving field(s) following an unpermitted MOVE statement are unpredictable.

An **elementary** MOVE is one that involves the transference of data from an elementary item to one or more elementary items and is governed by one of the following sets of rules depending upon the nature of the elementary items involved.

(1) *Alphanumeric to Alphanumeric*

Any alphanumeric elementary item may be MOVEd to any other alphanumeric elementary item. (Note in this context alphanumeric can be considered to include the alphabetic class.)

If the receiving field is larger than the sending field then padding with spaces will occur on the right of the receiving field. If the receiving field is smaller than the sending field then data are truncated at the right-hand end (after the receiving field has been filled). For example, suppose two fields have been defined thus:

```
77 AREA-1 PICTURE X(6) VALUE "ABCDEF".
77 AREA-2 PICTURE X(5) VALUE "VWXYZ".
```

Then the instruction

```
MOVE AREA-1 TO AREA-2.
```

would result in the value of AREA-2 being set to "ABCDE". (Note that the character "F" has been truncated.) The instruction

```
MOVE AREA-2 TO AREA-1.
```

would result in the value of AREA-1 being set to "VWXYZ♭". (Note that a space has been inserted to fill the area at the right-hand end.)

(2) *Numeric to Numeric*

Any numeric elementary item may be MOVEd to any other numeric elementary item. In this type of MOVE the data is aligned on the decimal point—which may be assumed (PICTURE string character V on right-hand end) or specified (period in edited numeric item). After decimal-point alignment unused character positions are set to zero and additional character positions are truncated. Note that because of decimal-point alignment zero filling or truncation may occur at either end of the receiving field.

For example, consider the two definitions below:

```
77 NUM-1 PICTURE 999V99 VALUE 217.34.
77 NUM-2 PICTURE 99V999 VALUE 69.423.
```

We can demonstrate truncation and zero filling in the same statement by using the statement:

```
MOVE NUM-2 TO NUM-1.
```

The value of NUM-1 after this statement was executed would be 069V42 (zero filling at the left-hand end and truncation on the right-hand end). When coding numeric MOVE statements it is most important to remember that the data items will be aligned on the decimal point—if this is forgotten important data may be lost. For example, consider these two definitions:

```
77 TOTAL PICTURE S9(6)V99.
77 SAVE PICTURE S9(8).
```

If the statement:

MOVE TOTAL TO SAVE.

was executed then the decimal portion of TOTAL would not be transferrred because of decimal-point alignment (the decimal point is assumed to be at the right-hand end of SAVE). Note that this truncation occurs despite the fact that TOTAL and SAVE would occupy the same number of storage locations. (If it was required to move the eight digits in TOTAL to the eight locations in SAVE without decimal-point alignment then the REDEFINES clause could be used.)

The programmer can avoid potential trouble-spots by making all his numeric fields the same length:

77 NUM-1 PICTURE S9(6)V99.
77 NUM-2 PICTURE S9(6)V99.

Then any MOVE statements, such as:

MOVE NUM-1 TO NUM-2.

will replace the original contents of NUM-2 with an exact copy of the contents of NUM-1.

(3) *Numeric to Alphanumeric*

A numeric elementary item may not be moved to an alphabetic elementary item but may be moved to an alphanumeric one, providing that the decimal point, in the numeric elementary item, is at the right-hand end. The absolute value of the numeric elementary item is transferred to the alphanumeric item, so therefore the result of this type of move is unsigned. For example, consider the following definitions:

77 NUM PICTURE S999 VALUE −127.
77 ALP PICTURE XXX.

the statement

MOVE NUM TO ALP.

would result in ALP containing the characters "127"—i.e. the numeric value is converted to an unsigned character string. Padding, if required, is with spaces as in (1) above.

(4) *Alphanumeric to Numeric*

An alphabetic elementary item cannot be moved to a numeric elementary item. A numeric elementary item may receive data from an alphanumeric elementary item providing the sending field contains only numeric digits. If an instruction attempts to move non-numeric data to a numeric elementary item the results will be unpredictable. This type of MOVE is not recommended.

When a MOVE statement is encountered with one or more non-elementary (i.e. group) items it is treated as if each group item were an alphanumeric elementary item and the rules in either (1) or (3) above will apply.

Examples: The rules specified above may seem rather daunting at first; however, they are quite simple and will soon be second-nature to you. In fact, the rules only really specify those situations which one would probably have inferred anyway:

1. If the sending and receiving fields are of unequal length padding or truncation will take place.
2. Numeric fields are aligned on a decimal point.
3. Moving alphanumeric values to numeric fields may produce odd results.

In use the MOVE statement will soon be recognized as one of the simplest statements appearing in the COBOL language.

Consider a card file record with this layout:

```
01 CARD.
    02 NAME PICTURE X(20).
    02 ACCNO PICTURE 9(6).
    02 SALES.
        03 ORDERS PICTURE 999.
        03 VALUE PICTURE 99999.
    02 FILLER PICTURE X(46).
```

Suppose a program was to read these cards and produce, for each card, a print-line showing the above details plus an average value per order, the print-line could be defined thus:

```
01 PRINT.
    02 FILLER PICTURE XXX VALUE SPACES.
    02 P-ACCNO PICTURE 9B9(5).
    02 FILLER PICTURE XX VALUE SPACES.
    02 P-NAME PICTURE X(20).
    02 FILLER PICTURE XX VALUE SPACES.
    02 P-ORDERS PICTURE ZZ9.
    02 FILLER PICTURE XX VALUE SPACES.
    02 P-VALUE PICTURE £££££9.
    02 FILLER PICTURE XX VALUE SPACES.
    02 P-AVERAGE PICTURE ££££9.
    02 FILLER PICTURE X(80) VALUE SPACES.
```

The coding to set up the print-line from each card file record could be as shown:

```
BUILD-PRINT.    MOVE ACCNO TO P-ACCNO.
                MOVE NAME TO P-NAME.
                MOVE ORDERS TO P-ORDERS.
                MOVE VALUE TO P-VALUE.
                DIVIDE VALUE BY ORDERS GIVING AVERAGE.
                MOVE AVERAGE TO P-AVERAGE.
```

A single data item value may be transferred to more than one other data field by use of the MOVE statement:

```
MOVE AREA-1 TO AREA-2, AREA-3, AREA-4.
```

Exercises

Consider the following part of a Working Storage section then, for each question, write down the value of the result field after the MOVE statement.

```
77 NUM-1 PICTURE S9999 VALUE 1234.
77 ALPHA PICTURE XXXX.
77 NUM-2 PICTURE S999.
77 NAME PICTURE XXXXX VALUE "SMITH".
```

1. MOVE NAME TO ALPHA.
2. MOVE NUM-1 TO NUM-2.
3. MOVE NUM-1 TO NAME.
4. MOVE "HELLO" TO ALPHA.
5. Write the statement to transfer the value of item DELTA to the item OMEGA.

CHAPTER THIRTY

DATA MANIPULATION—2

The examination, by program, of individual characters within a data field is possible with the knowledge so far acquired of COBOL (for example the field could be redefined as several single-character fields and each could then be manipulated on its own). However, to do so would be cumbersome and possibly difficult for the newcomer. Since it is not an uncommon requirement that individual characters be examined within a data field the COBOL language provides two powerful statements—EXAMINE and TRANSFORM —to make this type of task very simple indeed.

The EXAMINE Statement

The EXAMINE statement is used to count the number of times a particular character occurs within a data field and may optionally be used to replace that character with another, selected, character.

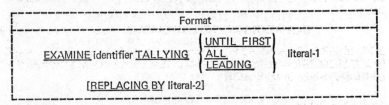

Let us first of all consider the use of this statement without the REPLAC- ING option. The field called identifier is examined, from left to right, character by character and a count is made according to the option specified. In all cases literal-1 must be a single-character literal with the same data class as identifier (i.e. if the field NUM PICTURE 999 is being examined then literal must be a numeric literal), additionally a figurative constant (e.g. ZERO, SPACE) may be used but again the data class must correspond with that of identifier.

UNTIL FIRST Option

The data field is examined and a count is made of the number of characters preceding the first (from left to right) occurrence of literal. For example, suppose we wish to know how many characters preceded the character "S" in the field defined:

77 ALPHA-LIST PICTURE X(1Ø).

Then we could use the following statement:

EXAMINE ALPHA-LIST TALLYING UNTIL FIRST "S".

If the content of ALPHA-LIST at the time this statement was executed was "ABEGJSMNST" then the result of the EXAMINE statement would be 5 (i.e. 5 characters precede the first "S" in this field). If the character "S" did not occur at all in the field then the result would be 10 (i.e. the total length of the field). Similarly, we can examine numeric fields:

EXAMINE NUMBER TALLYING UNTIL FIRST ZERO.

ALL Option

In this case the result of the EXAMINE statement is a count of all the specified characters occurring in the data field. For example, suppose we wish to discover how many times the character "." (period) occurs in the field:

77 NAME PICTURE X(2∅).

then we would write:

EXAMINE NAME TALLYING ALL ".".

If name contained, at the time this statement was executed, the value "A. B. JOHNSON AND CO." then the result of the EXAMINE statement would be 3. Again we can use figurative constants:

EXAMINE NAME TALLYING ALL SPACE.
EXAMINE NUMBER TALLYING ALL ZERO.

Or we can count the number of times a particular digit occurs in a numeric item:

EXAMINE NUMBER TALLYING ALL 7.

If NUMBER had the value 2467917 then the result of the EXAMINE would be 2. If NUMBER contained, say, 1234123 then the result would be zero (i.e. no 7's are present in the number).

LEADING Option

This will count the number of occurrences of literal prior to the occurrence of another character, i.e. the number of leading "literals". For example to discover the number of leading zeroes in the field PRINT-NO:

EXAMINE PRINT-NO TALLYING LEADING ZEROES.

If the value of PRINT-NO was ∅∅∅421 at the time the statement was executed then the result of the EXAMINE would be 3. Similarly, we might wish to discover how many cheque-protect symbols had been edited into a field:

EXAMINE AMOUNT TALLYING LEADING "*".

TALLY

The result (i.e. the count) of an EXAMINE statement is made available to the programmer in a special field called TALLY. This field is automatically defined by the COBOL compiler (and must not be defined by the programmer) and has the PICTURE attribute 9(5), (i.e. it is an unsigned 5 digit numeric item). If, therefore, the programmer wished to save the result of an EXAMINE statement he could write:

> EXAMINE AMOUNT TALLYING ALL "*".
> MOVE TALLY TO AST-COUNT.

The field TALLY may be operated upon as any other numeric item; however remember that each EXAMINE statement will overwrite the previous value of TALLY.

REPLACING Option

The counting is still done as above, with this option and, in addition the characters counted are replaced with literal-2. For example, if we wish to replace all the characters before the first "M", in a field ALPHA, with SPACE:

> EXAMINE ALPHA TALLYING UNTIL FIRST "M"
> REPLACING BY SPACE

we may use this option to perform simple editing:

> EXAMINE AMOUNT TALLYING LEADING SPACE
> REPLACING BY "*".

This statement would change a value in AMOUNT of "   123" to "****123". Similarly, we may replace all the occurrences of a character:

> EXAMINE Z-CHK TALLYING ALL Ø REPLACING BY 6.

The operation of the REPLACING option is illustrated in the table below:

Statement	AREA Before	AREA After	Value of TALLY
EXAMINE AREA TALLYING ALL Ø REPLACING BY 1	1ØØ1Ø1	111111	3
EXAMINE AREA TALLYING LEADING "*" REPLACING BY "M"	**P*P	MMP*P	2
EXAMINE AREA TALLYING UNTIL FIRST Ø REPLACING BY 1	234Ø12	111Ø12	3

The TRANSFORM Statement

The TRANSFORM statement is used to change characters in a field according to a specified rule.

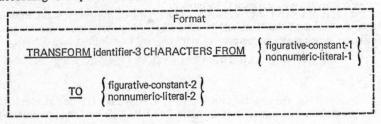

```
                        Format

  TRANSFORM identifier-3 CHARACTERS FROM  { figurative-constant-1 }
                                          { nonnumeric-literal-1  }

            TO  { figurative-constant-2 }
                { nonnumeric-literal-2  }
```

If a figurative-constant is specified in either the FROM or TO option then either figurative-constant or a single-character non-numeric literal must be specified in the other option. If non-numeric literal is specified in both the FROM and TO option then they must be of equal length.

Let us consider firstly the case of single-character or figurative literals. Each occurrence of the FROM literal in identifier is transformed to the TO literal. For example, to change each space in a field ALPHA to an asterisk the following could be used:

TRANSFORM ALPHA CHARACTERS FROM SPACE TO "*".

This would have the same effect on ALPHA as the statement:

EXAMINE ALPHA TALLYING ALL SPACE REPLACING BY "*".

Suppose, however, that we wish to change or transform more than one character; for example, we might wish to change all the spaces in a field to zeroes and all the *'s to X's. We could do this with two EXAMINE statements, of course; however we may do this with a single-transform statement:

TRANSFORM ALPHA CHARACTERS FROM "ƀ*" to "ØX".

In this case any character in ALPHA represented by a character in the FROM option is changed to the corresponding character in the TO option. As another example consider a field ALPHA-NUM containing the alphabetic characters A–F which we wish to change to the numeric characters 1–6 (such that A is replaced by 1, B is replaced by 2, and so on). We could therefore write the following statement:

TRANSFORM ALPHA CHARACTERS FROM
"ABCDEF" TO "123456".

If the contents of ALPHA prior to this statement had been "BBACFE" then the content after execution would have been "221365".

Exercises

1. Write the statement to count the number of zeroes in the field NUM.
2. Where would the result of the statement in question 1 be found and what would the field's attributes be?
3. Write the statement to count the number of leading spaces in the field CHQ and replace them with zeroes.
4. Write the statement to count the number of characters before the first 7 in the field STATUS (PICTURE 9999).
5. Write the statement to change the field ALPHA-X such that each A becomes 4, each B becomes 3, and each C becomes 2.

CHAPTER THIRTY-ONE

PREPARING DATA FILES

Almost all commercial programs will handle some form of input or output files on one or more of the available storage devices. We have already examined the File Description (FD) entries required to define these files in the Data Division. So now we come to the problem of accessing the data on our files within the Procedure Division.

Before a file can be manipulated it is necessary for the operating system to make certain checks on the file we are about to deal with and on the device containing the file. The operating system must verify that the required device is available to the system (i.e. that it is switched on) and that the file on the device is the correct one (this applies only to magnetic tape and magnetic disc files). The methods by which these checks are carried out are not the concern of the programmer; however, it is necessary for each COBOL program to issue an instruction requesting that the checks be carried out on the file(s) required by the program.

The OPEN Statement

The OPEN statement prepares a file for processing by the program.

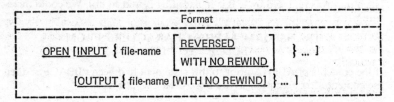

```
                                    Format

OPEN [INPUT { file-name  [ REVERSED        ]  } ... ]
                         [ WITH NO REWIND   ]

       [OUTPUT { file-name [WITH NO REWIND] } ... ]
```

When the FD for a particular file was written no indication was given as to whether the file was required for inputting data or for outputting data. This is in fact specified in the OPEN statement. Because of this it is possible, if required, to create a data file in one part of the program and then (by issuing a new OPEN statement) to read the same file in another part of the program.

A file can be prepared for input processing thus:

OPEN INPUT MASTER-FILE.

or for output thus:

OPEN OUTPUT PRINT-FILE.

Before any file can be accessed an OPEN statement must be specified and it must contain either the INPUT or the OUTPUT option. *Any attempt to access a file that has not been* OPEN*ed will result in a program failure*, as will an attempt to, say, OPEN INPUT on a file destined for a printer device.

Magnetic Tape Files. The other options in the OPEN statement general format apply only to files on magnetic tape devices. In the case above where a file is to be created and then read back by the same program, it is possible to read the tape backwards to avoid having to rewind the reel. (Note that, of course, the individual records on the file will be read in reverse order.) To achieve this the following statement could be used:

OPEN INPUT WORK-FILE REVERSED.

The REVERSED option indicating that the file is to be read in reverse order. Similarly, if the tape is not to be automatically rewound when it is opened the NO REWIND option can be specified:

OPEN INPUT FILE-A NO REWIND.
OPEN OUTPUT FILE-B NO REWIND.

The additional options available for magnetic tape files are very rarely used and the programmer will normally only be concerned with specifying whether the file is INPUT or OUTPUT.

For example, in the sample program discussed in Chapter Twenty-five the first paragraph in the Procedure Division would be to OPEN the files used by the program as shown below:

BEGIN. OPEN INPUT CARD-IN.
OPEN OUTPUT TAPOUT, PRINT.

Notice how one statement can be used to OPEN more than one file.

The programmer must remember to give an OPEN statement before attempting to input data from or output data to a file.

When a program has completed the processing of a particular file the operating system has to be informed in order that the device containing the file can be made available to other users (e.g. each magnetic tape file is rewound).

The CLOSE Statement

The CLOSE statement is used to inform the operating system that a file is no longer required for processing.

```
┌─────────────────────────────── Format ───────────────────────────────┐
│                                                                       │
│                              ┌─────────────┐                          │
│   CLOSE   file-name-1   [WITH │ NO REWIND  │ ]                        │
│                              │ LOCK        │                          │
│                              └─────────────┘                          │
└───────────────────────────────────────────────────────────────────────┘
```

In most cases the programmer simply specifies the file name(s):

CLOSE MASTER-FILE.
CLOSE CARDS, PRINT-FILE.

Following this statement the particular file(s) closed is no longer available to the program (unless it is opened again).

Magnetic Tape Files. The additional options once again apply only to magnetic tape files. The LOCK option specifies that the file is to be rewound and then unloaded automatically by the operating system—once this is done the file cannot be reopened:

CLOSE TAPE WITH LOCK.

The NO REWIND option specifies that the file is to be made unavailable for processing, but is not to be rewound. Hence it can be opened again with the REVERSED option. A program which creates a magnetic tape file and then wishes to read it in again in the reverse direction could therefore use the following sequence of statements:

OPEN OUTPUT WORK-FILE.

.
.
.
.
.
.

CLOSE WORK-FILE WITH NO REWIND.
OPEN INPUT WORK-FILE REVERSED.

.
.
.
.

CLOSE WORK-FILE WITH LOCK.

Once again these additional options will be rarely used—although the programmer must remember to CLOSE all his files when he has finished processing them. This will normally be done at the end of the program; if all the files are closed together then there is less danger of one being left open:

CLOSE CARD-IN, TAPOUT, PRINT.

Exercises

1. Write the statement to prepare a file PRINT for processing as an output file.
2. Write the statement to terminate the processing of two files—WORK-A, WORK-B.
3. Write the statement to open a magnetic tape file, WORK-FILE, that is to be read backwards.
4. Write the statement to terminate the processing of a magnetic tape file TAPE-1 without the tape being rewound.
5. Rewrite the answer to question 4 such that the tape will be unloaded.

CHAPTER THIRTY-TWO

DATA TRANSFER

The transfer of data from or to an external file is accomplished by means of input and output statements, the format of which is discussed below. Since this work is intended for the newcomer to computer programming we will only look in detail at files organized in a sequential manner. However, the reader should bear in mind that files can be organized, on a disc-backing store, in a direct (or random) access mode. A file, on a disc-backing store, organized in a direct-access manner can be accessed in any order the programmer desires. For example, if a file was organized in a specific manner the programmer could access a particular record merely by quoting, say, a customer account number to his program. The coding for handling direct-access disc files can be quite complicated, and since the use of such files tends to be restricted in commercial environments, their use is not described in the coding examples used in this book.

All the files referred to in the examples below will be organized in a sequential (also called serial) manner. Sequential files have already been described in Part One. However, it is important to remember that when inputting a sequential file every record on the file has to be read—if the programmer wishes to by-pass a number of records he must specifically write the necessary instructions to do so. If record number n has just been input then the next record accessed will be record number n + 1. Similarly, if record number n has been output to a file then the next record sent to that file must be record number n + 1. However, since the records on a sequential file are accessed one after another the programmer does not need to be concerned with the number of a particular record on a file.

The READ Statement

The READ statement is used to make available, to the program, the next record on the file and take specific action when the end-of-file condition is reached. (Note that, as already mentioned, the removal of logical records from physical file blocks is handled by the operating system and need not be the concern of the COBOL programmer.)

```
┌─────────────────────────────────────────────────────────────┐
│                          Format                               │
├─────────────────────────────────────────────────────────────┤
│  READ file-name RECORD [INTO identifier]   AT END  imperative-statement │
│                                                               │
└─────────────────────────────────────────────────────────────┘
```

Before the first READ statement is executed for any file the file must have been prepared for input with an OPEN INPUT statement.

When a READ statement is executed the next record on the file is input to storage and is made available to the program in the record-input area defined with the DATA RECORDS clause in the FD. Note that when more than one type of record exists on a file, each one is read into the same area which has been implicitly redefined with the DATA RECORDS clause.

Each READ statement must specify an AT END option—which will be executed when the **end-of-file** condition exists. The end-of-file condition is indicated by the presence of a special record located at the physical end of the file. For magnetic tape and magnetic disc files this end-of-file record is written automatically by the operating system when a CLOSE statement is encountered during file creation. End-of-file for a card file or paper tape file is indicated by a special record appended to the file by the computer operators.

Example: Consider the following file descriptions in the Data Division:

```
FD CARD-IN,
    BLOCK CONTAINS 1 RECORD,
    RECORDING MODE IS F,
    LABEL RECORDS ARE OMITTED,
    DATA RECORD IS CARD.

Ø1 CARD.
    Ø2 NAME PICTURE X(2Ø).
    Ø2 ADDRESS PICTURE X(6Ø).

FD TAPE-IN,
    BLOCK CONTAINS 4 RECORDS,
    RECORDING MODE IS F,
    LABEL RECORDS ARE STANDARD,
    DATA RECORDS ARE TAPE-1, TAPE-2.

Ø1 TAPE-1.
    Ø2 ACCNO-1 PICTURE 9(6).
    Ø2 STATUS PICTURE 9(4).
    Ø2 NAME PICTURE X(2Ø).
    Ø2 ADDRESS PICTURE X(6Ø).

Ø1 TAPE-2.
    Ø2 ACCNO-2 PICTURE 9(6).
    Ø2 PAYMENTS OCCURS 7.
        Ø3 AMOUNT PICTURE 9(6).
        Ø3 DATE PICTURE 9(6).
```

Before any data can be accessed from either of these files they must be opened with the following Procedure Division statement:

OPEN INPUT CARD-IN, TAPE-IN.

Since this statement specifies the INPUT option the READ statement can now be used to input data to the program.

READ CARD-IN AT END GO TO EOR.

This statement will cause the next record to be transferred to the area CARD in the Data Division. (Note—the first time this statement is executed then the first record on the file will be made available.)

The contents of the first record can now be manipulated as desired in the Procedure Division. For example, if we wish to move the value of the field NAME we could write:

MOVE NAME TO OTHER-AREA.

The execution of the READ statement again would transfer the second record to storage and so on. When the end-of-file card is read the AT END option will be executed and the statement GO TO EOR will be executed.

To see the entire run of a file consider this very trivial piece of coding to count the number of records in the file CARD. (Note—no other processing is done with the data from the file.)

```
BEGIN.    OPEN INPUT CARD-IN.
LOOP.     READ CARD-IN AT END GO TO EOR.
          ADD 1 TO COUNT.
          GO TO LOOP.
EOR.      STOP. CLOSE CARD-IN.
```

Let us now consider the inputting of data from the file TAPE-IN. The READ statement for this file will be similar to that already shown:

```
READ TAPE-IN AT END GO TO END-FILE.
```

The record read in by this statement will be in the area defined by TAPE-1 and TAPE-2 (since these two definitions refer to the same area), although so far the program has no indication of which type of record it has. The easiest way of doing this would be to add an additional field to each record, in the same relative location from the beginning of the file, which would identify the type of record. If this additional field was called TYPE (in TAPE-1) then the different processing of the two types of record could be achieved thus:

```
READ TAPE-IN AT END GO TO END-FILE.
IF TYPE = 1 GO TO PROCESS-TYPE-1.
IF TYPE = 2 GO TO PROCESS-TYPE-2.
```

Alternatively, the file might be organized in such a manner that each type-1 record was always followed by a type-2 record. To differentiate the processing we could write the following:

```
LOOP.   READ TAPE-IN AT END GO TO END-FILE.
PROCESS-TYPE-1.
          .
          .
          .
          .
          .
          READ TAPE-IN AT END GO TO END-FILE.
PROCESS-TYPE-2.
          .
          .
          .
          .
          .
        GO TO LOOP.
```

Whichever way the programmer determines which type of record he has in storage he will refer to it by the appropriate definition in the file record description. Once again when the end-of-file is reached control will be transferred to END-FILE (from the AT END option) where the programmer can specify any required end-of-file processing (including usually the instructions to CLOSE the file).

INTO option.

When this option is specified the next record is read into the DATA RECORDS area and is also transferred to the area specified in the INTO option. For example, using the file TAPE-IN above, the following statement:

READ TAPE-IN INTO WORK-AREA AT END GO TO EOF.

will cause the next record to be read into the area TAPE-1 and to be then moved to the area WORK-AREA. The record could then be manipulated in both areas.

The WRITE Statement

The WRITE statement is used to transmit a record to an output file. Additionally, when used with a file on a printer, the WRITE statement is used to advance the paper.

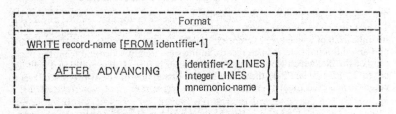

As with the READ statement the WRITE statement cannot be executed until the file has been opened with an OPEN OUTPUT statement.

The most important thing to notice with the WRITE statement is that a **record name** (as specified in a DATA RECORDS clause) must be used and not a file name. In this way the operating system can determine (from the layout of the data-record description) the length of the particular record to be written and can therefore write variable-length (RECORDING MODE V) type files.

Example:
Suppose the following file definition appears in the Data Division:

```
FD TAPE-OUT,
    RECORDING MODE IS V
    BLOCK CONTAINS 200 CHARACTERS,
    LABEL RECORDS ARE STANDARD,
    DATA RECORDS ARE TAPE-1, TAPE-2.

01 TAPE-1.
    02 FILLER PICTURE X(40).

01 TAPE-2
    02 FILLER PICTURE X(60).
```

Any WRITE statement for this file must specify that either a TAPE-1 or a TAPE-2 record is to be written to the file. Note that as far as the programmer is concerned the record is written to the output device although in fact it will be firstly placed in the current block and only when this block is full will any data be actually written to the output device. (This has been described fully in Chapter Eighteen.) For example, if the programmer has made up a TAPE-1 type record and now wishes to direct it to the output device, he can write:

WRITE TAPE-1.

Alternatively, if he had assembled a TAPE-2 type record he could write:

WRITE TAPE-2.

In each case above the appropriate amount (40 or 60 characters respectively) would be written, from the record-item area, to the output device. Note, however, that only one type of record can be built up at any one time since both TAPE-1 and TAPE-2 refer to the same area in core storage (because the DATA RECORDS clause implies redefinition of the same area).

If, then, the programmer wished to assemble both types of record before writing them to the output device he would have to build them up in some other areas in the Working-Storage Section. If, say, these areas were called ASSEMBLE-1 and ASSEMBLE-2 (40 and 60 characters in length respectively) the data records could be written to the output device using the FROM option:

WRITE TAPE-1 FROM ASSEMBLE-1,
WRITE TAPE-2 FROM ASSEMBLE-2.

The FROM option is therefore the reverse of the INTO option and causes data to be moved from the specified area into the data-record area, from where it is transferred to the output device.

Print Files

When a WRITE statement is executed for a printer-output device it causes the paper to advance, as specified in the statement, and a line to be printed (i.e. output). The required paper advancement can be specified in one of two ways. The programmer may specify the exact number of lines he wants the paper advanced as a numeric literal in the WRITE statement. For example, the following statement will cause the paper to advance two lines, and the line called LINE-A to be printed:

WRITE LINE-A AFTER ADVANCING 2 LINES.

Similarly, the programmer can write:

WRITE HEADING AFTER ADVANCING 1 LINE.
WRITE LINE-3 AFTER ADVANCING 16 LINES.

and so on up to a maximum of 100 lines. Alternatively, the programmer may specify that the paper is to be advanced according to the current value of a data item:

WRITE HEADER AFTER ADVANCING SKIP LINES.

The actual advancement will be determined from the value of SKIP according to the following rules:

Value	Paper Advancement
Space	One line (single spacing of print-out).
Ø (zero)	Two lines (double spacing of print-out).
- (hyphen)	Three lines (triple spacing of print-out).
1–9	Skip paper forward to channel 1–9 respectively.

Printing by Channel

As well as advancing a specific number of lines the paper may be advanced to a specified **channel**. Each channel represents a predetermined position on each page of print-out. These channels can be changed, by the computer operators, for use on particular pre-printed stationery although **channel one**, by convention, always represents the **top line of a page**.

The use of multiple channels for printing is outside the scope of this book; however, the beginner will obviously wish to be able to advance a printed report to the beginning of a new page. To do this the following statements could be used:

MOVE "1" TO SKIP.
WRITE HEADING AFTER ADVANCING SKIP LINES.

This will usually be required after the previous page has been filled with printing. Standard computer stationery can accommodate 64 lines of printing although it is not uncommon to only print, say, 58 lines to make the report neater. Suppose a program prints out its detail lines by PERFORMing the routine PRINT-OUT. This routine could take care of page-changing by a method such as that shown below:

PRINT-OUT.
    WRITE DETAIL AFTER ADVANCING 1 LINE.
    ADD 1 TO LINE-COUNT.
    IF LINE-COUNT EQUALS 58 PERFORM PAGE-CHANGE.

PAGE-CHANGE.
    MOVE "1" TO SKIP.
    WRITE HEADING AFTER ADVANCING SKIP LINES.
    MOVE ZERO TO LINE-COUNT.

NEXT-PARA.

Note, particularly, the fact that the paragraph PAGE-CHANGE sets the value of LINE-COUNT to zero so that the number of lines on the new page are counted correctly. Each time the routine PRINT-OUT is performed the value of LINE-COUNT will be incremented by 1; only when this field has a value of 58 will the routine PAGE-CHANGE be executed.

More detailed use of the WRITE statement, with examples for the sample program, is discussed in Chapters Thirty-four and Thirty-five.

Exercises

1. Write the statement to input the next record from the file CARDS, when the last card has been read set the value of SWITCH equal to "1".

2. Write the statement to input the next record from the file TAPE into an area called TAPE-SAVE, at end-of-file transfer control to the paragraph named TAPE-END.
3. Write the statement to output a record called NAME to the file CUSTOMER.
4. Write the statement to print the line DETAIL-1 after advancing the paper 1 line.
5. Write the statement to print the heading HEAD-UP on the next page of a report if the value of LINE-COUNT is 6∅. (N.B. SKIP has the value "1".)

CHAPTER THIRTY-THREE

COMMUNICATION WITH THE COMPUTER OPERATOR

It is often necessary for a program to give a message to the computer operator and on some of these occasions receive a reply from the operator. For example, the program may wish to ask the operator for the current date, or in the case of some type of error, ask what is the next action to be taken. In order to achieve this communication it would be possible to define a file for the operator's console (usually an electric typewriter) with an FD and use a READ or WRITE statement as appropriate.

However, rather than involve the programmer in additional coding for a straightforward and standard requirement the COBOL compiler provides two statements which can be used to send messages to and receive replies from the computer operator.

The DISPLAY Statement

The DISPLAY statement is used for transmitting data to the computer operator's console.

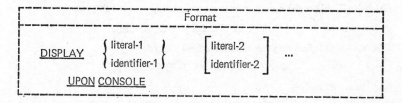

The value of the literals or the current value of each identifier used is transmitted to the operator's console. A mixture of literals and identifiers is permitted so that a message can be built up by the program.

Examples: For the program to send a straightforward message to the operator the following could be coded:

```
    DISPLAY "THIS PROGRAM HAS FINISHED" UPON CONSOLE.
or  DISPLAY "UP-DATE BEGINS" UPON CONSOLE.
```

A more complicated message can be output by mixing literals and identifiers:

MOVE 2 TO RUN-NO.
MOVE 3 TO RECORD-NO.
PERFORM OPERATOR.
OPERATOR. DISPLAY "RUN" RUN-NO "STARTS AT RECORD"
RECORD-NO UPON CONSOLE.

The PERFORM statement above when executed would produce the following message on the operator's console:

RUN 2 STARTS AT RECORD 3

Note that the compiler will automatically ensure that the relevant special characters are transmitted to create a **carriage return** after the DISPLAY message has been output.

The ACCEPT Statement

The ACCEPT statement is used to obtain data from the computer operator.

Format
ACCEPT identifier FROM   CONSOLE

When this command is executed the computer will output the message "AWAITING REPLY" following which the operator may type in his response. The number of characters which the program will accept from the operator is limited to the length of identifier specified in the ACCEPT statement. Note that until an ACCEPT statement is executed the keyboard of the operator's console remains locked. If the operator keys in fewer characters than the receiving field can contain then the field will be padded with spaces or zeroes (for alphanumeric or numeric fields respectively) as appropriate.

Example: To allow the operator to input a value for the field DATE:

ACCEPT DATE FROM CONSOLE.

Suppose the program requests data for a field defined:

77 RESULT PICTURE X(6)

with the statement

ACCEPT RESULT FROM CONSOLE.

If the operator replied with YES (note—no enclosing quotation-marks are required by the operator for an alphabetic reply), the field RESULT would be given a value of "YESꝑꝑꝑ" (i.e. 3 blanks would be inserted at the right-hand end as padding).
Similarly, for a field defined:

77 MANY PICTURE 999.

The programmer could code

ACCEPT MANY FROM CONSOLE.

If now the operator replied with the single character 7, then the resultant value of MANY would be 007 (i.e. zero filled).

The ACCEPT statement is normally used in conjunction with DISPLAY in order that the operator may be told what information is required of him before the keyboard is unlocked. For example, suppose the program wished to know a date to be used for processing before a run could be complete. The following sequence of statements could be used:

        DISPLAY "PLEASE TYPE DATE" UPON CONSOLE.

        ACCEPT DATE FROM CONSOLE.

        MOVE DATE TO PR-DATE.

Another use of these statements would be the case of a program which produced a number of different printed reports upon request from the operators. The statements used in this case might be as shown:

NEXT. DISPLAY "ANY MORE REPORTS REQD?" UPON CONSOLE.

        ACCEPT RESULT FROM CONSOLE.

        IF RESULT EQUALS "NO" GO TO PROG-END.

        DISPLAY "WHICH REPORT NUMBER?" UPON CONSOLE.

        ACCEPT RESULT FROM CONSOLE.

        GO TO PRINT-REPORTS.

The printing (with replies) on the operator's console from a run of this program might appear like this:

                    ANY MORE REPORTS REQD?

                    AWAITING REPLY

                    YES

                    WHICH REPORT NUMBER?

                    AWAITING REPLY

                    2

                    ANY MORE REPORTS REQD?

                    AWAITING REPLY

                    YES

                    WHICH REPORT NUMBER?

                    AWAITING REPLY

                    3

                    ANY MORE REPORTS REQD?

                    AWAITING REPLY

                    NO

The message AWAITING REPLY is automatically inserted by the compiler so that the computer operator is aware that a reply is required.

Exercises

1. Write the statement to tell the operator that program 2 has ended.
2. Write the statement to tell the operator the contents of MESSAGE.
3. Write the statement to input an operator reply into the field ANSWER.
4. Write the statements to ask the operator for a date, the reply being input to a field called IN-DATE.
5. Write the statements to ask the operator for the number of reports to be printed. Each report is to be printed using the paragraphs PRINT THRU PRINT-END.

CHAPTER THIRTY-FOUR

FILE PROCESSING

In this chapter we will extend the knowledge so far gained about the use of external files (excluding print files). To do this some practical examples of coding will be presented and discussed. The first example to be examined is the card-validation program first presented in Chapter Twenty-five. The file handling for this program is very simple indeed requiring only that cards be input, tape output, and lines printed.

The first paragraph in this program prepares the three files for processing:

> BEGIN. OPEN INPUT CARD-IN.
> OPEN OUTPUT TAPOUT, PRINT.

The first statement in the main body of the program will input records from the card file:

> READ-CARD. READ CARD-IN AT END GO TO PROGRAM-END.

When the card has been validated it will be written, if accepted as valid, to the tape output file:

> WRITE VALID FROM CARD.

Note how, in this instance, the record written to the file is identical in format to the card read and the FROM option can therefore be used. The file handling in this program is quite straightforward—one file is read in, some processing is done, and another file is written out. However, in a large proportion of cases the file handling will be more complicated because the program requires two input files to be **matched**.

File Matching

File matching consists of reading two files (which are organized in the same order) in parallel and comparing them on their key fields (e.g. if they are organized in account number sequence then the account numbers of the two files are compared). When a record from each file is read in both with the same key field then the files are said to be **matched**. File matching will become much clearer by studying an example of the use to which it is put. Suppose that a master file containing one record for each customer of an organization is to be updated according to the details contained on an amendment file. Both files are organized in sequence of the customer account numbers. The amendment file may contain one or more amendment records for each master file record or it may contain no amendment record for a particular master file record. For example the master file could contain records for customers with the following account numbers:

$$1, 2, 3, 4, 5, 6, 7, 8, 9$$

while, on a particular occasion the master file is to be updated, the amendment file might contain amendment records for the following master file records:

$$3, 4, 6, 6, 7, 9$$

(Note that a particular customer's details may be amended by more than one amendment record.)

The program that updates the master file has to read every master file record and either copy it straight out to the updated master file or, if an amendment is required, amend the record and then write the record to the updated master file. The program must cater for more than one amendment per master file record and must also cater for an amendment record for which no master file record exists.

This will be achieved by matching the two files. At the start of a file-matching procedure the first record of each file is read into storage. The two records are compared and if equal the master file record is updated, the next amendment record read in and the records compared again; if the master file record is less than the amendment file record then the master file record is copied to the updated master file, a new master file record is read in and the comparison procedure is repeated; if the amendment file record has a key less than the master file record then an error has occurred and the appropriate action can be taken (in this case the amendment file record is said to be **unmatched**). Once the first two records have been input the matching procedure described above will continue, in its correct sequence, until the end of the files is reached. Note that special consideration must be given to the end-of-file conditions on the two files since these may not occur at the same time. The basic file-matching procedure is illustrated in the flowchart Fig. 40.

In practice it will be necessary to cater for the end-of-file conditions on the two files. *Once a file has reached the end-of-file condition no further attempt must be made to* READ *the file*. A number of methods exist for checking these conditions and one of the more popular ones is described below.

The field on which the file is sequenced, e.g. customer account number, is not allowed in normal circumstances to have the value ALL "9". When the end-of-file condition is reached on a particular file the key field within the file record area is set equal to ALL "9"; then if the other file contains further records they will all appear less than the finished file and will therefore be processed correctly by the file-matching logic. The only other requirements are that, before each file is read, a check must be made to see if the end-of-file condition has occurred and, if it has, the READ statement for the file can be by-passed; when the key fields for both files are equal to ALL "9" then

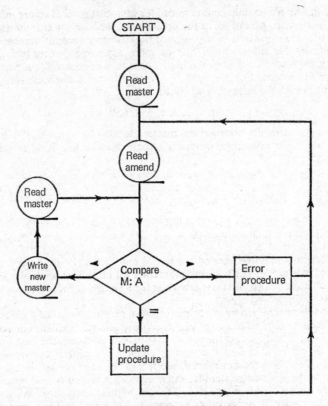

Fig. 40. Basic file matching logic

both files have been completely read and the program can be terminated. This is illustrated in the flowchart Fig. 41.

This full file-matching procedure is shown in the coding below. Assume that the three files required are MASTER-IN, MASTER-OUT, and AMENDS; the key fields for comparison are M-CUSTNO (in MASTER-IN) and A-CUSTNO (in AMENDS). Note that if the end-of-file condition is generated on the initial READ for MASTER-IN, then no records exist on the file and the program is immediately terminated.

PROCEDURE DIVISION.

    OPEN INPUT MASTER–IN, AMENDS.

    OPEN OUTPUT MASTER–OUT.

    READ MASTER–IN AT END GO TO CLOSE–FILES.

READ–AMENDS.

    IF A–CUSTNO EQUALS ALL "9" GO TO COMPARE.

    READ AMENDS AT END MOVE ALL "9" TO A–CUSTNO.

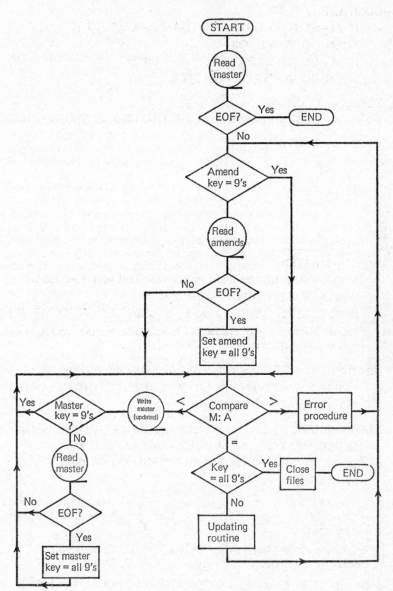

Fig. 41. Complete file matching logic

COMPARE.
    IF M – CUSTNO GREATER THAN A – CUSTNO
    THEN GO TO ERROR.
    IF M – CUSTNO LESS THAN A – CUSTNO
    THEN GO TO WRITE – MASTER.

EQUAL – RECORDS.
    IF M – CUSTNO EQUAL ALL "9" THEN GO TO CLOSE – FILES.

UPDATE – ROUTINE   .
                      .
                      .
                      .
                      .
                      .
                      .

    GO TO READ – AMENDS.
WRITE – MASTER.
    MOVE MASTER – IN – AREA TO MASTER – OUT – AREA.
    WRITE MASTER – OUT – AREA.
    IF M – CUSTNO EQUALS ALL "9" THEN GO TO COMPARE.
    READ MASTER – IN AT END MOVE ALL "9" TO M – CUSTNO.
    GO TO COMPARE.

ERROR.
    DISPLAY A – CUSTNO, "OUT OF SEQUENCE" UPON CONSOLE.
    GO TO READ – AMENDS.

CLOSE – FILES.
    CLOSE MASTER – IN, MASTER – OUT, AMENDS.
    DISPLAY "PROGRAM ENDED" UPON CONSOLE.
    STOP RUN.

In order to verify that this coding will correctly update a file the reader
may like to follow the coding through for a number of records. The following
could be used:

    records on MASTER-IN (M-CUSTNO)   10, 11, 12, 13, 15, 17 "EOF"
    records on AMENDS (A-CUSTNO)   10, 12, 12, 15, 16, 17 "EOF"

Note that in the paragraph COMPARE it is not necessary to specifically
check if M-CUSTNO is equal to A-CUSTNO since if the statements on the
previous two lines are false then these two values must be equal. When they
are equal it is only necessary to check one value for ALL "9" (paragraph
EQUAL-RECORDS) to see if both files have reached the end-of-file (EOF)
condition.

Exercises

Given the following file definitions:

```
FD  MAIN-IN,
        RECORDING MODE F, LABEL RECORDS STANDARD,
        BLOCK CONTAINS 4, DATA RECORD IS IN-AREA.
    01  IN-AREA.
        02  FILLER PICTURE X(6).
        02  M-KEY PICTURE X(4).
        02  FILLER PICTURE X(40).
FD  MAIN-OUT,
        RECORDING MODE F, LABEL RECORDS STANDARD,
        BLOCK CONTAINS 4, DATA RECORD IS OUT-AREA.
    01  OUT-AREA.
        02  FILLER PICTURE X(50).
FD  TRANSACTIONS,
        RECORDING MODE F, LABEL RECORDS STANDARD,
        BLOCK CONTAINS 2, DATA RECORD IS TRANS.
    01  TRANS.
        02  FILLER PICTURE X(6).
        02  T-KEY PICTURE X(4).
        02  FILLER PICTURE X(40).
```

Write the Procedure Division coding to match the files MAIN-IN and TRANS (sequenced on the fields M-KEY and T-KEY respectively). When the records are matched the record from TRANS should be used to replace that from MAIN-IN; each record on MAIN-IN that does not have a TRANS record should be written to the output file; if a record on TRANS does not match one on MAIN-IN then a message should be sent to the computer operator and the program terminated. When end-of-file is reached on MAIN-IN the program is to be terminated; when end-of-file is reached on TRANS an error has occurred (EOF on MAIN-IN should always occur first) and the program should be terminated.

CHAPTER THIRTY-FIVE

PROCESSING PRINT FILES

The printing of reports is an important facet of computer programming since it is only by the production of printed matter that programs can communicate with human beings. Because the majority of printed reports will be read by non-technical personnel a number of features are provided within the COBOL language to improve the readability of such reports. These facilities—editing, line, and page skipping—have already been described in detail. However, the purpose of this chapter is to expand the knowledge of these features in terms of their use in commercial programs.

We will look, therefore, at some of the requirements of computer programs which produce reports on plain (or standard) stationery and those which produce reports on pre-printed stationery.

Printing on Plain Stationery

Reports which are output on to **plain stationery** are usually confined to
those which have no circulation outside the computer department or cer-
tainly which have no circulation outside the company running the computer.
For instance a program concerned with payroll might produce an analysis of
wage costs for each department within a works; this report would be cir-
culated only among the management of the company and would not therefore
require specially prepared stationery.

As already mentioned each page of standard stationery can accommodate
64 lines of printing although a gap of a few lines is normally left at the bottom
of each page. The number of characters that can be printed across one line
depends on the particular computer in use although it is unlikely to be less
than the, popular, size of 132 characters.

The statements required to output a line to a printer device have already
been described in detail (Chapter Thirty-two) and do not need to be expanded
here. However, when dealing with standard stationery it is obviously necessary
for the program to produce any heading information at the top of each page.
The normal way of achieving consistent heading information is to print each
line of text by PERFORMing a print-output paragraph. This paragraph will
output a line to the printer and add 1 (or 2 depending on the line spacing used)
to a line-count, once this line-count equals a specified value (selected as the
maximum number of lines required per page) then the routine to advance the
paper to the next page and print the headings can be performed. Note that
this heading routine must reset the line-count to its initial value in order that
the next page will be correctly spaced. In its simplest form these two routines
(line print and heading print) could look like this:

```
PRINT-LINE.   WRITE  PRINT-DETAIL  AFTER  ADVANCING  1
    LINES.
    ADD 1 TO LINE-COUNT.
    IF LINE-COUNT = 58 PERFORM HEADINGS.
HEADINGS.     WRITE  PRINT-DETAIL  FROM  HEAD-1  AFTER
    ADVANCING SKIP LINES.
    WRITE PRINT-DETAIL FROM HEAD-2 AFTER ADVANCING
    2 LINES.
    MOVE ZERO TO LINE-COUNT.
```

There are a number of drawbacks to this basic routine: (*a*) each detail line
can only be printed on the line immediately following the previous line; (*b*)
the first detail line will immediately follow the second heading line; (*c*) the
WRITE verb is used three times (for reasons beyond the scope of this book
this can be inefficient). A more versatile method is shown below. In this routine
the number of lines to be spaced prior to printing a line is selected before the
routine PRINT-LINE is performed (the value required as described in
Chapter Thirty-two is placed in SPACING). It is possible therefore to split
up groups of lines on a single page, for example, when sub-totalling is
required. The checking for end-of-page routine is done before each line is
printed; in this way the first detail line on a page can be separated from the last
heading by the desired spacing.

General view of the ICL System/4 computer system installed at London Airport to control cargo handling. *Reproduced by courtesy of International Computers Ltd.*

ICL Magnetic Tape units with the tape transport vertical—note the loops of tape in the reservoir. *Reproduced by courtesy of International Computers Limited.*

IBM Operators Console type device (note similarity to IBM Golf Ball typewriter). *Reproduced by courtesy of International Business Machines (UK) Limited.*

A magnetic disc pack in its plastic storage container. *Reproduced by courtesy of International Business Machines (UK) Limited.*

Computer Operator loading a disc pack onto one spindle of a multi-spindle ICL disc unit. Each 'drawer' holds one disc pack. *Reproduced by courtesy of International Computers Limited.*

Disc pack mounted on ICL disc unit with the head assembly withdrawn and the lid raised (disc will not revolve until lid is shut). *Reproduced by courtesy of International Computers Limited.*

General view of a Honeywell 200 computer system installed at West Riding County Council. *Reproduced by courtesy of Honeywell Limited.*

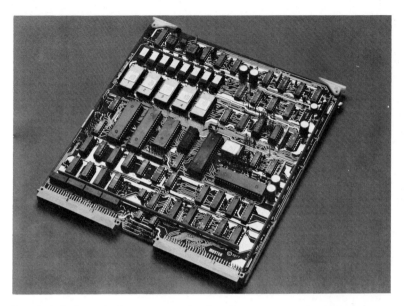

A typical single card microprocessor showing the many supporting chips required. *Reproduced by courtesy of Mostek.*

A Mostek development system featuring Z80-based microprocessor, visual display unit, printer and disc units. *Reproduced by courtesy of Mostek.*

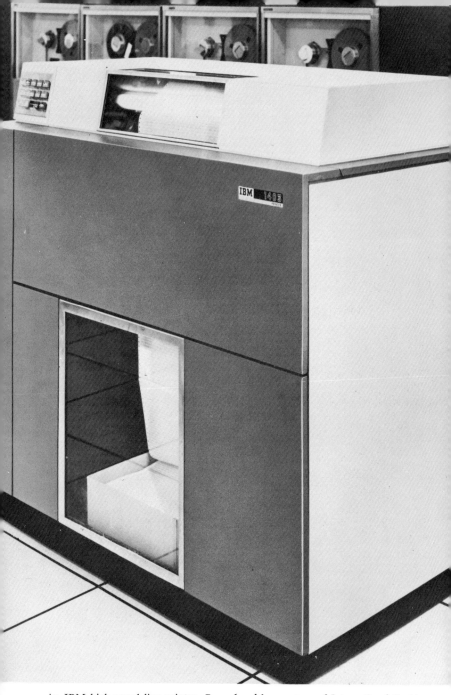

An IBM high speed line printer. *Reproduced by courtesy of International Business Machines (UK) Limited.*

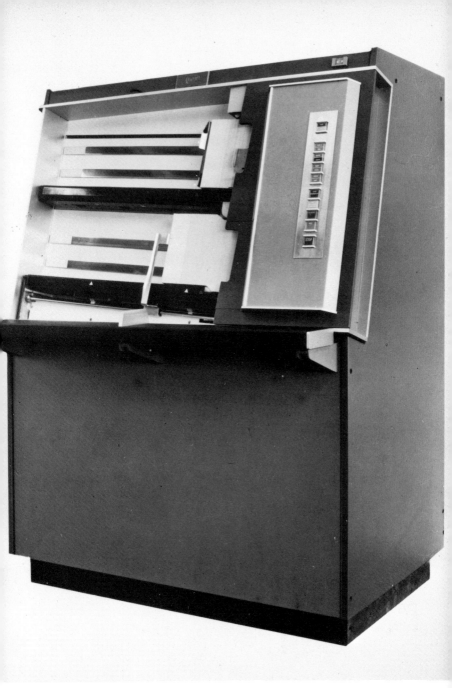

An ICL card reader with horizontal hoppers. The lower tray is the input hopper and the upper tray the output hopper. The read station is behind the panel containing the buttons. *Reproduced by courtesy of International Computers Limited.*

A general view of the GPO System/4 computer system. *Reproduced by courtesy of International Computers Limited.*

PRINT-LINE. IF SPACING EQUALS SPACE THEN ADD 1 TO LINE-COUNT.

IF SPACING EQUALS ZERO THEN ADD 2 TO LINE-COUNT.

IF SPACING EQUALS "-" THEN ADD 3 TO LINE-COUNT.

IF LINE-COUNT GREATER THAN 60 THEN PERFORM HEADINGS.

MOVE DETAIL-LINE TO PRINT-LINE; PERFORM PRINT.

HEADINGS. MOVE "1" TO SPACING; MOVE HEAD1 TO PRINT-LINE.

PERFORM PRINT.

MOVE "-" TO SPACING. MOVE 6 TO LINE-COUNT.

PRINT. WRITE PRINT-LINE AFTER ADVANCING SPACING LINES.

Note in this coding how the number added to LINE-COUNT is dependent on the spacing required by each line; note also that the line-count is tested to see if it is greater than 60 since it may never actually equal 60 (depending on the sequence in which the various line spacings are requested). As with the previous example if the value of LINE-COUNT does not satisfy the tested condition the heading routine will not be performed and control will be returned to the statement following the PERFORM when the paragraph PRINT-LINE has been executed. When the heading routine, in the example above, is performed the line spacing requested by the program (as specified in the field SPACING) is overwritten so that the first detail line on a page is always 3 spaces after the heading. In this example, the line-count is reset to 6 in the heading routine since this is the number of lines that have been used on the page at this point. The same result could be achieved by testing the line-count field in PRINT-LINE to see if it was greater than 54.

Printing on Pre-printed Stationery

Pre-printed stationery is that which has been overprinted, prior to use, with standard wording or some form of pattern. Pre-printed stationery is used for such things as invoices, statements, gas bills, promotional letters, and so on. In this case it is not necessary for the programmer to produce heading information (since this will already be on the stationery); however, he must ensure that his program prints within the format of the pre-printing. When pre-printed stationery is to be used the program specification must include a detailed layout of the positioning required for the printing. It is no use supplying a sample of the pre-printed stationery since this will not show the programmer accurately the relative positioning of the various boxes on each sheet (he could of course use an accurate ruler to measure the character and line spacing but this is considered undesirable). Instead the program specification should include a printer layout sheet marked with the required printing positions. Figure 42 illustrates the use of a printer layout sheet for a pay-slip. The left-hand column indicates the channels in use and as can be seen the first line to be printed is represented by channel 1 (head of page).

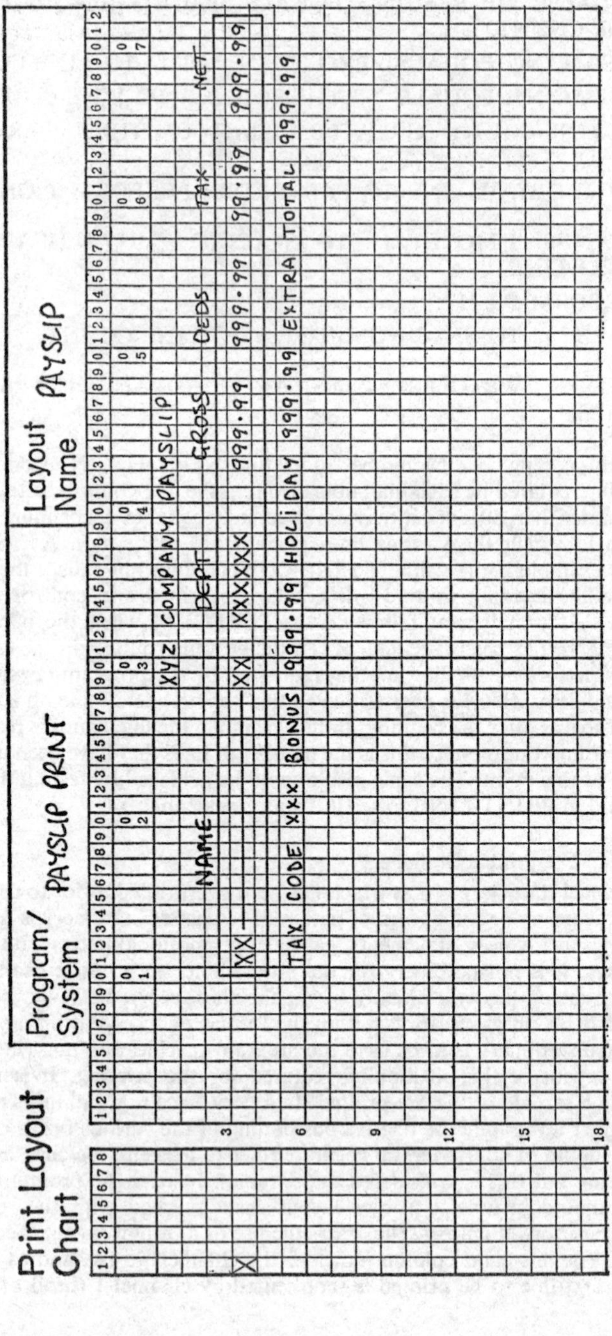

Fig. 42. Part of a Print Layout Sheet used to design a pay-slip

Given this program to code the programmer would transcribe the printer layout to a print-line definition in his program. The definitions for the sample pay-slip shown could appear thus:

```
Ø1  DETAIL-1.
    Ø2  FILLER              PICTURE X(1Ø).
    Ø2  EMPLOYEE-NAME       PICTURE X(2Ø).
    Ø2  FILLER              PICTURE XX.
    Ø2  DEPARTMENT          PICTURE X(6).
    Ø2  FILLER              PICTURE XXXX.
    Ø2  GROSS-WAGE          PICTURE ZZ9.99.
    Ø2  FILLER              PICTURE XX.
    Ø2  DEDUCTIONS          PICTURE ZZ9.99.
    Ø2  FILLER              PICTURE XX.
    Ø2  TAX                 PICTURE Z9.99.
    Ø2  FILLER              PICTURE XX.
    Ø2  NET-PAY             PICTURE ZZ9.99.

Ø1  DETAIL-2
    Ø2  FILLER              PICTURE X(19).
    Ø2  TAX-CODE            PICTURE XXX.
    Ø2  FILLER              PICTURE X(7).
    Ø2  BONUS-AMOUNT        PICTURE ZZ9.99.
    Ø2  FILLER              PICTURE X(9).
    Ø2  HOLIDAY-PAY         PICTURE ZZ9.99.
    Ø2  FILLER              PICTURE X(13).
    Ø2  TOTAL-EXTRAS        PICTURE ZZ9.99.
```

Having produced the necessary detail line record descriptions the use of pre-printed stationery requires no other special coding except that the line spacing is specific for each line (i.e. no heading routine checking is done) and that a **line-up routine** is included in the program.

Stationery Line-up

Each printing output device has a number of adjustments that can be made to the positioning of the stationery relative to the print-line. For example, the position of the first line on a page (i.e. the position of channel 1) can be moved relative to the actual top of the page and the paper can be moved from left to right (thus altering the size of the margins). The positioning of text on standard stationery is not critical; however pre-printed stationery must be lined up accurately before the program commences producing its data output. Each program that uses pre-printed stationery must therefore include a line-up routine before any data is printed. This line-up routine will print a dummy document (filled with, say, asterisks) and then ask the computer operator if the line-up is satisfactory. This procedure will be repeated until the operator responds that the stationery is ready; printing proper can then commence. A line-up routine suitable for the stationery shown in Fig. 42 is given below:

```
MOVE "1" TO SKIP.
MOVE ALL "*" TO EMPLOYEE-NAME, TAX-CODE.
MOVE 999.99 TO NET-PAY, TOTAL EXTRAS.
```

LINE-UP. MOVE DETAIL-1 TO PRINT-LINE.
      WRITE PRINT-LINE AFTER ADVANCING SKIP LINES.
      MOVE DETAIL-2 TO PRINT-LINE.
      WRITE PRINT-LINE AFTER ADVANCING 2 LINES.
      DISPLAY "LINE-UP OK?" UPON CONSOLE.
      ACCEPT ANSWER FROM CONSOLE.
         IF ANSWER NOT EQUAL "YES" GO TO LINE-UP.

Once the computer operator is satisfied that he has adjusted the stationery to
the correct positioning he will reply YES to the program's question and
printing of pay-slips will commence.

Exercises

There are no exercises for this chapter. Instead, you should now attempt Revision
Questions, Set 3, on page 212.

Revision
Questions, Set 3, on page 212.

CHAPTER THIRTY-SIX

QUALIFICATION

We have already encountered the case of a program containing two files
whose records have identical layouts. In order to distinguish the individual
fields between records we have given the names a unique suffix or prefix. For
example, we might have the following two sets of data names from a master
and a transaction file respectively:

          M-NAME   T-NAME
          M-AMOUNT   T-AMOUNT
          M-STATUS   T-STATUS

It is possible, however, to give identical names to elementary items within
record descriptions in the same program:

        Ø1 MASTER.
          Ø2 NAME   PICTURE X(2Ø).
          Ø2 AMOUNT PICTURE 9(6).
          Ø2 STATUS   PICTURE X.
        Ø1 TRANS.
          Ø2 NAME   PICTURE X(2Ø).
          Ø2 AMOUNT PICTURE 9(6).
          Ø2 STATUS   PICTURE X.

We cannot now refer to one of these elementary items just by its own name
since to do so would be ambiguous. Instead we will **qualify** each elementary
item name with the name of the record to which it belongs:

    MOVE NAME OF MASTER TO NAME OF TRANS.

The expression OF MASTER is said to be the **qualifier** for the elementary
item name. The keyword OF may be replaced with IN as desired:

    ADD AMOUNT IN MASTER TO AMOUNT IN TRANS.

Any number of record descriptions may contain identical elementary item names, however, the record names must be unique. *Duplicate elementary item names, when used, must be qualified with their respective record-description names.*

CORRESPONDING Option

When two record descriptions contain a number of identical elementary items shorthand versions of three COBOL statements are provided to enable these fields to be manipulated easily. Consider for example these two record descriptions:

```
        IN-REC.
        Ø2 AMOUNT-1  PICTURE 9(5).
        Ø2 AMOUNT-2  PICTURE 9(5).
        Ø2 AMOUNT-3  PICTURE 9(5).
        Ø2 STATUS    PICTURE XXX.
        Ø2 NAME      PICTURE X(2Ø).
        Ø2 ADDRESS   PICTURE X(6Ø).
    Ø1 OUT-REC.
        Ø2 AMOUNT-1  PICTURE 9(5).
        Ø2 AMOUNT-2  PICTURE 9(5).
        Ø2 AMOUNT-3  PICTURE 9(5).
        Ø2 STATUS    PICTURE XXX.
        Ø2 NEW-DATA PICTURE XX.
        Ø2 NAME      PICTURE X(2Ø).
        Ø2 ADDRESS   PICTURE X(6Ø).
```

Suppose we wish to transfer the values of the fields in IN-REC to the like-named fields in OUT-REC. We cannot simply say MOVE IN-REC TO OUT-REC because OUT-REC has an additional field NEW-DATA which would upset a group move. Rather than write out the six individual MOVE statements we can use the MOVE statement with the CORRESPONDING option:

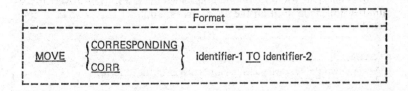

When this option is specified each elementary item within identifier-1 is moved to the elementary item with the identical name in identifier-2. Any elementary item in identifier-1 that does not have a corresponding name in identifier-2 is ignored.

For the example above we can move the six elementary items in IN-REC to their corresponding positions in OUT-REC by using the statement:

MOVE CORRESPONDING IN-REC TO OUT-REC.

The other two statements with the CORRESPONDING option are ADD and SUBTRACT.

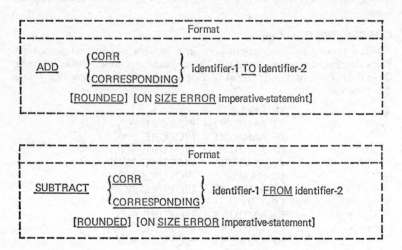

The statement

ADD CORRESPONDING IN-REC TO OUT-REC.

would be equivalent to the three statements:

ADD AMOUNT-1 OF IN-REC TO AMOUNT-1 OF OUT-REC.
ADD AMOUNT-2 OF IN-REC TO AMOUNT-2 OF OUT-REC.
ADD AMOUNT-3 OF IN-REC TO AMOUNT-3 OF OUT-REC.

Note that only **elementary numeric items** are corresponded when ADD or SUBTRACT is used with the CORRESPONDING option.

If the ON SIZE ERROR option is specified the test for the size-error condition is not made until all the additions (or subtractions) have been completed.

Exercises

1. Write down the following elementary items in qualified form:

```
Ø1 INREC.
    Ø2 AREA    PIC 999.
    Ø2 RADIUS  PIC 999.
    Ø2 DIAM    PIC 999.
```

2. Write down the qualified elementary items for the following:

```
Ø2 UPDATE.
    Ø2 AREA    PIC 999.
    Ø2 RADIUS  PIC 999.
    Ø2 DIAM    PIC 999.
```

3. Write the single statement to transfer the contents of the elementary item of INREC above to those of UPDATE (without using a group move).
4. What is the statement in question 3 the equivalent of when no CORRESPONDING option is used?
5. Write the single statement to subtract the values of the elementary items of UPDATE from those of INREC.

CHAPTER THIRTY-SEVEN

TABLE HANDLING

A **table** (or array) is a collection of ordered items having positional significance relative to each other and could be likened to a set of pigeon holes with each data element in the table corresponding to a single hole. We have already seen (Chapter Twenty-two) the use of the OCCURS clause to define tables. To recap consider this definition of a table:

Ø2 TABLE OCCURS 4 TIMES PICTURE 999.

This table could be pictorially represented thus:

TABLE	TABLE	TABLE	TABLE
(1)	(2)	(3)	(4)

We have already seen that individual table elements can be referenced by the use of literal **subscripts**:

ADD TABLE (1) TO TOTAL.

Subscripts may also be specified as variables, at execution time the variable is evaluated and its current value taken as the element number required. For example, suppose the element SUBS had the current value of 1 then the following statement is equivalent to that shown above:

ADD TABLE (SUBS) TO TOTAL.

Suppose we wish to add the value of each element in this table to the item TOTAL, we could write the following four statements:

ADD TABLE (1) TO TOTAL.
ADD TABLE (2) TO TOTAL.
ADD TABLE (3) TO TOTAL.
ADD TABLE (4) TO TOTAL.

To do this for a much larger table would be extremely tedious, to say the least, so instead we could use a variable subscript:

```
                MOVE 1 TO SUBS.

        LOOP. IF SUBS GREATER THAN 4 GO TO LOOP-END.
                ADD TABLE (SUBS) TO TOTAL.
                    ADD 1 TO SUBS.
                        GO TO LOOP.
        LOOP-END.       .
                        .
                        .
                        .
                        .
                        .
```

This coding can be improved upon by use of the PERFORM statement as shown:

```
                MOVE 1 TO SUBS.
                PERFORM LOOP 4 TIMES.

                    .
                    .
                    .
                    .
                    .

        LOOP. ADD TABLE (SUBS) TO TOTAL.
                ADD 1 TO SUBS.
```

This is a simple example of table handling and it is quite acceptable to use the type of coding shown. However, the programmer will often find a requirement for much more complicated table-handling features needing more coding to set up the initial conditions (in the case above MOVE 1 TO SUBS), the incrementing of the subscript (ADD 1 TO SUBS) and the termination of the loop. In the case above the paragraph will always be performed four times; however, instances may exist where the table handling is to be terminated if a specific condition arises.

PERFORM VARYING Option

An additional format of the PERFORM statement is provided for this more advanced table handling.

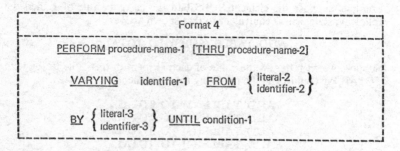

The sequence of events for this type of PERFORM statement is as shown below:

1. The value of identifier-1 is set equal to the current value of identifier-2, or the value of literal-2 (whichever is specified). This is called the starting or **initial value** of identifier-1.
2. Condition-1 is evaluated and if false the specified procedure(s) is executed (i.e. performed) once.
3. The value of identifier-1 is incremented by the value of identifier-3 (or literal-3) (the **increment**) and condition-1 is re-evaluated. (N.B. the value of identifier-1 may be decremented if identifier-3 (or literal-3) is specified as negative.)
4. Steps 2 and 3 are repeated, as necessary, until condition-1 is true. When this condition is true control is passed to the statement following the PERFORM. Note that if the condition is true prior to the first time the PERFORM is executed then the procedure(s) specified is not executed.

This sequence of operations is further illustrated by the following flowchart:

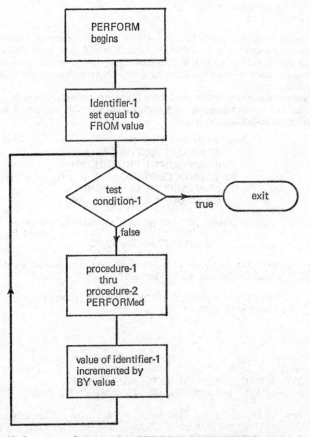

Fig. 43. Sequence of events when PERFORM VARYING is executed

Examples: The table coding shown above can be rewritten using this additional PERFORM feature:

> PERFORM LOOP VARYING SUBS FROM 1 BY 1
> UNTIL SUBS EQUALS 5.
> .
> .
> .

LOOP.   ADD TABLE (SUBS) TO TOTAL.

The first thing to note in this example is that the single PERFORM statement includes all coding necessary to set up the loop and execute it the required number of times. The sequence of operation for this coding is as follows:

1. SUBS is set to an initial value of 1 (FROM 1).
2. The condition (SUBS EQUALS 5) is evaluated.
3. The condition is false so LOOP is PERFORMed.
4. SUBS is incremented by 1 (BY 1).
5. Step 2 is repeated.

This sequence continues until SUBS is equal to 5 at which time control will be passed to the statement following the PERFORM. LOOP will have been performed for SUBS having the values 1, 2, 3, 4. The reader may like to verify this sequence of operations by following the flowchart above with the values used in the PERFORM statement example.

This type of statement will be used more frequently on larger tables or groups of tables where its use can save the programmer a considerable amount of work.

Consider the following two tables:

> Ø2 TAB1 OCCURS 2Ø.
> Ø3 NAME1 PICTURE X(1Ø).
> Ø3 AMOUNT-1 PICTURE 999.
> Ø2 TAB2 OCCURS 2Ø.
> Ø3 NAME2 PICTURE X(1Ø).
> Ø3 AMOUNT-2 PICTURE 999.

To transfer the entire contents of TAB1 to TAB2 we could simply write:

> MOVE TAB1 TO TAB2

However, suppose that we wished to transfer only, say, the odd-numbered elements of TAB1 to TAB2; the following could be used:

> PERFORM TABMOVE VARYING SUB FROM 1 BY 2
> UNTIL SUB EQUALS 21
> .
> .
> .
> .

TABMOVE. MOVE NAME1 (SUB) TO NAME2 (SUB).
MOVE AMOUNT-1 (SUB) TO AMOUNT-2 (SUB).

Notice how we are now using SUB itself as a subscript for the table elements. The first time TABMOVE is executed SUB will have the value 1 and the effect will be to execute the following:

MOVE NAME1 (1) TO NAME2 (1).
MOVE AMOUNT-1 (1) TO AMOUNT-2 (1).

The second time SUB will have the value 3 and so on. Suppose we wish to produce the total of all the amounts in TAB1; however not all the elements are necessarily used—the first occurrence of spaces in NAME1 will indicate the end of processing. We could use the following:

PERFORM TABADD VARYING SUB FROM 1 BY 1
UNTIL SUB = 21 OR NAME1 (SUB) = SPACES.

Note that we must still test for a terminal value of SUB (in addition to examining NAME1 for spaces) to cater for the case when all the elements of TAB1 contain a definite (non spaces) value.

Instead of checking for spaces we might have a field containing a count of the number of elements in TAB1 which are to be totalled:

PERFORM TABADD VARYING SUB FROM 1 BY 1
UNTIL SUB IS GREATER THAN TAB-COUNT.

In each of these cases the performed paragraph could be:

TABADD. ADD AMOUNT-1 (SUB) TO TOTAL.

The PERFORM VARYING statement is very useful for printing out details of table contents as the following example will demonstrate. Consider a variable length input record, read from tape, containing details of transactions carried out by a particular customer and having the following format:

```
Ø1 TRANS.
    Ø2 ACCNO PICTURE 9999.
    Ø2 NAME PICTURE X(2Ø).
    Ø2 NO-TRANS PICTURE 99.
    Ø2 TRANS-DETAILS OCCURS 2Ø.
        Ø3 DATE PICTURE X(6).
        Ø3 CODE PICTURE XXX.
        Ø3 AMOUNT PICTURE 9(4)V99.
```

These details are to be printed out with each transaction occupying one line, the first line is also to contain the customer account number and name. The number of the first transaction to be printed has already been computed and stored in the field START.

The print-line is defined thus:
```
Ø1 PRINT-LINE.
    Ø2 FILLER PICTURE XXX.
    Ø2 P-ACCNO PICTURE 9999.
    Ø2 FILLER PICTURE XX.
    Ø2 P-NAME PICTURE X(2Ø).
    Ø2 FILLER PICTURE XXXX.
    Ø2 P-DATE PICTURE XXBXXBXX.
    Ø2 FILLER PICTURE XX.
    Ø2 P-CODE PICTURE XXX.
    Ø2 FILLER PICTURE XX.
    Ø2 P-AMOUNT PICTURE £(4)9.99.
```

The following Procedure Division entries could be used to accomplish this printing:

```
        PERFORM PRINT THRU PRINT-END VARYING SUB FROM
        START BY 1 UNTIL SUB GREATER THAN NO-TRANS.
            .
            .
            .

PRINT.  MOVE SPACES TO PRINT-LINE.
        MOVE DATE (SUB) TO P-DATE.
        MOVE CODE (SUB) TO P-CODE.
        MOVE AMOUNT (SUB) TO P-AMOUNT.
PRINT-A.  IF SUB NOT = START GO TO PRINT-END.
        MOVE ACCNO TO P-ACCNO.
        MOVE NAME TO P-NAME.
PRINT-END.  WRITE PRINT-LINE AFTER ADVANCING 1 LINES.
        ADD 1 TO LINE-COUNT.
        IF LINE-COUNT EQUALS 60 PERFORM HEADINGS.
```

Exercises

1. Write the statement to add the element of TABLE referenced by SUB into the field TOTAL.
2. Write the statements to add the 6 elements of TABLE into TOTAL without using VARYING.
3. Repeat question 2 using the VARYING option.
4. Write the statement to execute PARA-X varying the subscript INC from an initial value of START to an end value of FINISH incrementing by STEP each time.
5. Write the statements to add the elements of the two tables shown together:

```
        02 TABA OCCURS 20 PICTURE 999.
        02 TABB OCCURS 20 PICTURE 999.
```

CHAPTER THIRTY-EIGHT

TABLE SEARCHING

Frequently it will be necessary to **search** a table for a particular entry rather than manipulate every entry in the table as in the previous chapter. For example, in a payroll program, we might have a table showing, for each department, the applicable bonus rate. As each employee's net pay is calculated the program must search the table until the department number corresponding with the employee is found and so extract the relevant bonus rate.

In other words, each department number in the table will be compared with the employee's department number and when a **match** is achieved the bonus rate will be extracted for calculation.

The table of bonus rates could have been defined like this in the Working-Storage Section:

```
Ø1 DEPARTMENTAL-BONUS.
   Ø2 DEPT1.
      Ø3 DEPTNO-1 PICTURE 9(5) VALUE 12345.
      Ø3 RATE-1 PICTURE V99 VALUE .1Ø.
   Ø2 DEPT2.
      Ø3 DEPTNO-2 PICTURE 9(5) VALUE 24567.
      Ø3 RATE-2 PICTURE V99 VALUE .Ø5.
   Ø2 DEPT3.
             .
             .
             .
             .
             .
             .
   Ø2 DEPT2Ø.
      Ø3 DEPTNO-2Ø PICTURE 9(5) VALUE 72341.
      Ø3 RATE-2Ø PICTURE V99 VALUE .1Ø.
Ø1 FILLER REDEFINES DEPARTMENTAL-BONUS.
   Ø2 RATES OCCURS 2Ø.
      Ø3 DEPT PICTURE 9(5).
      Ø3 RATE PICTURE V99.
```

In order to find the rate required for each employee the following coding could be used in the Procedure Division. (Note—the employee's department number is in the field EMP-DEPT.)

```
MOVE ZEROES TO EMP-RATE.
PERFORM DEPT-SEARCH VARYING SUB FROM 1 BY 1
UNTIL SUB = 21 OR EMP-RATE NOT = ZEROES.
IF EMP-RATE = ZEROES GO TO DEPT-NOT-FOUND.
```

COMPUTE BONUS = NET PAY * EMP-RATE.
```
             .
             .
             .
             .
```

```
DEPT-SEARCH.
   IF EMP-DEPT = DEPT (SUB) MOVE RATE(SUB)
   TO EMP-RATE.
```

In this coding the employee's department number (in EMP-DEPT) is compared with each entry in the table in turn. (In the paragraph DEPT-SEARCH.) If a match is found then the corresponding rate is moved to EMP-RATE. The paragraph DEPT-SEARCH is performed either 20 times (UNTIL SUB = 21) to examine every entry or until EMP-RATE is not equal to zeroes (in other words until a match is made). When either of these conditions is true the PERFORM is terminated. If then EMP-RATE is still equal to zeroes the table has been completely searched and no match has occurred this may indicate an error (depending upon the program) and control can be transferred to a special routine (i.e. DEPT-NOT-FOUND above).

Keys in Serial Order

If the key used to identify each table entry (i.e. department number above) is part of a consecutive series then it is not necessary to store the key with each table entry. For example if a program has to maintain a total of the number and value of sales in each of 12 sales areas numbered 1 to 12 the following table could be used:

```
Ø2 SALES-TOTALS OCCURS 12.
   Ø3 SALES-NO PICTURE 9(4).
   Ø3 SALES-VALUE PICTURE 9(6).
```

The first entry in the table represents the totals for sales-area1, the second for sales-area2, and so on. If each sales record is processed separately the following coding could be used to identify the correct table element in which to add the figures (assume the sales-area number is in the field called AREA-CODE):

```
ADD 1 TO SALES-NO (AREA-CODE).
ADD AMOUNT TO SALES-VALUE (AREA-CODE).
```

The field AREA-CODE is used as a variable subscript to access the elements required in the table. If the key items do not start at one, but are consecutive, this method can still be used. Suppose that a table has been set up to hold the names of the 20 branches of a company (each branch element called BRANCH-NAME) numbered from 21 to 40 the following coding could access the correct name (the number of the branch is held in BRANCH-NO):

```
SUBTRACT 2Ø FROM BRANCH-NO GIVING SUB.
MOVE BRANCH-NAME (SUB) TO PRINT-NAME.
```

Table Optimization

The programmer can often restructure tables or table-keys to obtain a more efficient means of accessing the table. If a direct method of accessing a table element (as shown above) can be utilized it will be much more efficient than searching a table, with keys included, for the relevant entry. For example, suppose the sales value for an area is to be added into an area group total. The sales area numbers are consecutive but the area groups do not contain consecutively numbered areas. For example, the areas contained in each group might be allocated thus:

Area No.	Group to which area belongs
1	11
2	12
3	11
4	12
5	13
6	11
7	12
8	13
9	11
1Ø	13

In order to accomplish the requirement to add a value into the correct area total two tables will be set up. The first will contain the information shown in the right-hand column above, i.e. for each area there will be a table entry showing the group to which it belongs. (Note that since the area numbers are consecutive the area number itself will not be held in the table.) Thus, using the area number as a search key, the required group number can be selected; this group number can then be used as a subscript (suitably adjusted) to access the group area table. The two tables would be defined thus:

```
Ø1 GROUP-CODE-TABLE.
   Ø2 FILLER  PICTURE  X(2Ø)
        VALUE "11121112131112131113".
Ø1 GROUP-TABLE-CODES REDEFINES GROUP-CODE-TABLE.
   Ø2 GROUP-NO OCCURS 1Ø PICTURE 99.
Ø1 GROUP-TOTALS.
   Ø2 GROUP-AMOUNT OCCURS 1Ø PICTURE 9(5).
```

Note how the group numbers are defined in GROUP-CODE-TABLE; when this is redefined each pair of "characters" becomes a two-digit numeric item (GROUP-NO) which will become a subscript for the table GROUP-TOTALS. The Procedure Division coding to add the area amount to its group total could be as shown:

```
SUBTRACT 1Ø FROM GROUP-NO (AREA-CODE) GIVING SUB.
ADD AREA-AMOUNT TO GROUP-AMOUNT (SUB).
```

In the first statement the group number for a particular area is extracted from the first table by using the area number (in the field AREA-CODE) as a subscript; it is decremented by 10, in the same statement, to make it usable directly as a subscript for the second table containing the group area totals. For example, if AREA-CODE was 4 then the group code extracted from the first table (GROUP-NO (4)) would be 12; the value of SUB would therefore be set to 2 and this would cause the second statement above to add the amount for area 4 into group 12 total (area 4 is as shown a member of group 12).

Exercises

1. Write the Working-Storage entry to define a table consisting of ten items each containing the 2 elements DATE (6 digits) and NAME (20 characters).
2. If the NAME entries in 1 above relate to salesmen coded 1 to 20 write the statement to access the date for the salesman whose number is held in MAN-NO (placing it in DATE-CHECK).
3. Repeat question 2 for salesmen numbers in the range 36–55.
4. Write the statements to search the table TAB:

```
Ø2 TAB OCCURS 2Ø.
   Ø3 CODE PICTURE 999.
   Ø3 STATUS PICTURE X.
```

to extract STATUS for the key held in SEARCH-CODE and place it in

COMPARE-STATUS, if present. Assume that TAB has been initialized with the required information at the start of the program. (Note that the possible values of CODE are neither sequential or consecutive.)
5. Rewrite the answer to question 4 assuming that CODE can only be in the range 1–20 and that TAB has been organized such that the entries for CODE = 20 are in element1, CODE = 19 in element2, and so on.

CHAPTER THIRTY-NINE

SUBROUTINES

A routine which is to be used a number of times within one program need only be coded once. Each part of the program requiring that coding can then use a PERFORM statement (see Chapter Sixteen) to cause one or more named paragraphs to be executed. A particular piece of coding may be required in a number of different programs within an installation. For example, each program within a sales accounting suite of programs may need to verify the check digit on inputted account numbers; rather than code this routine into each program (thereby introducing additional work) it can be written once (as a separate routine) and then called up by each program requiring it. This system can also be used to access routines written in other programming languages (e.g. a mathematical process coded in FORTRAN) and special routines supplied by the computer manufacturers (it is normal, for instance, for computer manufacturers to supply a routine for calculating PAYE tax).

Parameters

When a routine is written that is to be used by a number of programs, in the manner described above, it is obviously not possible for the programmer who is writing this routine to know the data names that will be used in the calling program (i.e. the program that will use the specially written routine). Additionally, the special routine (usually called a **sub-program**) will be compiled on its own and cannot therefore refer directly to names in the calling program. It is quite clear, however, that the sub-program must be given access to the data values in the calling program.

When a sub-program is initiated (see the CALL statement below) the names of the data areas, required by the sub-program (called **parameters**), are passed to the sub-program; usually group area names (i.e. 01 level entries) will be given—in this way an entire record can be passed rather than having to list every field within the record. Within the sub-program the data areas to be received from the calling program(s) are defined in the Linkage Section. Such entries are defined in exactly the same manner as those in a Working-Storage Section except that the VALUE clause cannot be used and the area can only be referenced if the sub-program has been called (i.e. a sub-program cannot run by itself). An area in the Linkage Section of a sub-program must have the same layout as the area to which it corresponds in the calling program although it does not necessarily have to have the same elementary item names.

The ENTRY Statement

A sub-program is identified by an ENTRY statement in the procedure division:

```
┌─────────────────────────────────────────────────────────────────┐
│                           Format                                │
├─────────────────────────────────────────────────────────────────┤
│                                                                 │
│     ENTRY literal [USING identifier-1 [identifier-2] ... ]      │
│                                                                 │
└─────────────────────────────────────────────────────────────────┘
```

The literal (which must begin with an alphabetic character) identifies the name by which the sub-program is to be called. The identifiers following the USING option refer to the data areas that are to be passed to the sub-program and each entry must correspond to a level 01 or level 77 entry in the Linkage Section of the sub-program.

For example, suppose we wish to code a sub-program to validate an account number. The validation checks to be made are (*a*) number is numeric; (*b*) if first digit of number is 1 then remaining 5 digits must be less than 60000; (*c*) if first digit is 2 then remaining 5 digits must be greater than 60000 —any other range of numbers is invalid; if the number is not valid a status flag will be set equal to 1, otherwise it will be set equal to zero. The following coding could be used:

```
DATA DIVISION.
LINKAGE SECTION.
77 FLAG          PICTURE 9.
Ø1 ACCOUNT-NO.
   Ø2 FIRST      PICTURE 9.
   Ø2 REST       PICTURE 9(5).
PROCEDURE DIVISION.
         ENTRY "SUBPROG" USING FLAG, ACCOUNT-NO.
         MOVE Ø TO FLAG.
         IF ACCOUNT-NO NOT NUMERIC THEN GO TO ERROR.
         IF FIRST EQUALS 1 THEN GO TO PARA-A.
         IF FIRST EQUALS 2 THEN GO TO PARA-B.
           GO TO ERROR.
PARA-A. IF REST LESS THAN 60000 GO TO LEAVE.
           GO TO ERROR.
PARA-B. IF REST GREATER THAN 6ØØØØ GO TO LEAVE.
ERROR. MOVE 1 TO FLAG.
LEAVE. GOBACK.
```

The statement GOBACK causes control to be returned to the **calling program** at the statement immediately following the **calling statement**. On some computer systems (e.g. ICL 1900 Series) this statement is replaced by

EXIT PROGRAM.

The effect of these two statements is identical as described above.

The CALL Statement

To invoke a sub-program the CALL statement is specified.

```
┌──────────────────────────────────────────────────────────────┐
│                           Format                             │
├──────────────────────────────────────────────────────────────┤
│                                                              │
│   CALL literal [USING identifier-1 [identifier-2] ... ]      │
│                                                              │
└──────────────────────────────────────────────────────────────┘
```

The sub-program to be called is specified by literal—this name will correspond with the name given in the sub-program's ENTRY statement. The data areas which are to be passed to the sub-program are specified following the USING option. (Note that in the rare case of a sub-program requiring no parameters the USING option is omitted.)

For example if the programmer wished to use the sub-program coded in the example above he could write:

CALL "SUBPROG" USING CUSTOMER-NO, STATUS-FLAG.

Notice that the names of the parameters do not correspond with the names used in the sub-program; however, the definitions of corresponding areas must be identical (i.e. CUSTOMER-NO must have the same definition as ACCOUNT-NO above and STATUS-FLAG the same as FLAG above) and the list of parameters must be in the same order in the CALL statement and the ENTRY statement (i.e. in the example above CUSTOMER-NO will always represent the area whose data is passed to ACCOUNT-NO and STATUS-FLAG the area whose data is passed to FLAG.

The most common use of sub-programs will be to gain access to facilities not available in COBOL. In these cases the programmer will not necessarily understand the working of the sub-program but he will have a user description which will describe the function of the sub-program and the number and format of the parameters which must be passed. Knowing this the programmer can issue the appropriate CALL statement. The operating system is responsible for ensuring that the called sub-programs are made available for execution as they are required.

The actual workings of CALL statements, etc., is beyond the scope of this book; however, the interested reader is referred to *Modular Programming* (London: Butterworths, 1971) by the same author.

Exercises

1. Write the statement to identify the sub-program CHECKNO which requires the two parameters NUMBER and INDICATOR.
2. Write the Linkage Section entries to define the fields required for question 1 above (6 numeric and 1 alphabetic characters respectively).
3. Write the statement to call the sub-program mentioned above, passing the parameters ITEM-NO and FLAG.
4. Write the Linkage Section and Procedure Division entries for a sub-program MEAN to calculate the average of three input values, the result to be placed in the last parameter of the following list:

```
77  INPUT-1  PICTURE  9(5).
77  INPUT-2  PICTURE  9(5).
77  INPUT-3  PICTURE  9(5).
77  RESULT  PICTURE  9(6).
```

5. Write a statement to invoke the routine written in question 4.

CHAPTER FORTY

PROGRAM TERMINATION

We have already covered the statements required to terminate programs. These being, for sub-programs:

> GOBACK
> or EXIT PROGRAM

and for programs:

> STOP RUN

The third statement above can be issued in a sub-program in which case the calling program is terminated and that particular job is finished. The other two statements however may only be issued in sub-programs. There is more to ending a program than just issuing a STOP RUN statement. When looking at the use of data files we have already noticed that each file in use must be closed before the program is ended. In most commercial programs there will be additional end-of-program processing required immediately before the file closing routine to produce the control totals.

Program Controls

As a safeguard against either manual error or computer failure it is usual, in commercial systems, to build in **batch** and **control** totalling procedures. Batch controls refer to raw input data such as punched cards or punched paper tape. When a set or batch of data has been prepared by the data-preparation department certain information relating to the data is totalled. Batch totals may consist of a simple count such as the number of cards actually punched or may be a more complicated procedure involving the total of the values contained in a given field in each card (for example, in a payroll application the batch total may refer to the total hours worked).

The **batch total** is punched into a special card which is placed at the end of the deck to be input to the program. When this card is read by the program the total it contains is compared with the computed figure and if any discrepancy occurs the program will be abandoned (when several batches of cards are input to a program then only the unbalanced batch need be rejected). The coding to perform a simple batch check might look like this:

CARD-READ. READ CARD-IN AT END GO TO CONTROLS.

    IF CARD-TYPE NOT = "BATCH"
    THEN ADD 1 TO CARD-COUNT GO TO PROCESS.

IF CARD-COUNT = BATCH-COUNT GO TO CONTROLS.
DISPLAY "BATCH TOTAL UNBALANCED JOB ABANDONED"
UPON CONSOLE.
GO TO END-OF-JOB.

The main purpose of batch totals is to ensure that all the input data has been supplied to the computer. It is not unknown for packs of data cards to be dropped and some lost!

Control totals are similar to batch totals except that they occur on the ends of tape or disc files. For example, a sales analysis file might contain, in its control total record, the total sales value and total outstanding debt for all the customers on the file. These figures can again be used to verify that all the data on the file has been correctly read (it is possible for a tape to be damaged in some way such that the data it contains will be corrupted). These totals are of more use for auditing purposes since their provision makes the investigation of cash totals a simple operation. When a file containing control totals is updated it is obviously important that the **control record** (i.e. the record containing the control totals) is also updated. This will normally be accomplished by adding the relevant fields from each record into an accumulator at the time the record is written to the updated file. When the control record for the input file has been verified the new control record for the updated file can be written to that file. The values in new control records will normally be summarized following the last page total on the program's printed report.

The steps mentioned above can be summarized as a check-list representing the normally required end-of-program functions:

> verify batch totals
> print grand totals for reports
> verify input control totals
> print output control totals
> write output control totals
> close all files
> issue STOP RUN statement.

Exercises

1. Why are program controls necessary?
2. Where would batch totals occur?
3. Where would control totals occur?

CHAPTER FORTY-ONE

DOCUMENTATION AIDS

Although a COBOL program is relatively easy to read because of its use of pseudo-English language syntax elements and the choice by the programmer of meaningful names, it is still useful to be able to annotate a COBOL program with comments. This facility is provided with the NOTE statement:

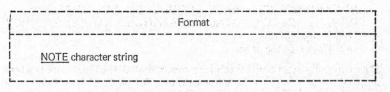

> NOTE character string

If a NOTE statement appears within a paragraph then the **comment** is terminated by the first period:

> CALC-A. MULTIPLY RATE BY HOURS GIVING GROSS.
>   NOTE NEXT LINE DETERMINES SEX.
>   IF FLAG-3 EQUALS 7 GO TO RATE-M.

When the NOTE statement is the first to appear after a paragraph name then the entire paragraph is treated as a **comment**:

> COMMENT. NOTE THE INSTRUCTION.
>   MOVE A TO B.
>   IS NEVER EXECUTED.
> NEXT.

As the note states the MOVE statement above is not executed because it is treated as a comment. The NOTE statement can be used to explain complicated coding, to explain special techniques used, and generally to improve the readability of your program. The NOTE statement can only appear in the Procedure Division.

The COPY Statement

When a suite of programs is being developed it is almost certain that certain of the files used will be required in more than one of the programs in the suite. When this is the case the record descriptions for the common files will appear in several programs and there is the possibility that mistakes will occur when transcribing the descriptions from one program to another. To avoid the possibility of such errors and to cut down the amount of work involved in writing the same description several times, the programmer may COPY the description into his program.

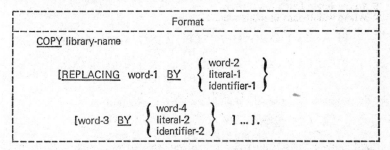

> Format
>
> COPY library-name
>
>   [REPLACING word-1 BY $\left\{ \begin{array}{l} \text{word-2} \\ \text{literal-1} \\ \text{identifier-1} \end{array} \right\}$
>
>   [word-3 BY $\left\{ \begin{array}{l} \text{word-4} \\ \text{literal-2} \\ \text{identifier-2} \end{array} \right\}$] ...].

The description to be copied must reside on a library available to the COBOL compiler. Knowing the name of the information the programmer can copy it into his program. The operating system in use will provide the facility to store record descriptions on a backing store in a file known as a **library**. The method by which record descriptions are written to the library is dependent upon the particular computer system in use and is therefore beyond the scope of this book. However, suffice to say that when a record description has been prepared it is a simple task to request the operating system to transfer it to the library from where it can be COPYed into any program as described.

For example, supposing the record description for a payroll file is held on the library under the name PAYFIL, the programmer can retrieve this into his program as shown:

> DATA RECORD IS PAY.
> Ø1 PAY COPY PAYFIL.

Suppose the description held on the library under the name PAYFIL was:

> Ø1 PAYROLL.
>   Ø2 NAME PICTURE X(2Ø).
>   Ø2 GROSS PICTURE 9(5).
>   Ø2 TAX   PICTURE 9(3).

The copy statement above (Ø1 PAY COPY PAYFIL) would result in the following definition appearing in the program:

> Ø1 PAY.
>   Ø2 NAME PICTURE X(2Ø).
>   Ø2 GROSS PICTURE 9(5).
>   Ø2 TAX   PICTURE 9(3).

Note that the Ø1 entry of the library description is replaced by the Ø1 entry in the program.

The REPLACING option may be used when general file layouts on the library are to be specialized for the program. Suppose the following description was on the library under the name GEN:

> Ø1 FILLER.
>   Ø2 A PICTURE X(2Ø).
>   Ø2 B PICTURE X(1Ø).

The following two copy statements:

> Ø1 AREA-1 COPY GEN REPLACING A BY NAME-1
>   B BY CODE-1.
> Ø1 AREA-2 COPY GEN REPLACING A BY NAME-2
>   B BY CODE-2.

would produce the following definitions in your program:

> Ø1 AREA-1.
>   Ø2 NAME-1 PICTURE X(2Ø).
>   Ø2 CODE-1 PICTURE X(1Ø).
> Ø1 AREA-2.
>   Ø2 NAME-2 PICTURE X(2Ø).
>   Ø2 CODE-2 PICTURE X(1Ø).

The REPLACING option will not be used very frequently although its availability should be borne in mind when working on a suite of programs containing several similar files.

Mixed Programming Languages

Some COBOL compilers provide the facility to write statements in other languages within the COBOL program. Obviously these statements are not actioned by the COBOL compiler. The ENTER statement is used to initiate the required compiler.

```
┌─────────────────────────────────────────────────────────────┐
│                          Format                              │
├─────────────────────────────────────────────────────────────┤
│   ENTER language-name                                        │
└─────────────────────────────────────────────────────────────┘
```

For example, to change to FORTRAN for part of a COBOL program the following could be used:

> ENTER FORTRAN.
> .
> .
> .   (FORTRAN statements)
> .
> .
> ENTER COBOL.

Notice how an ENTER COBOL statement is required to return to the COBOL compiler following the FORTRAN routine. This statement is very rarely used and is presented only for completeness.

Exercises

1. Write the statement to insert the comment "Read routine" in a paragraph.
2. Write the statement to retrieve FILEX from the library and use it for the definition of the record entry INPUT-AREA.
3. Rewrite the statement in question 2 such that any occurrence of the word XY in FILEX will be changed to NAME.
4. Write the statement to retrieve DATE from the library for use as the record entry WORK.
5. Write the statement to inform the compiler that the following statements are written in FORTRAN.

CHAPTER FORTY-TWO

THE SORT FEATURE

Sorting

The COBOL compiler contains facilities to enable the programmer to request that an input data file be **sorted** into order on one or more key fields. The programmer will specify an input file to be sorted, a sort file, and an output file for the sorted data. The input and output files are defined in the usual way with an FD (see Chapter Eighteen). The **sort file** must be defined in the File Section with an SD entry which is almost identical to the FD previously discussed:

```
┌────────────────────────── Format ──────────────────────────┐
│                                                             │
│  SD sort-file-name                                          │
│                                                             │
│      [RECORDING MODE IS mode]                               │
│                                                             │
│              ┌ RECORD IS   ┐                                │
│      [DATA   │             │ data-name-1 [data-name-2] ... ]│
│              └ RECORDS ARE ┘                                │
│                                                             │
│      [RECORD CONTAINS [integer-1 TO] integer-2 CHARACTERS]  │
│                                                             │
│              ┌ RECORD IS   ┐  ┌ STANDARD ┐                  │
│      [LABEL  │             │  │          │ ]                │
│              └ RECORDS ARE ┘  └ OMITTED  ┘                  │
│                                                             │
└─────────────────────────────────────────────────────────────┘
```

The description of the sort file, and of the data it contains, must be identical to the description given to the input and output file associated during the program with the sort.

The rules applying to the SD entry are as those relating to the FD as given in Chapters Eighteen and Nineteen. The following extract from a Data Division File Section illustrates the specification of the three files involved in a sorting procedure:

```
        FD SORTIN,
            RECORDING MODE IS F,
            LABEL RECORDS ARE STANDARD,
            DATA RECORD IS IN-AREA.
        Ø1 INAREA.
            Ø2 FILLER PICTURE X(76).
        FD SORTOUT,
            RECORDING MODE IS F,
            LABEL RECORDS ARE STANDARD,
            DATA RECORD IS OUT-AREA.
```

```
Ø1  OUT-AREA.
    Ø2  ACCOUNT-NO  PICTURE 9(6).
    Ø2  NAME         PICTURE X(2Ø).
    Ø2  DETAILS      OCCURS 1Ø PICTURE 9(5).

SD  SORTER,
    RECORDING MODE IS F,
    LABEL RECORDS ARE OMITTED,
    DATA RECORD IS SORT-AREA.

Ø1  SORT-AREA.
    Ø2  KEY-FIELD  PICTURE 9(6).
    Ø2  FILLER     PICTURE X(7Ø).
```

The input file records will not be individually accessed (since the data is not required until it has been sorted) and the record description does not need to be detailed. The output file will be used later in the program (after it has been sorted) as input data and needs, therefore, to have its record-description entry given in full. The sort file will only need the **key-fields** (i.e. those fields on which the file is to be sequenced) to be given; in this case the file is to be sorted on the single field ACCOUNT-NO, and as can be seen, the description of KEY-FIELD in the sort file record description corresponds with this item.

The sort operation is requested in the Procedure Division by means of the SORT statement:

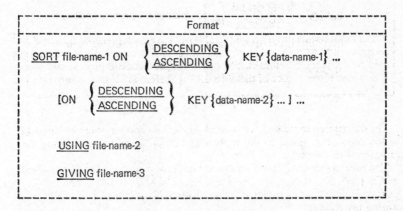

A sort operation can be requested on one or more fields although in the examples which follow only one key-field will be used for simplicity. The sort can be either ASCENDING in which case the lowest value key-field will be first (on the output file) with the remainder in ascending order or DESCEND-ING in which case the highest value key-field will be first with the remainder in descending order.

The USING option specifies the input file (i.e. the file which is to be sorted) and the GIVING option specifies the output file (i.e. the file on to which the sorted input file is to be written).

Using the files described above the following SORT statement could be used:

        SORT SORTER ON ASCENDING KEY KEY-FIELD
                    USING SORTIN, GIVING SORTOUT.

This will result in the input file SORTIN being read in and transferred to the sort file SORTER, sorted and the output (in the desired sequence) being written to SORTOUT.

Using the SORT Statement

The sequence of events within a program to use the SORT statement could be as follows (note that a sort file is not opened):

```
PROCEDURE DIVISION.
    OPEN INPUT SORTIN.
    OPEN OUTPUT SORTOUT.
    SORT SORTER ON ASCENDING KEY KEY-FIELD
        USING SORTIN, GIVING SORTOUT.
    CLOSE SORTIN, SORTOUT.
    OPEN INPUT SORTOUT.
    .
    .
    .                    (process sorted file)
    .
    .
    .
    CLOSE SORTOUT.
    STOP RUN.
```

The input to this program (SORTIN) will have been prepared by a previous program, it is read into this program sorted into ascending sequence on the field ACCOUNT-NO and is then processed, in this order, by the program.

Suppose the sequence of the file SORTIN before input to this program was as follows:

Record No.	Value of Account-No.
1	278491
2	279499
3	279498
4	456840
5	364128
6	667842
7	372231
8	123456

Then the sequence after the SORT statement had been executed would be:

Record No.	Value of Account-No.
1	123456
2	278491
3	279498
4	279499
5	364128
6	372231
7	456840
8	667842

When a file is sorted on two key-fields the second field appears in order within the order of the first key. This is illustrated by the record sequence below (sorted file).

Record No.	Key field 1	Key field 2
1	10	6
2	10	7
3	10	9
4	11	3
5	11	4
6	12	2

Exercises

1. Write the SD entry for a sort file (called SFKG) containing no labels, fixed-length records of 60 characters, the key field being the first 5 (numeric) characters of the record.
2. Write the statement to sort the above-mentioned file into descending sequence, using FILE-A as input and FILE-B as output.
3. Write the Procedure Division entries to sort file SORTX into ascending order on key field CODE, the input data is on IND and the output is to be on OUTD.

CHAPTER FORTY-THREE

PROGRAM TESTING FACILITIES

One of the most difficult aspects of computer programming is that involved in testing a program once it has been written. When a program is to be tested it will be compiled and then run with specially prepared **test data** (designed to check every path within the program). The output of the **test run** will be compared with the anticipated output to verify that the program is working correctly. Frequently, of course, the two things differ and the programmer must discover which part of his program has been incorrectly coded in order that corrections can be made and the program retested. To aid the programmer during testing the COBOL language provides three statements which can be incorporated during the testing stage to provide additional information about the running of the program.

The TRACE Statement

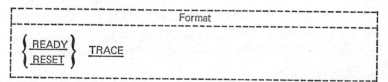

```
┌─────────────────────────────────────────────────────────┐
│                        Format                            │
├─────────────────────────────────────────────────────────┤
│  ⎰ READY ⎱   TRACE                                       │
│  ⎱ RESET ⎰                                               │
└─────────────────────────────────────────────────────────┘
```

Following the occurrence of a READY TRACE statement each paragraph name in the program which is executed causes a print-out to be made of that paragraph name.

The printing of paragraph names in the sequence they are executed will help the programmer trace the path or paths followed by data through his program. The RESET TRACE statement terminates the operation of a READY TRACE statement. Any number of combinations of READY and RESET TRACE statements may occur within a program under test enabling a number of small parts of a program to be examined for their logic paths.

The EXHIBIT Statement

The EXHIBIT statement is used to print-out the value of a data item or literal.

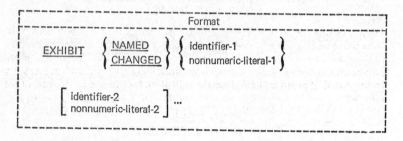

The EXHIBIT NAMED expression is effectively equivalent to a DISPLAY statement since it will cause the current value of identifier or literal to be printed out. (Note—depending upon the computer system in use the EXHIBIT statement may cause values to be printed either on the operator's console or on a printer device.) For example, if during testing the programmer wished to know the value of the item COUNT every time the paragraph LOOP was executed he could use the following:

LOOP.
EXHIBIT NAMED "LOOP NO", COUNT.

In this case he has preceded the value of COUNT with a literal to identify the meaning of the value to him (this would, of course, be particularly useful when a number of data items were to be listed during one test).

The EXHIBIT CHANGED statement causes the value of identifier to be listed only if it is different from the last time the EXHIBIT was executed. The values are all considered to have changed when the EXHIBIT CHANGED is first executed in a program.

This statement:

EXHIBIT CHANGED TOTAL.

will cause the value of TOTAL to be printed for each execution of the EXHIBIT statement for which the value of TOTAL has changed.

The DEBUG Statement

This statement is used to enable the programmer to insert additional coding into a paragraph, for use during testing, without altering the paragraph itself.

The DEBUG card specifies the name of the paragraph to contain the additional coding and is followed by that coding.

```
┌─────────────────────────────────────────────────────────────────┐
│                             Format                               │
├─────────────────────────────────────────────────────────────────┤
│                                                                  │
│   DEBUG    location                                              │
│                                                                  │
└─────────────────────────────────────────────────────────────────┘
```

For example, suppose we are testing a program containing the following coding:

> LOOP. PERFORM CALL SUB TIMES.
> MOVE 1 TO INDIC.

During testing the programmer may wish to insert a specific value into SUB before the PERFORM in paragraph LOOP is executed. He cannot insert a MOVE statement immediately before the paragraph LOOP since this paragraph is the subject of GO TO statement (and the MOVE would not therefore be executed). Instead he can place the following statements at the end of his program.

> DEBUG LOOP.
> MOVE 1 TO SUB.

The statement(s) following the DEBUG card is then executed as if it had been written between LOOP and PERFORM, i.e. it is equivalent to rewriting the paragraph LOOP thus:

> LOOP. MOVE 1 TO SUB.
> PERFORM CALC SUB TIMES.
> MOVE 1 TO INDIC.

Exercises

1. Write the statement to begin tracing the path taken by a program through its various paragraphs.
2. Write the statement to terminate the tracing implemented in question 1.
3. Write the statement to print out the value of the data item FIELD during testing.
4. Write the statement to print out the value of COUNT each time it has changed during a test run.
5. Write the statements to cause the statement ADD 1 TO COUNT to be executed immediately the paragraph BONUS-LOOP is entered.

CHAPTER FORTY-FOUR

EJECT AND SKIP

When a program is compiled the COBOL language compiler will produce what is known as a **source listing** of the input data. In other words it will print out all the **source statements** comprising the program. The programmer has available four **compiler directing commands** to improve the readability of this listing.

The EJECT Statement

The EJECT statement which, as shown in the format above, can appear anywhere in Area B instructs the compiler to advance the source listing to the top of the next page.

Where used the EJECT statement must be the only statement on a line and that line must contain no punctuation.

The SKIP Statement

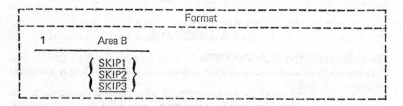

The SKIP statement which again may appear anywhere in Area B, instructs the compiler to advance the source listing 1, 2, or 3 lines (i.e. requests single, double, or triple spacing). The SKIP statement must be the only statement on a line and that line must contain no punctuation.

It is most important to remember that the EJECT and SKIP statements refer only to the listing of the COBOL program produced by the compiler (i.e. the source listing). They do not affect, in any way, the printed output of the program when that program is executed.

Exercises

1. Write the statement to advance the source listing two lines.
2. Write the statement to advance the source listing to the top of the next page.

CHAPTER FORTY-FIVE

THE IDENTIFICATION DIVISION

The Identification Division is used to identify the program and optionally certain information about its writing. This division must appear first in the source program and is identified by the following entry which must appear in Area A:

IDENTIFICATION DIVISION.

The possible entries that can be given in the Identification Division are shown below, and, when used, must appear in the sequence shown:

$$\left\{\begin{array}{l}\underline{\text{IDENTIFICATION DIVISION.}}\\ \underline{\text{ID DIVISION.}}\end{array}\right\}$$

<u>PROGRAM-ID</u>.   program-name.

[<u>AUTHOR</u>.   [comment-entry] . . .]

[<u>INSTALLATION</u>.   [comment-entry] . . .]

[<u>DATE-WRITTEN</u>.   [comment-entry] . . .]

[<u>DATE-COMPILED</u>.   [comment-entry] . . .]

[<u>SECURITY</u>.   [comment-entry] . . .]

[<u>REMARKS</u>.   [comment-entry] . . .]

Required Entries

Only the **PROGRAM-ID** paragraph is mandatory in this division:

```
Format

PROGRAM-ID.    program-name.
```

This entry gives the **name** to the program by which it will be **known** to the operating system. The format which this name may take is usually specific to the particular computer system in use. For example, when using IBM System 360 each program's name can be from 1 to 8 characters in length and must begin with an alphabetic character.

PROGRAM-ID. SAMPLE.

A program containing the above entry would be known to the operating system as SAMPLE and once compiled could be executed by giving this name in the appropriate command to the operating system. For example, depending on the computer system in use, one of the following commands could be given to the operating system to execute the program:

EXEC SAMPLE

RUN SAMPLE

GO SAMPLE

START SAMPLE

Each program written, therefore, must contain an Identification Division with a PROGRAM-ID entry to give a name to the program. *Each program within an installation must have a unique name.*

Optional Entries

The other entries in the Identification Division are for documentation purposes only. Their normal use is described below:

AUTHOR. The programmer who has coded the program can insert his name into the source listing by using this paragraph.

INSTALLATION. The name of the company for whom the programmer is working can be inserted in this paragraph. This is, of course, particularly helpful when programs are made available to a number of computer users.

DATE-WRITTEN. Self-explanatory.

DATE-COMPILED. When this entry is given the compiler will replace any comment entry made with the date on which the program was compiled. This may of course be different on each source listing of the program and can be useful for identifying the latest version of a program.

SECURITY. If the use of a program is in any way to be restricted a comment to that effect can be given in this paragraph. Note, however, that the appearance of an entry here does not itself restrict the use of a program in any way.

REMARKS. The programmer may insert any additional information here that he wishes. It is common to find this paragraph used to give a brief description of the processing performed by the program.

A sample Identification Division is shown below:

IDENTIFICATION DIVISION.
    PROGRAM-ID. EXAMPLE.
    AUTHOR. J. MAYNARD
    INSTALLATION. W. H. ALLEN
    DATE-WRITTEN. 1972
    DATE-COMPILED. THIS COMMENT WILL BE REPLACED
                   BY THE ACTUAL DATE.
    SECURITY. FREELY AVAILABLE.
    REMARKS. THIS IS THE IDENTIFICATION DIVISION
              FOR A SAMPLE PROGRAM TO ILLUSTRATE
              COMPUTER PROGRAMMING MADE SIMPLE

Exercise

1. Write the Identification Division for a program written by yourself called MINE.

CHAPTER FORTY-SIX

THE ENVIRONMENT DIVISION—1

The features of the COBOL language covered thus far in this book represent those areas which are common to the major computer systems currently in use. Some manufacturers provide additional facilities, often peculiar to their own machines, which because of their specific nature are outside the scope of this book. A program written in COBOL using the specification given in this book so far will be acceptable to the popular commercial computers.

The remaining COBOL division (the Environment Division) which is described in the remainder of Part Two is used to describe the computer system on which the COBOL program is to be run. This description will vary not only from manufacturer to manufacturer but also from installation to installation. It is not possible therefore to provide sufficient information to enable the reader to fully code this division. However, the division is relatively small and is quite straightforward; an outline is given of the type of information required in this division and the reader, faced with the task of coding a program for a specific installation, will have no difficulty referring to the appropriate computer manual to discover the precise format of the entries required.

The Environment Division

The Environment Division, which must immediately follow the Identification Division, is identified by the following heading appearing in Area A:

ENVIRONMENT DIVISION.

The Environment Division describes the type of computer on which the program is to be run (in the Configuration Section) and the nature of the input/output and backing store devices to be used by the program (in the Input-Output Section—see Chapter Forty-seven).

The Configuration Section

```
┌─────────────────────────────────────────────────────────────┐
│                       General Format                         │
├─────────────────────────────────────────────────────────────┤
│                                                              │
│   CONFIGURATION SECTION.                                     │
│   SOURCE-COMPUTER. source-computer-entry                     │
│   OBJECT-COMPUTER. object-computer-entry                     │
│   [SPECIAL-NAMES. special-names-entry]                       │
│                                                              │
└─────────────────────────────────────────────────────────────┘
```

The Configuration Section describes the type of computer on which the program is to be compiled, the type of computer on which it is to be run, and permits the user to change certain compiler function names.

The source and object computers required are described in a manner such as shown:

SOURCE-COMPUTER. IBM-360-30
OBJECT-COMPUTER. IBM-360-50

Special Names

The full use of this paragraph would require a detailed knowledge of the specific computer system on which the program was to be run. However, two common features of this paragraph are as described below.

The use of the word CONSOLE in a DISPLAY or ACCEPT statement may be changed thus:

SPECIAL-NAMES.
CONSOLE IS OPERATORS-DESK.

Messages to and from the computer operator could now be coded thus:

DISPLAY MESSAGE UPON OPERATORS-DESK.
ACCEPT RESPONSE FROM OPERATORS-DESK.

The functions of the period (decimal point) and comma may be transposed in PICTURE character strings by coding the following in the special names paragraph:

DECIMAL POINT IS COMMA.

However, the use of this last-mentioned option is not recommended because of the potential confusion it may cause when another programmer looks at the program containing it.

Exercise

1. Write the Configuration Section entries for a program compiled on an IBM-360-40 and to be run on an IBM-360-30. Change the name of CONSOLE to DESK.

CHAPTER FORTY-SEVEN

THE ENVIRONMENT DIVISION—2

Input-Output Section

The Input-Output Section is used to identify the external storage media used by each file in the program, to assign each file to a particular input/output or backing store device (File Control paragraph) and optionally to specify special input/output techniques in use (in the I-O-Control paragraph). The general format of the INPUT-OUTPUT SECTION is as shown:

```
┌─────────────────────────────────────────────────────────┐
│                     General Format                      │
├─────────────────────────────────────────────────────────┤
│   [INPUT-OUTPUT SECTION.                                 │
│    FILE-CONTROL. {file-control-entry} ...               │
│   [I-O-CONTROL. input-output-control-entry]]            │
└─────────────────────────────────────────────────────────┘
```

The FILE-CONTROL Paragraph

The format of the FILE-CONTROL paragraph is shown below:

```
┌─────────────────────────────────────────────────────────┐
│                     General Format                      │
├─────────────────────────────────────────────────────────┤
│   FILE-CONTROL.                                         │
│       SELECT Clause                                     │
│       ASSIGN Clause                                     │
│       [RESERVE Clause]                                  │
└─────────────────────────────────────────────────────────┘
```

Each file used in the program must have a SELECT clause of the form

SELECT file name

which is followed immediately by an ASSIGN clause describing the type of device to be used by the file (e.g. tape, printer, card-reader) and the particular device of that type. (N.B. an installation may have, say, two printers and the appropriate one must be selected.)

The nature of these entries is obviously dependent upon the computer system in use but a typical entry would be:

SELECT PRINT-FILE ASSIGN TO SYS030-UR-1403-S.
SELECT TAPE-IN ASSIGN TO SYS020-UT-2401-S.

Once the programmer has decided the devices he wishes to use it is a very simple task to look up the appropriate device-type code to be used in the ASSIGN clause. The newcomer to programming should not worry about these names—their selection makes no difference to the coding of the Data and Procedure Division which form 99% of any program.

The RESERVE clause can be used to request the compiler not to reserve two buffer areas in core for a file. If this clause is not specified then two buffers will automatically be allocated. To specify a single buffer the following is specified following the ASSIGN clause for a file:

RESERVE NO ALTERNATE AREA.

The I-O-CONTROL Paragraph

The general format of the I-O-Control paragraph is as shown below:

```
General Format

I-O-CONTROL.

    [SAME AREA Clause] ...
```

This can be used when the programmer wishes to use the same input/output areas in storage for more than one file. This can only be done if, of course, the files so selected will not be in use at the same time. When two or more files are used in the program but are open at different times the use of the SAME-AREA clause will reduce the overall size of the program (by avoiding the setting up of two sets of areas only one of which will ever be in use at one time).

I-O-CONTROL.
SAME AREA FOR FILE-1, FILE-2.

The I-O-Control paragraph is optional.

No attempt need be made by the reader to learn the Environment Division entries contained in this chapter—suffice from him to know they are required. However, for completeness a sample Environment Division is shown below:

ENVIRONMENT DIVISION.
CONFIGURATION SECTION.
    SOURCE-COMPUTER. IBM-360-30.
    OBJECT-COMPUTER. IBM-360-40.
INPUT-OUTPUT SECTION.
FILE-CONTROL.
    SELECT TAPE-IN ASSIGN TO SYS020-UT-2400-S.
    SELECT TAPE-OUT ASSIGN TO SYS030-UT-2400-S,
        RESERVE NO ALTERNATE AREA.
    SELECT PRINTER ASSIGN TO SYS025-UR-1403-S.
    SELECT DATA-FILE ASSIGN TO SYS027-UT-2400-S.

I-O CONTROL.
SAME AREA FOR TAPE-IN, DATA-FILE.

Exercises

There is no exercise for this chapter, however; you should now attempt the final and fourth set of COBOL Revision Questions. Once these have been correctly answered you are well on your way to becoming a proficient COBOL programmer.

Revision Questions. Set 1

1. Name the four COBOL divisions.
2. What punctuation-marks may be used to separate clauses?
3. What characters may be used to form a COBOL word?
4. List the figurative constants.
5. Describe the type of each of the following literals:
   (a) 123.7   (b) "123"   (c) "J. SMITH"   (d) QUOTE   (e) "QUOTE"
6. Where on the COBOL coding form can a sequence number occur?
7. Write the single statement to calculate $A = (B + C)/D \times E$.
8. Write the statement to calculate the sum of SALES and STANDING placing the result in TARGET.
9. Rewrite the answer to question 8 such that control would be transferred to ERROR if a size error condition occurs.

   For the following questions use these definitions:

   ```
   77 NUM-1 PICTURE S999V99.
   77 NUM-2 PICTURE S999V99.
   77 SALES PICTURE 9999.
   77 VALUE PICTURE 9999V99.
   77 WORK PICTURE 9999V99.
   ```

10. If NUM-1 contained 126V36 and NUM-2 contained ØV63 what would be the result of the statement:

    ADD NUM-1 TO NUM-2 GIVING SALES.

11. What would be the result if the statement in question 10 were rewritten:

    ADD NUM-1 TO NUM-2 GIVING SALES ROUNDED.

12. If VALUE now contained Ø627V30 and SALES the value from question 10 what would be the content of VALUE after this statement:

    SUBTRACT SALES FROM VALUE.

13. Write the statements (without using COMPUTE) to calculate the average value of SALES and VALUE. (Placing the result in WORK.)
14. Write the statements to calculate the average, in minutes, of the two times TA and TB, in hours, placing the result in AVG.
15. Write the single statement to calculate the result of the equation

    $$R = Y^2 + Z (A \times (B + C)).$$

16. Write the statement to transfer control to the paragraph MAIN.
17. Write the statements to transfer control to P-A if SUB = 1, P-B if SUB = 2, and P-C if SUB = 3.
18. What would be the result of question 17 if SUB = 4?

19. Write the statements to change the paragraph:

LOOP. GO TO MAIN.

to transfer control to SUBSID.

20. Write the statements to execute the statement:

ADDUP 6 times.

21. Write the statements to execute the paragraphs TOTA, TOTB, and TOTC (which are in separate parts of your program).
22. Rewrite question 21 assuming the three paragraphs are consecutive.
23. Write the statements to execute the paragraphs MAIN and MAIN-EXIT as long as SUB is not equal to zero.
24. Write the paragraph LOOP (which is to be the subject of a PERFORM) which will add 1 to SUB if TOTAL equals zero or add 1 to SUB-X if TOTAL is not zero.
25. Write the statements to PERFORM the answer to question 24 if the value of INDIC is equal to the value of CODE.

Revision Questions. Set 2

1. Name the sections comprising the Data Division.
2. What is the level number for record descriptions?
3. What is the maximum level number that can be used within a structure?
4. What are the special level numbers and their uses?
5. Write the file description for the file MAIN-IN which has 200 character fixed-length records, blocked in fours and standard labels. The file records are to be read into an area called IN-DATA.
6. Name the classes to which the following data values belong:
   (a) 1234 (b) "1234" (c) "FRED SMITH" (d) Ø (e) ZERO.
7. Define a twelve-character alphabetic item at level four which will not be referenced by name.
8. Define the record description entry for the following record layout:

Card					
Location		Payments			
Name	Address	Amount	Amount	Amount
(20)	(40)	(5)	(5)	(5)

(characters)

Not to Scale

9. Write the statement to add the last field in question 8 to the field TOTAL.
10. Write the statements to add each of the fields COST below to the item TOT:

Ø3 COST OCCURS 2Ø PICTURE 9(4).

11. Rewrite the definition of COST in question 10 such that it can be referenced in the format shown or as twenty alphabetic items called STATUS.
12. Define a non-contiguous field PI with an initial value of 3.142.
13. Define five areas called CHECK (group name CHECK-ALL) each 5 numeric digits and all with an initial value of zero.
14. Define a field called ALPHA with the value "ABCDEF" such that each letter can be accessed as LETTER (subscript).
15. The table below shows a number of editing PICTURE's and the value to be moved to each one. Write down the resulting value of each edited item after the moves.

	Picture	Value
(a)	£99999	13
(b)	£9,999	12
(c)	£9,999	2764
(d)	+99	12
(e)	+9999	−7
(f)	£9,99.99	8V61
(g)	££,££9	12
(h)	££,££9	1234
(i)	££,££9	Ø
(j)	£££,£££,££9.99	1234567V89
(k)	ZZ9	Ø
(l)	ZZ9	Ø27
(m)	***.**	Ø
(n)	**9.99	V2Ø
(o)	ZZ,ZZZ,ZZ9	3647

16. How many non-significant zeroes are in the value ØØØØ4Ø2Ø3Ø7?
17. Write down the classes of data and the PICTURE string characters used to represent their occurrence.
18. Write the record description for the following layout:

Customer				
Name	Status	Transactions		
		Type	Size	Total of 6 occurences of TYPE/SIZE
(No. of characters) (10)	(2)	(1)	(6)	

Not to Scale

19. Write the definition for the following record area:

Rec									
Location		Finance							
Name	Account-no	Payments		Flags					
		This-month	Last-month	Credit	Delivery	Switch			
(No. of characters) (20)	(6)	(6)	(6)	(1)	(1)	(1)	(1)	(1)	(1)

Not to Scale

20. Write the file description for TAPE consisting of 100 character fixed-length records, blocked in fives with standard labels. Data records to be read into IN-AREA.

Revision Questions. Set 3

1. Write the statement to transfer control to NUMBER if the data item QUERY is composed only of the digits Ø–9.
2. Write the statements to transfer control to PARA if NUM is in the range 36Ø to 512, PARB if it is less than this range, and PARC if it is greater than this range.
3. Rewrite the data and procedure division statements below using condition names:

77 STATUS PICTURE 9.

IF STATUS EQUALS 1 GO TO YES-LOOP.
IF STATUS EQUALS 2 GO TO NO-LOOP.
IF STATUS EQUALS 3 GO TO DOUBT-LOOP.

where the three values of STATUS indicate good credit, bad credit, and doubtful credit respectively.

4. Write the statement to transfer control to YES if STATUS has a value of 6 and CODE has a value other than 7.
5. Write the statements to subtract 1 from SUB if CODE is positive or add 1 to SUB if CODE is negative or zero.
6. Write the statements to perform the following calculation:
   "If SEX is male (=m) and RATE is 3 or higher move 1 to SUB; for all other values of RATE move 2 to SUB. If SEX is not male move 3 to sub."
7. Write the statement to transfer the contents of FIELDA to Z-CODE.
8. Write the statement to count the number of spaces preceding the alpha characters in ALPHA-2.
9. Write the statement to change each zero in ALPHA-1 to an asterisk.
10. Write the statement to transfer the count obtained in question 8 to SUB.
11. Write the Procedure Division statements to transfer the contents of file INA to file OUTB. The respective data record areas being AREA-1 and AREA-2.
12. Write the statements to request the run number from the computer operators, showing the reply in RUN-NO.
13. Write the Data Division and Procedure Division entries required to read the card file defined below printing the contents of each card. Each page is to have 60 lines of printing with a heading line ("CARD PRINT"). When all the cards have been read print the number read.
   card file—called CARDS, each card to be printed as it is read.
   print file—called PRINT.

Choose your own layout for the printing and define any additional data items required with your own identifiers.

Revision Questions. Set 4

1. Write the statement to add all the elements of group item SALES to those with like names in TOTALS.
2. Write the Data Division entries to define two tables, each consisting of twenty entries, called AREAS and AREA-TOTS under the group name TOTALS. Each element is to be 5 numeric digits signed.
3. Write the statement to add the odd-numbered elements of AREAS (in question 2 above) to the even-numbered in AREA-TOTS (i.e. element 1 in AREAS added to element 2 in AREA-TOTS and so on).
4. Write the statements to add the elements of AREAS (in question 2 above) to the elements of AREA-TOTS starting from the element whose number is contained in STARTS and continuing until the element whose number is contained in ENDS.
5. Write the statement to invoke the sub-program MODULE passing the parameters CODE, STATUS, and NUM.
6. Write the Data Division and Procedure Division entries for the sub-program MODX which receives three parameters (each 6 numeric characters). The sub-program calculates the average of the first two parameters and places the result in the third parameter.
7. Write the Data Division and Procedure Division for the following program:
   Input Files—*Master file* containing sequential records, blocked in fours, with the layout shown below. Only one record may exist for each customer.

Master File layout:
  Customer number   6 numeric digits
  Customer code   1 numeric digit
  Customer details 33 alphabetic digits.

Transaction File containing sequential records, blocked in six's, with the layout shown below. Only one record may exist for any customer although each customer does not necessarily have a record on this file. No record will exist on this file for which a master file record does not exist.

Transaction File Layout:
  Customer number   6 numeric digits
  Type   1 alphabetic digit
      value 1 =   delete
      value 2 =   replace
  Customer details   33 alphabetic digits.

Output Files—Updated master file (format as for master file in).

Processing. Read and match the Master and Transaction files. When a match occurs examine the transaction type—if it is equal to 1 then delete the master file record, if it is equal to 2 then replace the master file customer details with those from the transaction file.

At the end of the program inform the operator of the number of master file records deleted.

8. A sample Procedure Division for the program problem presented in Chapter Twenty-five is given as the answer to this question. However, prior to studying this answer the reader may wish to attempt the coding for this problem. If so the following additional Working-Storage Section entries should be assumed in addition to the Data Division entries shown in Chapter Twenty-five. (Note—these additional entries are those shown to be required when the Procedure Division was coded.)

        77 FLAG PICTURE X.
        77 SUB PICTURE S99.
        77 LINE-COUNT PICTURE S99 VALUE 58.
        77 SKIP PICTURE X VALUE "1".

N.B. To verify the check-digit in CUST-ACCNO use the following CALL statement:

    CALL "CHKDIG" USING CUST-ACCNO, CHK-DIGIT, FLAG.
    If the check-digit is not correct FLAG will be set to SPACE.

PART THREE

FORTRAN PROGRAMMING LANGUAGE

HISTORY

FORTRAN had its beginnings in the mid-1950s when computing, as well as programming, was very much in its infancy. At this time the number of compilers in development was small and little or no co-operation between compiler writers was attempted. Similarity between compilers thus developed was as much coincidental as planned. It was not until the mid-1950s that any attempt was made to formally define an industry wide standard for the FORTRAN programming language. FORTRAN and the standards relating to it have developed continually since this time and indeed seem likely to continue doing so for the foreseeable future. Currently, standards for FORTRAN are specified by ANSI—the American National Standards Institute (formerly USASI and ASA), ECMA—the European Computer Manufacturers Association, and ISO—the International Standards Organization. ISO further complicated the issue by producing three separate levels of "standard" FORTRAN; to each of these were suggested minor changes or amendments by many of the member states of ISO.

Each of the FORTRAN standards mentioned above describes only the minimum level that must be contained within a particular implementation of the language. Many of the computer manufacturers have written compilers containing their own ideas on the extensions required to the basic standard language. We can, therefore, see that while the concept of FORTRAN is internationally standardized its implementation varies, in varying degrees, from manufacturer to manufacturer.

It is clearly undesirable for a book of this nature to describe a language as implemented on a particular computer. The reader must be given a grounding in FORTRAN sufficient to enable him to use the language on any modern computer. However, from the foregoing it is clear that this could be difficult and extremely lengthy. The content of Part Three describes, therefore, the underlying principles behind FORTRAN, giving full details of the common statements available together with some of the more common extensions to the languages. These extensions, which are identified in the text, are not available on every FORTRAN compiler in the manner described but do represent a concise overview of the more common additions to standard FORTRAN.

Having studied the following text, and completed the exercises, the reader will be well prepared to undertake FORTRAN programming on any modern computer. The peculiarities of the particular machine chosen (including Job Control—see Part One—available peripherals and language extensions) will be readily apparent from the detailed reference manuals supplied by the manufacturer.

A common, and recommended, procedure for familiarizing oneself with a given compiler's implementation details and for learning more about program coding techniques is to study some source listings (see Part One) output from

215

that compiler. In doing so the reader may encounter some of the terms mentioned below; while these are part of the standard FORTRAN nucleus they represent some advanced and complicated procedures which are beyond the scope of this book. The terms are—PAUSE, REWIND, BACKSPACE, ENDFILE, COMMON, EQUIVALENCE, EXTERNAL, and BLOCK DATA.

CHAPTER FORTY-EIGHT

INTRODUCTION

The name FORTRAN is an acronym of FORmula TRANslation which hints at the major use for which this language was designed—i.e. the solution of **mathematics based** problems. Such is the simplicity of FORTRAN that non-computer personnel with only a brief introduction to computing, such as engineers, mathematicians, designers, and so forth, can write and run programs to solve the problems they encounter in their everyday work. A major problem with programming by non-programmers is that they must still learn the intricacies of the computer operating system in use and in particular the Job-Control Language required to run their programs (see Chapter Eight). To circumvent this problem a development utilizing facilities remote from the main computer is becoming increasingly popular. The development is called **Time-Sharing** and a brief description of it is given below prior to the FORTRAN language details. Note that the actual coding of FORTRAN programs is the same whether the job is to be run on a Time-Sharing System or directly on a commercial computer system.

Time-Sharing Computer Systems

A time-sharing system is so called because it involves several separate users sharing the time available on a large central computer (which in some circumstances may simultaneously be running ordinary local work). Each user is connected to the computer via a telephone line which can be either a permanent private wire circuit, or more commonly, a dialled STD connection. The equipment at the users' end of the telephone line is called a **terminal** and is basically an electric typewriter device. When any of the keys are depressed the relevant character is printed on the terminal and the code representing that character is transmitted, via the telephone line, to the computer. The computer can send messages back to the terminal as a series of electric pulses, along the telephone wire, which are converted at the terminal into printed characters. The user can therefore communicate with the computer by typing on the terminal. He will receive the computer's reply also on the terminal.

A typical time-sharing service may permit thirty different users to be connected to the computer at any one time. A smaller time-sharing network is illustrated in Fig. 44. The **modem**, shown attached to each **terminal telephone**, is used to eliminate the normal voice pick-up of the telephone handset once communication is established with the computer. The **multiplexor**, at the computer centre, is used to interface between the telephone lines and the computer system itself.

The major attraction of time-sharing systems is their simplicity of use which makes them ideally suited for use by people without a computer background. Before any programs can be written or run it is necessary to contact the computer centre, a typical procedure would be:

1. Dial the number of the computer.
2. Wait for a whistle to show that contact has been established.

3. Press the button provided on the telephone.
4. (At this point the computer will print an opening message on the terminal.)
5. The user will now type his identity code.
6. Programming may now proceed.

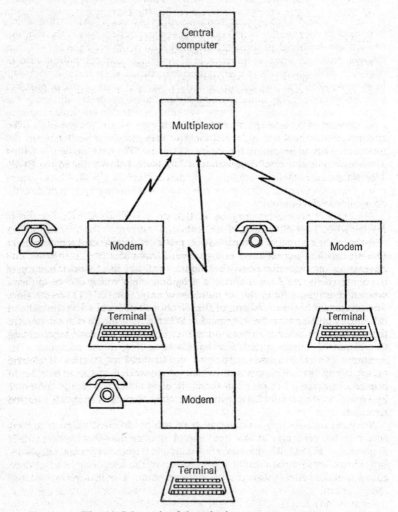

Fig. 44. Schematic of time-sharing computer system

Once the connection, or **log-in**, procedure has been completed the user can proceed with his programming. This is very simple and involves only typing in the various FORTRAN statements required and one or two simple commands to the system. These system commands are much easier to learn than the JCL for a large system. Some typical time-sharing system commands are shown below:

RUN   requests the computer to compile and then execute the FOR-TRAN program typed in on the terminal.

STOP   requests that the currently running program be terminated.

SAVE   instructs the computer to file the current program into its backing store for later retrieval and rerunning.

LOAD   (followed by a program name) causes the computer to retrieve the named program from its backing store.

NEW   permits the user to establish a new program name (prior to using the SAVE command for example).

EXECUTE   causes the computer to retrieve a named program from its backing store and immediately execute it.

The reader will no doubt appreciate that armed with a terminal and these simple commands, it would be a straightforward task to prepare and run his program. This of course is the major attraction of time-sharing—it allows easy and simple access to a large computer system for the person with a knowledge of FORTRAN.

FORTRAN Coding

FORTRAN statements may be written on a FORTRAN Coding Form (except when Time-Sharing is in use) although this is not absolutely necessary because of the straightforward layout permitted. Each statement may be preceded by a statement number if desired. These statement numbers do not have to be in sequence since their order does not effect the sequence of execution of the statements within a program. Statement numbers are used when it is desired to alter the normal flow of execution through the program (see Chapter Fifty-one). When the FORTRAN program is to be run directly on a computer system the statement number if present should occupy the first 5 character positions of each line with the statement itself commencing in position 7. Position 6 should be left blank.

When typing FORTRAN statements on a time-sharing terminal the layout is slightly different. The statement number when used must appear first on the line and be separated from the statement itself by at least one space character. However, when no statement number is given it is not necessary to leave spaces where it would have appeared.

When typing FORTRAN statements on a terminal or when writing them on coding sheets for input to a large computer it is important to differentiate between the *letter* O and the *number* 0. The code transmitted to the CPU must be different for these two characters since they are of course logically different. (Note—unlike some typewriters a computer terminal will have two distinct keys.)

It is not always possible to distinguish these two characters by their context so some standard for their writing must be adopted. Various methods have been tried in the computer industry but the method described below is the most common.

Letter "oh" written as   O

Number zero written as Ø

Throughout part three Ø will be used to indicate a zero in text representing computer input, output, or contents.

For clarity of reading the text of this part has also been set in standard printers' characters. In practice the characters available to the computer user are limited to those found on a typewriter. The reader will find, when studying computer print-out, that the quotation symbols and those for minus and hyphenation differ slightly from those shown herein.

CHAPTER FORTY-NINE

CONSTANTS AND VARIABLES

Constants

Being a mathematics based programming language FORTRAN makes great use of **numbers**. The numbers, as will be seen below, can be of several different types depending upon the type of calculation involved. Any amount specified as an actual quantity—such as 3, 10, or 327.4—has a fixed unvarying value throughout the program. Such a value is known therefore as a **constant**. In addition to **numeric constants** FORTRAN has three types of **non-numeric constants** specified with alphabetic characters. The language contains seven types of constants each of which is described below.

Integer Constant. An **integer constant** represents an **integral** or **whole number** and is made up of from 1 to about 11 digits* without a decimal point. Integer constants may be preceded by a sign indicator (+ for positive, − for negative) although if none is present the number is assumed to be positive. When a large number (such as 3,427,691) is to be used it must be written without the embedded commas. Examples of valid integer constants:

3
+27
−91
41638219

Examples of invalid integer constants:

4.   (decimal point included)
2,764   (embedded comma used).

Real Constants. A **real constant** represents an **integral number** or a number with a **decimal position**. It is written as a string of from 1 to about 9 digits* including a decimal point or as a **floating-point** value (see Chapter Nine). When written as a string of numbers a real constant may be signed (preceded by + or −) or unsigned in which case it is assumed to be positive. When a real constant has an integral value it must still be given a decimal point (i.e. 35. or 3.).

When specified in **floating-point** format the **mantissa** must be formatted as for the first type of real constant above (i.e. it must have a decimal point). The

---

* The actual upper limit will depend upon the computer in use and can be found in the manufacturer's manual.

mantissa is followed by the letter "E" which is followed by an integral **exponent**. This exponent may be signed or unsigned; if unsigned the exponent is assumed to be positive.

Examples of valid real constants:

> 4.
> 27.2196
> 2492.3
> 4.0E3   (equivalent to 4.0 × 10³ = 4000)
> 3.0E − 3   (equivalent to 3.0 × 10⁻³ = .003)
> 3.47E + 12

Examples of invalid real constants:

> 6   (no decimal point)
> 3,234.0   (embedded comma)
> E6   (no mantissa)
> 4.0E   (no exponent)

Double-precision constant. This type of constant is specified in the same manner as a real constant except that it must always have an exponent. The letter "D" (used instead of "E" to precede the exponent) differentiates a **double-precision** constant from a real constant. The letter "D" for double precision is interpreted in the same manner as an "E" for a real constant, with the exception that more **precision** is maintained within the CPU for the values of double-precision constants. For example, an "E"-type constant may use up to eight significant digits (e.g. 1.2456879E10) whereas a "D"-type may use 19 (e.g. 7.467213468291234678E26). The actual precision permitted in these two cases is dependent upon the computer system in use.

The rules for formatting double-precision constants are the same as for floating-point real constants above.

Complex Constant. Certain branches of mathematics require calculations to be performed using the square root of −1 as a factor. Since a negative number can never have a square root a special symbol—*i*—is used, in mathematics, to indicate the imaginary value of $\sqrt{-1}$. Values involving *i* are often called imaginary numbers although the more usual term is complex numbers.

A complex constant in FORTRAN is a representation of the value "a + b*i*" where a and b are real values. It is written as two real numbers separated by a comma and enclosed in parentheses. These two numbers represent a and b above respectively. Note the letter *i* is not written as part of the constant.

For example the complex constant (4.3, 7.0) represents the value 4.3 plus 7 times $\sqrt{-1}$. The constant (6.1, 2.7) has the expanded value 6.1 + 2.7*i*. It is most important that the **parentheses** are specified for a **complex** constant; where, as we shall see later, numbers are enclosed in parentheses for other purposes these must be in addition to those required for the specification of a complex constant.

Alpha or Literal Constant. Although FORTRAN is basically a mathematical language it is sometimes necessary to use non-numeric constants. For example, if a value were to be printed out with a name to identify it then an **alphabetic literal** constant would be used. Literal constants can usually be any length and are specified either as a character string enclosed in quotation marks or in the form nHa . . . a where n is the number of characters and a . . . a is the character string composing the constant.

Using quotation marks alpha constants could be written thus:

"TEST" "RUN6" "GO" "ANS"

The same alpha constants could be written in the more common alternative format thus:

4HTEST 4HRUN6 2HGO 3HANS

Note that digits may be stored in an alpha constant although even "1234" is not a number and cannot be used in arithmetic statements. Also, some compilers, especially in a time-sharing environment, limit the length of a literal (or alpha) constant.

File-name Constants. This type of constant specifies the name of an input/output file to which the program will refer. It is composed of from 1 to 8 characters enclosed in quotation marks. The following, for example, are valid **file-name** constants:

"TESTFILE" "RUNDATA" "ANSWERS"

The use of file names will become clearer when the statements used to transmit data to and from backing store devices are examined in Chapter Fifty-three. This type of constant is generally restricted to time-sharing compilers.

Logical Constant. This type is mentioned here for completeness only since its use will not become clear until later chapters have been studied. Suffice to say that a **logical** constant can have only one of two values:

.TRUE. or .FALSE.

Note that each value is preceded and followed by a period (full-stop).

Variables

Within his FORTRAN program the programmer must have areas in which he can store the intermediate and final results of his calculations. Rather than have the unchanging values of constants these new areas will have values which vary as the program progresses through its various stages. These areas are therefore known as **variables**. A variable is an area of core storage which can contain a value and to which the programmer can refer in his program by name (rather than value).

The name by which a variable is identified in a program is composed of alphanumeric characters the first of which must be alphabetic. The maximum length of a variable name is dependent upon the computer system in use but is usually set at 6 characters. Examples of valid variable names are:

COUNT RESULT A TOTAL7 D432

A name such as 4AB or 789 would, however, be invalid because it did not begin with an alphabetic character. When a statement refers to a variable by name the execution of that statement refers to the current value of the variable. A single statement may be executed several times with a particular variable having a different value each time.

Just as a constant may be of several different kinds so the value of a variable will be of a specific type. Each variable in fact is allocated a type of value and it may hold only this type throughout the execution of the program. There is a variable type corresponding to each constant kind as described above. Variables can therefore be of the following types:

> integer
> real
> double precision
> complex
> literal
> file-name
> logical

Before a variable can be used in a program it must be given a type either **explicitly** or **implicitly**. Explicit typing is done by means of the type statement which consists of a **type identifier** followed by the variable name(s) which are to have that type. Explicitly typing of the various variables is shown below:

> INTEGER COUNT, DIVISR, RESULT
> REAL INTER, NUMBER

In these two FORTRAN statements the variables COUNT, DIVISR, and RESULT are identified as integer variables and can therefore hold integral (i.e. whole-number) values during the execution of the program in which the type statement appears, while INTER and NUMBER are shown to be real variables and can therefore hold real-number values (i.e. values with fractional parts).

> DOUBLE PRECISION LONG
> COMPLEX X, Y

These statements define one double-precision variable (LONG) and two complex variables (X and Y). The values which these variables can hold will be of the same form as the respective constant types described above. (For example, X could have the value (3.0, 4.7) in one part of the program and (13.9, 0.43) in a later part.)

A logical variable (which could hold the value .TRUE. or .FALSE.) is defined thus:

> LOGICAL SWITCH

Literal (Alpha) and File-name variables are similarly typed, when available:

> ALPHA NAME, CODE
> FILENAME IN, OUT

The two variables NAME and CODE could each hold up to 4 alphanumeric characters while IN and OUT could each hold a file name (1 to 8 characters). (Note that the method of assigning and subsequently changing the values of variables is discussed in Chapter Fifty.)

If a type statement is not given for a variable then it has an **implied** use depending on the **first character** of the **name** given. The FORTRAN compiler assumes that variables whose names start with the letters I to N inclusive are **integer** variables and that variable names starting with any other letters are **real**. Thus the following are assumed to be integer variables:

INP, NUM, KOUNT, LOOP

whereas the following are assumed to be real:

A, B, COUNT, ZOO

It is important to realize that implied typing of variables is only effective if the particular variable name does not appear elsewhere. For example, if the statement

REAL INTER

appears in the program then the implied typing is overridden.

Only real and integer variables may be given implied types, all others must be explicitly expressed with the appropriate type statement as shown above. Only a single type statement (explicit or implicit) may appear for any single variable name and the type so given will apply throughout the entire program. The type of a variable cannot be changed during execution of a program. Since an explicit typing for a variable must appear before that variable is used it is useful to put all the type statements required at the beginning of each of your FORTRAN programs.

Note that it is not necessary to specify the number of storage locations required for a particular variable. The compiler will always allocate a sufficient number to hold the maximum value for a particular type of variable (which is dependent upon the computer system in use).

Initial Value (Time-Sharing)

At the beginning of your program (i.e. before any calculations have begun) all the variables used in the program (explicit and implicit) will be given an **initial value** by the compiler. This value will be zero for the numeric variables, .FALSE. for logical variables, and spaces for alpha and file-name variables.

Initial Value (Non-Time-Sharing)

The values assigned to variables will, in this case, be unpredictable at the start of processing. It is necessary, therefore, to assign such initial values as are required. For example, one would set zero values thus:

$$A = 0.0$$
$$B = 0.0$$
$$I = 0$$
$$N = 0$$

In the coding examples used in the remainder of Part Three initial values as for Time-Sharing will be assumed for ease of reading.

Exercises

1. Specify the type of each of the following constants:
    (*a*) 327 (*b*) 472.0 (*c*) 3.4E10 (*d*) 4.0D7 (*e*) (1.0, 7.2) (*f*) "RUN"
    (*g*) "INPUT" (*h*) 3HSET (*i*) .FALSE.
2. Write the FORTRAN statements to specify two double precision variables called A and B and one complex variable called ROOT.

3. What is the implied type of the following variables:
   (a) NUMBER (b) COMPLX (c) REAL (d) ZEUS (e) KLOWN (f) MANY.
4. Define an integer constant called REAL and a real constant called INTEGR.
5. What would the initial value of the following variables be:
   (a) LOGICAL SWITCH
   (b) INTEGER SEVEN
   (c) REAL LOOP
   (d) ALPHA NAME

CHAPTER FIFTY

THE ASSIGNMENT STATEMENT

The **assignment** or **replacement** statement is the most important in the FORTRAN language since it is this statement which is used to **assign** a value to a variable during execution of the program. The assignment statement is used for the performance of calculations, the result of the calculation being placed in a specified variable. The general form of the assignment statement is

$$\text{variable} = \text{expression}$$

This is not stating the fact that the variable is equal to the expression but is requesting the program to **evaluate the expression** and place the result of this evaluation into the variable named on the left of the equals sign (replacing the previous value of the variable in the process).

In its simplest form this statement will consist of a variable to the left and a constant to the right of the equals sign. The *value* of the constant replaces the previous value of the variable each time the statement is executed.

$$\text{KOUNT} = 37$$

In this example the constant value 37 will be assigned to the variable KOUNT (the previous value of KOUNT being destroyed).

$$\text{STARTE} = 2.34E3$$

In this example the variable STARTE assumes the value 2,340 (2.34×10^3) each time the statement is executed. The more normal use of the assignment statement, the performance of calculations, will involve an arithmetic expression to the right of the equals sign.

Arithmetic Expressions

An **arithmetic expression** consists of a combination of variables and/or constants interspersed with **arithmetic operators** and **parentheses**. The allowable arithmetic operators for this type of expression are as shown below.

**	exponentiation (or raised to the power of)
/	division
*	multiplication
+	addition
−	subtraction

The use of these operators is slightly different from standard mathematical notation since an operator cannot be assumed and two operators cannot appear consecutively. For example, the mathematical statement (W)(Z) is quite valid to indicate the multiplication of W by Z; however when using FORTRAN the required operator must be written thus:

$$(W)*(Z)$$

The use of two operators, as in ordinary mathematics, such as $P*-Q$ is not permitted in FORTRAN without the use of parentheses to separate the two requirements. The expression shown would be written:

$$P*(-Q)$$

(Note that the expression $-P*Q$ is quite acceptable.) In an expression containing a mixture of arithmetic operators such as

$$P/Q + 3.\emptyset*Z -2**R$$

a certain precedence of operator evaluation exists in order that the programmer may be aware that the expression will always be evaluated in the manner in which he intended. The desired calculation in this example is obvious to the reader; however, it is equally obvious that a totally different result could be obtained if, say, the subtraction were performed before the exponentiation.

The preferred order of arithmetic operation is as follows:
1. exponentiation
2. multiplication and division
3. addition and subtraction

The sequence of steps undergone to evaluate the expression shown above would be as shown below (parentheses indicating here previously calculated values)

$$2**R$$
$$P/Q$$
$$3.\emptyset*Z$$
$$(P/Q) + (3.0*Z)$$
$$((P/Q) + (3.\emptyset*Z)) -(2**R)$$

As can be seen from this sequence of events operators on the same level, i.e. all additions and subtractions, or all multiplications and divisions, are performed from left to right. However, if several exponentiations are included in an expression then they are evaluated from right to left. This latter rule is most important since totally wrong results can be obtained if it is not remembered.

For example, suppose we wish to evaluate 2^{3^4} (i.e. we wish to raise two to the third power and then raise the result to the fourth power), the FORTRAN expression

$$2**3**4$$

would give an incorrect result since it would be evaluated right to left (i.e. 3**4 would be the first calculation). The correct method of writing the expression would be:

$$(2**3)**4$$

Operations contained within parentheses are evaluated first. When sets of parentheses are contained within other parentheses the innermost level is evaluated first, followed by the next level, and so on. The use of parentheses allows us to amend the order in which the arithmetic operators are evaluated. For example, suppose we wish to multiply together the variables D, E and the difference between G and H. If we wrote the expression thus:

$$D*G -H*E$$

the result would be not as intended but would consist of the result of H multiplied by E subtracted from the result of D multiplied by G. The required evaluation can be obtained by using parentheses as shown:

$$D*(G -H)*E$$

In this instance H is first subtracted from G the result being multiplied by D and this result being multiplied by E.

More than one set of parentheses can be used to further modify the sequence of evaluation as shown·

$$((D -G)*(F -H) -R)*S$$

The innermost parenthesized operators will be evaluated first—giving D −G and F −H, the two results so obtained being within the outer set of parentheses will be multiplied in the third step. From the result of this multiplication will be subtracted R and this result will be multiplied by S. (Note—within the outer parentheses the evaluation is as per the table above.)

Parentheses can be used when not absolutely required in order to clarify the meaning of a complicated expression. For example, the expression:

$$(D*G -3) + (E*(2**R)) -(18*F**3)$$

will be evaluated in exactly the same manner as:

$$D*G -3 + E*2**R -18*F**3$$

although the former would be easier to follow.

When in doubt about the order in which operators will be evaluated use parentheses. Remember that it is very easy to misinterpret the way in which a complicated statement will be evaluated and such an error can be very difficult to detect when testing your program.

The Assignment Statement in Use

We have already seen the simplest form of assignment or replacement statement where a variable is given the value of a constant:

REAL KOUNT

·
·
·
·

·

KOUNT = 2.734E4

A variable can be made equal to the value of another variable in a similar manner:

$$NUMBER = MAJOR$$

In this example the value of NUMBER is replaced by the *current value* of MAJOR. Note, however, that the value of MAJOR is unchanged following the execution of this statement. The most important use of the assignment statement is the solving of calculations (which is basically the purpose of a FORTRAN program). For example, consider part of a program used to calculate the properties of pipes. One section of the program may be required to calculate the cross-sectional area and then the volume of metal in a hollow pipe. The parameters relating to the type of pipe whose data is required have already been input to the program (see Chapter Fifty-four) and are stored in the variables INNER (for inner radius), OUTER (for outer radius), and LENGTH (for length of tube under consideration). These factors are all real numbers and so the program would contain, at the front, the following statement:

$$REAL\ INNER,\ LENGTH$$

(Note—the variable OUTER is implicitly real.) For the purposes of this exercise the program must calculate the thickness of the pipe wall, its cross-sectional area, and the volume of metal in a given length. The following coding could be used:

$$AREA\quad = 3.142\ (OUTER\ **2 - INNER\ **2)$$
$$VOLUME = AREA * LENGTH$$

If a later part of the program did not require the values of thickness and area (computed above into THICK and AREA respectively) then a single statement could have been used to calculate the pipe volume:

$$VOLUME = 3.142 * (OUTER - INNER)\ **2* LENGTH$$

(The reader may care to verify that this statement will give the same answer in VOLUME as the three statements above—remember the sequence of evaluation of arithmetic operators.)

Consider a program which must calculate the arithmetic mean (average) of the values of five variables A, B, C, D, E, and then calculate the mean as a percentage of the value of variables A and E.

$$REAL\ MEAN$$
$$MEAN\quad = (A + B + C + D + E)/5$$
$$PERCNA = 100.0* MEAN/A$$
$$PERCNB = 100.0* MEAN/B$$

Note that when the calculations are completed the values for variables A, B, C, D, and E remain unchanged.

A literal variable may be given the value of a constant or of another literal variable by means of the assignment statement:

$$ALPHA\ NAME,\ IDENT$$
$$NAME = \text{“SWOP”}$$
$$IDENT = NAME$$

Similarly for file-name variables.

So far we have looked only at assignment statements in which the expression to the right of the equals sign is of the same type as that to the left. Clearly, however, there will be occasions when the result of the expression is to be of a different type to the variable to which the answer is to be assigned. When the result of the expression is of a different type to the variable it will be automatically converted to match the variable type providing the two types are compatible. Compatible types are shown in Fig. 45.

Variable	Expression
Real	Real, integer, double-precision
Integer	Real, integer, double-precision
Double-precision	Real, integer, double-precision
Complex	Complex, real, integer, double-precision
Logical	Logical
Literal	Literal
Filename	Alpha or filename

Fig. 45. Compatible assignment statement types

For example, consider the following statement:

$$RESULT = 27* (NUMBER + 7)$$

The result of the expression is of type integer (NUMBER is implicitly defined as being integral) which will be automatically converted to the equivalent real number (e.g. if the answer were 128 then RESULT would be given a value of 128.0).

When a real or integral value is to be assigned to a complex number the imaginary part of that number is given the value 0.0. For example the statements:

$$COMPLEX \ J, I$$
$$J = 39.7$$
$$I = 27$$

will result in the variable I having the value (27.0, 0.0) and J the value (39.7, 0.0).

When a real or double-precision result is to be assigned to an integral number the fractional part is dropped and the whole-number portion given to the variable without being rounded. For example this statement:

$$NUM = 2.999$$

will result in NUM (implicitly integral) having the value 2. Great care must therefore be exercised when using integral variables in assignment statements that contain non-integral values in the expression. (If in doubt always use real variables for the results of calculations.) When an expression contains variables and/or constants of different types the integral values will be converted to their equivalent real value for the duration of the calculation. An integral value so converted is given a zero fractional part. Once the calculation has been performed the result will then be converted again if necessary to match the type of the result variable. For example in the statement:

$$N = D*I/J$$

the variable I is converted to a real value before it is multiplied by D; the result of this calculation is then divided by the real equivalent of J. The real result is then assigned to N as an integral value. The type of I and J remains integral after the execution of this statement.

Exercises

1. Write down the order of evaluation of the arithmetic operators, noting the effect of parentheses.
2. Write down the statement to place in the variable R the value of P raised to the power Y the result of which is itself raised to the power W.
3. Given the following:

$$COMPLEX\ X$$
$$A = 2.4$$
$$B = 3.6$$
$$C = 0.1$$
$$I = 2$$
$$J = 6$$

what would be the result in the variable of each of the statements below?
   (a) R = I*J
   (b) M = A + B + C
   (c) M = (A + B)*I
   (d) M = A + B*I
   (e) R = A + B*I
   (f) R = (A + B)*I
   (g) X = A*J
   (h) M = (A + B + C)*K
4. Write the statements required to place the average of A, B, C, and D in MEAN, the square of the average in MSQR and the complex square in MCOM.
5. Write the statement to place in NUMBER the result of multiplying ONE by the negative of TWO (i.e.—TWO).

CHAPTER FIFTY-ONE

PROGRAM CONTROL STATEMENTS

The normal **flow of execution** of the statements in your FORTRAN program is **sequential**. In other words each statement is executed in the order in which it appears in the source program. It is often desired that the flow of execution is changed from this normal route, perhaps to execute a set of statements several times or to by-pass certain statements when specific conditions exist. A number of FORTRAN Control instructions or statements are available to the programmer to change the normal flow. These statements are discussed in this and the following chapters.

The GO TO Statement

The GO TO statement causes control to be transferred to the statement whose number immediately follows the words GO TO.

$$GO\ TO\ 17$$

This statement will cause control to be transferred to the statement which is preceded by the number 17. The sequential flow will continue therefore from statement 17 (until another control statement is executed). The statement number (17 in this example) is written thus:

$$17\ COUNT = TOTAL + 1$$

The following section of a FORTRAN program shows the GO TO statement used to repeat a set of statements:

$$10\ A = B*C + (D - F)$$
$$L = A**2$$
.
.
.
.
.
$$GO\ TO\ 10$$

The Computed GO TO Statement

This statement can be used to transfer control to one of a number of statements depending on the value of a variable at the time the statement is executed. The statement is written as the words GO TO followed by a list of statement numbers in parentheses followed by a variable name. When the statement is executed the value of the variable is examined (note—the integral value of this variable must be greater than zero and not greater than the number of statement numbers in parentheses) and control is transferred to the statement number with the position, in parentheses, corresponding to that value.

231

This sounds extremely complicated whereas it is a simple statement to understand and use and can be best explained by means of an example:

INTEGER SWITCH

GO TO (10, 20, 42), SWITCH

This statement has the effect of transferring control to statement 10 if the value of SWITCH is 1, statement 20 if the value of SWITCH is 2, and statement 42 if the value of SWITCH is 3. If SWITCH has any other value control will generally pass to the statement immediately following the GO TO (some compilers will cause the program to stop). The computed GO TO statement can be used to select one of a number of process paths depending upon the value of a parameter:

GO TO (4, 6, 8), JUMP

.
.
.
.

4 A = 90 + 7

.
.

GO TO 12
6 A = 90 + 9

.
.

GO TO 12
8 A = 90 −3

.
.

12 .
.
.
.

This statement can also be used to repeat a group of statements a set number of times. For example, suppose we wish to execute such a group four times, the following could be used:

A = 0
10 X = Y**2 + D*7 + R**Z
A = A + 1
GO TO (10, 10, 10, 10), A

Note the statement A = A + 1 which is used to increment the value of A by 1 each time the group of statements is executed. The computed GO TO will transfer control to statement 10 when A has the value 1, 2, 3, and 4. The group of statements between 10 and the GO TO will therefore be executed four times as required.

The Assigned GO TO Statement

The GO TO statement may be combined with a (real or integral) variable name which has previously been assigned a statement number by means of an ASSIGN statement (not to be confused with the assignment or replacement statement). In the following example the variable JUMP has been assigned to the statement number 25:

$$ASSIGN\ 25\ TO\ JUMP$$
$$GO\ TO\ JUMP$$

$$\cdot$$
$$\cdot$$
$$\cdot$$
$$\cdot$$

$$25\ \ldots$$

The statement GO TO JUMP will therefore cause control to be transferred to statement 25 (i.e. the value that has been assigned to JUMP). The assigned GO TO can be used to set up a **program switch** such that one of two paths is executed alternately during repeated execution:

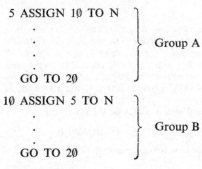

On the first time through this program control will transfer sequential to statements in group A, the end of which transfers control to statement 20. This is an assigned GO TO which will transfer control to statement 10 (group A having set N to 10) and the statements in group B will be executed. During the execution of this group the value of N will be changed to 5 so that on the next time through (or next **pass** as it is known) group A will be executed again. The two groups will therefore be executed alternately. This switching on alternate passes can also be accommodated with the computed GO TO as shown below:

$$5\ N = 1$$

$$\cdot$$
$$\cdot$$
$$\cdot$$

$$GO\ TO\ 20$$

Group A

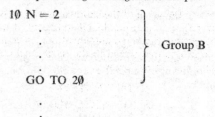

$$10 \ N = 2$$

Group B

$$\text{GO TO } 20$$

$$20 \ \text{GO TO } (10, \ 5), \ N$$

Care must be exercised with GO TO statements to ensure that **endless loops** are not set up inadvertently. For example, the following GO TO statement would produce a never-ending loop if the value of N was equal to 2:

$$10 \ \text{GO TO } (20, \ 10, \ 35, \ 4), \ N$$

Methods of terminating loops and alternative ways of setting them up are discussed in Chapter Fifty-two.

Exercises

1. Write the statement to transfer control to the statement numbered 37.
2. Write the statement (numbered 8) to transfer control to statement 6 if N has the value 1, statement 12 if N has the value 2, and statement 32 if N has the value 3.
3. In question 2 to which statement will control be transferred if N has the value 4.
4. Write the statements to transfer control to statement 8 if SWITCH has the value 7, statement 14 if SWITCH has the value 8, and statement 21 if SWITCH has the value 9.
5. Write the statement which will cause the statement

GO TO JUMPER

to transfer control to statement number 18.

CHAPTER FIFTY-TWO

PROGRAM DECISIONS AND LOOPS

Additional Program-Control Statements

The GO TO statements discussed in Chapter Fifty-one always cause the program flow to be altered. The IF statement allows the programmer to alter the program flow selectively depending on the state of a particular **condition**. It is possible therefore that if a tested condition does not exist the program flow will not be altered. An IF statement is called a **conditional statement** since its result depends upon the state of a particular condition.

The simplest form of the IF statement transfers control to one of three statements depending on the value of an expression. The statement consists of the word IF followed by an expression in parentheses followed by three statement numbers. If the value of the expression is negative (less than zero) control is transferred to the first-numbered statement, if it is zero control is transferred to the second-numbered statement, and if it is positive (greater than zero) then control is transferred to the third-numbered statement. For example, consider the statement below:

$$\text{IF (A) } 10, \ 20, \ 30$$

The expression in this case is simply the one variable, A. If the value of A is **negative** then control will be transferred to statement number 10, if the value of A is **zero** control will be transferred to statement 20, and if the value of A is **positive** control will be transferred to statement 30. The expression in parentheses following the word IF can be anything that is allowable in an assignment statement (Chapter Fifty) except that complex expressions are not permitted. Some further examples of IF statements of the form described are shown below:

$$\text{IF } (A**2 - D) \ 10, \ 20, \ 30$$
$$\text{IF } (A*B + C*D - R**Y) \ 1, \ 2, \ 7$$
$$\text{IF } (A + B + C + D + X - Y) \ 6, \ 7, \ 8$$

In each case the value of the expression will be evaluated and control transferred according to whether the value is negative, zero, or positive. The IF statement may also be written with a **relational expression** in parentheses followed by a single statement. If the relational expression is true control will be transferred to the statement specified, if the expression is false control will be transferred to the next sequential statement.

Relational Expressions

A **relational expression** consists of two arithmetic expressions separated by a relational operator. A relational expression can have only two values—.TRUE. and .FALSE. The expression is .TRUE. if the relation between the arithmetic expressions is satisfied and .FALSE. if it is not. The relational operators and their meanings are shown in Fig. 46.

Symbol	Meaning
.GT.	Greater than
.GE.	Greater than or equal to
.LT.	Less than
.LE.	Less than or equal to
.EQ.	Equal to
.NE.	Not equal to

Fig. 46. The FORTRAN relational operators

Note that only .EQ. and .NE. may be used with complex arithmetic expressions but all six relational operators may be used with integer, real, double-precision and alpha variable expressions.

The IF statement may therefore be used to evaluate the relationship between variables:

$$IF\ (A.GT.B)\ GO\ TO\ 1\emptyset$$

In this case if the value of A is *greater than* the value of B control will be transferred to statement number 10. A more complicated expression may be used:

$$IF\ (A**2 - B*X\ .EQ.\ 7\emptyset.\emptyset)\ GO\ TO\ 22$$

The value of the arithmetic expressions will be evaluated and compared according to the relational operator. If the relation is fulfilled or .TRUE. (in this case if the values are *equal*) then the statement GO TO 22 will be executed and control will be transferred. If the relation is not fulfilled (i.e. if it is .FALSE.) the statement GO TO 22 will not be executed and control will pass to the next sequential statement. The IF statement can be used to select different program paths depending upon the value of a variable:

$$IF\ (INDIC\ .EQ.\ 7)\ GO\ TO\ 2\emptyset$$
$$IF\ (INDIC\ .EQ.\ 12)\ GO\ TO\ 25$$
$$IF\ (INDIC\ .GT.\ 17)\ GO\ TO\ 35$$

Program paths can be selected depending upon the relationship existing between variables:

$$IF\ (SUMA\ .EQ.\ SUMB)\ GO\ TO\ 42$$
$$IF\ (SUMA\ .LT.\ SUMB)\ GO\ TO\ 47$$

Literal variables can also be examined:

$$IF\ (ALPH\ .EQ.\ ``NAME")\ GO\ TO\ 5\emptyset$$
$$IF\ (ALPH\ .LT.\ ALPH2)\ GO\ TO\ 47$$

The statement following the parenthesized relational expression does not have to be a GO TO. An assignment statement may appear in the IF statement:

$$IF\ (CODE.LE.DUMP)\ KOUNT = KOUNT + 1$$

In this example if the value of CODE is *less than* or is *equal to* the value of DUMP (i.e. if the relational expression is .TRUE.) then the statement KOUNT = KOUNT + 1 will be executed. If the relational expression is not true the statement will not be executed. In either case the next statement to be executed is the one immediately following the IF statement. Thus in the following example if the value of A is initially 1 the final value of B will be 20 whereas if the initial value of A is any value other than 1 the final value of B will be 10.

$$B = \emptyset$$
$$IF\ (A.EQ.1.\emptyset)\ B = B + 1\emptyset$$
$$B = B + 1\emptyset$$

Logical variables may be examined by means of the IF statement:

LOGICAL SW

.
.
.
.

IF (SW) GO TO 3Ø

If the value of SW is .TRUE. then the statement GO TO 3Ø will be executed.
If the value of SW is .FALSE. the GO TO statement will not be executed.

An IF statement can be used to set up a loop to be executed a set number
of times:

$$A = \emptyset$$
$$10 \ A = A + 1$$

.
.
.
.   (*loop statements here*)
.
.

IF (A.LT.1Ø) GO TO 1Ø

The above loop will be executed 10 times; note that the variable A is set to
zero before the loop is entered (the loop starts at 10) and is incremented by 1
for each pass of the loop. Such a loop could be used, for example, to work out
the factorial of a given number (note—factorial N, expressed as N!, is equal
to $1 \times 2 \times 3 \times 4 \dots (N - 1) \times (N)$). The following coding will calculate
the factorial of the number in I, prior to entering the loop, leaving the
solution in K.

$$A = 1$$
$$K = 1$$
$$10 \ K = K*A$$
$$A = A + 1$$
$$\text{IF } (A.LT.I + 1) \text{ GO TO } 1\emptyset$$

The IF statement may also be used to select alternative process paths depending on the value of a particular variable. For example, suppose the value of
CHOICE determines the processing path required for a set of values on which
certain calculations are to be performed. If the value of CHOICE is "A" then
the statements beginning at 10 are to be executed, if the value is "D" the
statements beginning at 16 are to be executed, otherwise the next sequential
statement is to be executed. The following coding could be used:

ALPHA CHOICE

.
.
.

IF (CHOICE .EQ. "A") GO TO 1Ø
IF (CHOICE .EQ. "B") GO TO 16

The DO Statement

The DO statement enables the programmer to set up and control a **loop** in a single statement. The format of the DO statement is the word DO followed by a statement number followed by a variable name and three values. Execution of the statement causes the statements between the DO and the numbered statement to be executed with the variable equal in value to the first of the numbers. After this first execution the value of the specified **variable** is **incremented** by the third number and the following statements executed again. This incrementing and executing will continue until the value of the variable exceeds the value of the second number. This sounds extremely complicated but is quite simple and very useful in practice. To clarify the operation of the DO statement we will examine the workings of an example:

$$DO\ 1\emptyset\ J = 1,\ 4,\ 1$$
.
.
.
.
$$1\emptyset\ A = A + 1$$

The statements between the DO and statement number 10 will be executed four times by the DO statement. When the DO is first encountered J will be set equal to the first number (1—the **initial value**) and the statements between the DO and statement number 10 (the **range of the** DO) will be executed. Control will be returned to the DO where the third number (1—the **increment**) will be added to J. The statements forming the range of the DO will be executed again (for J having the value 2). This will continue with J having the values 3 and 4; however when control next returns to the DO, J will be given the value of 5 (4 incremented by 1). Since this value exceeds the second number 4 (the **terminal value**) control will now pass to the statement following statement number 10.

The DO statement used to set up a loop requires fewer statements than the equivalent loop with an IF. Suppose we wish to execute a set of statements twenty times:

$$DO\ 35\ K = 1,\ 2\emptyset,\ 1$$
.
.
.
.
$$35\ .$$

During the execution of the DO loop the value of the **loop index** (the variable in the DO statement) may be used. For example, the following coding will total the numbers 1 to 20 and total the squares of these numbers:

$$DO\ 1\emptyset\ K = 1,\ 2\emptyset,\ 1$$
$$TOTALN = TOTALN + K$$
$$1\emptyset\ TOTALS = TOTALS + K**2$$

(Note, however, that the value of the index must not be altered within the range of the DO loop.)

The value of the increment does not have to be 1. For example we could repeat the above example for the odd numbers only (1 to 19 inclusive).

$$DO \ 10 \ K = 1, \ 20, \ 2$$
$$TOTALN = TOTALN + K$$
$$10 \ TOTALS = TOTALS + K**2$$

Similarly, the initial value can be other than 1 as the following variation of the above example will show (calculating the totals for the even numbers):

$$DO \ 10 \ K = 2, \ 20, \ 2$$
$$TOTALN = TOTALN + K$$
$$10 \ TOTALS = TOTALS + K**2$$

When the increment value is 1 it can be omitted if desired—1 being the assumed value. The initial value and the terminating value must always be present:

$$DO \ 12 \ N = 2, \ 15$$
$$I = A**2 + N$$
$$J = I**N$$
$$12 \ R = R + J$$

In this case the DO loop will be executed fourteen times (for N having the values 2 through 15 in increments of 1 (the assumed value)). The initial, terminating and increment values may all be specified, if desired, as a variable rather than as a constant. In this case the values used are those which the variables have at the time the DO statement is executed. You will recall that earlier, during the discussion of the IF statement, the following coding was given to calculate the factorial of the value in I:

$$A = 1$$
$$K = 1$$
$$10 \ K = K*A$$
$$A = A + 1$$
$$IF \ (A.LT.I + 1) \ GO \ TO \ 10$$

The same calculation could be accomplished in a much easier manner using a DO loop:

$$A = 1$$
$$DO \ 10 \ K = 1, \ I$$
$$10 \ K = A*K$$

The DO loop will be terminated when the value of K exceeds the value of I, in other words, therefore, if I has the value 12 when the DO statement is encountered the loop will be executed twelve times.

The following coding shows a method of calculating pi using Wallis' formula. The precision to which pi will be calculated depends upon the number of executions of the loop; suppose this value is specified in TA:

$$PI = 1$$
$$DO \ 17 \ F = 1, \ TA$$
$$17 \ PI = PI*F/(F - 1)*F/(F + 1)$$

Using different values in TA this coding could determine the rate at which the formula approaches the true value of pi.

Within the range of a DO statement it is permissible to include GO TO and IF statements:

$$DO\ 30\ R = 4,\ 32,\ 2$$
$$A = R*(K + 7)$$
$$IF\ (L.EQ.\ .FALSE.)\ GO\ TO\ 12$$
$$DX = B*(R**2)$$
$$GO\ TO\ 14$$
$$12\ DX = B/(R**2)$$
$$14\ P = P + I$$
$$30\ G = DX + A$$

Note, however, that it is not permissible to use a GO TO or an IF statement as the last in a DO range. If this is desired then a **dummy end statement** must be used. This is specified by the CONTINUE statement:

$$DO\ 15\ K = 1,\ 10$$
$$R = H*K$$
$$IF\ (R.GT.0.)P = P - R$$
$$15\ CONTINUE$$

More examples of the use of the DO statement will be found in Chapter Fifty-three.

Exercises

1. Write the statements to transfer control to statement 12 if the expression $A*B/(H - 2)$ is zero and statement 91 otherwise.
2. Write the statement to transfer control to statement 14 if the value of X is greater than the value of CNT.
3. Write the statements to add 1 to the value of KOUNT if the value of A squared is less than or equal to the value of B raised to the power 7.
4. Write the statement to transfer control to statement number 7.
5. Write the statements to repeat the equation $C = B**2/A + C$ for A having the values 1 to 100 without using a DO statement.
6. Repeat question 5 using a DO statement.
7. Write the statements to calculate the sum of the first 50 numbers and calculate the square of this total (results in the integer variables SUM and TOTAL respectively).
8. Interest on a loan can be calculated using the formula $I = (R/100) \times P$ where R is the rate and P the principal (or starting amount). The total amount after one year would be equal to the principal plus the interest. This new principal would be used to calculate the interest for the next year. Write the statements to calculate the interest on an amount (in P) over five years at a rate given by R.
9. Repeat question 8 with the number of years given by N.
10. Write the statements to calculate e (the base of natural logarithms) by adding together successive values of the expression $(1 + 1/N)^N$ for N having the values 1 to 1000.

CHAPTER FIFTY-THREE

ARRAYS

An **array**, or matrix as its mathematical equivalent is known, is a set of identical fields arranged, conceptually, in a row. An array can be considered as the computer's set of pigeon-holes. Each hole, or **element**, has the same attributes (i.e. can hold the same amount of like information, and has the same name (the method of referring to individual elements is discussed below)). An array can be used to hold a table of information—e.g. a set of parameters—or a series of similar results. These uses will become clearer when the examples following are studied.

The arrays required in a FORTRAN program are defined using the DIMENSION statement. This statement specifies the name of the array and the number of elements it is to contain. Any number of DIMENSION statements, each of which can define several arrays, can appear in your program; however, they must appear before any other statements used (except a TYPE statement). To define an array the programmer will write the word DIMEN-SION followed by the array name which is itself followed by the number of elements to be contained within the array in parentheses. For example, to define a twelve-element array called MONTH:

DIMENSION MONTH(12)

More than one array may be defined in a single statement:

DIMENSION DAY(7), WEEK(4), MONTH(12)

A twelve-element array consists of 12 identical variables with the same name. The type of these variables is specified in the same manner as for non-array variables:

DIMENSION A(4), K(7), R(6)
DOUBLE PRECISION R

The array A consists of 4 real variables, the array K of 7 integer variables, and the array R of 6 double precision variables. The initial value of each element of an array is zero (except a logical array for which each element has the initial value .FALSE.). Any variable name used in a DIMENSION statement may not appear in any other DIMENSION statement and can refer only to the array so defined.

The array TOTAL defined thus:

DIMENSION TOTAL(4)

can be represented diagrammatically thus:

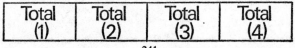

| Total (1) | Total (2) | Total (3) | Total (4) |

Each of the four elements has the same name, TOTAL, although they all have a unique element number. It is this element number that is used to distinguish between the different elements in an array. For example, to add 1 to the second element in the array TOTAL:

$$TOTAL(2) = TOTAL(2) + 1$$

The number enclosed in parentheses following the array name is called a **subscript** and identifies the particular array element required. A variable name which has appeared in a DIMENSION statement must always be followed by a subscript.

The following will add together the contents of the four elements of TOTAL and place the result in SUM:

$$SUM = TOTAL(1) + TOTAL(2) + TOTAL(3) + TOTAL(4)$$

To add the contents of the array defined thus

$$DIMENSION \ SETS(4)$$

to the array TOTAL (i.e. adding corresponding elements) the following could be used:

$$TOTAL(1) = TOTAL(1) + SETS(1)$$
$$TOTAL(2) = TOTAL(2) + SETS(2)$$
$$TOTAL(3) = TOTAL(3) + SETS(3)$$
$$TOTAL(4) = TOTAL(4) + SETS(4)$$

Variable Subscripting

Using constants as subscripts is quite acceptable for arrays with only a small number of elements. However, suppose we wished to add together two arrays each of 100 elements. Clearly an alternative method must be available. The subscript of an array name can be specified as a variable whose integral value is used to identify the particular element of the array. Since the value of the variable subscript can be different it is possible to refer to every element in an array within a small loop of instructions. Before looking at this technique consider the following statements and make certain that you understand their implications.

$$K = A(I)$$

This statement places in K the value of the array A element whose number is given by the current value of I. If the value of I, at the time of execution of the above statement, equalled 6 then the statement would be equivalent to

$$K = A(6)$$

Similarly, if the value of I equalled 3 the statement would be equivalent to

$$K = A(3)$$

A statement may contain reference to two arrays with variable subscripts:

$$B(I) = A(I) + 1$$

In this example the Ith element of B is made equal to the value of the Ith

element of A plus one. Similarly, the Ith element of two arrays could be compared:

$$IF \ (A(I).EQ.B(I) \ ) \ GO \ TO \ 17$$

It is clear from these examples that a loop of statements set up to vary the value of I through the complete number of elements of these arrays would enable all the elements to be processed in a single set of statements. The simplest way of achieving this is of course to use the DO statement.

Let us consider first of all a simple example. Suppose we wish to add 1 to each element of this array.

$$DIMENSION \ TOT(6)$$

the following DO loop will be sufficient:

```
       DO 10 I = 1, 6
10 TOT(I) = TOT(I) + 1
```

Since this loop will be executed for I having the values 1, 2, 3, 4, 5, and 6, it is evident that every element of the array TOT will be increased in value by 1. This technique can also be used to transfer the contents of one array to another:

```
       DO 10 I = 1, 6
    TOT(I) = ARR(I)
10 ARR(I) = 0.0
```

In this case the array ARR is set to zero after each element has been transferred to the corresponding element in TOT. The following coding examines the array R and counts the number of negative elements (result in N), the number of positive elements (result in P), and the number of zero elements (result in Z), and produces the total (in T) of all the element values:

```
       DO 20 K = 1, 20
    T = T + R(K)
    IF (R(K) ) 10, 11, 12
10 N = N + 1
    GO TO 20
11 Z = Z + 1
    GO TO 20
12 P = P + 1
20 CONTINUE
```

Arrays will be used frequently in FORTRAN because of the ease with which data stored therein can be manipulated. The mean (average) of a set of numbers can be worked out quite simply:

$$M = (A + B + C + D + E)/5$$

However, if the number of values was very large it would be very tedious to use this method. Instead the various values can be held in an array (rather than in individual variables), the mean can then be computed thus:

```
       DO 10 K = 1 TO 50
10 S = S + A(K)
    M = S/50
```

Another statistical problem could involve calculating the harmonic (as opposed to the arithmetic) mean of a group of values. The harmonic mean is given by the formula:

$$H = \frac{n}{\Sigma \left(\frac{1}{x}\right)}$$

where n is the number of values and x is the occurrence of each value. (Note that Σ—Greek letter sigma—denotes *the sum of* and indicates that all the values of x are to be taken.) Suppose that the values of x are held in the array A; the harmonic mean would be calculated thus:

```
        DO 10 K = 1, 50
10  W = W + 1/A(K)
        H = 50/W
```

The subscript specified with a variable name can be an expression rather than just a variable; the following could therefore be valid statements:

```
A(B + 3) = A(C − 2) + 1
K = A(B**2 + 1)
```

A useful application of this is in the so-called **rolling up** of tables of information. For example, suppose a program contains a table of twelve elements representing a sales figure for the preceding twelve months. Each time the program is run (monthly) a new figure is added to the end of the table and all the other entries are moved back one place; i.e. last month's becomes the last but one month and so on. The following coding could be used;

```
          DO 20 K = 1, 11
20  MONTH(K) = MONTH(K + 1)
      MONTH(12) = NEW
```

The first pass of this DO loop will move the content of MONTH(2) to MONTH(1), the second pass will move MONTH(3) to MONTH(2), and so on. When the loop has completed the original value of MONTH(1) will have been lost and the other values all moved back one element as required.

The DATA Statement

We have already seen that constant values can be placed in variables by means of the assignment statement:

```
A = 27
B = 6
C = 9 and so on
```

The DATA statement permits a number of variables to be **primed** with constant values at the start of your program. This statement consists of the word DATA followed by a list of variables followed by a list of constants enclosed in slash-marks (the slash-mark is the division symbol /). Values from the list of constants are assigned to the list of variables from left to right. The first value is assigned to the first variable, the second value to the second variable, and so on. The number of constants must equal the number of variables specified.

DATA I, A, K, R/6, 3.∅, 27, 6.∅/

In this case the value 6 is assigned to I, the value 3.∅ to A, the value 27 to K, and the value 6.∅ to R. Note that the type of each constant corresponds to the type of its associated variable.

Array element names may also appear in a DATA statement:

DATA A(7), A(4), A(9)/3.∅, 4.2, 6.9/

However, if every element in the array is to be assigned a value the array name can be specified once only without a subscript:

DIMENSION D(4)
INTEGER D
DATA D/6, 7, 8, 9/

In this case the value 6 is assigned to D(1), 7 to D(2), 8 to D(3), and 9 to D(4). When an array name is used in this way sufficient constant values must be specified to give each array element a value.

Exercises

1. Write the statements to define three arrays—R, Q, and Y—each of six elements. Array Y is to be integral, array Q complex, and array R real.
2. Write the statement to add the fourth element of array B to the third element of array Q.
3. Write the statements to add the contents of array R (DIMENSION R(6)) to the corresponding elements of array Z.
4. Write the statements to place the total of the elements of array B in the variable X and the square of this total in variable Y. The number of elements in array B is given in variable N.
5. Using the data computed in question 4 write the statements to calculate the average of the values of the elements in array B.
6. Write the statements to total (result in M) the negative values of array R (20 elements) into variable N and the positive values into variable P.
7. Given that the chi-square (χ^2) value is found from

$$\chi^2 = \frac{(O - E)^2}{E}$$

Where O is a set of observed frequencies and E is an expected frequency write the statements to calculate χ^2 for the frequencies held in the twelve-element array C. The expected frequency (E) is in the variable F.
8. Write the statement to set constant values of 1, 2, 3, 4, and 5 into the integral variables A, B, C, D, and E.
9. Rewrite question 8 placing the five constant values in the integral array Q.
10. Write the statement to transfer control to statement 12 if the nth element of array B is equal to the value of variable P.

CHAPTER FIFTY-FOUR

INPUT AND OUTPUT STATEMENTS

Before a FORTRAN program can process any data and produce the required computations it is necessary for data to be input to the program. Similarly the results of calculations must be communicated to the programmer by the program itself. When a FORTRAN program is being run from a time-sharing terminal the data will normally be inputted from the typewriter device in use and the results printed on the same device. (Note that when a FORTRAN program is run in an environment other than time-sharing the peripheral input/output commands discussed in Chapter Fifty-five will be used for the reading and printing of data.) The commands described in this chapter apply only to FORTRAN programs operated via a time-sharing system. Since these commands do not appear in standard FORTRAN the keywords used differ in different systems. Those used here (INPUT and PRINT) are the more common ones in the author's experience; they do indicate, however, the general format to be used.

The INPUT Statement

To enable data to be read into your program when it is executed you should use the INPUT command. This consists of the word INPUT followed by a comma, followed by one or more variable names. When the statement is executed, during program running, a question mark will be printed on the user's terminal and the keyboard will be unlocked. The user can then type in a list of values (separated by commas) which he wishes assigned to the variables in the INPUT statements. If the user does not specify enough values a further question mark will be printed; if he specifies too many the excess values will be ignored.

The simplest form of the INPUT command is with a single variable:

$$INPUT, A$$

When this statement is encountered during program execution the computer will print ? on the terminal and will unlock the keyboard; the user may type in his value for the variable A followed by a carriage return:

$$? \ 27.39 \ \textcircled{CR}$$

The value 27.39 will be assigned to the real variable A. On subsequent executions of the above statement different values may of course be given to the variable A by the user. Once the variable has been given a value by the operator it may be used for computation:

```
          INTEGER X
          INPUT, X
          DO 10 K = 1, X
          A = A + K**2
    10    A = A + K**3
```

The INPUT statement may contain more than one variable name:

INPUT, R, S, T

The computer will expect the user to respond to the ? with three values:

? 2.09, 4.0, 18.1 Ⓒ®

The value 2.09 will be assigned to R, the value 4.0 to S, and the value 18.1 to T. If the user gave only two values the computer would respond with a further ? which the user would follow with the third value:

? 2.09, 4.0 Ⓒ®
? 18.1 Ⓒ®

A null value (i.e. zero) may be indicated by the appearance just of a comma:

? 3, 4, Ⓒ®

would indicate the values 3, 4, and zero.

? 3, ,4 Ⓒ®

would indicate the values 3 zero and four.

An array may be filled by an INPUT statement within a DO loop:

DO 10 K = 1, 10
10 INPUT, A(K)

Each time the loop is passed the INPUT statement will request a value for A(K), thereby filling the elements 1 to 10 of the array (since the DO statement will cause the INPUT statement to be executed 10 times). Note, however, that each ? must be responded to with a single value—the computer will print 10 question marks; one for each execution of the loop.

If the INPUT statement within the loop contained more than one variable name then the user would have obviously to give more than one value:

DO 10 K = 1, 10
10 INPUT, A(K), B(K)

In this case the computer would still print ten question marks, but the user would give two values to each of these. The two values would represent one for array A and one for array B. For example, in the coding above the two values entered during the fourth pass of the loop would be assigned to A(4) and B(4) respectively.

The PRINT Statement

This statement allows the user to print the value of a variable on his terminal device during execution of his program. To use this statement the programmer writes the word PRINT followed by a comma, followed by one or more variable names. When the statement is encountered during program execution the current value of the variable(s) specified are printed on the user time-sharing teletype device.

PRINT, A

When this statement is executed the *current value* of variable A will be printed on the terminal. As with the INPUT statement above this statement may contain several variable names:

PRINT, R, Q, X

This statement will cause the current values of R, Q, and X to be printed on the terminal device. (Note—the three values will be automatically spaced out by the compiler.) Since alpha constants can be specified in a PRINT statement it is possible to give notations to the data being printed:

ALPH = "R IS"
PRINT, ALPH, R

The result of this PRINT statement will be the printing of the expression "R IS" (which is the current value of ALPH) followed by the actual value of R.

Using the INPUT and PRINT statements it is now possible for us to write complete working FORTRAN programs. For example, as a simple start, let us look at the program to input single values and print out the square and cube of these numbers:

```
10 INPUT, R
   S = R**2
   T = R**3
   PRINT, S, T
   GO TO 10
```

When this program is run the computer will ask for a value of R by typing a question mark. The value typed by the user will be assigned to R; the next two statements will calculate the square and the cube of R, and the PRINT statement will type out these values. The GO TO statement will cause the above steps to be repeated as long as the user desires. (Note—typing the word STOP, rather than a value, following the ? will cause the program to terminate.) Suppose that as well as calculating the square and cube of each of several values (say 10 in all) we wish also to calculate the square and cube of the total of the values:

```
   DO 10 K = 1, 10
   INPUT, R
   S = R**2
   T = R**3
   A = A + R
10 PRINT, S, T
   S = A**2
   T = A**3
   PRINT, S, T
   STOP
   END
```

Notice how in this example we have introduced two new statements—STOP and END. STOP is used to signify the logical end of our program to the compiler which will generate coding to automatically return to the operating system when the statement is encountered. END is used to signify the physical end of the program and causes compilation to terminate.

The following program will read in twelve values, representing the monthly stock figures, calculate a three-month moving average for each of the groups of three consecutive months, and calculate the average of the twelve months (output first).

```
        DIMENSION A(12)
        DO 10 K = 1, 12
        INPUT, A(K)
    10  T = T + A(K)
        M = T/12
        PRINT, M
        DO 20 J = 1, 10
        T = A(J) + A(J + 1) + A(J + 2)
        M = T/3
    20  PRINT, M
```

The calculation, within the second DO loop, for the three-month moving average could have been accomplished in one compact statement:

$$M = (A(J) + A(J + 1) + A(J + 2))/3$$

As a final example consider the program designed to input a series of 20 values each of which represents a temperature. The program will convert these figures from either Fahrenheit to Centigrade or Centigrade to Fahrenheit depending upon the nature of the input values. The program will determine which conversion is required by requesting an indicator value from the user. If the value is 1 the conversion required is Fahrenheit to Centigrade and if zero Centigrade to Fahrenheit.

Remember that $C = 5/9(F - 32)$
$F = 9/5C + 32$.

```
        ALPHA A
        DIMENSION T(20), C(20)
        DO 10 K = 1, 20
    10  INPUT, T(K)
        A = "F TO C"
        PRINT, A
        INPUT, I
        IF (I .EQ. 1) GO TO 12
        DO 14 K = 1, 20
    14  C(K) = T(K)*9/5 + 32
        GO TO 17
    12  DO 16 K = 1, 20
    16  C(K) = (5/9) *(T(K) - 32)
    17  DO 18 K = 1, 20
    18  PRINT, T(K), C(K)
        STOP
```

Notice how the message F TO C is printed before the user has to give his requirements for conversion; this will remind him that he has entered all the temperature values and now has to tell the program which way they are to be converted.

Formatting

When a PRINT statement contains a number of variable names such as this example:

PRINT, A, B, C, D

the values subsequently printed when the program is executed will be automatically tabulated into columns across the page. When the same (or similarly coded) PRINT statement is executed several times (in a DO loop for example) the tabulation will be the same each time thus producing neat columns of figures on the print-out.

Since FORTRAN is basically a language aimed at solving calculations its tabulation facilities, other than those mentioned above, are fairly complicated to master. They are therefore beyond the scope of this book; the reader will find the automatic column tabulation quite adequate while familiarizing himself with FORTRAN.

Exercises

1. Write the statement to read into your program values for the variables P, Q, and T.
2. Write the statement to print out the current values of variables SUM, TOTAL, and B.
3. Write a program to read 10 values into an array R, then calculate and print out the average of the 10 values.
4. Write a program to read in 10 numbers, sort them into order and print them out. Note—sorting can be achieved by comparing each successive pair of numbers and swopping them if out of order; when all the nine pairs have been examined without a swop being needed then the array will be in sequence.
5. Write a program to read in 8 values and print out the largest of these values.

CHAPTER FIFTY-FIVE

BACKING STORE HANDLING

The commands described in this chapter enable you to input data from or output data to a backing store device (normally a magnetic disc). In a non-time-sharing environment these statements can also be used in lieu of INPUT and PRINT to input data from punched cards (or paper tape) and output data to a line printer respectively.

File Layout

It is not necessary to define record or block layouts when reading or writing FORTRAN files. The blocking and deblocking is done by coding automatically generated by the FORTRAN compiler and each input or output statement will specify the layout required in a given record. Note that it is possible to generate different record layouts with different output statements; however, since the input statement must specify (before reading the data) the expected layout it is recommended that a single layout only be used on any given file.

Outputting Data

Data is written to files by means of the WRITE statement. The WRITE statement consists of the word WRITE followed by the name of the file to be written to (in parentheses), followed by the names of the variables to be written. For example, to transfer the values of the variables R, S, and T to the file called OUTLIST the following could be coded:

WRITE ("OUTLIST") R, S, T

The three values will be written as a single record to the named file (reading the data back into a program is discussed below), although the programmer does not explicitly have to state this within his program. A single variable may be so written:

WRITE ("OUTFILE") A

or a large number may be written:

WRITE ("FILE2") A, R, Q, X, Z, Y, P, D, F, G, H

In each case the variable(s) specified in the WRITE statement are grouped into a single record. (Note—the **blocking factors** are automatically determined by the compiler.)

The name of the file to which data is to be written may be specified by a file-name variable, enabling a single WRITE statement to transfer data to more than one file during execution of a program:

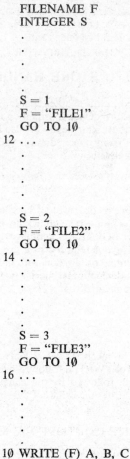

```
          FILENAME F
          INTEGER  S
          .
          .
          .
          .

          S = 1
          F = "FILE1"
          GO TO 10
     12 ...
          .
          .
          .
          .

          S = 2
          F = "FILE2"
          GO TO 10
     14 ...
          .
          .
          .
          .

          S = 3
          F = "FILE3"
          GO TO 10
     16 ...
          .
          .
          .
          .

     10 WRITE (F) A, B, C
          GO TO (12, 14, 16) S
```

The records written to the different files will all have the same layout—being made up of the three variables A, B, and C.

Inputting Data

Data is inputted, from backing store files, by means of the READ statement. This is similar to the WRITE statement except that within the parentheses must be specified an **end condition**. You will recall from Part One that the end of data on an input file is indicated by a special record; the program must detect this condition since any attempt to read beyond the marker will generate an error condition. The end-of-file condition is tested for by means of the expression

$$END = nn$$

where nn specifies the line number to which control is to be passed when the condition occurs. The statement to input the three variables written in the first WRITE statement above could be coded thus:

READ ("OUTLIST", END = 27) R, S, T

In this case the three variable names specified are identical to the ones used in the WRITE statement. Since the READ and WRITE statements are likely to be in different programs the names need not be the same in each case; however, they must specify variables of the same type. The above READ statement could be replaced by

READ ("OUTLIST", END = 27) A, B, C

In this case variable A must be of the same type as variable R in the file writing program. Similarly for S and B and T and C.

Arrays and Files

An array may be written to (and subsequently read from) a file by using the appropriate statement within a DO loop:

DIMENSION A(1∅)

.

.

.

.

DO 1∅ K = 1, 1∅
1∅ WRITE ("FILE1") A(K)

Using this method each element of the array will be the subject of a separate WRITE statement and will therefore occupy a separate record. With large arrays this will clearly be wasteful of file space (remember inter-block gaps). An alternative could be found for small arrays thus:

WRITE ("FILE2") B(1), B(2), B(3), B(4)

but this is clearly unsuitable for large arrays. Instead an implied DO facility is provided within the WRITE and READ statements. This is illustrated by the following example:

WRITE ("FILE1") (A(K), K = 1, 1∅)

The array to be output to the file is specified as the array name with a **variable subscript** together with the **initial, terminal,** and **increment** values required for the subscript. (Note—in the example shown the increment is assumed to be 1.) This WRITE statement will cause the ten elements of the array to be written as a **single record**. This will save file space and will reduce the time required for the operation (i.e. one record of ten elements takes less time to write than ten records each of one element). The array written above could be input to a program using a READ statement with an implied DO:

READ ("FILE1", END = 14) (A(K), K = 1, 1∅)

This statement will expect to read a single record containing ten elements of an array. Any number of such records may exist on the file being input and the program using it may therefore process a large number of array values. The following program will read sets of values from the user's terminal and write them as arrays to a file called ARR. In order that the user may keep track of his data values the program prints the array name (A) and the element number required prior to each input statement. (Note—the program will be completed by the programmer typing "STOP" which causes automatic termination.)

```
      DIMENSION A(10)
      INTEGER A
    5 DO 10 K = 1, 10
      PRINT, "A", K
   10 INPUT, A(K)
      WRITE ("ARR") (A(K), K = 1, 10)
      GO TO 5
      STOP
```

To read this file the following could be used:

```
      DIMENSION R(10)
      INTEGER R
   10 READ ("ARR", END = 12) (R(N), N = 1, 10)
      .
      .
      .                    (array processing)
      .
      .
      GO TO 10
   12 PRINT, "END"
      STOP
```

Exercises

1. Write the statement to transfer the values of the variables TOTAL, TIME, and MAIN to the file called OUTDATA.
2. Write the statement to input the data written by question 1 into the variables A, B, and C; file-name is in the file-name variable Q.
3. Write the statements to read groups of four values (2 real, 2 integer) from the terminal and transfer them to the file OUT4.
4. Write the program to read the file written in question 3 and print the values on the terminal.
5. Write the statement to assign the file-name FOURX to the file-name variable NAME.

CHAPTER FIFTY-SIX

SUBROUTINES

When writing a large program it is quite likely that a particular set of instructions will be required a number of times. For example in a statistical program it may be found that the calculation of the mean (average) of a series of values appears in different areas of the program logic. It would be wasteful of program space and the programmer's time to code this sequence every time it was required. To avoid this FORTRAN provides a facility called subroutining. This involves the writing of a set of instructions as a separate unit that can be executed from any part of the program as and when required. The separate unit of instructions (called a subroutine) is identified by the word SUBROUTINE which is followed by the name of the programmer wishing to give it:

SUBROUTINE CALC

This statement indicates that the statements following form part of a sub-routine to be known by the name CALC. The end of a subroutine is indicated by the word RETURN (the additional function of which is discussed later). The following statement could therefore be a subroutine to calculate the average of the values of the four variables A, B, C, and D.

SUBROUTINE MEAN
M = (A + B + C + D)/4
RETURN

This subroutine assumes that the values to be operated on are always in the same variables (i.e. A, B, C, and D). However, it is quite possible, in a large program, that the programmer wishes to calculate the average of different sets of variables. He could, of course, assign these values to the subroutine variables before passing control to the subroutine:

A = V1
B = V2
C = V3
D = V4

Passing Parameters

This method is quite feasible and does have some applications. However, in order to avoid the programmer in the additional work (of assigning values to the subroutine variables) the compiler provides a simple method of specifying the required assignment. The variables which are to be used by the sub-routine (and which are to be assigned the required values) are listed in parentheses after the subroutine name:

SUBROUTINE MEAN (A, B, C, D, M)

A corresponding list of variables is given in the CALL statement which is

255

used to **invoke** (or transfer control to) a subroutine. In its simplest form the CALL statement will specify only the subroutine name:

CALL SUBA

This statement will cause control to be transferred to the subroutine defined with the name SUBA. When the SUBROUTINE statement has a list of variables then the corresponding CALL statement must have an equivalent list. For example, to invoke the above-mentioned subroutine MEAN the following CALL statement could be used:

CALL MEAN (V1, V2, V3, V4, R)

This will transfer control to the subroutine MEAN and will assign the values of the variables named to those variables listed in the SUBROUTINE statement. In this case variable A will be assigned the value of V1, variable B the value of V2, variable C the value of V3, and variable D the value of V4; variable R will contain the result of the calculation, i.e. the final values of M in the subroutine. The execution of the subroutine MEAN will therefore calculate the average of the values of V1, V2, V3, and V4 and place the result in the variable R.

The execution of a subroutine is terminated by the RETURN statement which causes control to be transferred to the statement following the CALL statement that invoked the subroutine.

The coding below illustrates a program containing two subroutines each of which is invoked from different parts of the program:

```
INTEGER A
INPUT, A, B, C, D
CALL SUBA (A, B, R)
CALL SUBB (R, C, D, S)
     .
     .
     .
CALL SUBA (P, Q, R)
CALL SUBB (C, D, R, S)
     .
     .
     .
SUBROUTINE SUBA (X, Y, Z)
INTEGER X
Z = (X**2+(Y −3)**2)
RETURN
SUBROUTINE SUBB (F, G, H, J)
REAL J
J = F**2 + G**2
J = (J + H)**2
RETURN
STOP
```

(Note that the subroutine type statements appear within the subroutine itself.)

It is important to note that not only must the CALL statement specify the same number of variables as the SUBROUTINE statement but corresponding variables must be of the same type. A variable in the CALL statement list may be replaced with a constant value providing the corresponding variable in the SUBROUTINE is not the subject of an assignment statement.

For example, consider the following subroutine which raises a variable to a specified power:

```
SUBROUTINE RAISE (A, B, C)
C = A**B
RETURN
```

The value for the variable B may be specified, in the CALL statement, as a constant:

```
CALL RAISE (X, 3.0, R)
```

In this case execution of the subroutine RAISE would cause the value of X to be raised to the power 3.0 with the resultant values placed in the variable R.

Arrays in Subroutines

When a subroutine is to handle one or more arrays then the list of variables in the CALL and SUBROUTINE statements may specify just the array name (i.e. without a subscript). The entire array can then be considered to be passed to the subroutine. The subroutine must contain any required DIMENSION statements.

The following illustrates the handling of arrays within a subroutine:

```
DIMENSION X(100), Y(100), W(50), Z(50)
         .
         .
         .
CALL SWOP (X, Y, 100)
CALL SWOP (W, Z, 50)
         .
         .
         .
SUBROUTINE (A, B, N)
DIMENSION A(100), B(100)
DO 10 J = 1, N
10 A(J) = B(J)
RETURN
```

The subroutine SWOP is used to transfer the first n elements of one array to another (where n is specified in the CALL statement) up to a maximum of 100 elements. The first CALL statement shown does in fact transfer the 100 elements of array Y to the corresponding elements of array X. The second CALL statement, by specifying only 50 for the third entry in the variable list, causes only 50 elements to be transferred from array Z to array W (which happens to be the complete array). A single subroutine has therefore been used to manipulate arrays of different sizes merely by amending one of the values transferred to that subroutine at the time it was invoked.

A subroutine which handles only non-array variables can be made to function with an array by placing the CALL statement within a DO loop:

```
                    DIMENSION X(50)
                         .
                         .
                         .

                    DO 10 K = 1, 50
                 10 CALL SQUARE (X(K))
                         .
                         .
                         .

                    SUBROUTINE SQUARE (A)
                    A = A**2
                    RETURN
```

This coding, to square each element of an array, is equivalent to the following with the array in the subroutine:

```
                    DIMENSION X(50)
                         .
                         .
                         .

                    CALL SQUARE (X)
                         .
                         .
                         .

                    SUBROUTINE SQUARE (A)
                    DIMENSION A(50)
                    DO 10 K = 1, 50
                 10 A(K) = A(K)**2
                    RETURN
```

The reader will no doubt now appreciate the difference between setting up a loop to pass array elements one at a time to a single variable subroutine and passing complete arrays to a subroutine with its own looping.

Exercises

1. Write the statement to invoke the subroutine SUBR passing the variables A, B, and D.
2. Write the subroutine called AVG to calculate the average of three values (the subroutine being passed four variables).
3. Write the subroutine to calculate the average value of a fifty-element array.
4. Write the statement to invoke the subroutine written as the answer to question 3 (using the array given by DIMENSION P(50)).
5. Write the statements required to divide each element of the array X(20) by the corresponding element of the array Y(20) using the following subroutine:

```
                    SUBROUTINE DIV (A, B)
                    A = A/B
                    RETURN
```

CHAPTER FIFTY-SEVEN

FUNCTIONS

Within the mathematical environment normally associated with the use of FORTRAN there is a continuing requirement for a variety of **functions** to be evaluated. These will include such things as square root, logarithm, and the trigonometric functions (such as sine, cosine, tangent, etc.). The programming required to compute the values of this type of function would clearly be extremely difficult and costly in terms of development time (especially since they would be so frequently required).

To circumvent these problems FORTRAN provides a number of **built-in functions** whose purpose is to specify a complicated or frequently used computation in a concise manner. Functions are identified to the FORTRAN compiler by a 3, 4, or 5 character abbreviation of the required function in an arithmetic expression. This function identifier is followed, in parentheses, by the variable or variables which are the subject of the function computation.

For example, the square root function is identified by SQRT (expression). The expression will be evaluated and the square root calculated. The following statement demonstrates a simple example of the use of this function:

$$A = SQRT(B)$$

In the evaluation of this statement the square root of the expression (in this case the current value of the variable B) will be assigned to the variable A. A more complicated expression may be given:

$$R = SQRT \ (A**3 + 3*V2)$$

In this case the expression $(A**3 + 3*V2)$ will be evaluated using the *current values* of A and V2 and then the square root of the *resulting value* will be assigned to the variable R. A function or functions may be combined with other elements or functions to form a larger expression:

$$RESULT = SQRT \ (P/Q) + SQRT(Z/R)$$
$$ANSWER = SQRT \ (A/B + SQRT(C) \ )$$

Since a function may appear anywhere that an expression may be used it can be coded into output statements, loops, and control statements as the following examples will demonstrate.

$$PRINT, \ SQRT(A), \ SQRT(B)$$

This statement will cause the printing of the square roots of the current values of the variables A and B and is equivalent to the following three statements:

$$X = SQRT(A)$$
$$Y = SQRT(B)$$
$$PRINT, \ X, \ Y$$

It is clearly more efficient to use the functions within the **PRINT** statement rather than perform the calculations prior to that statement. The statements below show a function within a loop, which in this case converts each element of an array to its square root value if the original value was positive and zero if the original value was negative. (Note an attempt to take the square root of a negative number will generate an error condition):

```
        DO 10 K = 1, 20
        IF (A(K) .LT. 0.0) GO TO 12
        A(K) = SQRT(A(K))
        GO TO 10
     12 A(K) = 0.0
     10 CONTINUE
```

It is permissible to take the square root of the value zero (in which case the result is also zero) and the above loop could therefore be recoded more efficiently thus:

```
        DO 20 K = 1, 20
        IF (A(K) .LT. 0.0 A(K)) = 0.0
     20 A(K) = SQRT(A(K))
```

A function reference is also permissible in a control statement as the following examples will show:

```
        IF (SQRT(A) .LT. 7.2) GO TO 16
        IF (A .EQ. B) Z = SQRT(B + A)
        DO 10 K = 1, SQRT(X)
```

Built-in Functions

For illustrating the permitted contexts of function statements only the square root function has been shown. There are, however, a considerable number of standard or **built-in functions** available within various FORTRAN compilers and a description of some of the more commonly used ones follows. Note—the term **argument** indicates the value of the expression(s) following the function reference. Thus SQRT (arg) indicates that a single expression only may be in parentheses following the SQRT function, whereas MAX (arg 1, arg 2 . . .) indicates that at least two expressions must be present.

ALOG (arg)

Generates the natural logarithm (i.e. to the base e) of the expression given as the single argument.

$$R = ALOG(B)$$

This statement causes the natural log of B to be assigned to the variable R. The value of the argument must be a real value; the result of the function also being real.

ALOG10 (arg)

This function calculates the common (to the base 10) logarithm and is used in the same manner as ALOG.

ATAN (arg)

The result of this function is a value giving the angle (in radians) whose tangent is equal to the value of (arg). Thus if a tangent value is held in the variable T the following statement will assign the size of the corresponding angle to A:

$$A = ATAN(T)$$

CLK (arg)

The current time of day will be obtained from the computer's supervisor as the result of this function. The argument in this case is not evaluated but is merely a "dummy" to satisfy the compiler's requirement that all functions must be followed by a parenthesized expression. The result of this function is of the form HH:MM (i.e. hours and minutes) and needs to be assigned to a FILENAME type variable or an ALPHA (literal) variable. The following statements will cause the current time to be printed during execution of a program.

        ALPHA T
        T = CLK(X)
        PRINT, "TIME", T

CONJG (arg)

Two imaginary numbers are said to be conjugate if they differ only in the sign of their imaginary part; i.e. a + b*i* is conjugate to a − b*i*. This function will generate the conjugate of a complex number. (Both the argument and the result are therefore complex.)

        COMPLEX A, B
        A = (2.∅, 3.∅)
        B = CONJG(A)

The result of the third statement above would be B having the value (2.∅, −3.∅)

COS (arg)

The trigonometric cosine of the argument is computed:

$$C = COS (ANGLE)$$

The cosine of ANGLE will be assigned to the real variable C.

DBLE (arg)

The value of the argument is converted to a double-precision value.

        DOUBLE PRECISION D

$$D = DBLE (A^{**}2 + B)$$

DIM (arg1, arg2)

This function generates the positive difference between the two real values of the arguments, i.e. it subtracts the smaller of the two arguments from the other. Thus the two DIM function references shown below would generate the same result (+2.∅):

$$A = 6.0$$
$$B = 4.0$$
$$C = DIM(A, B)$$
$$A = 4.0$$
$$B = 6.0$$
$$C = DIM(A, B)$$

EXP (arg)

This is an exponential function—the value e (the base of natural logarithms) is raised to the power specified by the evaluation of the real argument. Thus the following statements will cause the value of $e^{2.0}$ to be printed:

$$A = 2.0$$
PRINT, EXP(A)

MAX (arg1, arg2 . . .)

The result of this function is the largest of the values of all the arguments specified:

$$C = MAX (A, B, D, E)$$

Suppose before execution of the above statement the values of the variables A, B, D, and E were 2.0, 16.3, 15.9, and 14.4 respectively. The result of the statement would be that the value 16.3 was assigned to the variable C. Note— some FORTRAN compilers require that this function be specified as MAX0 and MAX1 for integer and real argument lists respectively.

MIN (arg1, arg2 . . .)

This is the converse of the previous function, giving the minimum of the values of the arguments in the list. Likewise some compilers require that this be specified as MIN0 or MIN1 for integer and real argument list respectively.

SIGN (arg1, arg2)

When used in an assignment statement the result of this function will be the value of argument 1 with the sign of argument 2. Thus if the values of A and B were 2.0 and −3.0 respectively then the result of the statement below would be to give C the value −2.0:

$$C = SIGN(A, B)$$

SIN (arg)

The trigonometric sine of the angle specified by the value of the argument is computed and represents the result of this function.

SQRT (arg)

The square root of the argument values is computed.

TAN (arg)

The trigonometric tangent of the angle specified by the value of the argument is computed.

Functions in Use

A tremendous number of uses exist for functions and precisely where you will encounter them will depend upon your working environment. However, to clarify the method of using functions in FORTRAN some examples of their use are presented below:

A quadratic equation of the form $ax^2 + bx + c = 0$ has two roots given by the formula

$$x = \frac{-b \pm \sqrt{(b^2 - 4ac)}}{2a}$$

The following program will read in the values of a, b, and c and print out the roots of the equation:

```
10 INPUT, A, B, C
   PRINT, (−B + SQRT(B**2 − 4*A*C))/2*A
   PRINT, (−B − SQRT(B**2 − 4*A*C))/2*A
   GO TO 10
```

Given one angle and the length of the opposite side of a right-angled triangle the following program will calculate first the lengths of the other two sides and then the area of the triangle. (Note—L1 is length of side opposite angle A and so on):

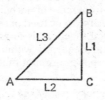

```
   REAL L1, L2, L3
10 INPUT, L1, A
   L2 = L1/TAN(A)
   L3 = SQRT(L1**2 + L2**2)
   A = L1*L2* 0.5
   PRINT, L1, L2, L3, A
   GO TO 10
```

Where the square root is to be taken of the difference between two numbers it is useful to use the DIM (Positive difference) function to avoid the possibility of supplying a negative number to the SQRT function:

```
    F = DIM(A, B)
    S = SQRT(F)
or  S = SQRT(DIM(A, B))
```

The trigonometric functions can be used to derive the co-ordinates of a variety of curves as shown below. The degree of accuracy of the subsequent plotting can be improved by increasing the number of executions of the DO loop. The program shown prints the x and y co-ordinates of the curve known as a cycloid (the path traced out by a point on the rim of a wheel) which are given by the equations:

$$x = a(\theta - \sin \theta), \; y = a(1 = \cos \theta)$$

where a is the radius of the wheel and θ the angle made by the radius of the wheel from a fixed starting-point.

```
        INPUT R
        PI = 3.142
        DO 10 K = 1, 4*PI, PI/180
        X = R*(K − SIN(K))
        Y = R*(1 − COS(K))
 10 PRINT, X, Y
        STOP
        END
```

The DO loop ensures that the x, y co-ordinates are generated at interval of 1° for θ although θ (K in the program) is specified in terms of radians (1 degree = $\pi/180$ radians).

User-Defined Functions

As well as using the built-in functions described above the programmer may define his own functions for use within any single program. Any function names so defined must differ from those of the built-in functions and must not be the same as any variable name to be used in the program.

The purpose of user-defined functions is to avoid repetition when a particular expression is to appear frequently within a program. A user-defined function is identified by the appearance of a function-type expression to the left of an equals sign:

$$MYFUNC(X) = A**2 + B**3$$

This identifies the user function to be known as MYFUNC which has a single argument—when encountered in an expression in the program the argument specified will be assigned the value of the expression on the right of the equals sign in the function definition.

For example the statement:

$$Y = MYFUNC(X)$$

is equivalent to $Y = A**2 + B**3$

(Note that the X in parentheses is a dummy argument and is not actually used although it must be present.)

The user-defined function can be used anywhere that a built-in function can be used:

$$R = A**2*(MYFUNC(X) + T**2 + Z)$$

In each case the appearance of MYFUNC(X) will be replaced by $A**2 + B**3$. As with built-in functions the user-defined functions are evaluated first when encountered in an arithmetic expression.

The type of a user-defined function is identified (and can be altered) in the same way as a variable—MYFUNC is therefore an INTEGER function unless specifically typed:

$$REAL \ MYFUNC$$
$$MYFUNC(X) = A**2 + B**3$$

A further example of a user-defined function is shown below where the function represents the current average of the values of three variables:

$$MEAN(X) = (A + B + C)/3$$
$$REAL \ MEAN$$

.
.
.
.
.
.

$$R = (D + E)/MEAN(X)$$

.
.
.
.

$$P = (F + G + K**2)/(MEAN(X) + 4)$$

.
.
.

STOP
END

Exercises

1. Write the statement to assign the value of the square root of variable A multiplied by variable B to the variable R.
2. Given that the formula for Standard Deviation is

$$S = \frac{\sqrt{\Sigma(x - \bar{x})^2}}{n}$$

where x is all the occurrence of the values under question, $\bar{x}$ is the average of those values, and n is the total number of them, write the statements to calculate the standard deviation for the values in the array P(DIMENSION (12)).
3. Write the statements to print out the square root of the difference between the largest and the smallest value of the variables A, B, C, F, G, H, P.
4. Define a real function MINE to represent the expression

$$(A**2 + 2*B + C)/D$$

5. Write the statements to assign to T the tangent of the angle whose size (in degrees) is held in A (1 degree = $\pi/180$ radians).

Revision Questions. Set 5

1. Identify the type of the following constants:
   (a) 27   (b) 27.0   (c) (4.1, 7.2)   (d) "HELP"   (e) 3H123   (f) .TRUE.
2. Write the statements to define the integer variables R, S, and T, the real variables K, L, and M, and the logical variable Y.
3. What will be the initial value of the variables defined in question 2.
4. Write the statement to assign the value of A multiplied by (B–C) to the variable D.
5. Write the statement to raise the variable R to the power 4.
6. Write the statement to calculate the average value of the variables J, K, L, and M placing the result in R.
7. Write the statement to transfer control to the statement numbered 12.
8. Write the statement to transfer control to the statement numbered 16 if the logical constant LOG is true.
9. Write the statement to square the value of A if that value is greater than 12.
10. Write the statements to add together the ten elements of the array B placing the result in S.
11. How many times will the loop initiated by the statement DO 10 K = 1, 20, 2 be executed?
12. Write the statements to total the values of the even-numbered elements of array A(DIMENSION A(16))
13. Write the statements to multiply each element of the array A by the corresponding element of B placing the result in array C (all arrays have twenty-four elements).
14. Write the statements to calculate the average of those elements of array A for which the corresponding element of array C is not equal to zero; both arrays have twelve elements.
15. Define a double precision array called DP with sixteen elements.
16. Write a program to read values from a user terminal and print for each one its square and cube.
17. Write the program to input from a user terminal the values for a twelve-element array IN. Calculate and print out the average of these values and the positive difference between each element and the average.
18. Write a program to input the values for a ten-element array F and write each set to a file SET as single record.
19. Write a program to read the file created in question 18 and print out the total of the values of each array.
20. Write a program to calculate and print the x and y co-ordinates for the curve specified by

$$x = a(\cos \theta + \tan \theta)$$
$$y = b \sin \theta$$

where a and b are constants supplied by the user and θ is an angle, specified in radians, for the range 0 to 2π (1 degree = $\pi/180$ radians).

PART FOUR

BASIC PROGRAMMING LANGUAGE

The word BASIC is an acronym of "Beginners All-purpose Symbolic Instruction Code" and although less elegant and less powerful than other programming languages does still fulfil its two main objectives. BASIC is for beginners—it can be used quite quickly by people who are not, and who do not wish to be, computer professionals. BASIC is also all-purpose: it can be used for simple computational work, for problem-solving, for small business applications and, increasingly, for home computing.

BASIC began life in 1964 at Dartmouth College, America, where it filled a need for a simple computer language for beginners. BASIC has proved to be very popular since then. This is particularly so in the case of time-sharing computer systems (see Chapter Forty-eight) where the language has been universally adopted. BASIC is also available on most mainframe computer systems.

The most recent development of the language has been in "home-computing". Microprocessor systems (discussed in detail in Part Five) have become very sophisticated in the last few years. Indeed, the latter half of the seventies will probably be well remembered as the microcomputer era. Early microcomputers used machine or assembly language and programming required a dedication found only in the most ardent enthusiast. As the systems developed and became larger and as the range of potential users widened it became necessary to supply a high-level language. BASIC proved to be the ideal choice; in its simplest form (see below) it can be implemented on a very small machine (unlike, say, COBOL) and yet it can provide for the most sophisticated file handling and so on. The problem with BASIC is that it has been extended and improved in different ways by different computer suppliers and users. This means that a program written in BASIC for one computer might not run on another machine from a different supplier.

Attempts have been made to produce an industry standard. The American National Standards Institute (ANSI) has produced a recommendation for "minimal BASIC" (ANSI X3JZ/76–0l); the National Computing Centre (U.K.) has published *Specification for Standard Basic*, by Bull, Freeman and Garland.

The fundamental part of BASIC (basic BASIC?) is reasonably standard throughout the computer industry. Programs written using the coding shown in the first part of the section will be "portable". They will run on almost any computer supporting the BASIC language.

The problem arises when the language is extended. Because there are no agreed standards, different computer suppliers have extended the language in different, non-compatible, ways. A number of books have tried to overcome this by giving an "average" BASIC or by listing the variations of all "major" suppliers. The problems with either of these approaches should not be too difficult to work out.

I have adopted a different approach. I have based the second section of Part Four (i.e. the non-standard BASIC) on a particular system. Readers who do not have access to such a system or who aquire a different piece of equipment will need to do a little re-learning for the extended features of BASIC. In my own experience this is less of a problem than it might appear. The differences are often only slight and the reader will at least have an understanding of the methods and techniques used.

The program examples given in this book are based on the BASIC compiler supplied with the MOSTEK SYS-80F described in more detail in Part Five. The author wishes to express his gratitude to MOSTEK for their help and understanding in the preparation of this text.

CHAPTER FIFTY-EIGHT

INTRODUCTION

In the text that follows the assumption is made that BASIC is being run via some form of interactive terminal device. The terminal may be of the visual display or printer-keyboard variety. In either case the programmer is in direct contact with the BASIC compiler in the computer and can interact with it. The programming may be for a time-sharing computer system or a stand-alone microcomputer.

BASIC can usually be run in either the direct or the indirect mode. In the **direct mode** the BASIC compiler will evaluate and execute each statement as it is typed (the end of each line or statement being signified by carriage-return). This facility can turn BASIC into a calculator to provide immediate computation. For example, if the programmer typed

$$\text{PRINT } (37*2) + (84/21)$$

the computer would respond immediately with

78

(Don't worry for the moment about the mechanism of formatting this particular statement.)

In the **indirect mode** the programmer types in all his program statements and then requests BASIC to run the complete program. All program examples following will be in the indirect mode.

Instruction Format

The fundamental unit of the BASIC program is the line. A line consists of three parts—the **line number**, the **BASIC statement** and an **optional comment**:

nnnn BASIC statement (remark)

The brackets around "remark" indicate that it is optional.

The line number may consist of two, three, four or five digits depending on the size of the program. The program will be executed in the order of the line numbers. This is a most important point that cannot be overstressed. Suppose a program was typed thus (don't worry about the statements at the moment):

300 PRINT A
200 LET A = P*2
100 INPUT P

the order of statement execution following a subsequent RUN command would be:

```
100 INPUT P
200 LET A = P*2
300 PRINT A
```

This feature can be very useful. If, in the example above, it was wished to add an extra calculation before the PRINT instruction, rather than retype the entire program the following can be added:

$$275 \text{ LET } A = A + 3.14$$

The BASIC compiler will automatically insert the line in the correct sequence before executing the program or before printing the complete program. Following the above entry a LIST command would produce:

```
100 INPUT P
200 LET A = P*2
275 LET A = A + 3.14
300 PRINT A
```

In order that lines can be subsequently inserted it is recommended that initial line numbers should include gaps. The simplest method is to increase line numbers by 10 each time:

```
110 ........
120 ........
130 ........
140 ........
```

It is then a simple matter to insert forgotten or additional lines.

The MOSTEK system will automatically provide line numbers, incremented as desired, by use of the AUTO command before program entry. The RENUM command will renumber all lines from any chosen starting line number and with any increment desired.

Note that if the same line number is entered more than once, the computer "remembers" only the last one:

```
210 PRINT "READY"
220 INPUT X
210 PRINT "READY?"
220
210 PRINT "READY"
```

In this case the result is that the computer holds only the line

```
210 PRINT "READY"
```

The use of a line number without a statement serves to delete that line from the program.

BASIC Statements

The variety of BASIC statements are dealt with in the following chapters. Before proceeding with those, however, some ground rules can be specified.

The keywords used to define the BASIC function required (such as PRINT, INPUT, GOTO) must be entered exactly as specified. The manner in which data can be entered into your program is covered in the next chapter. A space must be left between each line number and its BASIC statement although the statement may generally be devoid of spaces if desired. Note, however, that testing and correcting a program is much easier if it is neatly laid out and includes adequate comments.

It is important to stress the difference between the letter O and the number zero. As with earlier parts of this book the following text will follow this convention:

letter "oh" written as O

number zero written as Ø

when representing computer input, output or contents.

For clarity of reading the text of this part has also been set in standard printers' characters. In practice the characters available to the computer user are limited to those found on a typewriter. The reader will find, when studying computer print-out, that the quotation symbols and those for minus and hyphenation differ slightly from those shown here.

CHAPTER FIFTY-NINE

CONSTANTS AND VARIABLES

Data

Programs written in BASIC, like most other programs, handle data. Data can of course take many forms:

stock values

employee names

length of triangle sides

wages total

spacecraft velocity

your name and address

and each program must be ready to manipulate the particular data it needs. Despite the infinite number of meanings attributable to an item of data there are a very few types of data. BASIC is a simple language and so keeps its data types simple, recognizing just numerical and textual items.

Numbers

BASIC deals with three types of number only: integer form, real form and exponent form. An **integer form number** is simply a whole number—that is, a number without a decimal or fractional part. The following are examples of BASIC numbers in integer form:

$$2846$$
$$16$$
$$999$$

A **real form number** is one with a decimal part (i.e. the bit after the decimal point). The following are examples of BASIC numbers in real form:

$$28.96$$
$$3.141596$$
$$\emptyset.2$$

Numbers written in **exponent form** are slightly more complicated at first sight. Exponent form numbers are in two parts, the mantissa and the exponent. The mantissa gives the numeric part of the number and the exponent gives the order of magnitude. For example, the number 1.2E3 means "1.2 times 10 to the power 3" (equivalent to 1,200). Since exponent form numbers will not be used in the programming examples of this part no further examples will be given. The interested reader is referred to Chapters Nine and Forty-nine for further information.

(The manner in which numbers are printed depends on a number of factors discussed later when the PRINT statement is explained.)

Texts

As well as handling numbers BASIC will also deal with words or texts. An example in an earlier chapter included the BASIC settlement—PRINT "READY". The "READY" is an item of textual data. It might also be called text, string, literal, literal string or alphameric string. A **string** consists of all the characters, words or numbers enclosed by quotation marks. The only thing you cannot put in a string therefore is a quotation mark:

125 PRINT "IT'S 28. . . ."

(Some versions of BASIC allow the printing of quotation marks by differing methods but it is best to avoid this.)

Numbers can appear in strings:

"274"

but such numbers cannot be used for arithmetic.

The data examples shown above come into the general category of **constant**. A constant is something that does not change its value during execution of the program. As we have seen, constants can be numbers or texts. Although constants are required for initial values and factors and print layouts, it would be almost impossible to write useful programs without something that can have a variable value.

Variables

A variable is an area of computer storage within a program that can be referred to by a name. Any reference to that name is taken by the program as a reference to the current value of that storage area. Just as with constants, BASIC has numeric variables and string or text variables.

Numeric Variables

The most important point to note about numeric variables is that they can each hold a number in integer, real or exponent form. The particular form used depends on context.

BASIC provides 286 simple numeric variables as a standard feature. These

A	AØ	A1	A2	A3	A4	A5	A6	A7	A8	A9
B	BØ	B1	B2	B3	B4	B5	B6	B7	B8	B9
C	CØ	C1	C2	C3	C4	C5	C6	C7	C8	C9
D	DØ	D1	D2	D3	D4	D5	D6	D7	D8	D9
E	EØ	E1	E2	E3	E4	E5	E6	E7	E8	E9
F	FØ	F1	F2	F3	F4	F5	F6	F7	F8	F9
G	GØ	G1	G2	G3	G4	G5	G6	G7	G8	G9
H	HØ	H1	H2	H3	H4	H5	H6	H7	H8	H9
I	IØ	I1	I2	I3	I4	I5	I6	I7	I8	I9
J	JØ	J1	J2	J3	J4	J5	J6	J7	J8	J9
K	KØ	K1	K2	K3	K4	K5	K6	K7	K8	K9
L	LØ	L1	L2	L3	L4	L5	L6	L7	L8	L9
M	MØ	M1	M2	M3	M4	M5	M6	M7	M8	M9
N	NØ	N1	N2	N3	N4	N5	N6	N7	N8	N9
O	OØ	O1	O2	O3	O4	O5	O6	O7	O8	O9
P	PØ	P1	P2	P3	P4	P5	P6	P7	P8	P9
Q	QØ	Q1	Q2	Q3	Q4	Q5	Q6	Q7	Q8	Q9
R	RØ	R1	R2	R3	R4	R5	R6	R7	R8	R9
S	SØ	S1	S2	S3	S4	S5	S6	S7	S8	S9
T	TØ	T1	T2	T3	T4	T5	T6	T7	T8	T9
U	UØ	U1	U2	U3	U4	U5	U6	U7	U8	U9
V	VØ	V1	V2	V3	V4	V5	V6	V7	V8	V9
W	WØ	W1	W2	W3	W4	W5	W6	W7	W8	W9
X	XØ	X1	X2	X3	X4	X5	X6	X7	X8	X9
Y	YØ	Y1	Y2	Y3	Y4	Y5	Y6	Y7	Y8	Y9
Z	ZØ	Z1	Z2	Z3	Z4	Z5	Z6	Z7	Z8	Z9

Fig. 47. BASIC numerical variables

are in 26 groups represented by the letter of the alphabet. Each letter can be used on its own or with one of the digits 0–9. Fig. 47 illustrates the numeric variables; some programmers like to take a photocopy of this and annotate it with the use of each variable as it is used. This can avoid the use of a variable more than once.

When a number is put into a variable (see LET statement) it replaces the value already stored there. When a variable is used to supply a value (either to another variable or in, say, a PRINT statement) its value is not changed.

Do not assume that numeric variables are set to zero at the beginning of your program. If you are not sure or the manual for the BASIC you are using does not confirm that **initialization** of variables takes place you should clear all those used with the appropriate LET statements.

String Variables

BASIC provides 26 string variables called:

A$, B$, C$, D$, E$, F$, G$, H$, I$
J$, K$, L$, M$, N$, O$, P$, Q$, R$
S$, T$, U$, V$, W$, X$, Y$, Z$

each of which can contain a string or text value. The maximum size of string is dependent on the BASIC in use. The MOSTEK value of 255 is typical.

If the string "ABCDEF" is moved into a string variable then the length of the string becomes 6. If the string "ABC" is subsequently moved into the same variable its length becomes 3. If the length of 6 is to be retained the string "ABC   " must be used.

At the start of a program, string variables may or may not contain blanks (spaces). You can set the initial values—if the computer does not do it for you—using the LET statement (see Chapter Sixty).

Exercises

1. What would be the result of adding 2 to "2"?
2. How many numeric variables are available?
3. How many string or text variables are available?
4. What type of variable is M$?
5. Can the contents of C be added to the contents of M6?

CHAPTER SIXTY

THE LET STATEMENT

The LET statement, or **assignment statement** as it is sometimes known, is used to change the value of a variable; it is used to assign a value to a variable. The general form of the LET statement is:

$$nnnn \text{ LET } v = \text{expression}$$

where nnnn is the line number, v is a variable name and expression is any valid combination of variables, constants and operators that will define the new value of v. In its simplest form the LET statement will assign the value of a constant to a variable:

$$135 \text{ LET } A = 27$$
$$145 \text{ LET } A6 = 146.2416$$
$$155 \text{ LET } C\$ = \text{"STRING"}$$

Note that since the variable in line number 155 (C$) is of the string type it must be assigned a string value. Similarly, numeric variables must be assigned an expression whose value is also numeric.

The next simplest form of the LET statement is where a variable is assigned the current value of another variable:

$$215 \text{ LET } Q = P7$$
$$225 \text{ LET } G = G2$$
$$235 \text{ LET } G\$ = R\$$$

Note that the value of the variable on the right of the equals sign is not changed by the execution of the LET statement. The LET statement is easier to understand if the "=" is considered to mean "is replaced by" thus:

$$165 \text{ LET } A = 2$$

can be considered as "A is replaced by 2".

Expressions

BASIC will allow complex expressions to be written on the right-hand side of a LET statement. We have already seen that an expression is a combination of variables, constants and operators. The first two of these are already familiar from the previous chapter. Operators are simply the arithmetic symbols shown below and brackets:

Symbol	Function
+	addition
−	subtraction
*	multiplication
/	division
↑	exponentiation

Consider some simple examples first:

$$456 \text{ LET } A = A9 + B9$$

assigns to A the value of the sum of the values of A9 and B9.

$$567 \text{ LET } B = B9 - R$$

subtracts the value of R from B9 and places the result in B (B9 and R remain unaltered of course).

$$245 \text{ LET } G = H*3$$

replaces the current value of G with 3 times the current value of H.

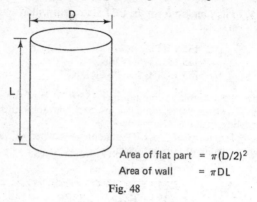

Area of flat part $= \pi(D/2)^2$
Area of wall $= \pi DL$

Fig. 48

Order of Evaluation

Consider now a more complex expression. Suppose you wish to calculate the surface area of a rod of length L and diameter D (Fig. 48). This is equal to:

$$2*3.14*D \uparrow 2/4 + 3.14*D*L$$

In working this out you would need to evaluate the component parts of the expression in the correct manner. For instance, you would clearly not begin by working out $4 + 3.14 = 7.14$, nor would you do $2/4 = 0.5$, then $0.5 + 3.14 = 3.64$.

Conventionally—and to mirror the problem—you would firstly evaluate the exponentiation function $D \uparrow 2$. Then you would do the multiplications, then the divisions and finally the additions and subtractions.

BASIC will evaluate an expression in the same way. Thus the order in which operators are handled is:

$\uparrow$	exponentiation
$*$ /	multiplication and division
$+$ —	addition and subtraction

Thus the following statement

$$169 \text{ LET A} = B*2 + C*3$$

is equivalent to

$$169 \text{ LET A} = (B*2) + (C*3)$$

and indeed brackets can be used like this to clarify an expression. Brackets can also be used to modify the evaluation of an expression because BASIC evaluates expressions in brackets first. If brackets are "nested" then evaluation begins with the innermost pair and works outwards.

Brackets should be used whenever there is a doubt as to the likely sequence of evaluation. For example, the expression $D/E/F$ could be interpreted as $(D/E)/F$ or as $D/(E/F)$ by different compilers. Similarly $M \uparrow R \uparrow S$ is ambiguous and could be interpreted as $(M \uparrow R) \uparrow S$ or $M \uparrow (R \uparrow S)$.

The following example illustrates the use of expressions with and without brackets.

Example: The monthly repayment on a mortgage loan of £A at an interest rate of I% for Y years can be calculated from the formula:

$$M = \frac{AP (1 + P)^Y}{12 [(1 + P)^Y - 1]} \text{ where } P = \frac{I}{100}$$

The BASIC routine to calculate M is as follows:

292 LET P = I/100
295 LET M = A*P*(1 + P) ↑ Y/(12* ((1 + P) ↑ Y−1))

Note that it is not possible to use implied multiplication; P(1 + P) is illegal—it is mandatory to write P * (1 + P) and so on. It is not permitted to put two operators (+ − */ ↑) together; brackets can be used to overcome this problem:

944 LET Z = 3 ↑ (− 3)

This statement will calculate the value of 3^{-3}.

Strings

We have seen already that strings can be manipulated using simple **LET** statements:

341 LET A$ = "NAME"
345 LET B$ = "DEPT"

Strings can also be assigned values from complex expressions but only the + operator may be used. In this case + is used to mean **concatenation** rather than addition. An example will best illustrate the point:

246 LET A$ = "ABC" + "DEF"

The resultant value of A$ after line number 246 has been executed is "ABCDEF".

String variables can be combined together or can be combined with string constants. Suppose that a man's name is held in N$; then the following will produce a value suitable for printing in P$:

147 LET P$ = "MR." + N$

An item of text could be surrounded with spaces using the following coding:

186 LET P$ = " " + I$ + " "

The word LET may be omitted from a LET statement if desired without affecting the BASIC interpretation:

214 LET A6 = B + R

is the same as:

214 A6 = B + R

Functions

BASIC includes a range of **intrinsic functions** that extend the scope of expressions in LET and other statements. Most BASICs include a wide range of functions many of which are unique to a particular implementation. However, the following 12 functions should be available in all versions of the language:

ABS (X)—returns the absolute value of the variable X. That is, if X is positive then ABS (X) = X; if X is negative then ABS (X) = − X. For example, in the statement

$$247 \text{ LET A} = \text{ABS (K)}$$

if K has the value −29 then A will be given the value 29.

EXP(X)—returns the value of e (2.71828) raised to the power X.

INT(X)—returns the largest integer (whole number) that is less than or equal to X. For example, the following two statements result in the integral value 412 being assigned to I:

$$66 \text{ LET A} = 412.76$$
$$68 \text{ LET I} = \text{INT(A)}$$

LOG(X)—calculates the natural logarithm (i.e. to the base e) of the number specified in X. Note that the value of X must be greater than zero.

SGN(X)—produces +1 if the value of X is greater than 0, 0 if the value of X is itself zero and −1 if the value of X is negative. This function is used therefore to determine the sign of a number.

SQR(X)—this function is used to calculate the square root of the value of X (which must not be negative). For example, to calculate the length of the side of a right-angled triangle, knowing the length of the other two sides and using the formula $L^2 = A^2 + B^2$:

$$246 \text{ LET I} = \text{A} \uparrow 2 + \text{B} \uparrow 2$$
$$248 \text{ LET L} = \text{SQR(I)}$$

This statement could have been written on one line thus:

$$245 \text{ LET L} = \text{SQR (A} \uparrow 2 + \text{B} \uparrow 2)$$

The following trigonometric functions are also available in BASIC:

ATN(X)—returns the angle (in radians) whose tangent has the value given by X.

COS(A)—calculates the cosine of the angle, measured in radians, specified by A.

SIN (A)—returns the sine of the angle (in radians) given by the value of A.

TAN(A)—calculates the tangent of the angle whose value in radians is given by A.

The use of the trig functions is best illustrated by a few calculations in respect of the triangle shown in Fig. 49. The area of the triangle ($\frac{1}{2}$AB sinK) is calculated thus:

$$244 \text{ LET } X = 0.5*A*B* \text{ SIN(K)}$$

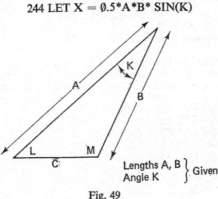

Lengths A, B ⎫ Given
Angle K ⎭

Fig. 49

The two unknown angles are calculated:

$$246 \text{ LET } L = \text{ATN } (B*SIN(K)/(A-B*COS(K)))$$
$$248 \text{ LET } M = \text{ATN } (A*SIN(K)/(B-A*COS(K)))$$

Finally, the length of the third side C can be computed using the formula $C = \sqrt{A^2 + B^2 - 2AB \cos K}$:

$$250 \text{ LET } C = \text{SQR } (A \uparrow 2 + B \uparrow 2 - 2*A*B*COS(K))$$

RND(X)—this is used to produce a "random" number between 0 and 1. If the value of X is less than 0 then a new sequence of numbers is started. If X is greater than 1 then RND(X) gives the next random number in the current sequence. A value of zero for X returns the last number again. Note that the number sequence is "pseudo-random"; sequences started with the same negative value of X will be the same.

The RND function can be used to "throw dice" for use, say, in playing a game with the computer:

$$561 \text{ LET } X = 1$$
$$563 \text{ LET } D = \text{INT } (1 + 6*RND(X))$$

VAL(X$)—returns the equivalent numerical value of the string variable X$. If X$ does not consist of digits (with or without a sign) then the returned value will be zero.

Exercises

1. Write the statements to:

   (i) Add the contents of A, B and C7 placing the result in D.
   (ii) Subtract 7 from G2.
   (iii) Put the square of G in A2.
   (iv) Divide A3 by G3 squared placing the result in A2.

2. Rewrite the statement:

$$240 \text{ LET } X = A/B + C$$

to divide A by the sum of B and C.

3. Write the statement to join strings X\$ and Y\$ in A\$.
4. Write the statement to produce a random number in the range 0 to 10.
5. What is the resultant value of A\$ following execution of these statements?

$$612 \text{ LET } X\$ = \text{"MR"}$$
$$614 \text{ LET } Y\$ = \text{"}\quad\text{"}$$
$$616 \text{ LET } Z\$ = \text{"JONES"}$$
$$618 \text{ LET } B\$ = \text{"B"}$$
$$622 \text{ LET } A\$ = X\$ + Y\$ + B\$ + Y\$ + Z\$$$

CHAPTER SIXTY-ONE

FURTHER FUNCTIONS

Most BASICs include a range of built-in functions additional to those described in Chapter Sixty. However, before considering some typical extra functions, a method for the programmer to define his own functions will be given.

A user function is specified using the command DEF (short for define) and BASIC provides for 26 such functions named FNA, FBN, etc., through to FNZ. For example, suppose you wish to define a function to convert an angular measurement in degrees to the equivalent in radians. The following function can be set up:

$$124 \text{ DEF } FNR(X) = 3.14159/180*X$$

Then the following statement will convert the angle in degrees held in variable A to its equivalent value in radians:

$$332 \text{ LET } Q = FNR(A)$$

In the definition of FNR (line 124 above) the variable X is called a **dummy argument** and is used only to indicate where a variable will go when the function is later evaluated. (The precise rules relating to function definitions vary from BASIC to BASIC and should always be checked before a program is **written**.)

More Intrinsic Functions

The following intrinsic functions form part of the BASIC system supplied with the MOSTEK system and illustrate the type of function available with the average system. Some BASICs have slightly different functions, others may have none.

ERL—returns the number of the line in which the last error occurred.

INSTR (X$, Y$)—finds the first occurrence of string Y$ in the string variable X$ and returns the position. For example, suppose the variable A$ contains the value "XXXXYXX". The statement:

$$212 \text{ LET C} = \text{INSTR (A\$, "Y")}$$

will set variable C to the value 5. (If the string Y$ is not found the value of C will be zero.)

LEFT $(X$, I)—returns the leftmost I characters of string variable X$.

LEN (X$)—calculates and returns the length of the string variable X$. Thus the value of R following these statements is 3:

$$814 \text{ A\$} = \text{"ABC"}$$
$$817 \text{ LET R} = \text{LEN (A\$)}$$

RIGHT $(X$, I)—returns the rightmost I characters of the string variable X$.

SPACE $(I)—returns a string variable of length I consisting entirely of spaces (blanks).

STR $(X)—returns a string variable representing the value of X.

Exercises
1. Define a function to find the area of a circle.
2. Write the statement to calculate the areas of the circle (radius in R) using the function from Q1.
3. Rewrite the answer to Q2 without the use of a function.
4. Find the string "MR" in the variable N$.
5. Write the statement to assign to variable M$ that part of string N$ following "MR".

CHAPTER SIXTY-TWO

INPUTTING DATA

Data for program variables can be input either from the program itself (in the form of constants) or read from the user's terminal device. The method used for loading program variables from within is considered first.

DATA and READ Statements

The DATA statement provides raw numbers or strings as constants for the READ statement to transfer to variables. The DATA statement stores the list of values in memory in a form suitable for later READing. Any number of DATA statements may appear in a program but, for the purposes of execution, they can be considered as one long list joined in order.

The READ statement always starts at the head of this list and picks up one item each time it is executed.

```
146 DATA "NAME", 2
148 READ N$
152 READ A
```

The string variable N$ now contains "NAME" and the value of A is 2. Note that the READ statement must encounter DATA values of the correct type otherwise a program error will occur.

```
146 DATA 2, "NAME"
148 READ N$
152 READ A
```

An error will occur at both statements 148 and 152 because the data type from the DATA statement in 146 will be incorrect.

After the following sequence of statements is executed the DATA list is "pointing" at the value 7 and this will be input by the next READ statement executed:

```
241 DATA 2, "ITEM", 2.14159, 16
243 DATA "JAN", "FEB", 7
245 READ A, I$, P, R
247 READ J$, F$
```

Note that a READ statement can contain a list of variables although the need to match variable type with DATA remains.

When a READ statement is executed the DATA list "pointer" is advanced to the next item but the DATA remains unaltered. Thus the items in the DATA lists can be read again by returning the "pointer" to the start of the list. This is done with the RESTORE command:

```
513 RESTORE
```

The next READ statement will input the first item following the first DATA statement of the program.

The INPUT Statement

This is used to request data values from the user terminal. As each value is typed in it is assigned to the appropriate variable. To input a single value:

244 INPUT A

When this statement is executed the terminal will print a ? (a question mark) and then await the user's response (note that program execution is suspended until the user enters a value and types carriage return). The value typed by the user must be of the correct sort (numeric or string) to match the variable name(s) quoted in the INPUT statement.

An INPUT statement can be used to input a number of values:

246 INPUT A, B, C

If the user does not enter enough values (which need to be separated by commas) BASIC will respond with further question marks. If too many values are entered the excess is ignored.

It is always a good idea to output a message prior to an INPUT statement so that the person subsequently running the program knows what is required. This is most often done with the PRINT statement discussed in the next chapter. Some BASICs, however, allow a prompt message to be included in the INPUT statement. In this case the message is printed prior to the question mark.

646 INPUT "GIVE STARTING YEAR", Y
648 INPUT "TYPE YOUR NAME", N$
652 INPUT "NEXT 3 VALUES", A, C, R

Exercises

1. Write the statement to prepare a data list with the values 28, 429.6, 3.14159 and your name.
2. Write the statements to start again at the head of the data list and put the name in N$.
3. Write the statement to assign your name to N$ from the user terminal.
4. What will be the result of typing 84, 5 in response to the statement:

INPUT A, C, R

5. What is wrong with these statements?

742 DATA 8, 12, "ONE"
744 READ A, C, R

CHAPTER SIXTY-THREE

THE PRINT STATEMENT

The PRINT statement is used, as its name implies, to print informatoin on the user's terminal. It can be used in a variety of ways to print string or numeric information and, with formatting control, can produce tabulations.

The simplest form of the PRINT statement uses the word PRINT and a single constant or variable:

```
142 PRINT "TEST PRINTING"
144 PRINT P
146 PRINT P$
148 PRINT R*3
```

Execution of line 142 will cause the words TEST PRINTING to appear on the user's terminal; line 144 will print the current value of the numeric variable P; line 146 prints the current value of the string variable P$ and line 148 computes the three times the current value of the numeric variable R and prints the answer. In each of these cases the PRINT statement is terminated with a carriage return and line feed so that only a single value is printed per line.

If you wish to print more than one value on a line then you should separate the items either with semi-colons or with commas. When separated with semi-colons the items in a PRINT statement will appear without intervening spaces:

```
412 LET L$ = " LEFT"
414 LET R$ = " RIGHT"
416 PRINT "MOVE"; L$; " OR"; R$
```

These statements will cause the following to be printed:

MOVE LEFT OR RIGHT

(Note the spaces within the string constants.)

When the last item in the list is followed by a space—as in line 416 above—the PRINT statement will terminate with a carriage return and line feed. If, however, a semi-colon follows the last item then the terminal print head remains in the current print position until the next PRINT statement. Thus the following statements will achieve the same result as line 416 above:

```
512 PRINT "MOVE";
514 PRINT " LEFT"; " OR";
516 PRINT " RIGHT"
```

Separating the PRINT statement items with commas causes BASIC to print in zones. For this the page width is divided by BASIC into 5 zones each of

14 characters. Thus zone 1 begins in print position 1, zone 2 in print position 15, zone 3 in print position 29, zone 4 in print position 43 and zone 5 in print position 57.

Each comma in a PRINT statement is regarded as an instruction to move to the first print position of the next available zone before commencing printing. If the print head is currently somewhere in zone 5 then the next comma will move it to zone 1 of the next line. The use of zones for tabulation is illustrated in the following coding showing part of a print-out of salesman's expenses:

```
241 PRINT "MONTH", "JONES", "SMITH", "WOOLEY"
243 PRINT, "(MANAGER)"
244 PRINT "JAN", J(1), J(2), J(3)
246 PRINT "FEB", F(1), F(2), F(3)
```

The resultant print-out is as shown:

MONTH	JONES	SMITH	WOOLEY
	(MANAGER)		
JAN	16	18	14
FEB	20	24	13

Note the use in line 243 of a comma as the first item to step the PRINT statement on to zone 2.

PRINT statements can contain both semi-colons and commas. When a semi-colon is encountered the next constant or variable is printed immediately; when a comma is encountered the print position moves to the beginning of the next zone. As an example, suppose that pound signs are to be added to the expenses program above; lines 244 and 246 can be amended as follows:

```
244 PRINT "JAN", "£"; J(1), "£"; J(2), "£"; J(3)
246 PRINT "FEB", "£"; F(1), "£"; F(2), "£"; F(3)
```

The resultant print-out is now as follows:

MONTH	JONES	SMITH	WOOLEY
	(MANAGER)		
JAN	£16	£18	£14
FEB	£20	£24	£13

The TAB Feature

This enables the next print position to be selected under program control:

```
281 PRINT TAB(1Ø); "TEN"
```

In this statement the expression TAB(1Ø) causes the print position to be set at 10 before the constant "TEN" is printed. (Note the first—left-hand—print position is 0, zero.)

The TAB expression may be calculated from a variable:

```
412 PRINT TAB (A); B$
414 PRINT TAB (C*2 + 1); B$
```

Thus, if in statement 414 the value of C was 10, then the printing of variable B$ would commence at print position 21.

PRINT USING

The PRINT USING statement allows the user to specify the **format** of a printed line by defining a print image. The user defines the print image for each line format he requires; then any PRINT USING statement can call upon this image with its own variables. Suppose, for example, that string variable A$ contains a print format:

> 116 PRINT USING A$; C; B; R$

The three variable C, B and R$ will be printed across the page according to the rules outlined below.

Consider first numeric fields, represented in the simplest form by a succession of # signs:

> 122 LET A$ = "####"
> 124 PRINT USING A$; C

The value of C is allowed 4 print spaces. The value of C will be right-justified and leading spaces will be inserted as necessary. If a decimal point is specified in the print format:

> 122 A$ = "##.##"

then the variable value is aligned to the decimal point, rounded if necessary. If the value is less than 1 then BASIC will insert a leading zero:

> 122 LET C = 4.5/5
> 124 PRINT USING A$, C

The printed value of C will be:

> Ø.9

(Note the trailing space inserted by BASIC.)

Numeric values can be spaced as desired across a page and aligned on their decimal points, thus:

> 482 LET A$ = "##.##   #.###   #.#"
> 484 PRINT USING A$; 27; .Ø246; 8

The resultant printout would be:

> 27.Ø   Ø.Ø25   8.Ø

(Note the rounding of .Ø246 to Ø.Ø25.)

If a plus sign is included in a numeric field format then either a + or − will be printed to indicate the sign of the value:

> 512 LET B$ = "+##   ###+"
> 514 PRINT USING B$; 29; −18

results in the following:

> +29   18−

If a minus sign is used in the format then it will be printed only if the value is negative; otherwise a space will appear.

A value in pounds can be preceded with a £ sign by using the following format:

> 694 LET P$ = "££###"
> 696 PRINT USING P$; 27
> 698 PRINT USING P$; 4162

which produces the following:

> £27
> £4162

Note that the £ sign is "floated" to the position immediately to the left of the leading digit.

Some BASIC compilers, including that supplied by MOSTEK, include a range of facilities for PRINT USING numeric formats including:

> floating asterisks (cheque protection)
> exponential format
> comma every third digit

Specific rules for these formats should be checked in the supplier's manual.

String items can be accommodated in print formats either as constants or variables. For example:

> 142 LET A$ = "RESULT IS ##.##"
> 144 LET C = 2.746
> 146 PRINT USING A$, C

results in a printout thus:

> RESULT IS 2.75

String variables are accommodated either by a ! (exclamation mark) for a single character or two / (slash marks) for 2 or more characters. Thus /   / (2 spaces between slash marks) represents a 4-character string variable.

Print formatting can usually be ignored at first and it only comes into its own when printing detailed reports or using preprinted stationery.

Blank Lines

Note that to print a blank line—for report spacing—use the PRINT statement without an operand:

224 PRINT
226 PRINT

This will produce two blank lines.

Exercises

1. Write the statement to print your name on the terminal.
2. Write the statement to print the values of the variables A, B, C each multiplied by 3 (print the answers in zones).
3. Rewrite the answer to number 2, printing the values without spaces between.
4. Rewrite the answer to number 3, printing the first value with a floating £ sign, the second with sign and the third rounded to two decimal places.
5. Write the statement(s) to produce two blank lines.

CHAPTER SIXTY-FOUR

PROGRAM CONTROL

This chapter looks at some of the ways in which you can change the normal flow of instructions in your program. Without any program control instructions execution will be in ascending sequence of line number. Program control instructions allow you to change this sequence either **unconditionally** (the change always takes place) or **conditionally** (the change only takes place if a particular condition is met).

The GO TO Statement

Unconditional program changes are made with the GO TO statement which instructs the program to go immediately to a specified line number:

142 GO TO 246

When line number 142 is reached the program moves or **jumps** to line 246, which will be the next statement executed. The following small program illustrates the use of GO TO (which may also be written GOTO) to create a continuous loop:

122 PRINT "INPUT THE RADIUS"
124 INPUT R
126 PRINT "AREA IS"; R ↑ 2*3.142
128 GO TO 122

The program will repeatedly request a value for the radius of a circle, then compute and print out the area of the circle. To stop program execution the terminal "break" key (or equivalent) should be pressed.

The IF THEN Statement

This is used to change the flow of program control only if a specified condition is met. This is best illustrated with a simple example:

282 IF R = S THEN 288

This statement says: if the value of R is equal to the value of S then transfer control to line 288, otherwise continue with the next sequential line number.

The general form of the statement is:

IF condition THEN line number

where condition is a combination of numbers or expressions and a conditional operator:

> = equals
> \> is greater than
> \< is less than
> \> = is greater than or equal to
> \< = is less than or equal to
> \<\> is not equal to

Some examples:

216 IF A = 29 THEN 218
217 IF B > = R*2 THEN 226
218 IF A <> B THEN 224
22Ø IF SQR(A + B) > Ø.35 THEN 226
222 IF 1Ø > A*2.5 THEN 226

The examples given so far relate to numeric variables or expressions. String expressions can be used only with the conditional operators = (equals) and <> (not equals):

214 IF A$ = "YES" THEN 226
226 IF R$ <> S$ THEN 234

Using the IF THEN statement the earlier sample program to calculate circle areas can be improved. Now the coding will loop only until a zero is entered:

122 PRINT "INPUT THE RADIUS"
124 INPUT R
126 IF R <> Ø THEN 128
127 STOP
128 PRINT "AREA IS"; R ↑ 2*3.142
129 GO TO 122

Note the use of the STOP statement in line 127. This has the effect of reverting control to the system, having terminated program execution.

Extensions to the IF THEN Statement

Some more advanced BASIC compilers, such as that provided by MOSTEK, extend the range of program control instructions with the following:

IF condition THEN line number ELSE line number

For example, the following statement will transfer control to statement 214 if A and B are equal and to statement 464 otherwise:

112 IF A = B THEN 214 ELSE 464

A further extension is to allow BASIC statements instead of line numbers:

414 IF A = B THEN PRINT "EQUAL"

or even

414 IF A = B THEN PRINT "EQUAL" ELSE PRINT "NOT EQUAL"

or

426 IF A > Ø THEN 428 ELSE PRINT "ERROR"
427 STOP
428 . . . . . .

In the last example the IF THEN ELSE statement has been used to verify that a variable is positive ($> Ø$) before processing continues.

Example. The use of GO TO and IF THEN is very important because of the way the statements allow complete programs to be constructed. It is always necessary to include some decisions in even the simplest of programs and the reader should take the time to understand fully the working of the program example given below. The purpose of this program is to calculate the area of a triangle, rectangle or circle (as selected by the user) from data supplied by the user.

```
100 PRINT "CALCULATE AREA OF GIVEN SHAPE"
110 PRINT
120 PRINT "TRIANGLE, RECTANGLE OR CIRCLE?"
130 INPUT S$
140 IF S$ = "STOP" THEN 340
150 IF S$ = "TRIANGLE" THEN 230
160 IF S$ = "RECTANGLE" THEN 190
170 IF S$ = "CIRCLE" THEN 280
180 GO TO 120
190 PRINT "GIVE HEIGHT AND WIDTH"
200 INPUT H, W
210 LET Z = H*W
220 GO TO 310
230 PRINT "GIVE LENGTHS OF THREE SIDES"
240 INPUT A, B, C
250 LET X = 0.5* (A + B + C)
260 LET Z = SQR (X* (X - A) * (X - B) * (X - C))
270 GO TO 310
280 PRINT "GIVE THE DIAMETER"
290 INPUT D
300 LET Z = 3.142*D↑2/4
310 PRINT
320 PRINT "AREA OF     "; S$; "IS"; Z
330 GO TO 110
340 STOP
```

The ON . . . GO TO Statement

This is another way of causing the program sequence to change depending on the value of a variable or expression. The general form of the statement is:

ON expression GO TO list of line numbers

When executed the expression is evaluated to an integer *i* (rounded if necessary) and control passes to the *i*th line number in the list. For example, consider this statement:

ON A GO TO 214, 226, 244

If A has the value 1 control passes to line 214, for a value of 2 to line 226 and for a value of 3 to 244. If the value of A is less than 1 or more than the number of line numbers (3 in this case) execution continues with the next sequential line number.

Example. The following simple program illustrates the use of ON . . . GO TO:

```
210 PRINT "TYPE A DIGIT Ø TO 3"
212 INPUT A
214 IF A < Ø THEN 238
216 IF A> 3 THEN 238
218 IF A − INT(A) <> Ø THEN 238
220 ON A GO TO 226, 23Ø, 234
222 PRINT "ZERO"
224 GO TO 212
226 PRINT "ONE"
228 GO TO 212
23Ø PRINT "TWO"
232 GO TO 212
234 PRINT "THREE"
236 GO TO 212
238 PRINT "ILLEGAL ENTRY"
24Ø GO TO 212
25Ø STOP
```

Exercises

1. Write the statement to transfer control to line 462.
2. Write the statement to transfer control to line 462 only if the value of A$ is "YES".
3. Write the statement to transfer control to line number 866 if the value of A divided by B is more than 96.
4. Write the statement to transfer control to line number 86 if the value of B is 6, 89 if the value is 7 or 94 if the value is 8.
5. Write the statements to print an error message if the value of A is not 1, 2 or 3.

CHAPTER SIXTY-FIVE

LOOPS AND SUBROUTINES

The FOR and NEXT Statements

It is often necessary to execute a series of statements repeatedly, perhaps with a counter to determine the sequence. For example, the following coding is executed up to 6 times depending on the value of A:

```
124 DATA "ONE", "TWO", "THREE", "FOUR", "FIVE", "SIX"
126 INPUT A
128 LET L = Ø
132 LET L = L + 1
134 READ P$
136 IF L <> A THEN 132
138 PRINT P$
```

(*Note:* for clarity it is assumed that the value of A is always in the range 1 to 6.)

The instructions on line numbers 132 to 136 inclusive are called a **loop** and use a "counter" L to control **iteration**. The same effect can be achieved in a simpler way with the FOR and NEXT statements as shown:

```
124 DATA "ONE", "TWO", "THREE", "FOUR", "FIVE", "SIX"
126 INPUT A
128 FOR L = 1 TO 6 STEP 1
132 READ P$
134 IF L = A THEN 138
136 NEXT L
138 PRINT P$
```

The statement in line 128 **initiates** a FOR/NEXT loop. This says: set the variable L at 1 (the **initial value**) and increase it by 1 (the **increment** or step value) until it reaches 6 (the **terminal value**).

For the first iteration, variable L will be given the value 1 and the statements following will be executed. When the NEXT statement is encountered control will pass back to the FOR, the value of L will be incremented and, if it is not more than the terminal value, the loop will be executed again.

When the increment or step value is 1 it can be omitted:

$$128 \text{ FOR L} = 1 \text{ TO } 6$$

The values in a FOR statement can be variables or expressions:

```
142 FOR A = B TO C
244 FOR R = 2 TO B*3 STEP 1Ø
472 FOR J = K TO L STEP −1
566 FOR K = R*2 TO 12 STEP B/1Ø
```

FOR/NEXT statements can be written within other FOR/NEXT statements; this is called **nesting**. The following program extracts a series of numbers from a DATA list and, for each number that is positive, prints the corresponding number of asterisks (i.e. if the value READ is 3 then three asterisks are printed):

```
120 FOR J = 1 TO 6
122 READ A
124 PRINT A;
126 IF A< = 0 THEN 136
128 FOR K = 1 TO A
132 PRINT "*";
134 NEXT K
136 PRINT
138 NEXT J
142 DATA 6, −1, 0, 2, 2, 4
```

With the DATA values shown this program will give the following result:

```
6 ******
−1
0
2 **
2 **
4 ****
```

Note that the inner or nested loop (statements 128–134) are only executed if the current value of A is positive (greater than 0).

To ensure correct operation of FOR/NEXT loops the following rules should be adhered to:

Never jump (via a GO TO) into the middle of a loop.
Do not assume anything about the value of the loop variable after dropping out of the loop.
Do not interleave nested loops.
Take care when using expressions in the FOR statement.
Never change the value of the loop variable within the loop.

Further examples of the FOR/NEXT statement are given in the next chapter covering arrays.

The GOSUB Statement

It is often found that the same sequence of statements is required a number of times in the one program. Rather than reproduce the sequence each time it is needed it can be included as a **subroutine**. This is a sequence of instructions that can be executed or called from any point in the program and which returns control to the statement following that which called it.

For example, suppose that in a program concerned with printing the following sequence of instructions is required each time a page is completed:

```
424 PRINT
426 PRINT
428 PRINT "-------------------------"
429 PRINT
433 PRINT "PAGE NO    "; N
434 PRINT
```

Rather than reproduce it each time it can be converted to a subroutine by the very simple process of adding a single line with the expression RETURN:

```
424 PRINT
426 PRINT
428 PRINT "-------------------------"
429 PRINT
433 PRINT "PAGE NO    "; N
434 PRINT
435 LET N = N + 1
436 RETURN
```

Now each time it is necessary to execute the end-of-page sequence the GOSUB statement can be used:

174 GOSUB 424

.
.
.

212 GOSUB 424

.
.
.

287 GOSUB 424

The RETURN statement will pass control back to the statement following that which called the subroutine. (Note the addition of line 435 LET N = N + 1, which includes the page number calculation in the subroutine and further reduces the coding requirements in the main line program.)

Subroutine calls may be nested, i.e. a subroutine may contain a call to another subroutine (some BASICs even allow a subroutine to call itself!). Care should be taken to ensure that the main line program does not "fall through" to a subroutine (in which case an error occurs when the RETURN statement is executed).

If a sequence of statements is found several times in a program using different variables it is often beneficial to convert this to a subroutine also. However, it will be necessary to pass the appropriate values to the subroutine as parameters. For example, suppose a program being written includes the requirement frequently to INPUT a value and check that it is in the range 1–10. Rather than repeat the coding each time the following subroutine could be coded:

```
920 E = 0
922 INPUT A
924 IF A < 1 THEN E = 1
926 IF A > 10 THEN E = 1
928 IF A − ABS(A) <> 0 THEN E = 1
929 RETURN
```

To invoke this subroutine it is only necessary to code the following:

```
122 GOSBU 920
124 IF E = 0 THEN 129
126 R = A
127 GO TO 133
129 PRINT "ERROR"
131 GO TO 122
133 . . . .
```

Note that following the return from the subroutine the program checks for an error by examining the value of E. If no error has occurred the inputted value is assigned to the current variable (R in this case) and processing continues.

Exercises

1. Write the statements to execute the following coding 3 times, varying the value of J from zero to 2:

> PRINT "INPUT TEST NO   "; J
> INPUT R

2. What will be the increment value for the following FOR statements?

   (*a*) FOR J = 1 TO 6 STEP 1
   (*b*) FOR J = 1 TO 6
   (*c*) FOR J = 1 TO 6 STEP C

3. Write the statement to perform the subroutine beginning at statement number 612 and ending at statement number 744.
4. Code a subroutine to calculate the area of circle when the radius of that circle is in variable R. The result should be placed in variable G.
5. What is wrong with the following?

> FOR I = 1 TO 4
> FOR J = 2 TO 6
> .
> .
> .
> NEXT I
> NEXT J

CHAPTER SIXTY-SIX

ARRAYS AND SUBSCRIPTS

Arrays

An array is a set of like variables arranged in sequence and referred to by a single name, qualified as necessary. A simple way to think of an array is as a set of pigeon holes. For example, Fig. 50 shows four boxes which could

1	2	3	4

Fig. 50. One-dimensional array B

represent an array called, say, B. Then the four "boxes" would be known as:

$$B(1), B(2), B(3) \text{ and } B(4)$$

Each **element** of the array (as the "boxes" are known) has the same properties as any simple numeric variable in respect of its value:

$$112 \text{ LET } B(1) = 2.19$$
$$114 \text{ LET } B(2) = 3.142$$
$$116 \text{ LET } B(3) = B(2)*2$$
$$118 \text{ LET } B(4) = B(3) + B(1)$$

The qualifier for the array name—the number in brackets following the name—is known as the **subscript**. The name of an array element is sometimes known as a singly-subscripted variable or just a **subscripted variable**.

The array discussed thus far is called one-dimensional. It has a single subscript to identify each element of the array. A two-dimensional array would need two subscripts to identify each element. Fig. 51 shows a two-dimensional array called C. This array has three rows each of four columns. The individual elements are referenced by the row and column number. For example, the top left-hand element is C(1, 1)—i.e. row one, column one—the bottom right-hand element is C(3, 4)—i.e. row three, column four. For a

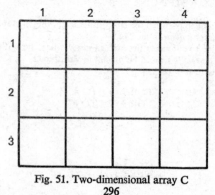

Fig. 51. Two-dimensional array C

double-subscripted variable, the row number is specified first and the column number second.

The elements of a two-dimensional array can also hold the same values as simple numerical variables:

$$226 \text{ LET } C(1, 2) = 3.14$$
$$228 \text{ LET } C(2, 3) = 29.8$$
$$232 \text{ LET } C(2, 4) = B(1) + C(2, 3)$$
$$234 \text{ LET } C(3, 1) = C(2, 4)*7$$

BASIC also allows the use of text or string variable arrays whose elements can hold the same type of strings as simple string variables:

$$\text{LET F\$ (1)} = \text{"TEST}\qquad\text{"}$$
$$\text{LET F\$ (2)} = \text{"PROGRAM"}$$
$$\text{LET F\$ (3)} = \text{F\$ (1)} + \text{F\$ (2)}$$

(Two-dimensional string variables are also available if required.)

The number of dimensions and the number of elements of an array (its size and shape) are specified in a DIM statement. The DIM statement (short for "dimension") gives the array name and the maximum subscript number in each dimension. (*Note:* although only one- and two-dimensional arrays are shown here, some BASICs allow many more dimensions.)

$$448 \text{ DIM A(20)}$$

This specifies an array called A( ) which has 20 elements A(1) through A(20): note that the variable A is quite distinct from this array.

$$124 \text{ DIM B(4), C(3, 4)}$$

In this statement two arrays are dimensioned; array B( ) has 4 elements and array C( ) has 12 (3 rows and 4 columns). String arrays are similarly dimensioned:

$$126 \text{ DIM A\$(16), B\$(2, 4)}$$

DIM statements should ideally be placed near the beginning of a program and should occur before the first reference to each array.

BASIC alows the use of up to 26 numerical arrays—A( ) through Z( )—and up to 26 string arrays—A\$( ) through Z\$( ).

Subscripts

It has already been shown that a subscripted variable may appear anywhere that a simple variable may appear. However, the real advantage of arrays comes from the fact that the subscripts themselves may be given as variables or expressions. For example, knowing that the following statement does not set the arrays to zeroes:

$$122 \text{ DIM A(6), B(10, 10)}$$

it would be possible to **initalize** each element to zero by writing a total of 106 LET statements; consider instead the following two sets of code:

```
124 FOR J = 1 TO 6
126 A(J) = Ø
128 NEXT J
        .
        .
        .
        .
142 FOR J = 1 TO 1Ø
144 FOR K = 1 TO 1Ø
146 B(J, K) = Ø
148 NEXT K
15Ø NEXT J
```

In the first example, the variable J takes successive values 1 through 6, thus setting each of the 6 elements of the array to zero in turn. The second example is a little more complicated: for each value of J (1 through 10) the variable K assumes the value 1 through 10; thus the loop moves along each row element by element. Do not proceed until you are sure you understand this example—if necessary write down the successive values of J and K to see how the array is scanned (left to right, top to bottom).

Where an expression is to be used as a subscript,

```
144 LET A(B/2) = Ø
```

care should be taken to ensure that the resulting subscript value is always an integral value.

By changing the order of FOR/NEXT statements the direction of scan of a two-dimensional array can be changed. For example, the following coding will print the contents of the array F( ) in rows across the page:

```
112 FOR J = 1 TO 3
114 FOR K = 1 TO 4
116 PRINT F(J, K),
118 NEXT K
12Ø PRINT
122 NEXT J
```

(Note the PRINT statement in line 12Ø to move to print head to the next line.)

To print the same array in columns across the page the following coding is necessary:

```
112 FOR K = 1 TO 4
114 FOR J = 1 TO 3
116 PRINT F(J, K),
118 NEXT J
12Ø PRINT
122 NEXT K
```

As a final illustration of arrays and FOR/NEXT loops the following coding will sort the numbers in the array A( ) into ascending sequence. The number of numbers to be sorted is contained in N.

```
112 FOR S = 1 TO N − 1
114 LET X = Ø
116 FOR I = 1 TO N − S
118 IF A(I)< = A(I + 1) THEN 128
12Ø LET T = A(I)
122 LET A(I) = A(I + 1)
124 LET A(I + 1) = T
126 LET X = 1
128 NEXT I
13Ø IF X = Ø THEN 134
132 NEXT S
134 FOR I = 1 TO N
136 PRINT A(I)
138 NEXT I
999 STOP
```

Notes on the program: Variable X is a "swop indicator"; it is set to zero before each **pass** of the array and set non-zero each time two elements are swopped (when there are no swops the array is in order). Variable T is a temporary store to enable elements A(I) and A(I + 1) to be swopped.

If the operation of the sort is not clear you should step through on paper, writing down the values of each array element after each program step. Start with the following values:

```
1Ø2 DATA 6, 4, 3, 7, 1, 2
1Ø4 LET N = 6
1Ø7 FOR J = 1 TO 6
1Ø8 READ A(J)
11Ø NEXT J
```

Exercises
1. Write the statement to define a numerical array with 10 elements and a string array with 8 elements.
2. Write the statements to clear the numeric array defined in question 1 to zeroes.
3. Write the statement to define a numeric array with 23 rows each of 6 columns.
4. Write the statements to set each element of the array defined in question 3 to 1.
5 How many elements are defined by the statement.

$$112 \text{ DIM A\$}(16, 1Ø)$$

Revision Questions. Set 6
1. Say which type of data is each of the following:

(a) 267.Ø
(b) "267.Ø"
(c) "NUMERIC"
(d) A\$

2. How many string variables are available for use?
3. What is the difference between the variables A and A(1)?
4. Write the coding to multiply the contents of variable C by 7.
5. Write the coding to join together the contents of string variables A$ and R$ and print the result.
6. What is the purpose of the following functions?

    (*a*) INT (X)
    (*b*) SGN (X)
    (*c*) COS (X)

7. Write the statement to assign the square root of Y to A.
8. Write the statement to calculate the area of a triangle from the formula area $= \frac{1}{2}$ AB sin *a*, where *a* is the angle (in variable K) between the two sides whose lengths are in variables A and B?
9. Write the statements to initialize the variables A, B, C, D with a list of values (hint: use the READ statement).
10. What is the purpose of the RESTORE statement?
11. Write the statements to input a value and print out that value, its square, square root, and cube using print zones.
12. Write the statement to move the print head to position 20.
13. Can a GOTO statement use a variable or expression to determine the line number?
14. Write the statements to transfer control to line number 184 if the value of A is not in the range 10–20.
15. Write the statements to stop the program if a "NO" is inputted, otherwise continue at line 244.
16. Write the statements to input a value and, if it is has the value 1, 2 or 3, transfer control to line 186, 194 or 266 respectively.
17. Write the statements to define two arrays, B and C, each of 20 elements and set them to zeroes.
18. Write a subroutine (starting at line number 612) to print two blank lines, and the heading "page number —".
19. Write the statement to invoke the subroutine coded in the previous question.
20. Write the statements to transfer the contents of array M(4, 6) to array P(6, 4), swopping rows and columns.

PART FIVE

THE MICROPROCESSOR EXPLAINED

A microprocessor is just another **integrated circuit**, albeit a complicated one. On its own a microprocessor is not very useful; it must be integrated into a complete system in order to function.

This opening paragraph is the expert's view of the microprocessor but in everyday use the term microprocessor has come to mean small computer. Small enough (and cheap enough of course) to be used in the home, in school or in the small one- or two-man business. (Note that it is the "expert's microprocessor" explained above that is used increasingly in washing machines and so on.)

This confusion over terms can be readily appreciated by comparing it with an earlier misuse of technical terms. In everyday use a transistor is a small, often battery operated, radio that happens to contain, amongst other things, transistors. To the technician a transistor is a small electronic switch about the size of a match-head; to the layman it is a fully functioning radio receiver.

To avoid a similar confusion—at least in this book—between microprocessor (tiny integrated circuit) and microprocessor (small computer) the latter will be referred to as a **home computer**.

The Home Computer

It is important to realize that the home computer is built along the same lines as the huge mainframe machines costing millions of pounds. The theory of operation is the same, the architecture is the same and the principles of operation are the same. Two things are different (apart from the cost).

First, the home computer is on a much smaller scale. It is not just physically smaller but it operates more slowly, it can store fewer items of data and it can execute smaller programs. Secondly, the home computer is used differently. It is often an adult toy (in the widest sense of the word) and is seldom purchased for any of the normal commercial (i.e. cost-saving) reasons.

This second point is, in the author's view, the most important one in respect of home computing and is one often missed by other writers on the subject. The home computer user wants to enjoy his "toy". This means that he wants to know how to use it without bothering too much why it does what it does. This can perhaps be made clearer with an analogy.

A person training to be a garage mechanic or a racing driver needs to know intimately the theory and practice of the motorcar. He needs to know every aspect of engines, gearboxes, suspension and so on. He must not only understand the theory but be able to dismantle, repair and rebuild each part. The average driver, on the other hand, interested in driving to work each day and making the odd pleasure trip to the country, has a different requirement. He might like to know roughly which bits are which and he needs to know and understand the car controls and how to drive the car.

Similarly the computer professional will need a detailed knowledge of the theory and the mechanics of the computer machine. The home computer user only needs to know how to drive it. In this part of the book the basic building blocks of the home computer are explained. The languages for programming computers are explained in other parts. This does not of course preclude the home computer user from being or becoming an electronic expert and building his system from scratch. Such detail is, however, beyond the scope of this work.

CHAPTER SIXTY-SEVEN

THE HOME COMPUTER

A home computer is defined in the same way as any stored program computer as a machine capable of manipulating data according to predefined rules. The rules are the instructions; the collection of instructions is the program. The program and the data are stored in the memory which is connected to the **Central Processing Unit (CPU)** as shown in Fig. 52. Notice

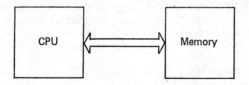

Fig. 52. Stored program computer

from this that the connection between the CPU and memory (the data bus, as explained below) is bi-directional.

The CPU encompasses the arithmetic unit, the control unit and the logic unit as described in Part One. The CPU actually does the computing; it will fetch an instruction from memory and execute it, often retrieving data from memory to do so. The CPU of a home computer will be contained in a single integrated circuit (such as the MOSTEK Z80).

Memory consists of one or more integrated circuits each of which can hold a pre-defined amount of data. The size of memory is given as so many **K**, each of which is 1024 storage units. Thus an 8K memory would hold 8×1024 units. The unit of storage varies with the type of system but is commonly the **word**, each word holding 8 or 16 bits. Each bit can be 0 or 1 and an 8-bit word stores an 8-bit binary number. (A detailed discussion on the binary system will be found in Chapter Nine.) The home computer user is usually interested only in the amount of memory he has as the limiting factor for program sizes. Memory is of different types each of which has its own place in the home computer user's repertoire and is described below.

Random Access Memory—RAM

This is the "normal" type of memory associated with a home computer system. RAM is accessible by the user for storage of data and programs. When using a high-level language such as BASIC (see Part Four) the allocation and subsequent addressing of RAM space (with commands such as DATA and READ) is a function of the compiler; the user does not need to worry about the physical organization of the RAM.

When using a low-level language (such as the Z80 assembler) or machine code the user will need to allocate and address RAM directly. Depending on the addressing capability of the CPU, the RAM addresses will consist of 2,

3, 4 or 5 hexadecimal digits (see Chapter Nine for a discussion of the hexadecimal system). Typical RAM addresses could therefore be 0010, 0AF2 and so on. A home computer will normally have a reset control that sets the program location counter to a pre-determined RAM address (such as 0000).

Read Only Memory—ROM

This is a memory unit that has been programmed during manufacture with data or program or both and can only be read. No matter what the program currently executing tries to do the data in ROM cannot be overwritten or changed.

ROM is used extensively by home computer manufacturers to provide operating systems or compilers. In the case of a compiler in ROM the user cannot alter or decipher the program, only obey it. Systems using microprocessors for specific control jobs (such as in a washing machine or electric typewriter) will have their control programs stored in ROM.

Programmable Read Only Memory—PROM

This is a type of ROM that can be programmed with a special machine after manufacture. Thus a PROM can be set up for a small or one-off application at low cost (ROM programming being economical only for large manufacturing quantities).

A number of specialized electronic outlets will program PROMs to a customer's specification for a few pounds. A typical application for a PROM would be to identify a machine or terminal with a unique identity or name so that it could be identified by a remote computer.

Erasable PROM—EPROM

This is the same as a PROM but the programming can be erased and a fresh one substituted. The erasing cannot be done by program (this would make it a RAM) but requires a special process such as exposure to ultraviolet light (often giving rise to the expression UVPROM). An EPROM can be used anywhere a PROM might be and where a change in program is likely to be required.

The CPU itself often contains a small amount of very high-speed memory (relative to the bulk of memory). This is often called **scratchpad memory** or working memory or accumulators. This area is usually divided into a number of, typically, two-word long **registers**. When a particular function has to be performed under program control, say an ADD, the data to be manipulated is brought from memory into a register; the arithmetic is performed in the register and the result is returned to RAM. Registers are also used to keep track of the current program location (the program counter register) and for program offsets (index register). Registers can be accessed directly in low-level or machine languages but are taken care of automatically by high-level languages.

The relative location of the registers is shown in Fig. 53, which also shows that the CPU and Memory are linked (via the data bus) to an input/output unit (I/O). This I/O unit provides the interface between the computer system and the outside world.

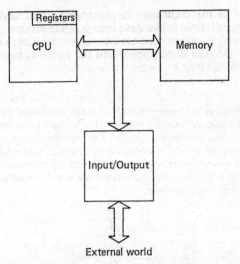

Fig. 53. Outside world interface

A large mainframe computer system such as that described in Part One will interface with the real world via a host of devices: paper tape, magnetic tape, visual display units, printed forms and so on. The home computer is clearly much more limited and yet, without a real world interface, it is quite useless. The typical home computer I/O system is discussed in the next chapter.

CHAPTER SIXTY-EIGHT

THE HOME COMPUTER I/O SYSTEM

Mainframe computer systems have multiple input/output systems but home computers are often lacking in this area. This is largely because of the relatively high cost of such things as keyboards and printers.

Input

The simplest and indeed the most popular home computer input mechanism is the **keyboard**. Early systems used a very simple keyboard—which may even have consisted of toggle switches rather than keys—with only 16 keys. These represented the hexadecimal digits 0–9 and A–F (for a discussion on the hexadecimal system see Chapter Nine). Using such a keyboard is quite difficult because all entries—program and data—must be entered directly in machine language.

Clearly, a full typewriter-like keyboard is required for high-level language-type input of the sort shown in Part Four. As the home computer market has increased so the availability of reasonably priced keyboards has improved. Further cost reductions have been possible because of developments in manufacturing techniques that have brought in keyboards with few, if any, moving parts. As with many applications the **electronic keyboard** is cheaper (and more reliable) than its mechanical counterpart.

Output

Home computing has been noticeable for the absence of the printed output so loved by mainframe computer users. This is almost entirely because of the relatively high cost of printing devices. The standard home computer output device has become the **video screen**—not, however, a specialized computer-type video but a modified television set. The reasoning behind this is that most home computer users would already possess a television set and would therefore be spared a major expense.

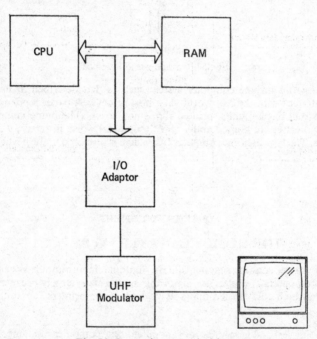

Fig. 54. Outputting to a television set

Fig. 54 shows the outline schematic for a home computer video output. An output adaptor is connected to the data bus and receives messages and control signals intended for the screen. These are converted from parallel to serial form (see next chapter) and passed to a **UHF modulator**. The function of this device is to generate a signal which can be fed into the TV aerial socket and which the television will think is a normal off-air programme.

Backing Storage

Programs developed by the user are stored in RAM; when power is removed from the home computer system this data is lost. Even if some form of battery back-up system was available, the user is unlikely to have sufficient RAM to save all his programs. Some simple and cheap **backing storage is** required therefore that can be used to store and retrieve data and programs.

This is provided with a special interface to a conventional audio cassette recorder. The data to be stored is firstly converted from parallel to serial form (in much the same way as the TV interface previously described). Then each bit of data is converted into one of two audio tones depending on whether it is 0 or 1. The tones are recorded on tape.

To load data from tape to RAM the reverse process is used. Each tone incoming to the **interface unit** is detected by an electronic filter and converted to the appropriate bit. Fig. 55 shows the cassette storage system in block form.

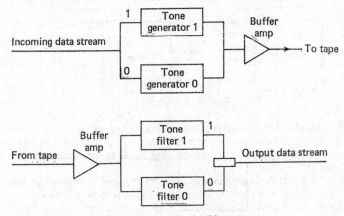

Fig. 55. Cassette tape backing storage

Other Input/Output

A number of other input/output mechanisms are available to the home computer user. These include **floppy discs** (so called because they are flexible), which are similar in concept to the disc storage discussed in Part One. As floppy discs tend to be used by only the more advanced home computer user they are not discussed further here.

To provide for a variety of input/output devices (such as printers, paper tape readers, model train controllers and so on) the home computer uses a standard interface type RS232 (also known as V24).

The **standard interface** is a general input/output route consisting of 25 pins. Of these one each is for transmitted and received data and (apart from a common earth) the remainder are control lines. The more important of these control lines, shown in Fig. 56, may or may not be used depending on the application. For example, a simple home-built model train controller would just accept data whereas a line printer would expect to indicate its readiness with a "clear to send" signal.

Pin No.	Description	Comments
1	Protective earth	
2	Transmitted data	
3	Received data	
4	Request to send	From terminal to computer
5	Clear to send	Computer ready to receive
6	Data set ready	
7	Signal ground	
9	+12V	
10	−12V	
15	Timing pulse	Transmitted data
17	Timing pulse	Received data
20	Data terminal ready	

Fig. 56. Input/output interface pin connections

CHAPTER SIXTY-NINE

THE BUS SYSTEM

A home computer, as we have already determined, consists of a number of separate integrated circuits. In order that data and instructions can be passed as required each integrated circuit or chip needs to be connected to every other one in the system.

Fig. 57 shows that six such connections are required for four chips whereas for just two more chips a total of 15 connections is required. As the number of chips increases so the required total of interconnections rises. The simplest home computer can contain 20 chips for which no less than 190 interconnections are needed.

Each of these interconnections needs to carry each of the eight bits of the computer word on a separate connection. The above figures must be multiplied by 8 to arrive at the total number of interconnections. Clearly this method would impose severe practical limitations very quickly. An alternative method of interconnection is therefore required. The bus system involves all chips being connected in parallel rather than directly to each other. Consider an 8-bit "highway" running round the chips; each chip is connected, via eight links, to this highway or bus. Fig. 58 shows such a method of interconnecting four chips and Fig. 59 shows the same interconnection as usually drawn.

Data put on to a bus can be read by all the chips connected to that bus. But usually the data is only intended for one other chip. So how does this chip know that a particular item of data is for it? The chips are connected to a second bus for addressing as shown in Fig. 60.

A chip will now accept data from the **data bus** only when it is addressed via the **address bus**. In practice a **control bus** of only one or two bits may also be added to prevent data acquisition whilst the bus is changing.

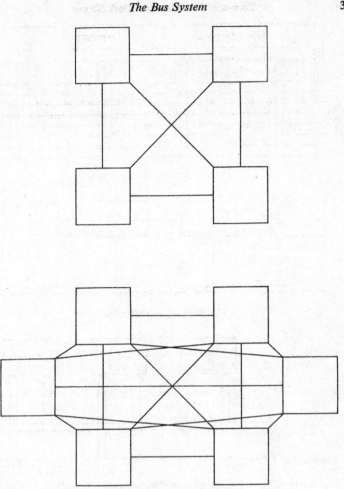

Fig. 57. Chip interconnections

The bus system overcomes the problem of interconnection between a large number of chips but it also has another attribute of great benefit to the home computer user. Additional chips can be added to the bus at any time. So, for example, home computer printed circuit boards invariably have spare integrated sockets for the addition of additional RAM or PROM as the user needs (and can afford!).

The individual bits of a computer word travel in parallel on a bus. The receiving chip accepts all eight bits together. This form of distribution—called **parallel transmission**—is always used within a computer but is not suitable for some peripheral devices. A slow printer, for example, will only

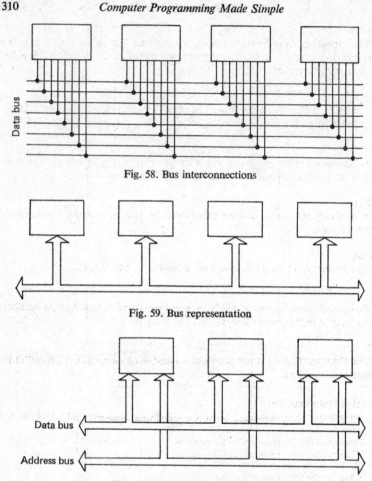

Fig. 58. Bus interconnections

Fig. 59. Bus representation

Fig. 60. Multiple bus arrangement

accept a single bit at a time. The individual bits of a character travel one behind the other. This is known as **serial transmission**.

A useful analogy is to think of a group of soldiers marching abreast (parallel transmission) or in single file (serial transmission). To change the direction of a group of soldiers they will stop, turn 90°, left or right, and continue. To convert from serial to parallel data transmission (or the reverse) requires only a special chip. The chip in question (a serial input/output interface) is really beyond the scope of this book and is not something the home computer user needs to understand. However, to assist the reader in understanding some of the advertising literature relating to home computers, a few of the more popular chips are described below (note that most of them are known by their initials):

UART

The Universal Asynchrous Receiver Transmitter acts as a serial to parallel and speed converter. It is generally used to interface to slow-speed devices such as teletypewriters.

FIFO

The First In First Out ram is used to expand a CPU register capacity. Data is retrieved from the fifo in the order in which it is put in.

UPC

A Universal Peripheral Controller is used to control high-speed peripherals. It is often programmable and a powerful CPU in its own right.

MMU

A Memory Management Unit takes over the task of memory bus control from the main CPU.

DMA

The Directory Memory Access unit is similar to the MMU.

PIO

Peripheral Input Output to medium- and high-speed devices having parallel input/output requirements is controlled by the PIO.

CTC

The Counter Timer Circuit provides a number of independent pre-settable timers and counters.

Revision Questions. Set 7

1. What is the major difference between a mainframe computer and a home computer?
2. Where are the program and data stored?
3. Where is the computing done?
4. How many words in a K?
5. What do the following stand for:

RAM
ROM
PROM

6. What type of memory would be used for user program storage?
7. How many keys on a hexadecimal keyboard?
8. Is data storage on an audio cassette done with serial or parallel data transmission?
9. How is data sent to a particular chip on a bus?
10. What chip could be used for serial to parallel conversion?

GLOSSARY OF TERMS USED

access, direct—The ability to retrieve a single data record from a backing store device without reference to any other record.

accumulator—An intermediate storage area used during arithmetic computation.

address, record—The location of a record on a backing store device—required for direct access of that record.

address, storage—A number specifying the location of a particular unit of core storage. Storage locations are usually addressed from zero up to the highest numbered location (this being equal to the storage size).

address, symbolic—A label or meaningful name attached, by the programmer, to a unit or units of core storage to enable easier referencing. Translation from symbols to actual storage addresses is accomplished by the compiler.

alphabetic—Using the character set consisting of the letters A to Z plus certain special symbols (e.g. period, comma, blank, etc.).

alphameric—same as alphanumeric.

alphanumeric—Using the complete character set, i.e. the alphabetic and the numeric sets.

analysis, systems—*see* systems analysis

annotation—Added descriptive comments or explanatory notes (often used when flowcharting).

application program—A program or routine to solve a particular commercial or mathematical problem. Application programs for statistical, design, and engineering work, etc. are usually supplied by the computer manufacturer.

area—A section of storage known by a particular name.

area, input—A section of storage reserved by the compiler for the receipt and processing of input data.

area, output—A section of storage reserved by the compiler for the processing and transmission of output data.

argument—A variable or variable expression on whose value the value of a FORTRAN function depends.

arithmetic, floating-point—A method of calculation which automatically accounts for the location of a decimal point in terms of a multiplication power. A floating-point number is expressed as a mantissa (giving the decimal value) and an exponent (giving the magnitude of the number).

array—A series of identical items arranged in continuous pattern. Each element of an array has the same name but is uniquely identified by a subscript.

assignment statement—A FORTRAN facility which allows the value of an arithmetic expression to be assigned to a variable, e.g. $TOT = (A + B)**3$.

assumed decimal point—The location within a numeric item at which the decimal point is assumed to be. A period (used to represent a decimal point) is not actually stored in a numeric item.

background processing—Work which has a low priority and is handled by the computer when higher priority work (such as time-sharing) is not occurring.

base—The weight to be applied to each character position in a number system (equal in value to the number of marks required by any number system). The decimal system has the base 10 and uses therefore 10 marks (0, 1, 2, 3, 4, 5, 6, 7, 8, 9). Each character position in a decimal number represents the number of occurrences of successive powers of ten. E.g. the decimal number 367 represents $3 \times 10^2 + 6 \times 10^1 + 7 \times 10^0$. Same as radix.

batch total—The sum of a certain field or fields in a group of records used to verify that the batch of records has been successfully transcribed. A group of payroll cards may have a batch total based on the gross pay on each card. As the computer reads each card it will total this field; the last card read will contain the batch total (prepared by the data-preparation department) which the computer will check against its own total.

batch work—Those computer programs which are collected into groups prior to running as background processing carried out in any commerical computer installation.

binary—A numbering system with the base (or radix) of 2 using the marks 0 and 1 when written.

bit—(from binary digit) a numeral in the binary scale of notation—may have the value 0 or 1.

bit-rate—The speed at which bits are transmitted. Usually only used for long-distance data transmission, e.g. over telephone lines.

blank—A character used to indicate a location where nothing is printed. Same as space.

block—A group of consecutive fields or records transferred into or out of the CPU as a single unit.

block diagram—A form of flowchart showing only the major steps or processes rather than the detailed logic. Often indicates only the various peripheral units to be used by a program.

blocking—The combination of two or more records into one backing store block.

block, input—A unit of data read from a backing store—may contain one or more records.

block length—A field containing a count of the number of characters in a block.

block, output—A unit of data written to a backing store—may contain one or more records.

buffer—An area of storage used to hold input or output data prior to it being processed by a program.

buffering, double—The technique of using two input (or output) areas for an input/output device to the CPU. As the program processes data in one buffer the other buffer is primed with the next record and vice versa.

bug—An error in the coding of a program which causes it to fail.

call—The transferring of control to a subroutine. A call always includes the ability to return to the statement following the call.

card—A machine-readable input medium consisting of special quality paper $7\frac{3}{8}'' \times 3\frac{1}{4}''$. Information is stored as a series of holes punched in twelve rows across eighty columns. Same as punched card.

card-code—The combination of punched holes which represent the characters on a punched card.

card column—One of the eighty vertical lines of punching in a card.

card-hopper—A tray-like mechanism which holds cards prior to their being read, or collects them after reading.

card-punch—A data-preparation machine for punching holes into cards.

card, punched—*see* card

card-reader—A device for transcribing the holes in a card into computer readable data.

card row—One of the twelve horizontal lines of punching in a card.

carriage return—Often written as ⓒⓇ the operation (key depression) that causes a typewriter type printer to return its print head to the left-hand margin. Usually accompanied by a line feed.

catalogue—A list of items with descriptive data to permit the speedy retrieval of data stored in a library. Similar to index.

central processing unit–(CPU)—That part of a computer system containing the memory unit, the arithmetic unit, and the control unit.

chad—The piece of material removed when a hole is punched in a card or tape.

channel—The path along which data is transferred from or to an input/output unit.

character—A symbol in a set which a

computer can recognize. Usually consists of the letters A–Z, the numerals 0–9, and various punctuation and special symbols. Each character is represented in the computer as a unique combination of bits.

check digit—A digit added to a numeric code to enable the computer to detect errors in that code.

COBOL–COmmon Business Oriented Language. A programming language designed for the solution of commercial problems.

coding—The act of writing programming language statements.

coding sheet—A pre-printed form on which programming statements can be coded.

collate—To merge two or more ordered sets of data (or cards) into a single set retaining the original ordering relationship.

column—*see* card column

compare—To determine whether the value of one item is higher, equal to, or lower than the value of another item.

compile—To process a source deck through a compiler.

compiler—A program which translates statements of a high-level language into computer executable instructions. A compiler will introduce additional coding of its own depending upon the options selected by the programmer in coding his program. A separate compiler will exist for each high-level language in use.

computer—A device capable of accepting information, processing it according to a prescribed set of rules and supplying the results of the processing.

condition—One of a set of specified values that a data item may assume (COBOL). An expression which, taken as a whole, may be either true or false.

condition-name—A name assigned by a programmer to a value representing one of the conditions of a data item.

console—The unit attached to a computer which may be used by the computer operator to communicate directly with the Operating System.

The console may also contain the computer power and start/stop switches.

constant—A quantity present in a program which has a fixed value throughout execution of the program and is specified as its actual numerical value.

constant, figurative (COBOL)—A constant which may be used without prior definition (in the Data Division) by reference to its name (e.g. ZERO).

constant, integer (FORTRAN)—A constant which has no decimal part and is written as a whole number.

constant, real (FORTRAN)—A constant which has a decimal part and must always contain an embedded decimal point.

control card—A card which contains parameters or job-control information.

conversion—The process of changing data from one form of representation to another.

copy, hand—A printed copy of machine output, e.g. listings, printed reports, etc.

core dump—A listing of the contents of the computer's core storage or part of it.

core storage—A form of high-speed storage used to make up the CPU. So called because it is made up of tiny magnetic cores each of which can represent one of two states (representing the binary digits 0 and 1). Each character held in core storage is represented by a unique pattern of these two states.

counter—A data item used to record the number of occurrences of a particular sequence of instruction statements.

cps—Abbreviation for characters per second or cycles per second.

CPU—*see* Central Processor Unit

cylinder—For magnetic disc backing stores, all the recording bands (or tracks) which can be accessed by a single movement of the read/write head assembly.

data—A general term used to denote any or all the facts, numbers, symbols, and letters that refer to or describe an idea, situation, or condition. Indicates basic elements of information which a computer can process. Plural of the term datum.

data, control—Items of data used to identify or verify a record, file, or processing operation.

data description—An entry in the Data Division of a COBOL program describing the characteristics of a data item.

data division—A division of a COBOL program describing the characteristics of the data (files, data items, etc.) processed by the program.

data element—A group of characters forming an item at the basic level—an elementary item.

data name—A name assigned by the programmer to a data item or variable for use in a program.

data processing—A procedure for receiving data, processing it, and producing a specific result. This processing is now accepted to be by computer when the term is used.

data, test—A set of data developed specifically to test the working of a computer program.

debug—To locate and correct errors in a computer program.

deck—A collection of cards forming a logical set.

diagram, flow—same as flowchart

digit, check—*see* check digit

direct access—*see* access, direct

disc, magnetic—A storage device on which information is recorded on the magnetized surface of rotating discs. A single disc pack may have ten recording surfaces all traversed by a single read/write head assembly.

disc pack—The exchangeable portion of a magnetic disc assembly consisting of a number of circular magnetized plates mounted on a common shaft or spindle.

disc storage—The storage of data on magnetic discs.

display—Visible representation of data on a console.

dividend—The quantity that is divided by another quantity.

division—The parts into which a COBOL program is divided. The Identification Division provides information to identify the program. The Environment Division specifies the hardware used for compiling and running the program. The Data Division defines the nature of the data to be processed by the program. The Procedure Division defines the instruction statements forming the programs' processing.

divisor—A quantity by which the dividend is divided.

document—A medium containing a representation of some stored information such as a sheet of paper, a punched card, etc.

documentation—The set of data (flowchart, description, etc.) describing the working and layout of a finished program.

double precision—Relating to a quantity having twice as many significant digits as are normally carried.

down time—The period during which a computer is not operating due to machine errors or failures.

drive—A device that moves tape past a read/write head assembly

dummy—An artificial address, instruction, or record inserted solely to fulfil prescribed conditions.

dump—To produce a core dump.

edit—To rearrange data for further machine processing by selecting, deleting, or inserting data. A data edit program may also check the validity of input data. Editing prior to outputting data can involve the insertion of special characters (blanks, periods, etc.) and the removal of unwanted characters (leading zeroes for example).

EDP—Electronic Data Processing.

element—A component part—typically one location comprising an array.

element, data—A specific item of information at the lowest level in a set of data.

end-of-file—The end of data marker on a file; may be a special record or a physical marker (e.g. reflective spot on back of magnetic tape). Automatically detected during file reading.

environment division—*see* division

EOF—*see* end-of-file

erase head—A device on a magnetic

backing store to erase previously recorded information.

error condition—An indication that a deviation from normal processing has occurred.

error message—A textual description of an error.

execute—To carry out an instruction or routine.

executive—*see* supervisor

exit—The place at which control is transferred out of a subroutine or program.

expression—A valid series of constants, variables, and functions that may be connected by operators symbols and punctuation.

expression, arithmetic—An expression containing a valid combination of constants, variables; functions and arithmetic operators.

field—A set of one or more characters which is treated as a whole; a set of one or more columns on a card which is treated as a whole.
   A specified area of a record used for a particular category of data; e.g. a set of columns representing gross pay in a payroll input card.

field, control—A constant (predetermined) location where information used for control purposes is held.

figurative constant—*see* constant, figurative

file—A collection of related records treated as a unit. For example one line of an invoice forms an item, a complete invoice forms a record, and the complete set of such records forms a file.

file label—A set of characters in a special record which uniquely identify a particular backing store file.

file, master—A file containing relatively permanent information.

file organization—The process of organizing information on a file to facilitate its later retrieval.

fixed-length—Pertaining to a record which contains a fixed number of characters.

flag—An indicator used frequently to tell some later part of a program that some condition occurred earlier. A flag may be set by giving a predetermined value (often 1) to a variable; it will be unset by being given another value (0).

floating-point—A form of number representation in which quantities are represented by a number multiplied by a number base raised to a power. For example the notational form 3.0E4 represents 3.0×10^4 which is equivalent to the decimal value 30,000.

flowchart—A graphical representation of the steps involved in a procedure.

flowchart symbols—The boxes used to indicate the various operations in a flowchart.

FORTRAN—A programming system, consisting of a language and a compiler, allowing programs to be written for solving arithmetic-based problems. Derived from FORmula TRANslation.

function—A means of referring to a type or sequence of calculations by a single statement in an arithmetic expression (FORTRAN).

gap—An interval of space to delimit between successive blocks on a backing store.

generation—Pertaining to the system of keeping old master files after an updated copy has been produced to provide back-up in case of loss of the most recent version.

hard copy—Typewritten or printed characters on paper. Usually produced at the same time as information is converted into a machine readable format.

hardware—The mechanical, magnetic, electromagnetic, electronic, and electrical devices or components of a computer system.

head—A device that reads, records, or erases information in a storage medium.

hexadecimal—Pertaining to the number system with the base 16.

hierarchy—A specified rank or order of items.

hit—The occurrence of a match of transaction items with master file items in the process of file updating.

hopper—A device that holds cards and makes them available to a feed mechanism.

housekeeping—Pertaining to administration or overhead operations or functions which are necessary in order to maintain control of a situation.

IBM—International Business Machines Corporation.

ICL—International Computers Limited.

identification division—*see* division

identifier—A symbol whose purpose is to identify a set of data.

idle time—The time that a computer is available for use but not in operation.

increment—The quantity by which another is modified. To modify a quantity by adding a smaller quantity.

index—An ordered reference list of the contents of a document, array, or file.

initialize—To set various counters, flags, indicators, etc. to their starting value, usually at the beginning of a program.

input—Information or data transferred from an external storage medium to the internal storage of the computer.

input area—*see* area, input

input block—A block which is to be transferred into the computer.

input units—Devices for feeding information into a computer.

instruction—A coded program step that tells the computer what to do for a single operation in a program.

integer—A whole (not fractional) number, e.g. 27, 3, etc.

integer variable (FORTRAN)—A variable whose value can only be an integral number.

interblock gap—*see* gap

interrupt—A break in the normal flow of a routine such that the flow can be resumed from that point at a later time. An interrupt is usually caused by a signal from an external source.

I/O—Abbreviation for Input/Output.

item—A field-holding data that concerns an individual object, event, or operation. The lowest level in a hierarchy of data.

jam, card—A pile-up of cards in a machine.

JCL—Job Control Language.

job control—That part of an operating system concerned with loading and running programs.

job control language—The commands and instructions used to instruct job control.

key—A group of characters, usually defined as a field, that identifies a record. For example the key for records on a payroll master file might be the clock-no. field.

keyboard—A device for encoding data by depression of a key, which causes the generation of a bit pattern.

keypunch—A device for recording information on cards or paper tape by punching holes in the card or tape to represent letters, digits, and special symbols.

keyword—An informative word that has a special meaning to a compiler and cannot be used as a data name (the COBOL verbs are all keywords).

label—*see* file label

language—A defined set of words, symbols, characters, etc. for communication (e.g. English, German, COBOL, FORTRAN, etc.). *See also* COBOL, FORTRAN.

language, object—The language used to specify object decks.

language, source—The language used to specify source decks.

length—The number of characters in a word or record.

level—A COBOL term indicating the status of one data item relative to another.

level indicator—A COBOL expression indicating the level of a Data Division entry.

library—A collection of programs or routines organized in a definite order and managed by the Operating System.

line printer—A printer output service in which an entire line is composed in the device prior to printing.

list—A string of data items written in a meaningful format.

listing—The printed output from a line printer.

literal—A word, number or symbol which describes or defines itself and not something it might represent.

load—Pertaining to the retrieval of a program from a library or input device.

log—A record of the status of a computer at various points during its operation.

logic—The process of determining the relationship between events.

loop—The repeated execution of a series of instructions a fixed number of times or until a terminal condition exists.

machine—A common or slang term for the computer.

magnetic core—*see* core storage

magnetic disc—*see* disc, magnetic

magnetic tape—*see* tape, magnetic

main frame—The main part of a computer system, i.e. the CPU.

mark—A symbol used to indicate the magnitude of each weight in a number system (e.g. the decimal system uses the marks 0, 1, 2, 3, 4, 5, 6, 7, 8, 9).

master file—*see* file, master

match—The occurrence of identical keys on two files which are being passed against each other. Same as Hit.

matrix—*see* array

memory—*see* storage

merge—To combine two or more files into one, usually in a specified order.

message—A group of words transmitted as a unit.

multiprogramming—A technique for handling more than one program simultaneously by interleaving their execution.

name—A term of one or more words to identify a specific item.

name, data—A name used to identify an item of data.

notation—The process of representing facts or quantities by a system of marks, symbols, or characters.

object deck—The output, in executable form, of a compiler.

object language—*see* language, object

object program—same as object deck

octal—Pertaining to the number system with the base 8.

off-line—Descriptive of the equipment of a computer environment which is not under control of the CPU.

on-line—Descriptive of the equipment directly controlled by the CPU.

operand—A piece of data on which an operation is performed. Any one of the quantities entering into an operation.

operating system—A collection of programs and techniques for controlling the operation of a computer.

option—Pertaining to a choice in the supply of parameters.

order—A defined sequence of events or elements.

output—Computer results or information transmitted to an output device.

output device—*see* device, output

overflow—In arithmetic, the generation of a result too large to fit into the result field.

pack—A combination of punched cards into a set or file to be input to a computer.

paper tape—A strip of paper capable of recording information as a series of punched holes.

paper tape reader—A device for reading paper tape and transmitting the information it contains to the computer.

parameter—A quantity passed to a subroutine which may be given different values from different parts of the program. A piece of information specified to the Operating System to indicate a required option.

pass—The process of reading a complete file sequentially. An execution of a loop.

path—The course taken by the computer through a program.

peripherals—Input, Output, and Backing Store devices connected to the CPU

point—The character, or implied character, that separates the integral part of a number from its fractional part.

precision—The degree of exactness with which a value is determined. *See also* double precision.

printer, line—*see* line printer

printout—A listing produced on a line printer.

procedure—The step-by-step method evolved for effecting a solution to a problem.

procedure division—*see* division

processing—Pertaining to the operation of a CPU.

processor—*see* CPU

program—A set of instructions or steps that tells a computer exactly how to solve a given problem. Most programs include alternate steps to cater for variations.

programmer—One who prepares programs for a computer system.

programming language—*see* language

program, object—same as object deck

program, source—same as source deck

program step—A single instruction within a program.

program, utility—A generalized program designed to assist in the running of the computer by performing frequently required tasks.

punch card—*see* card

punched card—A card that has information recorded on it.

punched tape—Paper tape that has information recorded on it.

qualification—In COBOL, the technique of making a name unique by adding IN or ON and another name according to the language rules.

quantity—A constant, variable, function name or expression.

radix—same as base

random access—same as access, direct

range—All the values that a function or variable may have.

read—The process of introducing data into a computer from an input device or backing store.

reader—A device that converts information in one form of storage to information in another form of storage.

real constant—*see* constant, real

real variable—*see* variable, real

record—A set of one or more consecutive fields on a related subject (e.g. an employee's payroll record).

reel—A spool of tape; generally refers to magnetic tape.

rerun—To repeat all or part of a program on a computer.

retrieve—To find and select a specific record in a storage media.

rewind—The process of returning a magnetic tape to its starting-point.

routine—A sequence of computer statements that carry out a well-defined function.

row—*see* card row

run—One performance of a computer program.

section—In COBOL, a sequence of one or more paragraphs designated as a section in accordance with the language rules.

section number—A number that identifies a particular section.

seek—The process of moving a disc read/write head assembly to the required cylinder to read a particular record.

sequence—To put a set of data into a defined order. A defined order of a set of data.

serial—The handling of data in a sequential fashion.

set—A collection of elements or data having some common feature or bearing some relation to one another.

sign—In arithmetic, the symbol or identification that distinguishes positive from negative numbers.

significant digit—A digit that contributes to the precision of an accurate number. The number of significant digits is counted beginning with the digit contributing the most value (the most significant digit) and ending with the one contributing the least value (called the least significant digit).

sign position—The position, in a numeric field, in which the sign is stored.

software—The internal programs and routines, prepared by the computer manufacturer, to simplify programming and computer operations. Software will include Operating Systems, Compilers (COBOL, FORTRAN, etc.), Utilities, and Library Maintenance programs.

sort—To arrange items of information according to rules dependent upon a key or keys contained in the items.

A program designed to arrange a file according to rules dependent upon a key or keys contained in each record of the file.

The dependent rule will usually specify either an ascending or descending sequence of keys.

source deck—A set of cards containing a source language program.

source language—*see* language, source

source program—*see* program, source

space—One or more blanks.

special character—A character other than a digit or a letter (e.g. * ? £).

specification—For programming, a definition of the data and procedures necessary to carry out a particular function.

spool—The mounting for a magnetic tape; usually plastic.

statement—In programming, a meaningful expression or a generalized instruction in a source language.

step—One instruction in a computer program.

storage—A general term for any device capable of retaining information. *See also* core storage.

storage, core—*see* core storage

string—A connected sequence of characters, words, or other elements.

subroutine—A sequence of statements which perform a definite function and which may be invoked from any part of a program by means of a call.

subroutine call—*see* call

subscript—A constant or variable (usually in parentheses) to identify a particular element of an array when each element has only the name of the array.

supervisor—A permanently resident program designed to control the work flow through a computer. The supervisor will load programs, schedule peripheral operations, organize multiprogramming, and handle error conditions.

symbolic—Pertaining to source language.

system, computer—A collection of equipment centred on a CPU plus its associated software designed to solve a range of business or scientific problems.

system, operating—*see* operating system

systems analysis—The examination of an activity or procedure, generally in business, to determine the optimum method of achieving the aims of the activity or procedure. Usually results in the specification of program specifications when the procedure is to be computerized.

table—A collection of data elements in a form suitable for ready reference. Similar to an array.

tabulator—An early mechanical device for listing the information on punched cards.

tag—A data item used as a marker or label.

tape, magnetic—*see* magnetic tape

tape, paper—*see* paper tape

terminal—same as console

time, object—The time at which a program is executed.

time, run—same as time, object

total, batch—*see* batch total

track—That portion of a magnetic disc available to a single read/write head.

update—To modify a master file with current information according to a defined procedure.

utility program—*see* program, utility

validate—The verification that a data item satisfies predetermined conditions.

value—In COBOL the information represented by a data item.

variable—A data item in storage that assumes different values during execution of the program. Referred to by a programmer defined name.

variable-length field—A field in a record whose length may differ from one record to the next.

variable-length record—A record in a file whose length may differ from one occurrence to the next.

verb—In COBOL, an instruction word (keyword) that specifies an operation to be performed by the program.

working storage—A portion of program storage reserved for intermediate results.

write—To transfer information from the CPU to an output medium or output device.

COBOL—LIST OF RESERVED WORDS

The following words are all reserved for indicating the various functions and elements of COBOL and may not be used as data names by the programmer.

ACCEPT	DATE-WRITTEN	LABEL
ADD	DEBUG	LEADING
ADVANCING	DECIMAL-POINT	LEAVING
AFTER	DEPENDING	LEFT
ALL	DESCENDING	LESS
ALPHABETIC	DISPLAY	LINES
ALPHANUMERIC	DIVIDE	LINKAGE
ALTER	DIVISION	LOCK
ALTERNATE	EJECT	LOW-VALUE
AN	ELSE	LOW-VALUES
AND	END	MEMORY
ARE	ENTER	MODE
AREA	ENTRY	MOVE
AREAS	ENVIRONMENT	MULTIPLY
ASCENDING	EQUAL	NAMED
ASSIGN	EQUALS	NEGATIVE
AT	ERROR	NEXT
AUTHOR	EVERY	NO
BEFORE	EXAMINE	NOT
BLANK	EXHIBIT	NOTE
BLOCK	EXIT	NUMERIC
BY	FD	OBJECT-COMPUTER
CALL	FILE	OBJECT-PROGRAM
CARD-PUNCH	FILE-CONTROL	OCCURS
CARD-READER	FILLER	OF
CHANGED	FIRST	OFF
CHARACTERS	FROM	OMITTED
CHEQUE	GIVING	ON
CLASS	GO	OPEN
CLOSE	GOBACK	OR
COMP	GREATER	OUTPUT
COMPUTATIONAL	HIGH-VALUE	PAPER-PUNCH
COMPUTE	HIGH-VALUES	PAPER-READER
CONFIGURATION	ID	PERFORM
CONSOLE	IDENTIFICATION	PIC
CONSTANT	IF	PICTURE
CONTAINS	IN	POSITIVE
CONTROL	INDEX	PROCEDURE
COMMA	INPUT	PROCEED
COPY	INPUT-OUTPUT	PROGRAM
CORR	INSTALLATION	PROGRAM-ID
CORRESPONDING	INTO	QUOTE
DATA	I-O-CONTROL	QUOTES
DATE	IS	READ
DATE-COMPILED	KEY	READY

RECORD	SELECT	TIMES
RECORDING	SENTENCE	TO
RECORDS	SIZE	TRACE
REDEFINES	SIZE ERROR	TRANSFORM
REMARKS	SKIP-1	TYPE
REMAINDER	SKIP-2	UNEQUAL
REPLACING	SKIP-3	UNTIL
RELEASE	SORT	UPON
REJECT	SOURCE-COMPUTER	USAGE
RESERVE	SPACE	USING
RETURN	SPACES	VALUE
REWIND	SPECIAL-NAMES	VALUES
REVERSED	STANDARD	VARYING
RIGHT	STOP	WHEN
ROUNDED	SUBTRACT	WITH
RUN	TALLY	WORDS
SAME	TALLYING	WORKING-STORAGE
SD	THAN	WRITE
SEARCH	THEN	ZERO
SECTION	THROUGH	ZEROES
SECURITY	THRU	ZEROS
SET		

ANSWERS TO EXERCISES

PART ONE

Chapter 1
No exercise.

Chapter 2
1. Central Processor Unit.
2. Memory Unit, Control unit, Arithmetic unit.
3. Program logic errors and invalid data.
4. In the memory unit of the CPU ("in the CPU" is acceptable).
5. Input unit, Output unit, Backing store.

Chapter 3
1. 80.
2. 12.
3. At the read-station.
4. 3 (made up of a total of 56 columns).
5. 8 (the sprocket hole is not used in the character code).

Chapter 4
1. The barrel printer.
2. 132.
3. One.
4. By means of sprocket holes in either side of the paper.
5. 15″ wide by 11″ deep.

Chapter 5
1. Magnetic tape and magnetic disc devices.
2. By a metallic strip at the load-point.
3. By an inter-block gap.
4. The amount of Core Storage available for data transfer.
5. Double-buffering.
6. 10.
7. 100.
8. 10 tracks or 1 cylinder.
9. File, Block, Record, Field.
10. Three at least.

Chapter 6
1. One of each.
2. No—the employee names will be held on the payroll master file.
3. By the drawing of a flowchart.
4. (*a*) Process
   (*b*) Decision or Comparison
   (*c*) Punched card input or output
   (*d*) Printed report.
5. (*a*) Magnetic disc input or output
   (*b*) Magnetic tape input or output
   (*c*) Paper tape input or output
   (*d*) Start or end point of program.

Chapter 7
1. Introduction, Input, Output, Throughput (or Processing).
2. Media used, record and block layouts.
3. Input, Processing, Output.
4. It must be checked for correct logic (i.e. lack of omissions, ambiguities, etc.).
5. Check the flowchart against the program specification.

Chapter 8
1. Multi-programming
2. The Supervisor (also called the Executive).
3. By the Supervisor. (Note–the Supervisor itself is loaded by a special facility built into the CPU.)
4. By pressing the interrupt button on his console typewriter.
5. The Job Control Language used to communicate requests to the Operating System.
6. By use of the COBOL Compiler.
7. Input—source program; output—source listing and object program.
8. Four of—Supervisor, Compilers, Sort, Utilities, Library maintenance, Error Recovery.
9. Because of its pseudo-English language format.
10. The relatively slow operation of input/output devices compared with the processing speed of the CPU.

Chapter 9
1. 7.
2. One array is contained within the structure—it consists of three elements each called TRANS. The array has the group name DETAILS.
3. (a) 11   (b) 5   (c) 3   (d) 57.
4.

Decimal	Binary	Octal	Hexadecimal
16	10000	20	10
25	11001	31	19
8	1000	10	8
46	101110	56	2E

5. (a) 1.23E5   (b) 6.0E1   (c) 2.0E6   (d) 8.12E−3.

PART TWO

Chapter 10
1. To improve readability and indicate coding elements to the compiler.
2. The commas are preceded by a space and not followed by a space.
3. IDENTIFICATION DIVISION, ENVIRONMENT DIVISION, DATA DIVISION, PROCEDURE DIVISION.
4. In the Identification Division.
5. By using commas or semi-colons.

Chapter 11
1. None.
2. b, d, f, h.
3. (a) 18   (b) 120.
4. ZERO, SPACE, HIGH-VALUE, LOW-VALUE, QUOTE, ALL "literal".
5. b, d, e, f, g, h.

Chapter 12
1. 8–11, 12–72.
2. 7.
3. (*a*) A　(*b*) A　(*c*) A　(*d*) A or B.
4. 1–6.
5. No.

Chapter 13
1. (*a*) 27.5Ø.　(*b*) 27.49.
2. ADD FIELD-1 TO FIELD-2.
3. ADD FIELD-1 TO FIELD-2 GIVING FIELD-X.
4. SUBTRACT SA, SB, SC FROM TOT GIVING RESULT.
5. ADD 327.6 TO AA, AB, AC ROUNDED, AD.

Chapter 14
1. In the data item DEPTH.
2. MULTIPLY AREA BY DEPTH GIVING VOLUME.
3. COMPUTE VOLUME = AREA * DEPTH.
4. − (minus sign), **, * and/, + and − (addition and subtraction).
5. The size error condition will be raised (attempted division by zero).

Chapter 15
1. GO TO END-OF-RUN.
2. GO TO CARD-1, ERROR, CARD-2, CARD-1 DEPENDING ON TYPE.
3. The second GO TO will never be executed.
4. ALTER MAIN-LOOP TO PROCEED TO SUBSID-LOOP.
5. The subject of an ALTER statement must be a paragraph containing only a GO TO statement.

Chapter 16
1. PERFORM BONUS THRU RATE.
2. 6 times.
3. PERFORM PAY UNTIL RATE-CODE LESS THAN 7.
4. (*a*) STOP RUN　(*b*) STOP "ERROR HAS OCCURRED".
5. An embedded PERFORM must have its range either totally included or totally excluded from the range of the original PERFORM.

Chapter 17
1. File Section, Working-Storage Section, Linkage Section.
2. Level 49.
3. Level 77 used for defining non-contiguous data items and level 88 used for defining conditions.
4. Level Ø1.
5. As blocked. Blocking factor is 3.

Chapter 18
1. (*a*) BLOCK CONTAINS 4 RECORDS.
   (*b*) BLOCK CONTAINS 1ØØ TO 37Ø CHARACTERS.
2. RECORD CONTAINS 8Ø CHARACTERS.
3. Fixed-length-F, Variable-length-V, Undefined-length-U, Spanned-length-S.
4. No.
5. FD MASTER.

Chapter 19
1. LABEL RECORDS ARE STANDARD.
2. DATA RECORDS ARE ONE, TWO.

3. None.
4. LABEL RECORDS ARE OMITTED.
5. FD MAIN-IN.
   BLOCK CONTAINS 4 RECORDS
   RECORD CONTAINS 7∅ CHARACTERS
   RECORDING MODE IS F
   LABEL RECORDS ARE STANDARD
   DATA RECORDS ARE DATA-B, DATA-C.

Chapter 20
1. (*a*) Numeric (*b*) Alphanumeric (*c*) Alphanumeric or Alphabetic.
2. 3. (Note—no space is required for the sign or the decimal point in a numeric item.)
3. A group item is always alphanumeric.
4. FILLER.
5. Decimal and Binary.

Chapter 21
1. Alphabetic—A, Numeric—9, Alphanumeric—X.
2. 77 FIELD PICTURE IS S9999V99.
3. 77 NAME PICTURE IS X(9∅).
4. ∅1 RECORD-1.
      ∅2 ACCOUNT.
         ∅3 ACC-NO PICTURE IS 9(5).
         ∅3 ACC-STATUS PICTURE IS X.
      ∅2 PAYMENTS USAGE IS COMPUTATIONAL.
         ∅3 PAY-1 PICTURE IS 999.
         ∅3 PAY-2 PICTURE IS 999.
         ∅3 PAY-3 PICTURE IS 999.
5. A to Z and space.

Chapter 22
1. ∅1 TOTAL.
      ∅2 TOT PICTURE S9(6) OCCURS 6.
2. ADD 1 TO TOT (2).
3. ∅1 TOTAL-X REDEFINES TOTAL.
      ∅2 TOT-X PICTURE A(36).
4. In the DATA RECORDS clause in the File Section.
5.   ∅2 MAIN OCCURS 6 TIMES.
         ∅3 GROUP.
            ∅4 ONE PICTURE XXX.
            ∅4 TWO PICTURE XXX.
         ∅3 GROUP-X REDEFINES GROUP.
            ∅4 THREE PICTURE X(6).

Chapter 23
1. 77 NUM PICTURE S9(7) VALUE IS 6.
2. ∅∅∅∅∅∅6.
3. ∅2 TOTALS VALUE IS ZERO.
      ∅3 TOTS PICTURE S9(5) OCCURS 6.
4. 77 NON-NUM PICTURE X(11) VALUE IS "HEADING ONE".
5. 77 EDIT PICTURE 9(6) BLANK WHEN ZERO.

Chapter 24
1. (a) 0.00
   (b) 2.00
   (c) 307.30
   (d) 2196.32.
2. (a) £**, ***, *37.20
   (b) £21,364,789.31.
3. (a) 01
   (b) 3,174
   (c) 00
   (d) 1,234,567.
4. 77 EDIT PICTURE —ZZZZ99.
5. 77 POUNDS PICTURE ££,££9.99.

Chapter 25
No Exercise

Chapter 26
1. 12.
2. 8.
3. 4.
4. 2.
5. One.

Chapter 27
1. (a) True   (b) true   (c) false   (d) false   (e) false.
2. (a) False.   (b) False.   (c) True.   (d) True.

Chapter 28
1. IF ACC NUMERIC THEN GO TO END ELSE ADD 1 TO ERR-COUNT.
2. IF C = ZERO THEN MULTIPLY A BY B.
3. Neither, zero is a special case.
4. IF A = B THEN IF D > E THEN ADD D TO C
                            ELSE ADD E TO C.
5. IF A NOT = B THEN GO TO PARA-A.
   IF D > E THEN ADD D TO C
               ELSE ADD E TO C.
   PARA-A. next sentence . . .

Chapter 29
1. "SMIT".
2. 234.
3. "1234".
4. "HELL".
5. MOVE DELTA TO OMEGA.

Chapter 30
1. EXAMINE NUM TALLYING ALL SPACES.
2. In the field TALLY which is a five digit unsigned numeric item.
3. EXAMINE CHQ TALLYING LEADING SPACES REPLACING BY ZEROES.
4. EXAMINE STATUS TALLYING UNTIL FIRST 7.
5. TRANSFORM ALPHA-X CHARACTERS FROM "ABC" TO "432".

Chapter 31
1. OPEN INPUT PRINT.
2. CLOSE WORK-A, WORK-B.
3. OPEN INPUT WORK-FILE REVERSED.
4. CLOSE TAPE-1 WITH NO REWIND.
5. CLOSE TAPE-1 WITH LOCK.

Chapter 32
1. READ CARDS AT END MOVE "1" TO SWITCH.
2. READ TAPE INTO TAPE-SAVE AT END GO TO TAPE-END.
3. WRITE NAME.
4. WRITE DETAIL-1 AFTER ADVANCING 1 LINES.
5. IF LINE-COUNT EQUALS 60 THEN
       WRITE HEAD-UP AFTER ADVANCING SKIP LINES.

Chapter 33
1. DISPLAY "PROGRAM 2 HAS ENDED" UPON CONSOLE.
2. DISPLAY MESSAGE UPON CONSOLE.
3. ACCEPT ANSWER FROM CONSOLE.
4. DISPLAY "PLEASE TYPE DATE" UPON CONSOLE.
   ACCEPT IN-DATE FROM CONSOLE.
5. DISPLAY "HOW MANY REPORTS REQD?" UPON CONSOLE.
   ACCEPT ANSWER FROM CONSOLE.
   PERFORM PRINT THRU PRINT-END ANSWER TIMES.

Chapter 34
PROCEDURE DIVISION. OPEN INPUT MAIN-IN, TRANSACTIONS.
                    OPEN OUTPUT MAIN-OUT.
                    READ MAIN-IN AT END GO TO FINISH.

READ-TRANS.   READ TRANSACTIONS AT END GO TO ERROR.

COMPARE.   IF M-KEY GREATER THAN T-KEY GO TO ERROR.
              IF M-KEY LESS THAN T-KEY GO TO WRITE-MAIN.

EQUAL.   MOVE TRANS TO IN-AREA.
              GO TO READ-TRANS.

WRITE-MAIN.   WRITE OUT-AREA FROM IN-AREA.
              READ MAIN-IN AT END GO TO FINISH.
              GO TO COMPARE.

ERROR.   DISPLAY "TRANSACTION FILE ERROR" UPON
                                              CONSOLE.

FINISH.   CLOSE MAIN-IN, MAIN-OUT, TRANSACTIONS.
              STOP-RUN.

Chapter 35
No exercise.

Chapter 36
1. AREA OF INREC, RADIUS OF INREC, DIAM IN INREC.
2. AREA OF UPDATE, RADIUS OF UPDATE, DIAM OF UPDATE.
3. MOVE CORRESPONDING INREC TO UPDATE.
4. MOVE AREA OF INREC TO AREA OF UPDATE.
   MOVE RADIUS OF INREC TO RADIUS OF UPDATE.
   MOVE DIAM OF INREC TO DIAM OF UPDATE.
5. SUBTRACT CORRESPONDING UPDATE FROM INREC.

Chapter 37

1. ADD TABLE (SUB) TO TOTAL.
2. MOVE 1 TO SUB.
   PERFORM TABADD 6 TIMES.

   .
   .
   .

   TABADD. ADD TABLE (SUB) TO TOTAL.
   ADD 1 TO SUB.
3. PERFORM TABADD VARYING SUB FROM 1 BY 1
                           UNTIL SUB = 7.

   .
   .

   TABADD. ADD TABLE (SUB) TO TOTAL.
4. PERFORM PARA-X VARYING INC FROM START BY JUMP UNTIL
                           INC GREATER THAN FINISH.
5. PERFORM TABADD VARYING SUB FROM 1 BY 1 UNTIL SUB = 21.

   .
   .

   TABADD. ADD TABA (SUB) TO TABB (SUB).

Chapter 38

1. Ø1 TABLE OCCURS 1Ø.
   Ø3 DATE PICTURE 9(6).
   Ø3 NAME PICTURE X(2Ø).
2. MOVE DATE (MAN-NO) TO DATE-CHECK.
3. SUBTRACT 35 FROM MAN-NO GIVING SUB.
   MOVE DATE (SUB) TO DATE-CHECK.
4. MOVE SPACES TO COMPARE-STATUS.
   PERFORM SEARCH VARYING SUB FROM 1 BY 1 UNTIL SUB = 21
   OR COMPARE-STATUS NOT = SPACES.
   SEARCH. IF SEARCH-CODE = CODE (SUB) MOVE STATUS (SUB)
   TO COMPARE-STATUS.
5. MOVE 21 TO SUB.
   SUBTRACT SEARCH-CODE FROM SUB.
   MOVE STATUS (SUB) TO COMPARE-STATUS.

Chapter 39

1. ENTRY "CHECKNO" USING NUMBER, INDICATOR.
2. LINKAGE SECTION.
   77 NUMBER PICTURE 9(6).
   77 INDICATOR PICTURE X.
3. CALL "CHECKNO" USING ITEM-NO, FLAG.
4. LINKAGE SECTION.
   77 INPUT-1 PICTURE 9(5).
   77 INPUT-2 PICTURE 9(5).
   77 INPUT-3 PICTURE 9(5).
   77 RESULT PICTURE 9(6).
   PROCEDURE DIVISION.
     ENTRY "MEAN" USING INPUT-1, INPUT-2, INPUT-3, RESULT.
     COMPUTE RESULT = (INPUT-1 + INPUT-2 + INPUT-3)/3
       GO BACK.
5. CALL "MEAN" USING INA, INB, INC, OUT.

Chapter 40
1. To safeguard against manual errors and computer failures.
2. At the end of card or paper tape input data.
3. At the end of tape or disc files.

Chapter 41
1. NOTE READ ROUTINE.
2. Ø1 INPUT-AREA COPY FILEX.
3. Ø1 INPUT-AREA COPY FILEX REPLACING XY BY NAME.
4. Ø1 WORK COPY DATE.
5. ENTER FORTRAN.

Chapter 42
1. SD SFILE,
      LABEL RECORDS ARE OMITTED,
      RECORDING MODE IS F,
      DATA RECORD IS SORT-AREA.
   Ø1 SORT-AREA.
      Ø2 KEY-FIELD PICTURE 9(5).
      Ø2 FILLER PICTURE X(55).
2. SORT SFILE ON DESCENDING KEY KEY-FIELD,
                  USING FILE-A, GIVING FILE-B.
3.   OPEN INPUT IND.
     OPEN OUTPUT OUTD.
   SORT SORTX ON ASCENDING KEY CODE
                  USING IND, GIVING OUTD.
     CLOSE IND, OUTD.
     STOP RUN.

Chapter 43
1. READY TRACE.
2. RESET TRACE.
3. EXHIBIT NAMED FIELD.
4. EXHIBIT CHANGED COUNT.
5. DEBUG BONUS-LOOP.
      ADD 1 TO COUNT.

Chapter 44
1. SKIP 2.
2. EJECT.

Chapter 45
1. IDENTIFICATION DIVISION.
      PROGRAM-ID. MINE.
      AUTHOR. YOUR NAME.
      INSTALLATION. ANYWHERE.
      DATE-WRITTEN. TODAY.
      DATE-COMPILED. TOMORROW.
      SECURITY. NONE.
      REMARKS. ONLY THE FIRST TWO LINES OF THIS ANSWER NEED
            BE AS SHOWN.

Chapter 46
1. CONFIGURATION SECTION.
      SOURCE-COMPUTER. IBM-36Ø-4Ø.
      OBJECT-COMPUTER. IBM-36Ø-3Ø.
      SPECIAL-NAMES. CONSOLE IS DESK.

Chapter 47
No exercise.

ANSWERS TO REVISION QUESTIONS

SET 1

1. Identification Division, Environment Division, Data Division, Procedure Division.
2. Comma and semi-colon.
3. A–Z, Ø–9, - (hyphen).
4. ZERO, SPACE, HIGH-VALUE, LOW-VALUE, QUOTE, ALL "literal".
5. (a) numeric (b) non-numeric (c) non-numeric (d) figurative (e) non-numeric.
6. In columns 1 to 6.
7. COMPUTE A = (B + C)/D*E.
8. ADD SALES TO STANDING GIVING TARGET.
9. ADD SALES TO STANDING GIVING TARGET ON SIZE ERROR
   GO TO ERROR.
10. 126.
11. 127.
12. Ø5ØØV3Ø.
13. ADD SALES TO VALUE GIVING WORK.
    DIVIDE WORK BY 2.
14. ADD TA TO TB GIVING AVG.
    MULTIPLY AVG BY 6Ø.
    DIVIDE AVG BY 2.
15. COMPUTE R = Y**2 + Z*(A*(B + C)).
16. GO TO MAIN.
17. GO TO P-A, P-B, P-C, DEPENDING ON SUB.
18. Control would be transferred to the next sentence.
19. ALTER LOOP TO PROCEED TO SUBSID.
20. PERFORM ADDUP 6 TIMES.
21. PERFORM TOTA, PERFORM TOTB, PERFORM TOTC.
22. PERFORM TOTA THRU TOTC.
23. PERFORM MAIN THRU MAIN-EXIT UNTIL SUB EQUALS ZERO.
24. LOOP. IF TOTAL EQUALS ZERO ADD 1 TO SUB GO TO LOOP-EXIT.
         ADD 1 TO SUB-X.
    LOOP-EXIT. EXIT.
25. IF INDIC EQUALS CODE PERFORM LOOP THRU LOOP-EXIT.

SET 2

1. File Section, Working-Storage Section, Linkage Section.
2. Ø1.
3. 49.
4. 77—non-contiguous items, 88—conditions.
5. FD MAIN-IN,
       BLOCK CONTAINS 4 RECORDS,
       RECORD CONTAINS 2ØØ CHARACTERS,
       LABEL RECORDS ARE STANDARD,
       RECORDING MODE IS F,
       DATA RECORD IS IN-DATA.
6. (a) numeric
   (b) alphanumeric
   (c) alphanumeric or alphabetic
   (d) numeric
   (e) numeric or alphanumeric depending on context.

7. Ø4 FILLER PICTURE X(12).
8. Ø1 CARD.
    Ø3 LOCATION.
        Ø5 NAME PICTURE X(2Ø).
        Ø5 ADDRESS PICTURE X(4Ø).
    Ø3 PAYMENTS OCCURS 3.
    Ø5 AMOUNT PICTURE 9(5).

Note that level numbers, other than Ø1, in your answer may be different from those shown providing your structure is the same as that shown.

9. ADD AMOUNT (3) TO TOTAL.
10.   MOVE 1 TO SUB. PERFORM ADDUP 20 TIMES
                                .
                                .
                                .

    ADDUP.   ADD COST (SUB) TO TOT.
                    ADD 1 TO SUB.

11. Ø2 COSTX.
    Ø3 COST OCCURS 2Ø PICTURE 9(4).
    Ø2 STATUSX REDEFINES COSTX.
    Ø3 STATUS OCCURS 2Ø PICTURE A(4).
12. 77 PI PICTURE 9V999 VALUE 3.142.
13. Ø2 CHECK-ALL VALUE ZERO OCCURS 5.
    Ø3 CHECK PICTURE 9(5).
14. Ø2 ALPHA PICTURE X(6) VALUE "ABCDEF".
    Ø2 LET REDEFINES ALPHA.
    Ø3 LETTER OCCURS 6 PICTURE X.
15. (a) £ØØØ13
    (b) £Ø,Ø12
    (c) £2,764
    (d) +12
    (e) −ØØØ7
    (f) £Ø,ØØ8.61
    (g) £12
    (h) £1,234
    (i) £Ø
    (j) £1,234,567.89
    (k) Ø
    (l) 27
    (m) ***.**
    (n) **Ø.2Ø
    (o) 3,647.
16. Four (i.e. those preceding the first non-zero character—which are those that can be removed without altering the value of the item).
17. Numeric—9
    Alphabetic—A
    Alphanumeric—X
18. Ø1 CUSTOMER.
    Ø2 NAME PICTURE X(1Ø).
    Ø2 STATUS PICTURE XX.
    Ø2 TRANSACTIONS OCCURS 6.
    Ø3 TYPE PICTURE X.
    Ø3 SIZE PICTURE 9(6).

19. Ø1 REC.
       Ø2 LOCATION.
           Ø3 NAME PICTURE X(2Ø).
           Ø3 ACCOUNT-NO PICTURE X(6).
       Ø2 FINANCE.
           Ø3 PAYMENTS.
               Ø4 THIS-MONTH PICTURE 9(6).
               Ø4 LAST-MONTH PICTURE 9(6).
           Ø3 FLAGS.
               Ø4 CREDIT PICTURE X.
               Ø4 DELIVERY PICTURE X.
               Ø4 SWITCH PICTURE X OCCURS 4.
20. FD TAPE,
    BLOCK CONTAINS 4 RECORDS,
        RECORD CONTAINS 1ØØ CHARACTERS,
        RECORDING MODE IS F,
        LABEL RECORDS ARE STANDARD,
        DATA RECORD IS IN-AREA.

                        SET 3
1. IF QUERY IS NUMERIC THEN GO TO NUMBER.
2. IF NUM IS LESS THAN 36Ø GO TO PARB.
   IF NUM IS GREATER THAN 512 GO TO PARC.
   GO TO PARA.
3. 77 STATUS PICTURE 9.
       88 GOOD-CREDIT VALUE 1.
       88 BAD-CREDIT VALUE 2.
       88 DOUBTFUL VALUE 3.
                    .
                    .
                    .

   IF GOOD-CREDIT GO TO YES-LOOP.
   IF BAD-CREDIT GO TO NO-LOOP.
   IF DOUBTFUL GO TO DOUBT-LOOP.
4. IF STATUS EQUALS 6 AND CODE NOT EQUAL 7 GO TO YES.
5. IF CODE IS POSITIVE THEN SUBTRACT 1 FROM SUB,
                        ELSE ADD 1 TO SUB.
6. IF SEX EQUALS M THEN IF RATE IS GREATER THAN 2 MOVE
                        1 TO SUB,
                        ELSE MOVE 2 TO SUB,
                        ELSE MOVE 3 TO SUB.
7. MOVE FIELDA TO Z-CODE.
8. EXAMINE ALPHA-2 TALLYING LEADING SPACES.
9. EXAMINE ALPHA-1 TALLYING ALL ZEROES REPLACING BY "*."
10. MOVE TALLY TO SUB.
11. PROCEDURE DIVISION.
                OPEN INPUT INA.
                OPEN OUTPUT OUTB.
    LOOP.   READ INA AT END GO TO FINISH.
                MOVE AREA-1 TO AREA-2.
                WRITE AREA-2.
                GO TO LOOP.
    FINISH.   CLOSE INA, OUTB.
                STOP RUN.

12. DISPLAY "PLEASE GIVE RUN NUMBER" UPON CONSOLE.
ACCEPT RUN-NO FROM CONSOLE.

13. DATA DIVISION.
FILE SECTION.
FD CARDS.
   LABEL RECORDS ARE OMITTED,
   DATA RECORD IS CARD-IN.
Ø1 CARD-IN.
   Ø2 FILLER PICTURE X(8Ø).
FD PRINT.
   LABEL RECORDS ARE OMITTED,
   DATA RECORD IS PRINT-LINE.
Ø1 PRINT-LINE.
   Ø2 FILLER PICTURE X(4) VALUE IS SPACES.
   Ø2 CARD-IMAGE PICTURE X(8Ø).
   Ø2 FILLER PICTURE X(48).
WORKING-STORAGE SECTION.
77 CARD-COUNT PICTURE 9(5).
77 SKIP PICTURE X VALUE "1".
77 LINE-COUNT PICTURE 99 VALUE 6Ø.
Ø1 HEADER.
   Ø2 FILLER PICTURE X(4) VALUE SPACES.
   Ø2 FILLER PICTURE X(1Ø),
     VALUE IS "CARD PRINT".
   Ø2 FILLER PICTURE X(118), VALUE IS SPACES.
Ø1 TRAILER.
   Ø2 FILLER PICTURE X(17),
     VALUE IS "NO OF CARDS READ".
   Ø2 P-COUNT PICTURE ZZZZ9.
   Ø2 FILLER PICTURE X(110), VALUE IS SPACES.
   PROCEDURE DIVISION.
   OPEN INPUT CARDS.
   OPEN OUTPUT PRINT.
LOOP.   READ CARDS AT END GO TO FINISH.
  MOVE CARD-IN TO CARD-IMAGE.
  ADD 1 TO CARD-COUNT.
  PERFORM PRINTING. GO TO LOOP.
PRINTING.   WRITE PRINT-LINE AFTER ADVANCING 1 LINES.
  IF LINE-COUNT EQUALS 60 PERFORM HEADING.
  ADD 1 TO LINE-COUNT.
HEADING. WRITE PRINT-LINE FROM HEADING AFTER
  ADVANCING SKIP LINES.
  MOVE Ø TO LINE-COUNT.
FINISH.   MOVE CARD-COUNT TO P-COUNT.
  WRITE PRINT-LINE FROM TRAILER AFTER ADVANCING 1 LINES.
  CLOSE CARDS, PRINT.

SET 4

1. ADD CORRESPONDING SALES TO TOTAL.

2. Ø1 TOTALS.
   Ø2 AREAS OCCURS 2Ø PICTURE S9(5).
   Ø2 AREA-TOTS OCCURS 2Ø PICTURE S9(5).

3. PERFORM ADDUP VARYING SUB FROM 1 BY 2
   UNTIL SUB EQUALS 2Ø.
   .
   .
   .

   ADDUP. ADD 1 TO SUB GIVING SUBX.
   ADD AREAS (SUB) TO AREA-TOTS (SUBX).

4. PERFORM ADD-RTN VARYING SUB FROM STARTS BY 1
   UNTIL SUB IS GREATER THAN ENDS.
   .
   .
   .

   ADD-RTN. ADD AREAS (SUB) TO AREA-TOTS (SUB).

5. CALL "MODULE" USING CODE, STATUS, NUM.

6. DATA DIVISION.
      LINKAGE SECTION.
      77 FIRST PICTURE 9(6).
      77 SECOND PICTURE 9(6).
      77 AVGE PICTURE 9(6).

   PROCEDURE DIVISION.

      ENTRY "MODX" USING FIRST, SECOND, AVGE.
      COMPUTE AVGE = (FIRST + SECOND)/2.
      GO BACK.

7. DATA DIVISION.

   FILE SECTION.

   FD MASTER,
      BLOCK CONTAINS 4 RECORDS,
      LABEL RECORDS ARE STANDARD,
      RECORDING MODE IS F,
      DATA RECORD IS M-IN.

   Ø1 M-IN.
      Ø2 M-CUSTNO PICTURE 9(6).
      Ø2 M-CODE PICTURE 9.
      Ø2 M-DETAILS PICTURE X(33).

   FD MASTER-OUT,
      BLOCK CONTAINS 4 RECORDS,
      LABEL RECORDS ARE STANDARD,
      RECORDING MODE IS F,
      DATA RECORD IS M-OUT.

   Ø1 M-OUT.
      Ø2 FILLER PICTURE X(4Ø).

   FD TRANS.
      Ø2 T-CUSTNO PICTURE 9(6).
      Ø2 T-TYPE PICTURE X.
      Ø2 T-DETAILS PICTURE X(33).

   WORKING-STORAGE SECTION.

   77 COUNT PICTURE 999.

   PROCEDURE DIVISION.

```
              OPEN INPUT MASTER, TRANS.
              OPEN OUTPUT MASTER-OUT.
READ-T.    READ TRANS AT END MOVE ALL 9 TO T-CUSTNO.
READ-M.    READ MASTER AT END GO TO FINISH.
              IF M-CUSTNO LESS THAN T-CUSTNO THEN
              PERFORM WRITE, GO TO READ-M.
EQUAL-RECS. IF T-TYPE EQUALS "1" THEN ADD 1 TO COUNT,
              GO TO READ-T.
NOTE THE PREVIOUS STATEMENT HAS THE EFFECT OF DELETING
   THE MASTER FILE RECORD.
              MOVE DETAILS TO M-DETAILS.
              PERFORM WRITE-M.
              GO TO READ-T.
WRITE-M.   WRITE M-OUT FROM M-IN.
FINISH.    CLOSE MASTER, MASTER-OUT, TRANS.
              DISPLAY COUNT "RECORDS DELETED" UPON CONSOLE.
              STOP RUN.
```

8. (Procedure Division for problem presented in Chapter Twenty-five.)
```
PROCEDURE DIVISION.
BEGIN.     OPEN INPUT CARD-IN.
              OPEN OUTPUT TAPOUT, PRINT.
              PERFORM HEADINGS.
READ-CARD.     READ CARD-IN AT END GO TO PROGRAM-END.
VALIDATE.
              IF CARD-TYPE NOT = "307" AND CARD-TYPE NOT = "308"
              THEN MOVE ALL "*" TO A-TYPE.
              CALL "CHKDIG" USING CUST-ACCNO, CHK-DIGIT, FLAG.
              IF FLAG NOT=SPACE THEN MOVE ALL"*" TO A-NUMBER.
VAL-AMOUNTS.   PERFORM AMOUNTS THRU AMOUNTS-END
   VARYING SUB FROM 1 TO 4.
              IF PRINT-ASTERISKS NOT = SPACES THEN GO TO REJECT.
              PERFORM ADD-AMOUNTS VARYING SUB FROM 1 TO 4.
              WRITE VALID FROM CARD.
              GO TO READ-CARD.
AMOUNTS.
              EXAMINE ENTRY-AMOUNT (SUB) TALLYING
              LEADING SPACES REPLACING BY ZEROES.
              IF ENTRY-AMOUNT (SUB) = ZEROES GO TO AMOUNTS-
              END.
              IF ENTRY-DATE (SUB) IS NOT NUMERIC
              MOVE ALL "*" TO A-ENTRY (SUB).
              IF ENTRY-AMOUNT (SUB) IS NOT NUMERIC
              MOVE ALL "*" TO A-AMOUNT (SUB).
AMOUNTS-END.   EXIT.
ADD-AMOUNTS.  IF CARD-TYPE = "307" THEN
              ADD ENTRY-AMOUNT (SUB) TO TOTAL-PAYMENTS
              ELSE ADD ENTRY-AMOUNT (SUB) TO TOTAL-CREDITS.
```

REJECT.   MOVE CARD TO CARD-IMAGE.
          MOVE PRINT-CARD-DETAIL TO PRINT-OUT.
          PERFORM PRINT-LINE.

          MOVE PRINT-ERROR-FIELDS TO PRINT-OUT.

          PERFORM PRINT-LINE.

          ADD 2 TO LINE-COUNT.

          IF LINE-COUNT = 58 THEN PERFORM HEADINGS.

          GO TO READ-CARD.

HEADINGS.   MOVE ZERO TO LINE-COUNT.
          MOVE PRINT-HEAD TO PRINT-OUT.
          WRITE PRINT-OUT AFTER ADVANCING SKIP LINES.

PRINT-LINE.   WRITE PRINT-OUT AFTER ADVANCING 1 LINES.

PROGRAM-END. MOVE TOTAL-PAYMENTS TO P-TOTAL-PAYS.
          MOVE TOTAL-CREDITS TO P-TOTAL-CRS.
          MOVE PRINT-TOTALS TO PRINT-OUT.

          PERFORM PRINT-LINE.

          CLOSE CARD-IN, TAPOUT, PRINT.

          STOP RUN.

ANSWERS TO EXERCISES

PART THREE

Chapter 48
No exercise.

Chapter 49
1. (a) integer (b) real (c) real (d) double precision (e) complex (f) literal (g) file name or literal (h) literal (i) logical.
2. DOUBLE-PRECISION A, B
   COMPLEX ROOT.
3. (a) integer (b) real (c) real (d) real (e) integer (f) integer.
4. INTEGER REAL
   REAL INTEGR.
5. (a) .FALSE. (b) $\emptyset$ (c) $\emptyset.\emptyset$ (d) spaces.

Chapter 50
1.   *1.* Exponentiation.
     2. Multiplication and division.
     3. Addition and subtraction (expressions in parentheses are evaluated first).
2. R = (P**Y)**W.
3. (a) 12.$\emptyset$ (b) 6 (c) 12 (d) 9 (e) 9.6 (f) 12.$\emptyset$ (g) (14.4, $\emptyset.\emptyset$) (h) $\emptyset$
(remember the initial value of K will be set by the compiler to $\emptyset$).
4. REAL MSQR
   COMPLEX MCOM
   MEAN = (A + B + C + D)/2
   MSQR = MEAN**2
   MCOM = MSQR.
5. NUMBER = ONE*(−TWO).

Chapter 51
1. GO TO 37.
2. 8 GO TO (6, 12, 32), N.
3. To the statement following statement number 8 (i.e. to the next sequential statement).
4. SWITCH = SWITCH-6.
   GO TO (8, 14, 21), SWITCH.
5. ASSIGN 18 TO JUMPER.

Chapter 52
1.   IF (A*B/(H − 2)) 91, 12, 91
2.   IF (X.GT.CNT) GO TO 14
3.   IF (A**2.LE.B**7) KOUNT = KOUNT + 1
4.   GO TO 7
5.   A = 1
     10 C = B**Z/A + C
       A = A + 1
       IF (A.LT.101) GO TO 10
6.   DO 10 A = 1,100
     10 C = B**2/A + C
7.   DO 20 A = 1, 50
     20 SUM = SUM + A
       TOTAL = SUM**2
8.   DO 10 X = 1, 5
     10 P = P(R/100*P)
9.   DO 10 X = 1, N
     10 P = P + (R/100*P)
10.   DO 20 N = 1,1000
     20 E = E + (1 + 1/N)**N

Chapter 53
1.   DIMENSION R(6), Q(6), Y(6)
       INTEGER Y
       COMPLEX Q
2.   Q(3) = Q(3) + B(4)
3.   DO 10 K = 1, 6
     10 Z(K) = Z(K) + R(K)
4.   DO 10 K = 1, N
     10 X = X+B(K)
       Y = X**2
5.   M = X/2
6.   DO 10 K = 1, 20
       IF (R(K) .LT.0.0) GO TO 19
       P = P + R(K)
       GO TO 20
     19 N = N + R(K)
     20 CONTINUE
7.   DO 10 K = 1, 12
     10 CHI = CHI + (C(K) − F)**2/F
8.   DATA A, B, C, D, E/1, 2, 3, 4, 5/
9.   DATA Q/1, 2, 3, 4, 5/
18.   IF (B(N).EQ.P) GO TO 12

Chapter 54

1. INPUT, P, Q, T
2. PRINT, SUM, TOTAL, B
3. DIMENSION R(1∅)
   DO 1∅ K = 1, 1∅
   10 INPUT R(K)
   DO 12K = 1, 1∅
   12 S = S + R(K)
   A = S/10
   PRINT, A
   STOP
4. DIMENSION T(1∅)
   INTEGER T, S, R
   10 DO 2∅ K = 1, 1∅
   20 INPUT T(K)
   23 R = ∅
   DO 25K = 1, 9
   IF (T(K) .LT. T(K + 1) GO TO 26
   S = T(K)
   T(K) = T(K + 1)
   T(K + 1) = S
   R = 1
   26 CONTINUE
   IF (R.EQ.1) GO TO 23
   DO 3∅ K = 1, 1∅
   30 PRINT T(K)
   STOP
5. INTEGER R, S
   DO 1∅ J = 1, 8
   INPUT R
   10 IF (R.GT.S)S = R
   PRINT S
   STOP

Chapter 55

1. WRITE ("OUTDATA") TOTAL, TIME, MAIN
2. FILENAME Q
   INTEGER C
   READ (Q, END = 1∅) A, B, C
3. 10 INPUT, R, S, I, N
   WRITE ("OUT4") R, S, I, N
   GO TO 1∅
4. 20 READ ("OUT4", END = 1∅) R, S, T, N
   PRINT, R, S, I, N
   GO TO 2∅
   10 STOP
5. FILENAME NAME
   NAME = "FOURX"

Chapter 56

1. CALL SUBR (A, B, D)
2 SUBROUTINE AVG (W, X, Y, Z)
   Z = (W + X + Y)/3
   RETURN

3.   SUBROUTINE MEAN (A, S)
          DIMENSION A(50)
          DO 10 K = 1, 50
   10   S + A(K)
          S = S/50
          RETURN
4.   CALL MEAN (P, R)
5.   DIMENSION X(20), Y(20)
                .
                .
                .
          DO 10 K = 1, 20
   10   CALL DIV (X(K), Y(K))

Chapter 57
1.   R = SQRT(A*B)
2.   DIMENSION P(12)
          DO 10 K = 1, 12
   10   Q = Q + P(K)
          M = Q/12
          Q = 0.0
          DO 12K = 1, 12
   12   Q = (P(K) − M)**2
          S = SQRT (Q/12)
          PRINT,S
          STOP
3.   X = MAX (A, B, C, F, G, H, P)
          Y = MIN (A, B, C, F, G, H, P)
          PRINT SQRT (X − Y)
4.   REAL MINE
          MINE (X) = (A**2 + 2 + B +C)/D
5.   PI = 3.142
          T = TAN (180*A/PI)

ANSWERS TO REVISION QUESTIONS

SET 5

1. (*a*) integer (*b*) real (*c*) complex (*d*) alpha (*e*) alpha (*f*) logical.
2. INTEGER R, S, T
   REAL K, L, M
   LOGICAL Y
3. integer—0
   real—0.0
   logical .FALSE.
4. D = A*(B − C)
5. R = R**4
6. R = (J + K + L + M)/4
7. GO TO 12
8. IF (LOG.EQ. .TRUE.) GO TO 16
9. IF (A.GT.12)A = A**2

```
10.      DO 10 K = 1, 10
      10 S = S + B(K)
11. Ten
12.      DO 10 K = 2, 16, 2
      10 S = S + A(K)
13.      DO  10 K = 1, 24
      10 C(K) = A(K) *B(K)
14.      DO 10  K = 1, 12
         IF (C(K) .EQ.0.0) GO TO 10
         S = S + A(K)
         I = I + 1
      10 CONTINUE
         A = S/I
15.      DIMENSION DP(16)
         DOUBLE PRECISION DP
16. 10   INPUT, Z
         PRINT, Z, Z**2, Z**3
         GO TO 10
17.      DIMENSION IN (12)
         DO 10 K = 1, 12
         INPUT, IN(K)
      10 J = J + IN(K)
         I = J/12
         DO 12 K = 1, 12
      12 PRINT, DIM(I, IN(K))
         STOP
18.      DIMENSION F(10)
       5 DO 10 K = 1, 10
      10 INPUT, F(K)
         WRITE ("SET") (F(K), K = 1, 10)
         GO TO 5
         STOP
19.      DIMENSION F(10)
      10 READ ("SET") (F(K), K = 1, 10)
         S = 0.0
         DO 12K = 1, 10
      12 S = S + F(K)
         PRINT, S
         GO TO 10
20.      INPUT, A, B
         PI = 3.142
         DO 10 K = 0,2*PI, PI/180
         PRINT, "X =", A*COS(K) + TAN(K)
      10 PRINT, "Y =", B*SIN(K)
         STOP
```

ANSWERS TO EXERCISES

PART FOUR

Chapter 58
No Exercise.

Chapter 59
1. An error. Textual constants, such as "2", cannot be used in arithmetic.
2. 286 A–Z, A∅–A9, B∅–B9 and so on.
3. 26 A$–Z$
4. Textual or string.
5. Yes, both are numeric variables.

Chapter 60
1. (i) LET D = A + B + C7
   (ii) LET G2 = G2–7
   (iii) LET A2 = G↑2
   (iv) LET A2 = A3/G3↑2
2. 240 LET X = A/(B + C)
3. 242 LET A$ = X$ + Y$
4. 244 LET X = 1
   246 LET N = INT (1 + 10*RND (X))
5. "MR B JONES"

Chapter 61
1. DEF FNA(X) = 3.14159*X*X
2. LET A = FNA(R)
3. LET A = 3.14159*R*R
4. LET C = INSTR (N$, "MR")
5. LET M$ = RIGHT $(N$, LEN $ (N$) −C + 1)

Chapter 62
1. 112 DATA 28, 429.6, 3.14159, "MAYNARD"
2. 114 RESTORE
   115 READ A, B, C   dummy
   117 READ N$
3. 119 INPUT "YOUR NAME", N$
4. A request for more data (a second?).
5. The variable R does not match the DATA entry "ONE" (which is a string).

Chapter 63
1. 112 PRINT "MAYNARD"
2. 114 PRINT A*3, B*3, C*3
3. 114 PRINT A*3; B*3; C*3
4. 114 LET A$ = "££## +#### ####.##"
   116 PRINT USING A$; A*3; B*3; C*3
5. 214 PRINT
   216 PRINT

343

Chapter 64
1. 112 GO TO 462
2. 112 IF A$ = "YES" THEN 462
3. 114 IF A/B > 96 THEN 866
4. 116 ON B − 5 GO TO 86, 89, 94
5. 122 ON A GO TO 126, 126, 126
   123 PRINT "ERROR"
   124 STOP
   126 . . . . .

Chapter 65
1. 112 FOR J = 0̸ TO 2
   114 PRINT "INPUT TEST NO   "; J
   116 INPUT R
   118 NEXT J
2. (*a*) one   (*b*) one   (*c*) the current value of c.
3. GOSUB 612
4. 112 G = 3.142 * R ↑ 2
   114 RETURN
5. The FOR/NEXT loops are interleaved.

Chapter 66
1. 112 DIM A(10̸), A$(8)
2. 114 FOR J = 1 TO 10̸
   116 A(J) = 0̸
   118 NEXT J
3. 120̸ DIM B(3, 6)
4. 122 FOR J = 1 TO 3
   124 FOR K = 1 TO 6
   126 B(J, K) = 1
   128 NEXT K
   132 NEXT J
5. 160 (16 rows each of 10 columns).

ANSWERS TO REVISION QUESTIONS

SET 6

1. (*a*) numeric   (*b*) string   (*c*) string   (*d*) string variable name.
2. 26 (A$ to Z$)
3. A(1) is the first element of the array A(   ) and is distinct from simple variable A.
4. 112 LET C = C*7
5. 114 PRINT A$ + R$
6. (*a*) to return the largest integer less than or equal to X.
   (*b*) to indicate the sign of the value of X.
   (*c*) to return the cosine of the angle X.
7. 244 LET A = SQR(Y)
8. 248 LET X = 0̸.5*A*B*SIN(K)
9. 331 DATA 87, 16, 4, 29.0
   527 READ A, B, C, D
10. To return the READ "pointer" to the first DATA statement.
11. 441 INPUT X
    442 PRINT X, SQR(X), X ↑ 2, X ↑ 3

12. 446 PRINT TAB(20);
13. NO
14. 151 IF A < 10 THEN 184
    153 IF A > 20 THEN 184
15. 182 PRINT "CONTINUE?";
    184 INPUT N$
    186 IF N$ <> "NO" THEN 244
    186 STOP
16. 112 INPUT A
    114 ON A GO TO 186, 194, 266
    116 PRINT "ERROR"
    118 GO TO 112
17. 212 DIM A(20), B(20)
    214 FOR J = 1 TO 20
    216 LET A(J) = 0
    217 LET B(J) = 0
    219 NEXT J
18. 612 PRINT
    614 PRINT
    616 PRINT "PAGE NUMBER   "; N
    618 LET N = N + 1
    620 RETURN
19. 412 GOSUB 612
20. 122 FOR J = 1 TO 4
    124 FOR K = 1 TO 6
    126 LET X = M (J, K)
    128 LET M(J, K) = P(K, J)
    130 LET P(K, J) = X
    132 NEXT K
    134 NEXT J

ANSWERS TO REVISION QUESTIONS

SET 7

1. That of scale.
2. In memory connected to the CPU.
3. In the CPU (central processor unit).
4. 1024.
5. Random Access Memory.
   Read Only Memory.
   Programmable Read Only Memory.
6. RAM.
7. 16.
8. Serial.
9. By putting the chip address on the address bus.
10. UART.

Index

ACCEPT, 166–8
ADD, 78–9
  CORRESPONDING, 180
  ON SIZE ERROR, 79
  ROUNDED, 79
Address bus, 308
Alignment, 77, 116
ALL, 71
ALPHA, 223
ALPHABETIC CLASS, 112
ALPHANUMERIC CLASS, 112–13
ALTER, 88–90
  for switching, 89
Amendment file, 169
AND, 143
Answers
  exercises, 324, 338, 343
  revision questions, 332, 341, 344
Area A, 73, 204, 207
Area B, 73
Arithmetic expressions, 84–5, 225–7
  parentheses in, 85
Arithmetic operators, 84, 225
  BASIC, 275
  functions, 264
  order of evaluation, 85, 226
Arrays, 53–4, 120–3, 181–6, 241–4
  BASIC, 296–9
  elementary items, 54
  elements, 53
  priming, 245
  with DO, 243–4
ASCENDING, 199
ASSIGN (COBOL), 208
Assignment statements, 225–30
  compatibilities, 229
  examples, 227–9
Assumed decimal point, 116
AT END, see READ
Auditing, 194
AUTHOR, 205–6
AUTO, 270
AWAITING REPLY, see ACCEPT

Babbage, 1
Backing storage, home computer, 307
Barrel printer, see Line printer
BASIC, compiler, 269
  introduction to, 267
  statements, 271
Batch totals, 193
Binary arithmetic, 56
Binary subtraction, 57
BLANK LINES, 76
BLANK WHEN ZERO, 126–7
BLOCK CONTAINS, 102–3
  CHARACTERS, 103
  RECORDS, 103
BLOCK SIZE, 27
Blocking, 22, 25–7, 98, 103
  factor, 98
  FORTRAN, 251
  schematic, 98
  variable length, 26–7
Bus system, 308–9

CALL, 192
  FORTRAN, 256
Card columns, 10
  as field, 11
Card pack, 11
Card rows, 10
Carriage return, 166, 246

Central control unit, 5
Central processor unit, 7–9
  interrupting, 48
Chip, see Microprocessor
CLASS condition, 140
CLOSE, 157–8
  LOCK, 158
  NO REWIND, 158
COBOL, 2, 49
  arithmetic statements, 77–80
  character set, 65
  coding form, 73
  divisions, 67
  language structure, 65
  punctuation, 66–7
  verbs, 68
  word set, 68
Coding form, 73–6, 219
  sequence numbers, 73
COMMA, 66
Comments, 195
Comparing, 31–2
Compilation, 49
Compilers, 49
  functions, 49–50
COMPLEX, 223
COMPLEX constants, 221
COMPUTATIONAL, see USAGE
COMPUTE, 84–6
Computer
  components, 5
  human analogy, 5
  structure, 5
Computer operator, 15, 48, 165–8, 177
  flowchart symbol, 38
Computer system
  functional units, 6
  sample application, 8
  status, 48
Condition names, 69, 142–3
Conditional statements, 234–5
Conditions, 139–44, 234–5
  ALPHABETIC, 140
  compound, 143–4
  NEGATIVE, 141
  NOT, 140
  NUMERIC, 140
  POSITIVE, 141
  relational, 141–2
  results table, 144
  with IF, 145
CONFIGURATION SECTION, 207–8
Constants in BASIC, 271–2
Constants in COBOL, 112, 125–7
  figurative, 71
  file name, 222
  LITERAL, 70
  non-numeric, 70
  NUMERIC, 70
Constants in FORTRAN, 220–2
  COMPLEX, 221
  DOUBLE PRECISION, 221
  INTEGER, 220
  LITERAL, 221–2
  LOGICAL, 222
  REAL, 220
Continuation lines, 73
CONTINUE, 240
Control bus, 308
Control record, 194
Control totals, 194
COPY, 195
  REPLACING, 196–7

346

CORRESPONDING, 179–80
CPU, *see* Central processor unit
CTC, 311

Data, 244–5
DATA, 282
Data bus, 308
Data classes, 111–13, 115, *see also* PICTURE
Data description entries, 113–14
DATA DIVISION, 67
  example, 132–6
  layout, 99
  organization, 97
  SECTION headers, 98–9
Data in BASIC, 272
Data names, 69, 113
  qualification, 178–9
Data preparation, 10
Data-preparation department, 193
DATA-RECORD descriptions, 109
DATA RECORDS, 109, 198
Data representation, 9
Data structures, 99
Data transformation, 154–5
DATE-COMPILED, 206
DATE-WRITTEN, 206
De-blocking, 26
DEBUG, 202–3
DECIMAL POINT
  assumed, 61
Decision box, 31
DEF (BASIC), 280–1
DESCENDING, 199
Device selection, 208–9
DIM (BASIC), 297
Dimension (BASIC), *see* DIM
DIMENSION, 241
Direct access storage devices, 24
Disc pack, *see* Magnetic discs
DISPLAY, 165–6
DIVIDE, 82–4
  BY, 84
  INTO, 83
  ON SIZE ERROR, 84
  REMAINDER, 84
Division by zero, 78
DIVISION headers, 73–6
DMA, 311
DO, 238–40, 257–8, 264
  examples, 239–40
  implied, 253
  range, 238
Documentation, 194–7
Double buffering, 22
Double precision, 223
Double precision constants, 221
Dummy statements, 88

Editing, 127–31
  cheque protect, 129–30
  example, 130–1
  floating £, 129
  insertion, 128
  suppression, 128
EDP, *see* Electronic data processing
EJECT, 204
Electronic data processing, 5
Elementary items, 52, 100, 111, 180
  non-contiguous, 101
ELSE, *see* IF
END, 248
End of file, 160, 169, 252–3
ENTER, 197
ENTRY, 191
ENVIRONMENT DIVISION, 67, 206–10
EPROM, 304
Erase head, 20
Error flagging, 50
Error recovery, 51
EXAMINE, 152–4
  ALL, 153
  LEADING, 153
  REPLACING, 154
  TALLYING, 152–4
  UNTIL FIRST, 152–3
EXHIBIT, 202, *see also* DISPLAY
  CHANGED, 202
  NAMED, 202
EXIT, 95–6
Explicit typing, 223
Exponent, 221
Exponentiation, 226
Exponentiation in COBOL, 84–5
Expressions
  BASIC, 275
  relational, 235–6
External data, 97

F, *see* Recording mode
FD, *see* File descriptions
FIFO, 311
Figurative constants, 126
File descriptions, 98, 102–11
  FD, 102
  sample, 110–11
File matching
  example, 170–2
  flowchart, 170
FILE SECTION, 98, 133–4
File updating, 169
FILE-CONTROL, 208
FILE-NAME, 223
Files, 19, 159, 168–73
  amendments, 28
  controls, 194
  definition levels, 27
  fixed length, 10
  FORTRAN, 251–4
  FORTRAN arrays, 253–4
  generation numbers, 107–8
  labels, 106–8
  master, 28
  matching, 28, 168–73
  physical organization, 26
  preparation, 156
  PRINT, 163–4
  security, 28
  sequencing, 27–8
  sequential, 28
  serial, 28
  sorting, 198–201
  updating, 28
  variable length, 27, 103, 162
FILLER, 114
Floating, *see* Editing
Floating point arithmetic, 61
Floating point numbers, 220–1
Flowchart symbols, 30–8
Flowchart
  sample, 33–6
Flowcharting, 30–8, 42–4
  check list, 44
FOR (BASIC), 292
FORTRAN, 3, 49
  background, 215
  coding forms, 219
FROM CONSOLE, *see* ACCEPT
Full stop, *see* Period
Functions, 259–65
  agruments, 260
  BASIC, 278–9
  built-in, 259–62
  examples, 263–4
  user defined, 264–5

General format notation, 71–2
Generation number, 28
GIVING option, 77
GIVING
  SORT, 199
Glossary, 313
GO TO, 86–8, 231
  assigned, 233–4
  BASIC, 288–9

GO TO (*cont'd*)
  computed, 231–2
  DEPENDING ON, 87
  for ALTER, 88
  in range of PERFORM, 95
GOBACK, 191–3
GOSUB, 293–5
GOTO, *see* GO TO
Group items, 100
Group names, 53

Hardware, 51
Head of page, 164, 174
High level languages, 49
HIGH-VALUE, 71
Home computing, 303

I-O-CONTROL, 209–10
IDENTIFICATION DIVISION, 67, 204–6
  example, 206
IF, 145–8
IF (BASIC), *see* IF THEN
IF (FORTRAN), 235
IF, nested, 146–8
IF THEN (BASIC), 289
Implicit typing, 223–4
Initial value, 183
INPUT, 246–7
INPUT (BASIC), 283
INPUT (COBOL), *see* OPEN
Input devices, *see* Input units
Input hopper, 11
Input units, 7, 9–16
Inputting in BASIC, 282
Input/output, home computer, 305–7
INPUT-OUTPUT, 45
INPUT-OUTPUT SECTION, 208–9
INSTALLATION, 206
Instruction format (BASIC), 269
INTEGER, 223
INTEGER constants, 220
Integral numbers (BASIC), 272
Inter-block gaps, 21, 24, 25–7
Interface, home computer, 305

JCL, *see* Job-control language
Job-control cards, 47
Job-control language, 47

Keyboards, 15
Keyfields, 28, 188, 199
  multiple, 201
Keywords, 68, 72

Label checking, 107
LABEL RECORDS, 108
Labels, *see* Files
LEADING, *see* EXAMINE
LEADING ZEROES, 127
LET (BASIC), 274–9
Level indicator, 99
Level numbers, 76, 99–101, 113–14
  01, 100
  77, 101, 114
  88, 101, 142–3
  special, 101
Levels, *see* Level numbers
Libraries, 195–6
Line numbers (BASIC), 270
Line-printer, 16–18
  flowchart symbol, 37
LINKAGE SECTION, 99, 190
Literals, 125–6, 221–2
Logic, 139
Logic paths, 30
Logical, 223
Logical RECORDS, 97–8
Loops, 233–4, 237
  example, 184
  in BASIC, 292
  INDEX, 238
  initial value, 183, 238

terminal value, 185, 238
LOW-VALUE, 71

Magnetic discs, 22–5
  cartridge, 22
  construction, 22–3
  cylinder concept, 23–4
  flowchart symbol, 37
  home address marker, 23
  transfer speeds, 25
  transport mechanism, 23
Magnetic ink character recognition, 15
Magnetic tape, 19–22, 156–7
  end of file, 21
  end of reel, 21
  flowchart symbols, 37
  load point, 20
  recording density, 21
  transfer speeds, 21
Mantissa, 220
Master files, 169
Matching
  files, 168–73
  tables, 186–7
Memory unit, 7
Microprocessor, 301
Mistakes, 9, 193
Mixed programming languages, 197
MMU, 311
Modem, 217
MOVE, 148–51
  CORRESPONDING, 179
  elementary, 148–50
  group, 150
Multi-access, *see* Time sharing
Multi-programming, 45–6
  schematic, 46
  storage division, 47
Multiplexor, 217
Multiplication in COBOL, *see* MULTIPLY
Multiplication in FORTRAN, *see* Assignment statements
MULTIPLY, 81–2
  SIZE ERROR, 82

Names, 69–70
  choice of, 69
Negative sign, 65
Nested IF, 146–8
  flowchart, 147
Nested PERFORM, *see* PERFORM
NEXT SENTENCE, *see* IF
Nesting (BASIC), 293
NEXT (BASIC), 292
NEXT SENTENCE, *see* IF
Non-contiguous items, 99–101
NOTE, 195
Number systems
  base, 55
  binary, 55–8
  decimal, 54–5
  hexadecimal, 59–60
  notation, 61
  octal, 58–9
  weights, 55
Numbers in BASIC, 272
NUMERIC CLASS, 112

Object program, 50
OBJECT-COMPUTER, 207
OCCURS, 120–2, 181–2
ON . . . GO TO (BASIC), 291
OPEN, 156–7
  NO REWIND, 157
  REVERSED, 157
Operating systems, 50–1
Optical character recognition, 15
Optical mark reading, 15
Optional words, 68, 72
OR, 143

Otherwise, *see* IF
OUTPUT, *see* OPEN
Output units, 7, 16

Paper tape reader, 12
Paper tape, 12
  flowchart symbol, 36
Paragraph names, 70, 76
Parallel transmission, 309
Parameters, 190, 255–6
Parentheses, 66, 221, 225
PERFORM, 91–5, 190
  EXIT, 95–6
  nested, 94–5
  TIMES, 92–3
  UNTIL, 93
  VARYING, 182–6
Period, 65–6
Physical records, 97–8
PIC, *see* PICTURE
PICTURE, 115–18, 127–9
  9, 115
  A, 115
  B, 128
  examples, 117–18
  S, 115
  symbol repetition, 117
  V, 116
  X, 115
PIO, 311
Plus sign, 65
Positional significance, 55
PRINT, 247–50
PRINT (BASIC), 284–5
Print barrel, 16–17
Print format (BASIC), 286
Printing, 16–18, 173–8, 204
  channels, 164, 175
  FORTRAN, 247–50
  FORTRAN examples, 248–9
  FORTRAN formatting, 250
  headings, 174–5
  in zones, 284
  line count, 174
  line-up, 177–8
  readability, 131
  sample routine, 175
PRINT USING, 286
Procedure branching instructions, 86
PROCEDURE DIVISION, 67
  organization, 136–7
PROCEDURE names, 70, 86
PROCEED, *see* ALTER
Process box, 30
Program, 7, 29–30
  calling, 190
  coding, 8
  control (BASIC), 288–95
  execution, 205
  library, 50
  name, 205
  sequence, 231
  sequence of execution, 86
  termination, 193–4, 248, *see also* STOP
  termination check list, 194
  testing, 201
Program libraries, 50
Program scheduling, 47–8
Program specifications, 39–45, 132–3
  input, 40
  output, 40
  throughput, 41
PROGRAM-ID, 205
PROM, 304
Punched cards, 10–12, 35
Punctuation mark, 66–7

Qualification, 178–9
Qualifier, 178
Quotation marks, 70
Quote, 71

RAM, 303
Random access memory, *see* RAM
READ, 159–62, 253
  AT END, 160
  example, 160
  INTO, 162
READ (BASIC), 282
Read only memory, *see* ROM
Read station
  card reader, 11
  paper tape reader, 12
Read-write head, 20, 23
READY TRACE, 202
Real numbers (BASIC), 272
REAL, 223
REAL constants, 220
RECORD CONTAINS, 103–4
Record descriptions, 196
RECORDING MODE, 104–6, 198
  fixed length, 104
  variable length, 104
REDEFINES, 123–4
Relational conditions, 141–2
Relational operators
  FORTRAN, 235
REMAINDER after DIVIDE, 84
REMARKS, 206
RENUM, 270
REPLACING, *see* EXAMINE
Required words, 68
Reserved words, 68, 72
  list, 322
RESET TRACE, 202
RETURN, 255
RETURN (BASIC), 294
RESTORE (BASIC), 282
Revision questions
  set 1, 210
  set 2, 211
  set 3, 212
  set 4, 213
  set 5, 266
  set 6, 299
  set 7, 311
ROM, 304
ROUNDED option, 77

S, *see* Recording mode
SAME AREA, 209
SD, 198
Searching, 186–8
  example, 187
SECTION headers, 76
SECURITY, 206
SELECT, 208
Semi-colon, 66
Sentences, 136, 137
Serial transmission, 310
Sign condition, 140–1
Single blocking, 25
Single buffering, 209
SIZE-ERROR option, 78, 138
SKIP, 204
Software, 51
Sorting, 198–201
  example, 200–1
Source listing, 50, 203
Source program, 49
SOURCE-COMPUTER, 207
SPACE, 71
Special level numbers, 101
Special words, 68
SPECIAL-NAMES, 207–8
Sprocket holes, 18
Statements, 136–7
  compiler directing, 139, 204
  conditional, 138
  imperative, 138
Stationery
  layout sheets, 176
  line-up, 177–8

Staionary (*cont'd*)
  plain, 174–5
  preprinted, 18, 131, 164, 175–7
STOP, 96, 248
STOP RUN, 96, 193
Strings in BASIC, 272–7
Structures, 52–3, 100–1
  block diagram, 53
  redefinition, 124
Sub-programs, 190, *see also* Subroutines
  FORTRAN, *see* Subroutines
  invocation, 192
  samples, 191
Subroutines, 190–2, 255–8
  arrays, 257–8
  BASIC, 292–5
  COBOL, *see* Sub-programs
  flowchart symbol, 38
  typing, 256–7
Subscripting, 122–3
Subscripts, 181–2, 188, 242
  BASIC, 296–9
  variable, 181–2, 242–4
SUBTRACT, 80–1, 108
  ROUNDED, 80
Supervisor, 47–9
  communication, 47
Switching, 233

TAB (BASIC), 285
Tables, 181–6
  optimization, 188–9
  printing, 185
  searching, 186–8
TALLY, 153–4, *see also* EXAMINE
TALLYING, *see* EXAMINE
Tape reservoirs, 20
Terminals, 217
  inputing from, 246–7
Terminator box, 33
Test data, 201
Testing aids, 201–3
Texts (BASIC), 272
Time sharing, 217–19
  commands, 219

logging in, 217–18
schematic, 218
Timing lines, 16
TRACE, 201–2
TRANSFORM, 154–5
Truncation, 77, 149

U, *see* Recording mode
UART, 311
Unblocking, 98
UNTIL FIRST, *see* EXAMINE
UPC, 311
UPON CONSOLE, *see* DISPLAY
USAGE, 118
  COMPUTATIONAL, 119
  DISPLAY, 118
User-defined functions, *see* Functions
User labels, 108
USING, 191
  SORT, 199
Utility programs, 51

V, *see* Recording mode
VALUE, 125–6, 142
VALUE OF, 109
Variables, 222–4
  BASIC, 271–4
  FORTRAN types, 223
  initial values, 224
  numeric (BASIC), 273
  priming, 244–5
  string (BASIC), 274
VARYING, *see* PERFORM

Words, 68
WORKING-STORAGE SECTION, 98–9,
  134–5
WRITE, 162–4, 251–2
  ADVANCING, 163–4
  FROM, 163

ZERO, 71

.FALSE., 235
.TRUE., 235